Lecture Notes in Computer Science 9539

Commenced Publication in 1973
Founding and Former Series Editors:
Gerhard Goos, Juris Hartmanis, and Jan van Leeuwen

More information about this series at http://www.springer.com/series/7408

Christiano Braga · Peter Csaba Ölveczky (Eds.)

Formal Aspects of Component Software

12th International Conference, FACS 2015
Niterói, Brazil, October 14–16, 2015
Revised Selected Papers

 Springer

Editors
Christiano Braga
Universidade Federal Fluminense
Niterói
Brazil

Peter Csaba Ölveczky
University of Oslo
Oslo
Norway

ISSN 0302-9743   ISSN 1611-3349   (electronic)
Lecture Notes in Computer Science
ISBN 978-3-319-28933-5   ISBN 978-3-319-28934-2   (eBook)
DOI 10.1007/978-3-319-28934-2

Library of Congress Control Number: 2015960400

LNCS Sublibrary: SL2 – Programming and Software Engineering

Printed on acid-free paper

This Springer imprint is published by SpringerNature
The registered company is Springer International Publishing AG Switzerland

Preface

This volume contains the proceedings of the 12th International Conference on Formal Aspects of Component Software (FACS 2015), held at the Universidade Federal Fluminense, Niterói, Brazil, during October 14–16, 2015.

Component-based software development proposes sound engineering principles and techniques to cope with the complexity of software systems. However, many challenging conceptual and technological issues remain. The advent of service-oriented and cloud computing has also brought to the fore new dimensions, such as quality of service and robustness to withstand faults. As software applications themselves become components of wider socio-technical systems, further challenges arise from the need to create and manage interactions.

The FACS series of events addresses the application of formal methods in all aspects of software components and services. Formal methods have provided foundations for component-based software development through research on mathematical models for components, composition and adaptation, and rigorous approaches to verification, deployment, testing, and certification.

FACS 2015 received 33 regular paper submissions, each of which was reviewed by at least three reviewers. Based on the reviews and extensive discussions, the program committee decided to accept 15 regular papers. This volume contains the revised versions of the 15 regular papers, as well as invited papers by Martin Wirsing and David Déharbe.

Many colleagues and friends contributed to FACS 2015. We thank Martin Wirsing, David Déharbe, and Renato Cerqueira for accepting our invitations to give invited talks, and the authors who submitted their work to FACS 2015. We are grateful to the members of the program committee for providing timely and insightful reviews as well as for their involvement in the post-reviewing discussions. Finally, we thank Bruno Lopes for his assistance in organizing FACS 2015, and acknowledge partial financial support from CAPES and CNPq.

November 2015

Christiano Braga
Peter Csaba Ölveczky

Organization

Program Chairs

Christiano Braga	Universidade Federal Fluminense, Brazil
Peter Csaba Ölveczky	University of Oslo, Norway

Steering Committee

Farhad Arbab (chair)	CWI and Leiden University, The Netherlands
Luís Barbosa	University of Minho, Portugal
Christiano Braga	Universidade Federal Fluminense, Brazil
Carlos Canal	University of Málaga, Spain
Ivan Lanese	University of Bologna, Italy, and Inria, France
Zhiming Liu	Birmingham City University, UK
Markus Lumpe	Swinburne University of Technology, Australia
Eric Madelaine	Inria, France
Peter Csaba Ölveczky	University of Oslo, Norway
Corina Pasareanu	CMU/NASA Ames Research Center, USA
Bernhard Schätz	fortiss GmbH, Germany

Program Committee

Dalal Alrajeh	Imperial College London, UK
Farhad Arbab	CWI and Leiden University, The Netherlands
Cyrille Artho	AIST, Japan
Kyungmin Bae	SRI International, USA
Luís Barbosa	University of Minho, Portugal
Christiano Braga	Universidade Federal Fluminense, Brazil
Roberto Bruni	University of Pisa, Italy
Carlos Canal	University of Málaga, Spain
Ana Cavalcanti	University of York, UK
José Fiadeiro	Royal Holloway, University of London, UK
Bernd Fischer	Stellenbosch University, South Africa
Marcelo Frias	Buenos Aires Institute of Technology, Argentina
Rolf Hennicker	Ludwig-Maximilians-Universität München, Germany
Ramtin Khosravi	University of Tehran, Iran
Ivan Lanese	University of Bologna, Italy, and Inria, France
Axel Legay	IRISA/Inria, Rennes, France
Zhiming Liu	Birmingham City University, UK
Alberto Lluch Lafuente	Technical University of Denmark, Denmark
Markus Lumpe	Swinburne University of Technology, Australia

Eric Madelaine	Inria, France
Robi Malik	University of Waikato, New Zealand
Hernán Melgratti	University of Buenos Aires, Argentina
Alvaro Moreira	Federal Univeristy of Rio Grande do Sul, Brazil
Arnaldo Moura	IC/UNICAMP, Brazil
Thomas Noll	RWTH Aachen University, Germany
Peter Csaba Ölveczky	University of Oslo, Norway
Corina Pasareanu	CMU/NASA Ames Research Center, USA
František Plášil	Charles University, Czech Republic
Camilo Rocha	Escuela Colombiana de Ingeniería, Colombia
Gwen Salaün	Grenoble INP - Inria - LIG, France
Augusto Sampaio	Federal University of Pernambuco, Brazil
Ralf Sasse	ETH Zürich, Switzerland
Bernhard Schätz	fortiss GmbH, Germany

Additional Reviewers

Aravantinos, Vincent	Majster-Cederbaum, Mila
Biondi, Fabrizio	Marti-Oliet, Narciso
Bonifácio, Adilson	Moggi, Eugenio
Castor, Fernando	Quilbeuf, Jean
Ciolek, Daniel	Rosa, Nelson
Dan, Li	Ruz, Cristian
Daniel, Jakub	Sanchez, Alejandro
Dimovski, Aleksandar S.	Soldani, Jacopo
Francalanza, Adrian	Stolz, Volker
Igna, Georgeta	Tcheukam Siwe, Alain
Inoue, Jun	Traonouez, Louis-Marie
Iyoda, Juliano	Verdejo, Alberto
Jancik, Pavel	Vinarek, Jiri
Lima, Lucas	Ye, Lina
Ma, Lei	Zalinescu, Eugen

Contents

OnPlan: A Framework for Simulation-Based Online Planning

Lenz Belzner[(✉)], Rolf Hennicker, and Martin Wirsing

Institut für Informatik, Ludwig-Maximilians-Universität München,
Munich, Germany
belzner@ifi.lmu.de

Abstract. This paper proposes the ONPLAN framework for modeling
autonomous systems operating in domains with large probabilistic state
spaces and high branching factors. The framework defines components
for acting and deliberation, and specifies their interactions. It comprises a
mathematical specification of requirements for autonomous systems. We
discuss the role of such a specification in the context of simulation-based
online planning. We also consider two instantiations of the framework:
Monte Carlo Tree Search for discrete domains, and Cross Entropy Open
Loop Planning for continuous state and action spaces. The framework's
ability to provide system autonomy is illustrated empirically on a robotic
rescue example.

1 Introduction

Modern application domains such as machine-aided robotic rescue operations
require software systems to cope with uncertainty and rapid and continuous
change at runtime. The complexity of application domains renders it impossible to deterministically and completely specify the knowledge about domain
dynamics at design time. Instead, high-level descriptions such as probabilistic
predictive models are provided to the system that give an approximate definition of chances and risks inherent to the domain that are relevant for the task
at hand.

Also, in contrast to classical systems, in many cases there are numerous different ways for a system to achieve its task. Additionally, the environment may
rapidly change at runtime, so that completely deterministic behavioral specifications are likely to fail. Thus, providing a system with the ability to compile a
sensible course of actions at runtime from a high-level description of its interaction capabilities is a necessary requirement to cope with uncertainty and change.

One approach to deal with this kind of uncertain and changing environments
is *online planning*. It enables system autonomy in large (or even infinite) state
spaces with high branching factors by interleaving planning and system action
execution (see e.g. [1–3]). In many domains, action and reaction are required very
often, if not permanently. Resources such as planning time and computational
power are often limited. In such domains, online planning replaces the requirement of absolute optimality of actions with the idea that in many situations it

© Springer International Publishing Switzerland 2016
C. Braga and P.C. Ölveczky (Eds.): FACS 2015, LNCS 9539, pp. 1–30, 2016.
DOI: 10.1007/978-3-319-28934-2_1

is sufficient and more sensible to conclude as much as possible from currently available information within the given restricted resources. One particular way to perform this form of rapid deliberation is based on simulation: The system is provided with a generative model of its environment. This enables it to evaluate potential consequences of its actions by generating execution traces from the generative model. The key idea to scale this approach is to use information from past simulations to guide the future ones to directions of the search space that seem both likely to happen and valuable to reach.

In this paper we propose the ONPLAN framework for modeling autonomous systems operating in domains with large or infinite probabilistic state spaces and high branching factors. The remainder of the paper is outlined as follows. In Sect. 2 we introduce the ONPLAN framework for online planning, define components for acting and deliberation, and specify their interactions. We then extend this framework to simulation-based online planning. In Sects. 3 and 4 we discuss two instantiations of the framework: Monte Carlo Tree Search for discrete domains (Sect. 3), and Cross Entropy Open Loop Planning for continuous state and action spaces (Sect. 4). We illustrate each with empirical evaluations on a robotic rescue example. Section 5 concludes the paper and outlines potential lines of further research in the field.

2   A Framework for Simulation-Based Online Planning

In this Section we propose the ONPLAN framework for modeling autonomous systems based on online planning. We introduce the basic concept in Sect. 2.1. In Sect. 2.2, we will refine the basic framework to systems that achieve autonomy performing rapidly repeated simulations to decide on their course of action.

2.1   Online Planning

Planning is typically formulated as a search task, where search is performed on sequences of actions. The continuously growing scale of application domains both in terms of state and action spaces requires techniques that are able to (a) reduce the search space effectively and (b) compile as much useful information as possible from the search given constrained resources. Classical techniques for planning have been exhaustively searching the search space. In modern application scenarios, the number of possible execution traces is too large (potentially even infinite) to get exhaustively searched within a reasonable amount of time or computational resources.

The key idea of online planning is to perform planning and execution of an action iteratively at runtime. This effectively reduces the search space: A transition that has been executed in reality does not have to be searched or evaluated by the planner any more. Online planning aims at effectively gathering information about the *next* action that the system should execute, exploiting the available resources such as deliberation time and capabilities as much as possible. Algorithm 1 captures this idea informally. In the following, we will introduce the ONPLAN framework that formalizes the idea of online planning.

Algorithm 1. Online Planning (Informally)
1: **while** true **do**
2:      observe state
3:      plan action
4:      execute action
5: **end while**

Framework Specification. The ONPLAN framework is based on the following requirements specification.

1. A set S_{real} which represents states of real environments. While this is a part of the mathematical formulation of the problem domain, it is not represented by a software artifact in the framework.
2. A set *Agent* that represents deliberating and acting entities.
3. Representations of the agent's observable state space S and the agent's action space A. The observable state space S represents information about the environment S_{real} that is relevant for an agent and its planning process. It is in fact an abstraction of the environment.
4. A function *observe* : $Agent \times S_{real} \to S$ that specifies how an agent perceives the current state of its environment. This function defines the abstraction and aggregation of information available to an agent in its real environment to an abstract representation of currently relevant information. In some sense, the function *observe* comprises the monitor and analyze phases of the MAPE-K framework for autonomous computing [4].
5. A function *actionRequired* : $Agent \times S \to Bool$ that is used to define triggering of action execution by an agent. A typical example is to require execution of an action after a certain amount of time has passed since the last executed action.
6. For each action in A, we require a specification of how to execute it in the real domain. To this end, the framework specification comprises a function *execute* : $A \times S_{real} \to S_{real}$. This function defines the real (e.g. physical) execution of an agent's action.
7. We define a set *RewardFunction* of reward functions of the form $R : S \to \mathbb{R}$. A reward function is an encoding of the system goals. States that are valuable should be mapped to high values by this function. States that should be avoided or even are hazardous should provide low values.
8. We define a set *Strategy* of strategies. Each strategy is a probability distribution $P_{act}(A|S)$ of actions over states. In the following, we will often omit the signature and simply write P_{act} for $P_{act}(A|S)$. It defines the probability that an agent executes a particular action in a given state. If an agent $a \in Agent$ in state $s_{current} \in S$ is required to act (i.e. when *actionRequired*$(a, s_{current})$ returns true), then the action that is executed is sampled from the distribution: $a \sim P_{act}(\cdot|s_{current})$, where $P_{act}(\cdot|s_{current})$ denotes the probability distribution of actions in state $s_{current}$ and $\sim$ denotes sampling from this distribution. Sampling can be seen as non-deterministic choice proportional to a distribution.

9. A set *Planner* of planning entities. Planning is defined by a function *plan* : *Planner*× $\mathcal{S}$ × *RewardFunction*× *Strategy* → *Strategy*. A planning entity refines its strategy P_{act} w.r.t. its currently observed abstract state and a reward function to maximize the expected cumulative future reward. It is usually defined as the sum of rewards gathered when following a strategy.

Framework Model. Figure 1 shows a class diagram for the ONPLAN framework derived from the mathematical specification. It comprises classes for the main components *Agent* and *Planner*. States and actions are also represented by a class each: states $s \in \mathcal{S}$ are represented by objects of class *State*, actions $a \in \mathcal{A}$ by objects of class *Action*. Probability distributions of actions over states (defining potential agent strategies) are modeled by the class *Strategy*. Reward functions are represented by object of class *RewardFunction*. All classes are abstract and must be implemented in a concrete online planning system.

Note that ONPLAN supports multiple instances of agents to operate in the same domain. While inter-agent communication is not explicitly expressed in the framework, coordination of agents can be realized by emergent system behavior: As agents interact with the environment, the corresponding changes will be observed by other agents and incorporated into their planning processes due to the online planning approach.

Component Behavior. Given the specification and the component model, we are able to define two main behavioral algorithms for *Agent* and *Planner* that are executed in parallel: *Agent* ∥ *Planner*. I.e., this design decouples information aggregation and execution (performed by the agent) from the deliberation process (performed by the planner).

Algorithms 2 and 3 show the behavior of the respective components. We assume that all references shown in the class diagram have been initialized. Both behaviors are infinitely looping. An agent observes the (real) environment, encodes the observation to its (abstract) state and passes the state to its corresponding planning component, as long as no action is required (Algorithm 2, lines 2–5). When an action is required – e.g. due to passing of a certain time frame or occurrence of a particular situation/event – the agent queries the planner's current strategy for an action to execute (line 6). Finally, the action proposed by the strategy is executed (line 7) and the loop repeats.

The behavior of the planning component (Algorithm 3) repeatedly calls a particular planning algorithm that refines the strategy w.r.t. current state and specified reward function. We will define a particular class of planning algorithms in more detail in Sect. 2.2.

Framework Plug Points. The ONPLAN framework provides the following plug points derived from the mathematical specification. They are represented by abstract operations such that domain specific details have to be implemented by any instantiation.

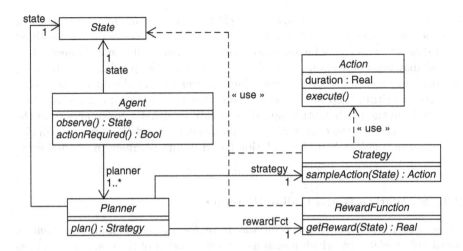

Fig. 1. Basic components of ONPLAN

Algorithm 2. Agent Component Behavior

Require: Local variable action : *Action*
1: **while** true **do**
2:      **while** !actionRequired() **do**
3:           state ← observe()   ▷ observe environment
4:           planner.state ← state   ▷ inform planner
5:      **end while**
6:      action ← planner.strategy.sampleAction(state)   ▷ sample from strategy
7:      action.execute()   ▷ execute sampled action
8: **end while**

Algorithm 3. Planner Component Behavior

1: **while** true **do**
2:      strategy ← plan()
3: **end while**

---

1. The operation *Agent::observe() : State*. This operation is highly dependent on the sensory information available and is therefore implemented in a framework instantiation.
2. The operation *Agent::actionRequired() : Bool*. The events and conditions that require an agent to act are highly depending on the application domain. The timing of action execution may even be an optimization problem for itself. The state parameter of the mathematical definition is implicitly given by the reference of an agent to its state.
3. The operation *Action::execute()*. Action execution is also highly dependent on technical infrastructure and physical capabilities of an agent.
4. The operation *RewardFunction::getReward(State) : Real*. Any concrete implementation of this operation models a particular reward function.

5. The operation *Strategy::sampleAction(State)* : *Action* should realize sampling of actions from the strategy w.r.t. to a given state. It depends on the used kind of strategy, which may be discrete or continuous, unconditional or conditional, and may even be a complex combination of many independent distributions.
6. Any implementation of the operation *Planner::plan()* should realize a concrete algorithm used for planning. Note that the arguments of the function *plan* from the mathematical specification are modeled as references from the *Planner* class to the classes *State*, *RewardFunction* and *Strategy*. We will discuss a particular class of simulation-based online planners in the following Sect. 2.2.

2.2   Simulation-Based Online Planning

We now turn our focus on a specific way to perform online planning: *simulation based online planning*, which makes use of a simulation of the domain. It is used by the planner to gather information about potential system episodes (i.e. execution traces). Simulation provides information about probability and value of the different state space regions, thus guiding system behavior execution. After simulating its possible choices and behavioral alternatives, the agent executes an action (in reality) that performed well in simulation. The process of planning using information from the simulation and action execution is iteratively repeated at runtime, thus realizing online planning.

A simple simulation based online planner would generate a number of randomly chosen episodes and average the information about the obtained reward. However, as it is valuable to generate as much information as possible with given resources, it is a good idea to guide the simulation process to high value regions of the search space. Using variance reduction techniques such as importance sampling, this guidance can be realized using information from previously generated episodes [5–7].

Framework Specification. In addition to the specification from Sect. 2.1, we extend the ONPLAN framework requirements to support simulation-based online planning.

1. For simulation based planning, actions $a \in \mathcal{A}$ require a duration parameter. If no such parameter is specified explicitly, the framework assumes a duration of one for the action. We define a function $d : \mathcal{A} \to \mathbb{R}$ that returns the duration of an action.
2. ONPLAN requires a set *Simulation* of simulations of the environment. Each simulation is a probability distribution of the form $P_{\text{sim}}(\mathcal{S}|\mathcal{S} \times \mathcal{A})$. It takes the current state and the action to be executed as input, and returns a potential successor state according to the transition probability. Simulating the execution of an action $a \in \mathcal{A}$ in a state $s \in \mathcal{S}$ yields a successor state $s' \in \mathcal{S}$. Simulation is performed by sampling from the distribution P_{sim}: $s' \sim P_{\text{sim}}(\cdot|(s,a))$, where $P_{\text{sim}}(\cdot|(s,a))$ denotes the probability distribution of successor states

when executing action a in state s and $\sim$ denotes sampling from this distribution. Note that the instantiations of the framework we discuss in Sects. 3 and 4 work with a fixed simulation of the environment. It does not change in the course of system execution, in contrast to the strategy.

3. We require a set $SimPlanner \subseteq Planner$ of simulation based planners.

4. Any simulation based planner defines a number $e_{\max} \in \mathbb{N}^+$ of episodes generated for each refinement step of its strategy.

5. Any simulation based planner defines a maximum planning horizon $h_{\max} \in \mathbb{N}^+$ that provides an upper bound to its simulation depth. A low planning horizon results in fast but shallow planning – long term effects of actions are not taken into account when making a decision. The planning horizon lends itself to be dynamically adapted, providing flexibility by allowing to choose between fast and shallow or more time consuming, but deep planning taking into account long term consequences of actions.

6. Any simulation based planner defines a discount factor $\gamma \in [0; 1]$. This factor defines how much a planner prefers immediate rewards over long term ones when refining a strategy. The lower the discount factor, the more likely the planner will built a strategy that obtains reward as fast as possible, even if this means an overall degradation of payoff in the long run. See Algorithm 5 for details on discounting.

7. We define a set $\mathcal{E} \subseteq (\mathcal{S} \times \mathcal{A})^*$ of episodes to capture simulated system execution traces. We also define a set $\mathcal{E}_w \subseteq \mathcal{E} \times \mathbb{R}$ of episodes weighted by the discounted sum of rewards gathered in an execution trace. The weight of an episode is defined as its cumulative discounted reward, which is given by the recursive function $R_{\mathcal{E}} : \mathcal{E} \to \mathbb{R}$ as shown in Eq. 1. Let $s \in \mathcal{S}$, $a \in \mathcal{A}$, $e, e' \in \mathcal{E}$ where $e = (s, a) :: e'$, and let $R : \mathcal{S} \to \mathbb{R}$ be a reward function.

$$R_{\mathcal{E}}(\text{nil}) = 0$$
$$R_{\mathcal{E}}(e) = R(s) + \gamma^{d(a)} R_{\mathcal{E}}(e') \qquad (1)$$

An element of $\mathcal{E}_w$ is then uniquely defined by $(e, R_{\mathcal{E}}(e))$.

8. In the ONPLAN framework, the simulation-based planner uses the simulation P_{sim} to generate a number of episodes. The resulting episodes are weighted according to rewards gathered in each episode, w.r.t. the given reward function of the planner. Simulation is driven by the current strategy P_{act}. This process is reflected by following function.

$$generateEpisode :$$
$$SimPlanner \times Simulation \times Strategy \times RewardFunction \to \mathcal{E}_w$$

9. Importance sampling in high value regions of the search space is realized by using the resulting weighted episodes to refine the strategy such that its expected return (see Sect. 2.1) is maximized. The goal is to incrementally increase the expected reward when acting according to the strategy by gathering information from simulation episodes in an efficient way. This updating of the strategy is modeled by the following function.

$$updateStrategy : SimPlanner \times 2^{\mathcal{E}_w} \times Strategy \to Strategy$$

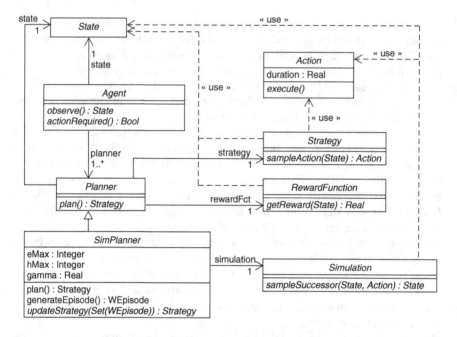

Fig. 2. Components of the ONPLAN framework

Algorithm 4. Simulation-based planning

Require: Local variable E_w : *Set(WEpisode)*
1: **procedure** PLAN
2:    $E_w \leftarrow \emptyset$
3:    **for** 0 ... eMax **do**
4:        $E_w \leftarrow E_w \cup$ generateEpisode()
5:    **end for**
6:    **return** updateStrategy(E_w)
7: **end procedure**

Framework Model. Using mathematically justified approaches for strategy refinement provides a solution to the notorious exploration-exploitation tradeoff (see e.g. [8]): While learning (or planning), an agent has to decide whether it should exploit knowledge about high-value regions of the state space, or whether it should use its resources to explore previously unknown regions to potentially discover even better options. We will discuss two instances of ONPLAN that provide principled and mathematically founded methods that deal with the question where to put simulation effort in Sects. 3 and 4.

Figure 2 shows the components of the ONPLAN framework for simulation-based online planning. It comprises the components of the basic ONPLAN framework (Sect. 2.1), and additionally defines a specialization *SimPlanner* of the *Planner* class, and a class *Simulation* that models simulations of the form P_{sim}. The parameters $e_{\text{max}}, h_{\text{max}}$ and γ are modeled as attributes of the *SimPlanner* class.

Algorithm 5. Generating weighted episodes

Require: Local variables s : *State*, r, t : *Real*, e : *Episode*, a : *Action*

1: **procedure** GENERATEEPISODE
2:     s ← state
3:     r ← rewardFct.getReward(s)
4:     t ← 0
5:     e ← nil
6:     **for** 0 ... hMax **do**
7:         a ← strategy.sampleAction(s)
8:         e ← e::(s, a)
9:         s ← simulation.sampleSuccessor(s, a)
10:         t ← t + a.duration
11:         r ← r + gamma^t · rewardFct.getReward(s)
12:     **end for**
13:     **return** (e, r)
14: **end procedure**

We further assume a class *WEpisode* that models weighted episodes. As it is a pure data container, it is omitted in the class diagram shown in Fig. 2.

The *SimPlanner* class also provides two concrete operations. The operation *SimPlanner::plan() : Strategy* realizes the corresponding abstract operation of the *Planner* class and is a template method for simulation based planning (see Algorithm 4). Episodes are modeled by a type *Episode*, weighted episodes by a type *WEpisode* respectively. The function *generateEpisode* is realized by the concrete operation *generateEpisode() : WEpisode* of the *SimPlanner* class and used by the *plan* operation. The function *updateStrategy* from the mathematical specification is realized as abstract operation *updateStrategy(Set(WEpisode))* in the class *SimPlanner*.

Simulation-Based Planning. *SimPlanner* realizes the *plan* operation by using a simulation to refine its associated strategy. We formalize the algorithm of the *plan* operation in the following. Algorithm 4 shows the simulation-based planning procedure. The algorithm generates a set of episodes weighted by rewards (lines 2–5). This set is the used to refine the strategy (line 6). The concrete method to update the strategy remains unspecified by ONPLAN.

Algorithm 5 shows the generation of a weighted episode. After initialization (lines 2–5), an episode is built by repeating the following steps for h_{max} times.

1. Sample an action $a \in \mathcal{A}$ from the current strategy w.r.t. the current simulation state $s \in \mathcal{S}$, i.e. $a \sim P_{act}(s)$ (line 7).
2. Store the current simulation state and selected action in the episode (line 8).
3. Simulate the execution of a. That is, use the action a sampled from the strategy in the previous step to progress the current simulation state s, i.e. $s \sim P_{sim}(s, a)$ (line 9).
4. Add the duration of a to the current episode time $t \in \mathbb{R}$. This is used for time-based discounting of rewards gathered in an episode (line 10).

5. Compute the reward of the resulting successor state discounted w.r.t. current episode time t and the specified discount factor γ, and add it to the reward aggregation (line 11).

After simulation of $h_{\max}$ steps, the episode is returned weighted by the aggregated reward (line 13).

Framework Plug Points. In addition to the plug points given by the basic framework (see Sect. 2.1), the framework extension for simulation-based online planning provides the following plug points.

1. The operation *sampleSuccessor(State, Action): State* of class *Simulation*. This operation is the interface for any implementation of a simulation P_{sim}. The concrete design of this implementation is left to the designer of an instance of the framework. Both simulations for discrete and continuous state and action spaces can instantiate ONPLAN. Note that, as P_{sim} may be learned from runtime observations of domain dynamics, this operation may be intentionally underspecified even by an instantiated system. Also note that the implementation of this operation does not necessarily have to implement the real domain dynamics. As simulation based planning typically relies on statistical estimation, any delta of simulation and reality just decreases estimation quality. While this also usually decreases planning effectiveness, it does not necessarily break planning completely. Thus, our framework provides a robust mechanism to deal with potentially imprecise or even erroneous specifications of P_{sim}.
2. The operation *updateStrategy(Set(WEpisode)): Strategy* of class *SimPlanner*. In principle, any kind of stochastic optimization technique can be used here. Examples include Monte Carlo estimation (see e.g. [6]) or genetic algorithms. We will discuss two effective instances of this operation in the following: Monte Carlo Tree Search for discrete domains in Sect. 3, and Cross Entropy Open Loop Planning for domains with continuous state-action spaces in Sect. 4.

Figure 3 shows an informal, high-level summary of ONPLAN concepts and their mutual influence. Observations result in the starting state of the simulations.

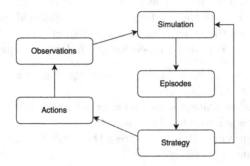

Fig. 3. Mutual influence of ONPLAN concepts

Simulations are driven by the current strategy and yield episodes. The (weighted) episodes are used to update the strategy. The strategy yields actions to be executed. Executed actions influence observations made by an agent.

In the following Sections, we will discuss two state-of-the-art instances of the ONPLAN framework for simulation-based online planning introduced in Sect. 2. In Sect. 3, we will illustrate Monte Carlo Tree Search (MCTS) [9] and its variant UCT [10] as an instantiation of ONPLAN in discrete domains. in Sect. 4, we will discuss Cross Entropy Open Loop Planning (CEOLP) [3,11] as an instance of ONPLAN for simulation based online planning in continuous domains with infinite state-actions spaces and branching factors.

3   Framework Instantiation in Discrete Domains

In this Section we discuss Monte Carlo Tree Search (MCTS) as an instantiation of the ONPLAN framework in discrete domains.

3.1   Monte Carlo Tree Search

Monte Carlo Tree Search (MCTS) provided a framework for the first discrete planning approaches to achieve human master-level performance in playing the game Go autonomously [12]. MCTS algorithms are applied to a vast field of application domains, including state-of-the-art reinforcement learning and planning approaches in discrete domains [2,9,13].

MCTS builds a search tree incrementally. Nodes in the tree represent states and action choices, and in each node information about the number of episodes an its expected payoff is stored. MCTS iteratively chooses a path from the root to leaf according to these statistics. When reaching a leaf, it simulates a potential episode until search depth is reached. A new node is added to the tree as a child of the leaf, and the statistics of all nodes that were traversed in this episode are updated according to the simulation result.

Figure 4 illustrates an iteration of MCTS. Each iteration consists of the following steps.

1. Nodes are selected w.r.t. node statistics until a leaf is reached (Fig. 4a).
2. When a leaf is reached, simulation is performed and the aggregated reward is observed (Fig. 4b).
3. A new node is added per simulation, and node statistics of the path selected in step (a) are updated according to simulation result (Fig. 4c).

Steps (1) to (3) are repeated iteratively, yielding a tree that is skewed towards high value regions of the state space. This guides simulation effort towards currently promising search areas.

3.2   UCT

UCT (upper confidence bounds applied to trees) is an instantiation of MCTS that uses a particular mechanism for action selection in tree nodes based on

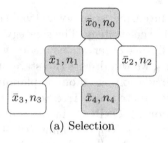

(a) Selection

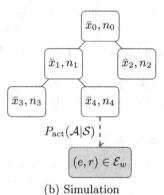

(b) Simulation

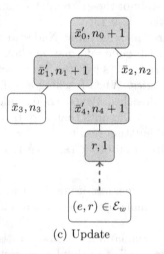

(c) Update

Fig. 4. Illustration of Monte Carlo Tree Search. $(e, r) \in \mathcal{E}_w$ is a weighted episode as generated by Algorithm 5. Nodes' mean values can be updated incrementally (see e.g. [14]): $\bar{x}_i' = \bar{x}_i + \frac{r - \bar{x}_i}{n_i + 1}$.

regret minimization [10]. UCT treats action choices in states as multi-armed bandit problems. Simulation effort is distributed according to the principle of *optimism in the face of uncertainty* [15]: Areas of the search space that have shown promising value in past iterations are more likely to be explored in future ones. UCT uses the mathematically motivated upper confidence bound for regret minimization UCB1 [16] to formalize this intuition. The algorithm stores the following statistics in each node.

1. $\bar{x}_a$ is the average accumulated reward in past episodes that contained the tuple (s, a), where s is the state represented by the current node.
2. n_s is the number of episodes that passed the current state $s \in \mathcal{S}$.
3. n_a is the corresponding statistic for each action a that can be executed in s.

Equation 2 shows the selection rule for actions in UCT based on node statistics. Here, $c \in \mathbb{R}$ is a constant argument that defines the weight of exploration (second term) against exploitation (first term). The equation provides a formalization of the exploration-exploitation tradeoff – the higher the previously observed reward of a child node, the higher the corresponding UCT score. However, the more often a particular child node is chosen by the search algorithm, the smaller the second term becomes. At the same time, the second term increases for all other child nodes. Thus, child nodes that have not been visited for some time become more and more likely to be included into future search episodes.

$$UCT(s, a) = \bar{x}_a + 2c\sqrt{\frac{2 \ln n_s}{n_a}} \qquad (2)$$

3.3 Framework Instantiation

Monte Carlo Tree Search instantiates the ONPLAN framework for simulation-based online planning based on the following considerations.

1. *Strategy::sampleAction(State): Action* is instantiated by the action selection mechanism used in MCTS. As MCTS is a framework itself, the particular choice is left underspecified. Examples of action selection mechanisms include uniform selection (all actions are chosen equally often), ϵ-greedy selection (the action with best average payoff is selected, with an ϵ probability to chose a random action) or selection according to UCT (see Eq. 2). Note that also probabilistic action selection strategies can be used, providing support for mixed strategies in a game-theoretic sense. Simulation outside the tree is performed according to an initial strategy. Typically, this is a uniformly random action selection. However, given expert knowledge can also be integrated here to yield potentially more valuable episodes with a higher probability.
2. *SimPlanner::updateStrategy(Set(WEpisode)): Strategy* adds the new node to the tree and updates all node statistics w.r.t. the simulated episode weighted by accumulated reward. Note that a single episode suffices to perform an update. Different mechanisms for updating can be used. One example is averaging rewards as described above. Another option is to set nodes' values to the maximum values of their child nodes, yielding a Monte Carlo Bellman update of the partial state value function induced by the search tree [2].

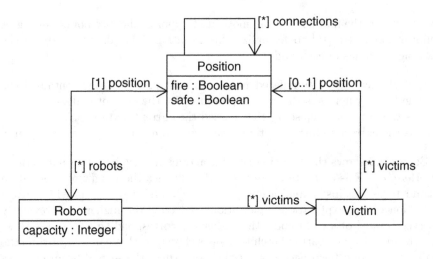

Fig. 5. Class diagram of the example domain.

3. While multiple simulations may be performed from a node when leaving the tree, typically the update (adding a node and updating all traversed nodes' statistics) is performed after each iteration. Thus, when using mcts for simulation-based planning, the number of episodes per strategy update e_{max} is usually set to 1.
4. The remaining plug-points – *execute* of class *Action*, *getReward* of class *RewardFunction* and *sampleSuccessor* of class *Simulation* – have to be instantiated individually for each domain and/or system use case.

3.4   Empirical Results

We implemented an instantiation of ONPLAN with UCT in an example search-and-rescue scenario to show its ability to generate autonomous goal-driven behavior and its robustness w.r.t. unexpected events and changes of system goals at runtime.

Example Domain. Figure 5 shows a class diagram of the scenario. A number of arbitrarily connected positions defines the domains topology. At some positions there is an ambulance (pos.safe = true). Positions may be on fire, except those that host an ambulance, i.e. class *Position* has the following invariant: pos.safe implies not(pos.fire) for all pos ∈ *Position*. Fires ignite or cease probabilistically depending on the number of fires at connected neighbor positions. A position may host any number of robots and victims. A robot can carry a number of victims that is bounded by its capacity. A carried victim does not have a position. A robot has five types of actions available.

1. Do nothing.
2. Move to a neighbor position that is not on fire.

3. Extinguish a fire at a neighbor position.
4. Pick up a victim at the robot's position if capacity is left.
5. Drop a carried victim at the robot's position.

All actions have unit duration. Each action may fail with a certain probability, resulting in no effect. Note that the number of actions available to a robot in a particular situation may vary due to various possible instantiations of action parameters (such as the particular victim that is picked up or the concrete target position of movement).

Experimental Setup. In all experiments, we generated randomly connected topologies with 20 positions and a connectivity of 30 %, resulting in 6 to 7 connections per position on average. We randomly chose 3 safe positions, and 10 that were initially on fire. 10 victims were randomly distributed on the non-safe positions. We placed a single robot agent at a random starting position. All positions were reachable from the start. Robot capacity was set to 2. The robot's actions could fail with a probability of up to 5 %, chosen uniformly distributed for each run. One run consisted of 80 actions executed by the agent. Results for all experiments have been measured with the statistical model checker MULTI-VESTA [17]. In all experiments, we set the maximum planning depth $h_{\max} = 20$. The discount factor was set to $\gamma = 0.9$. As MCTS was used for planning, we set $e_{\max} = 1$: The tree representing $P_{\mathrm{act}}(\mathcal{A}|\mathcal{S})$ is updated after every episode. UCT's exploratory constant was set to $c = 20$ in all experiments.

In the following experiments, we let the agent deliberate for 0.2 s. That is, *actionRequired()* returned true once every 0.2 s; i.e. each action was planned for 0.2 s, incorporating information from past planning steps.

As long as not stated otherwise, we provided a reward of 100 to the planning agent for each victim that was located at a safe position. Let $I : Bool \rightarrow \{0, 1\}$ be an indicator function that yields 1 if the argument is defined and true and 0, otherwise. Let *victims* $: \mathcal{S} \rightarrow 2^{Victim}$ be the set of all victims present in a given state. Then, for any state $s \in \mathcal{S}$ the reward function was defined as follows.

$$R(s) = 100 \cdot \sum_{v \in victims(s)} I(v.position.safe) \tag{3}$$

The reward function instantiates the *getReward* operation of class *Reward-Function* in the ONPLAN framework. Action implementations instantiate the *execute* operations of the corresponding subclasses of the *Action* class (e.g. move, pick up victim, etc.). A simulation about domain dynamics is provided to the simulation-based planner. It instantiates the *sampleSuccessor* operation of the *Simulation* class.

Estimation of Expected Future Reward. In a preliminary experiment, we observed the estimation of mean expected future reward. The MCTS planner increases the expected future reward up to step 60. Onwards from step 60 it decreases as the agent was informed about the end of the experiment after 80 steps.

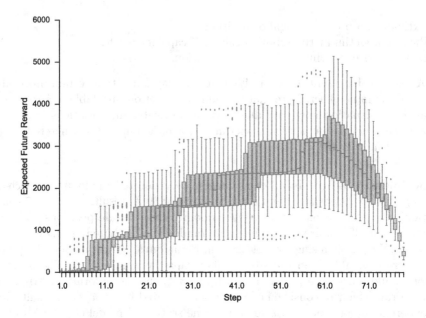

Fig. 6. Expected accumulated future reward at each step by the MCTS planner.

The planning depth $h_{max} = 20$ thus detects the end of an experiment at step 60. The mean expected reward for executed actions is shown in Fig. 6.

We also measured the increase in accuracy of the estimation of expected reward by MCTS. We measured the normalized coefficient of variation (CV) to investigate estimation accuracy, as the mean of expected future reward is highly fluctuating in the course of planning. The CV is a standardized measure of dispersion of data from a given distribution and independent from the scale of the mean, in contrast to standard deviation. Normalization of the CV renders the measurement robust to the number of samples. The normalized CV of a sample set is defined as quotient of the samples' standard deviation s and their mean $\bar{x}$, divided by the square root of available samples n. Note that the CV decreases as n increases, reflecting the increased accuracy of estimation as more samples become available.

$$\frac{s/\bar{x}}{\sqrt{n}} \tag{4}$$

We recorded mean $\bar{r}$ and standard deviation s_a of the expected reward gathered from simulation episodes for each potential action a, along with the number of episodes where a was executed at the particular step n_a. The normalized CV of an action then computes as follows.

$$\frac{s_a/\bar{r}}{\sqrt{n_a}} \tag{5}$$

Figure 7 shows the normalized CV w.r.t. expected reward of the actions executed by the agent at a given step in the experiment. We observed that MCTS

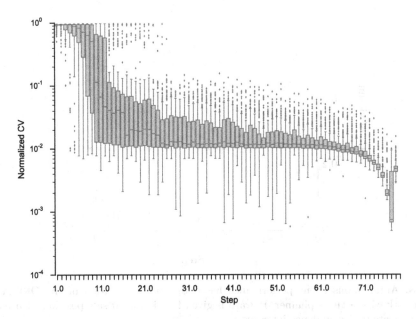

Fig. 7. Normalized coefficient of variation of expected reward estimation for actions executed by the MCTS planner. Note the logarithmic scale on the y-axis. After about 20 steps, estimation noise resembles the noise level inherent to the domain (up to 5 % action failures and average spread of fires).

steadily improves its estimation accuracy of expected reward. After about 20 steps, estimation noise resembles the noise level inherent to the domain (up to 5 % action failures and average spread of fires).

Autonomous System Behavior. In a baseline experiment, we evaluated ONPLAN's ability to synthesize autonomous behavior according to the given reward function. Figure 8 shows the average ratio of victims that was at a safe position w.r.t. to the number of actions performed by the agent, within a 95 % confidence interval. Also, the ratio of victims that are located at a burning position is displayed. No behavioral specification besides the instantiation of our planning framework has been provided to the agent. It can be seen that the planning component is able to generate a strategy that yields sensitive behavior: The robot transports victims to safe positions autonomously.

Robustness to Unexpected Events. In a second experiment we exposed the planning agent to unexpected events. This experiment is designed to illustrate robustness of the ONPLAN framework to events that are not reflected by the simulation P_{sim} provided to the planning component. In this experiment, all victims currently carried by the robot fall to the robot's current position every 20 steps. Also, a number of fires ignite such that the total number of fires accumulates to 10. Note that these events are not simulated by the agent while

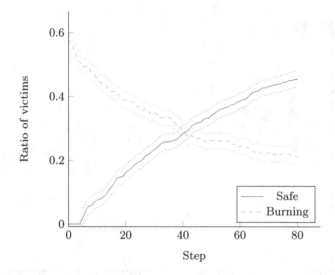

Fig. 8. Autonomous agent performance based on an instantiation of the ONPLAN framework with a MCTS planner. Reward is given for victims at safe positions. Dotted lines indicate 0.95 confidence intervals.

planning. Figure 9 shows the agent's performance in the presence of unexpected events with their 95 % confidence intervals. It can be seen that transportation of victims to safety is only marginally impaired by the sudden unexpected changes of the situation. As MCTS is used in an online manner that is based on replanning at each step, the planning framework is able to recover from the unexpected events efficiently.

System Goal Respecification. A third experiment highlights the framework's ability to adapt behavior synthesis to a system goal that changes at runtime. Before step 40, the agent was given a reward for keeping the number of fires low, resulting in a reduction of the number of burning victims. Onwards from step 40, reward was instead provided for victims that have been transported to safety. Besides respecification of the reward function to reflect the change of system goal no additional changes have been made to the running system. I.e., only the *rewardFct* reference of the planner was changed. This change impacts the weighting of episodes (see Algorithm 5, lines 3 and 11). The different weighting in turn impacts the updating of the planner's current strategy.

Figure 10 shows system performance in this experiment, together with 95 % confidence intervals. The results indicate that the framework indeed is able to react adequately to the respecification of system goals. As system capabilities and domain dynamics remain the same throughout the experimental runtime, all high-level specifications such as action capabilities (i.e. the action space $\mathcal{A}$) and knowledge about domain dynamics (i.e. the generative model P_{sim}) are sensibly employed to derive valuable courses of actions, regardless of the current system goal. ONPLAN thus provides a robust system adaptation mechanism for runtime goal respecifications.

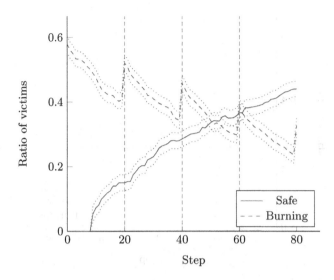

Fig. 9. Autonomous agent performance despite unexpected events at runtime. Every 20th step, all victims carried by the agent fall to the ground, and the number of fires raises to 10. Dotted lines indicate 0.95 confidence intervals.

4 Framework Instantiation in Continuous Domains

We now focus on an instantiation of the ONPLAN framework that works in continuous space and action domains. I.e. states and actions are represented as vectors of real numbers $\mathbb{R}^n$, for some $n \in \mathbb{N}$. This means that state and action spaces are of infinite size. In this section we show how Cross Entropy Open Loop Planning (CEOLP) [3,11] instantiates our planning framework, and illustrate how information obtained from simulations in the planning process can be used to identify promising ares of the search space in continuous domains. CEOLP works by optimizing action parameters w.r.t. expected payoff by application of the cross entropy method.

4.1 Cross Entropy Optimization

The cross entropy method for optimization [7,18] allows to efficiently estimate extrema of an unknown function $f : X \to Y$ via importance sampling. To do so, an initial probability distribution (that we call sampling distribution) $P_{\text{sample}}(X)$ is defined in a way that covers a large region of the function's domain. For estimating extrema of f, a set of samples $x \in X$ is generated w.r.t. the sampling distribution (i.e. $x \sim P_{\text{sample}}(X)$). The size of the sample set is a parameter of the cross entropy method. For all x in the set, the corresponding $y = f(x) \in Y$ is computed. Then samples are weighted w.r.t. their relevance for finding the function extrema. For example, when trying to find maxima of f, samples x are weighted according to $y = f(x)$. Typically this involves normalization to keep sample weights in the $[0; 1]$ interval. We denote the weight of a sample x_i by w_i.

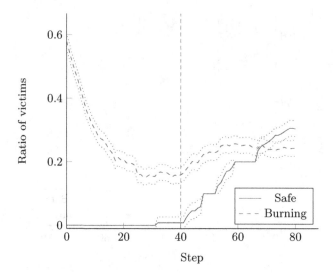

Fig. 10. Autonomous agent performance with a respecification of system goal at run-time. Before step 40, the agent is given a reward for keeping the number of fires low, resulting in a reduction of the number of burning victims. Onwards from step 40, reward is provided for victims that have been transported to safety. Dotted lines indicate 0.95 confidence intervals.

The weighted sample set is used to update the sampling distribution $P_{\text{sample}}(X)$ by minimizing the distributions' cross entropy. Minimizing cross entropy yields a distribution that is more likely to generate samples in X that are located close to the maxima of f. Minimizing of cross entropy has been shown to be equivalent to maximizing the likelihood of the samples x weighted by $f(x)$ [18]. Sampling, weighting and building new sampling distributions by maximum likelihood estimation are repeated iteratively. This yields an iterative refinement of the sampling distribution which increases the probability to sample in the region of the maxima of f, thus providing a potentially better estimate thereof. While convergence of the CE method has been proven for certain conditions, it is not easy to establish these conditions in the most practically relevant settings [19]. However, empirical results indicate that the CE method provides a robust optimization algorithm which has been applied successfully in a variety of domains (see e.g. [18,20,21])

Figure 11 illustrates the idea of iterative refinement of the sampling distribution to increase the probability to generate samples in the region of the maxima of the unknown function f. In this example, a Gaußian sampling distribution was chosen. The sampling distribution is shown as solid line, while the unknown target function is shown as dashed line. While in this Figure the target function has a Gaußian form as well, this is not required for the cross entropy method to work. Initially, the sampling distribution has a large variance, providing a well spread set of samples in the initial generation. Then the samples are weighted w.r.t. their value $f(x)$ and a maximum likelihood estimate is built from the weighted samples. This yields a Gaußian sampling distribution that exposes less variance than the initial one. Repeating this process finally yields a distribution that is very likely to produce samples that are close to the maximum of the unknown target function.

Sampling from a Gaußian distribution can for example be done via the Box-Muller method [22]. Equation 6 shows a maximum likelihood estimator for a Gaußian distribution (μ, σ^2), given a set I of n samples $\boldsymbol{a}_i \in \mathcal{A}, i \in \{0, ..., n\}$, each weighted by $w_i \in \mathbb{R}$. This yields a new Gaußian distribution that concentrates its probability mass in the region of samples with high weights. Samples with low weights are less influential on the probability mass of the new distribution.

$$\mu = \frac{\sum_{(\boldsymbol{a}_i, w_i) \in I} w_i \boldsymbol{a}_i}{\sum_{(\boldsymbol{a}_j, w_j) \in I} w_j}$$
$$\sigma^2 = \frac{\sum_{(\boldsymbol{a}_i, w_i) \in I} w_i (\boldsymbol{a}_i - \mu)^T (\boldsymbol{a}_i - \mu)}{\sum_{(\boldsymbol{a}_j, w_j) \in I} w_j} \tag{6}$$

Summarizing, the requirements for the cross entropy method are as follows.

1. A way to weight the samples, i.e. a way to compute $f(x)$ for any given $x \in X$.
2. An update mechanism for the distribution based on the weighted samples has to be provided. Typically, this is a maximum likelihood estimator for the sampling distribution.

Note that the cross entropy method is not restricted to a particular form of probability distribution. Also discrete distributions or other continuous ones than a Gaußian can be used to model the sampling distribution [18].

4.2   Online Planning with Cross Entropy Optimization

The key idea of CEOLP is to use cross entropy optimization on a *sequence* of actions. The agent's strategy $P_{\text{act}}(\mathcal{A}|\mathcal{S})$ is thus represented by a *vector* of multivariate Gaußian distributions over the parameter space of the actions $\mathcal{A} \subseteq \mathbb{R}^N$.

In the context of our framework for simulation-based planning, we want to find the maxima of a function that maps sequences of actions to expected rewards, that is $f : \mathcal{A}^* \to \mathbb{R}$. The simulation $P_{\text{sim}}(\mathcal{S}|\mathcal{S} \times \mathcal{A})$ and the reward function $R : \mathcal{S} \to \mathbb{R}$ allow us to estimate $f(\boldsymbol{a})$ for any given $\boldsymbol{a} \in \mathcal{A}^*$: We can generate a sequence of states $\boldsymbol{s} \in \mathcal{S}^*$ by sampling from the simulation and build an episode $e \in \mathcal{E}$ from $\boldsymbol{a}$ and $\boldsymbol{s}$. We can then evaluate the accumulated reward of this episode by computing the discounted sum of gathered rewards $R_{\mathcal{E}}(e)$ (see Eq. 1).

In ONPLAN, we generate e_{max} episodes and weight them by accumulated reward as shown in Algorithm 5. The sampling of actions from the strategy (Algorithm 5, line 9) is done by generating a sample from the Gaußian distribution over action parameters at the position of the strategy vector that matches the current planning depth (i.e. the number of iteration of

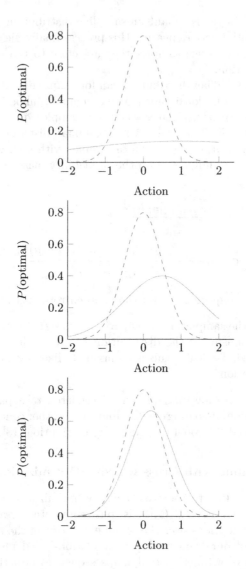

Fig. 11. Illustration of the cross entropy method with a Gaußian sampling distribution. The dashed line represents the unknown target function. The solid line represents the Gaußian sampling distribution that is iteratively refined by maximum likelihood estimation based on samples from the previous iteration, weighted by their target function values.

the for-loop in Algorithm 5, line 6). The Gaußians that form the strategy $P_{\mathrm{act}}(\mathcal{A}|\mathcal{S})$ are updated after generating and weighting $e_{\max}$ episodes, as stated in Algorithm 4. The update is performed via maximum likelihood estimation for each Gaußian in the strategy vector as defined in Eq. 6.

4.3   Framework Instantiation

Cross Entropy Open Loop Planning instantiates the ONPLAN framework based on the following considerations.

1. *Strategy::sampleAction(State): Action* generates samples from the current vector of Gaußians that represents P_{act}. As CEOLP is state agnostic and only accumulates action parameters w.r.t. planning depth, this depth is the only information that is used for conditioning the distribution: I.e. when sampling at depth d, the d-th component of the plan distribution is used to generate a value for the action.
2. *SimPlanner::updateStrategy(Set(WEpisode)): Strategy* refines the Gaußians in the strategy by maximum likelihood estimation w.r.t. the samples from the previous generation, weighted by the accumulated reward (see Eq. 6). This yields a strategy that is likely to produce high-reward episodes.
3. The remaining plug-points – *execute* of class *Action*, *getReward* of class *RewardFunction* and *sampleSuccessor* of class *Simulation* – have to be instantiated individually for each domain and/or system use case.

4.4   Empirical Results

We compared an instantiation of our framework with CEOLP with a vanilla Monte Carlo planner that does not perform iterative update of its strategy. The latter proposes actions from a strategy distribution that is the best average w.r.t. weighted simulation episodes. However, in contrast to the CEOLP planner, it does not refine the strategy iteratively while simulating to concentrate its effort on promising parts of the search space.

Experimental Setup. We provided the same number of simulations per action to each planner. The one that instantiates ONPLAN updates the strategy distribution every 30 simulations (i.e. $e_{max} = 30$) and does this 10 times before executing an action. Planning depth was set to $h_{max} = 50$. The vanilla Monte Carlo planner uses the aggregated result of 300 episodes generated w.r.t. the initial strategy to decide on an action, without updating the strategy within the planning process. It only builds a distribution once after all samples have been generated and evaluated to decide on an action. Action duration was fixed at one second. The discount factor was set to $\gamma = 0.95$ in all experiments.

Example Domain. Figure 12 depicts our evaluation scenario. The circle bottom left represents our agent. Dark rectangular areas are static obstacles, and small boxes are victims to be collected by the planning agent. The agent is provided with unit reward on collecting a victim. Victims move with Gaußian random motion (i.e. their velocity and rotation are randomly changed based on a normal distribution). Note that this yields a highly fluctuating value function of the state space – a plan that was good a second ago could be a bad idea to

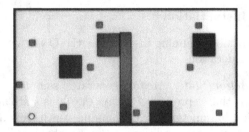

Fig. 12. The continuous sample domain.

realize a second later. This means that information aggregation from simulations should be as efficient as possible to be able to react to these changes in real time.

An agent can perform an action by first rotating for a second and then moving forward for the same amount of time. Rotation rate and movement speed are action parameters to be optimized by the planner in order to collect the victims as fast as possible. The agent is provided with a simulation of the environment as described above. Note that this simulation is an abstraction of the real environment. This means that reality and simulation may differ in their dynamics, even if performing the exactly same set of actions. Also, the simulation is not informed about the movement model of the victims.

The reward function providing unit reward to a planner on collecting a victim instantiates the *getReward* operation of class *RewardFunction* in the ONPLAN framework. Action implementations instantiate the *execute* operations of the corresponding subclasses of class *Action*. The simulation provided to the simulation-based planner instantiates the *sampleSuccessor* operation of the *Simulation* class.

Iterative Parameter Variance Reduction. Figure 13 shows an exemplary set of actions sampled from P_{act} for the first action to be executed. Here, the effect of updating the sampling strategy can be seen for the two-dimensional Gaußian distribution over the action parameters speed (x axis) and rotation rate (y axis). While the distribution is spread widely in the initial set of samples, updating the strategies according to the samples' weights yields distributions that increasingly concentrate around regions of the sample space that yield higher expected reward. The figures also show Spearman's rank correlation coefficient of the sampled action parameters to measure the dependency between the two action variables (speed and rotation rate). It can be seen that the degree of correlation increases with iterations. Also, the probability that there is no statistically significant correlation of the parameters decreases: From 0.94 in the initial set of samples to 0.089 in the tenth set.

Estimation of Expected Reward. Figures 14 and 15 show the effect of iteratively updating the strategy on simulation episode quality. We evaluated the

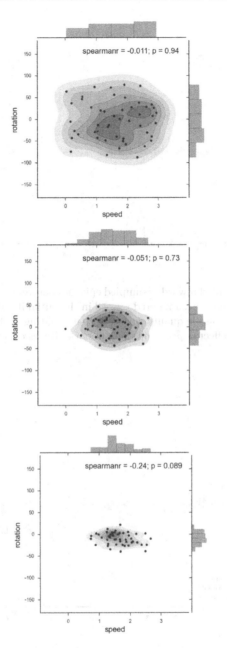

Fig. 13. Actions sampled from P_{act} for the first action to execute at iterations one, five and ten.

magnitude of effect depending on the degree of domain noise. Domain noise is given by movement speed of victims in our example. We compared victim speed of 0.1 and 1.0 (m/s). Figure 14 shows the average accumulated reward of

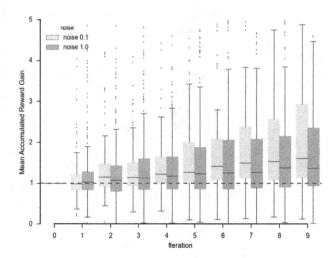

Fig. 14. Mean accumulated reward of sampled episodes per iteration. Results are shown as factor (i.e. gain) of mean accumulated reward in the initial iteration. The data shows a tendency to increase episode quality with iterative updating of the sampling strategy. The magnitude of the effect depends on domain noise. Boxes contain 50 % of measured data, whiskers 99.3 %.

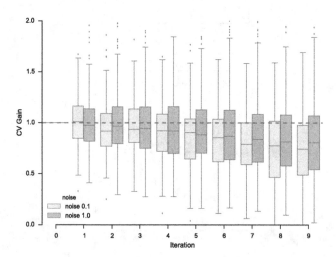

Fig. 15. Coefficient of variation (CV) of mean accumulated reward from the sampled episodes per iteration. Results are shown as factor (i.e. gain) of CV of mean accumulated reward in the initial iteration. The data shows a tendency to increase estimation accuracy with iterative updating of the sampling strategy (i.e. decreasing CV). The magnitude of the effect depends on domain noise. Boxes contain 50 % of measured data, whiskers 99.3 %.

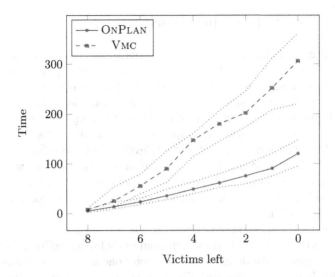

Fig. 16. Comparison of an instance of ONPLAN using CEOLP with a vanilla Monte Carlo planner (VMC). Lines show the median, dotted lines indicate interquartile range (comprising 50 % of measured data).

the episodes generated in a particular iteration, grouped by domain noise. The result is shown as a factor of the value in the initial iteration. The data shows that the episodes' average accumulated reward increases with iterations of strategy updates. The magnitude of the effect depends on domain noise. Figure 15 shows the corresponding coefficient of variation (CV), the quotient of standard deviation and mean of a sample set. This data is also grouped by domain noise. The CV of accumulated reward per episode shows a tendency to be reduced with iterations. This means that the estimation of the target value (accumulated reward per episode) is likely to increase its accuracy due to iterative strategy refinement. Again, the magnitude of the effect depends on domain noise.

Comparison with Vanilla Monte Carlo. Figure 16 shows the time needed to collect the victims by the ONPLAN and vanilla Monte Carlo (VMC) planners. Both are able to autonomously synthesize behavior that leads to successful completion of their task. System autonomy is achieved in a highly dynamic continuous state-action space with infinite branching factor and despite the noisy simulation. However, the planner using our framework is collecting victims more effectively. The benefit of making efficient use of simulation data by cross entropy optimization to drive decisions about actions becomes particularly clear when only a few victims are left. In these situations, only a few combinations of actions yield goal-oriented behavior. Therefore it is valuable to identify uninformative regions of the sampling space fast in order to distribute simulations more likely towards informative and valuable regions.

5   Conclusion and Further Work

Modern application domains such as cyber-physical systems are characterized by their immense complexity and high degrees of uncertainty. This renders unfeasible classical approaches to system autonomy which compile a single solution from available information at design-time. Instead, the idea is to provide a system with a high-level representation of its capabilities and the dynamics of its environment. The system then is equipped with mechanisms that allow to compile sensible behavior according to this high-level model and information that is currently available at runtime. I.e., instead of providing a system with a single predefined behavioral routine it is given a *space* of solutions and a way to evaluate individual choices in this space. This enables systems to autonomously cope with complexity and change.

In this paper we proposed the ONPLAN framework for realizing this approach. It provides simulation-based system autonomy employing online planning and importance sampling. We defined the core components for the framework and illustrated its behavioral skeleton. We showed two concrete instantiations of our framework: Monte Carlo Tree Search for domains with discrete state-action spaces, and Cross Entropy Open Loop Planning for continuous domains. We discussed how each instantiates the plug points of ONPLAN. We showed the ability of our framework to enable system autonomy empirically in a search and rescue domain example.

An important direction of future work is to extend ONPLAN to support learning of simulations from observations at runtime. Machine learning techniques such as probabilistic classification or regression provide potential tools to accomplish this task (see e.g. [23]). Also, other potential instantiations of the framework should be explored, such as the GOURMAND planner based on labeled real-time dynamic programming [1,24], sequential halving applied to trees (SHOT) [25,26], hierarchical optimistic optimization applied to trees (HOOT) [27] or hierarchical open-loop optimistic planning (HOLOP) [3,28]. It would also be interesting to investigate possibilities to extend specification logics such as LTL or CTL [29] with abilities for reasoning about uncertainty and solution quality. Model checking of systems acting autonomously in environments with complexity and runtime dynamics such as the domains considered in this paper provides potential for further research. Another direction of potential further research is simulation-based planning in collectives of autonomous entities that are able to form or dissolve collaborations at runtime, so-called ensembles [30,31]. Here, the importance sampling approach may provide even more effectiveness as in a single-agent context, as the search space typically grows exponentially in the number of agents involved. Mathematically identifying information that is relevant in a particular ensemble could provide a principled way to counter this combinatorial explosion of the search space in multi-agent settings.

Acknowledgements. The authors thank Andrea Vandin for his help with the MULTIVESTA statistical model checker [17].

References

1. Kolobov, A., Dai, P., Mausam, M., Weld, D.S.: Reverse iterative deepening for finite-horizon MDPS with large branching factors. In: Proceedings of the 22nd International Conference on Automated Planning and Scheduling, ICAPS (2012)
2. Keller, T., Helmert, M.: Trial-based Heuristic Tree Search for Finite Horizon MDPs. In: Proceedings of the 23rd International Conference on Automated Planning and Scheduling (ICAPS 2013), pp. 135–143. AAAI Press, June 2013
3. Weinstein, A.: Local Planning for Continuous Markov Decision Processes. Ph.D. thesis, Rutgers, The State University of New Jersey (2014)
4. Kephart, J.: An architectural blueprint for autonomic computing. IBM (2003)
5. Hastings, W.K.: Monte Carlo sampling methods using Markov chains and their applications. Biometrika $57(1)$, 97–109 (1970)
6. Rubinstein, R.Y., Kroese, D.P.: Simulation and the Monte Carlo Method, vol. 707. Wiley, New York (2011)
7. Rubinstein, R.Y., Kroese, D.P.: The Cross-Entropy Method: A Unified Approach to Combinatorial Optimization, Monte-Carlo Simulation and Machine Learning. Springer Science & Business Media, New York (2013)
8. Audibert, J.Y., Munos, R., Szepesvári, C.: Exploration-exploitation tradeoff using variance estimates in multi-armed bandits. Theor. Comput. Sci. $410(19)$, 1876–1902 (2009)
9. Browne, C.B., Powley, E., Whitehouse, D., Lucas, S.M., Cowling, P.I., Rohlfshagen, P., Tavener, S., Perez, D., Samothrakis, S., Colton, S.: A survey of monte carlo tree search methods. IEEE Trans. Comput. Intell. AI Game $4(1)$, 1–43 (2012)
10. Kocsis, L., Szepesvári, C.: Bandit based monte-carlo planning. In: Fürnkranz, J., Scheffer, T., Spiliopoulou, M. (eds.) ECML 2006. LNCS (LNAI), vol. 4212, pp. 282–293. Springer, Heidelberg (2006)
11. Weinstein, A., Littman, M.L.: Open-loop planning in large-scale stochastic domains. In: Proceedings of the Twenty-Seventh AAAI Conference on Artificial Intelligence (2013)
12. Gelly, S., Kocsis, L., Schoenauer, M., Sebag, M., Silver, D., Szepesvári, C., Teytaud, O.: The grand challenge of computer go: Monte carlo tree search and extensions. Commun. ACM $55(3)$, 106–113 (2012)
13. Silver, D., Sutton, R.S., Müller, M.: Temporal-difference search in computer go. In: Borrajo, D., Kambhampati, S., Oddi, A., Fratini, S. (eds.) Proceedings of the Twenty-Third International Conference on Automated Planning and Scheduling, ICAPS 2013, Rome, Italy, June 10–14, 2013. AAAI (2013)
14. Gelly, S., Silver, D.: Monte-carlo tree search and rapid action value estimation in computer go. Artif. Intell. $175(11)$, 1856–1875 (2011)
15. Bubeck, S., Cesa-Bianchi, N.: Regret analysis of stochastic and nonstochastic multi-armed bandit problems. Found. Trends Mach. Learn. $5(1)$, 1–122 (2012)
16. Auer, P., Cesa-Bianchi, N., Fischer, P.: Finite-time analysis of the multiarmed bandit problem. Mach. Learn. $47(2$–$3)$, 235–256 (2002)
17. Sebastio, S., Vandin, A.: Multivesta: Statistical model checking for discrete event simulators. In: Proceedings of the 7th International Conference on Performance Evaluation Methodologies and Tools, ICST (Institute for Computer Sciences, Social-Informatics and Telecommunications Engineering), pp. 310–315 (2013)
18. de Boer, P., Kroese, D.P., Mannor, S., Rubinstein, R.Y.: A tutorial on the cross-entropy method. Annals OR $134(1)$, 19–67 (2005)

19. Margolin, L.: On the convergence of the cross-entropy method. Ann. Oper. Res. **134**(1), 201–214 (2005)
20. Kobilarov, M.: Cross-entropy motion planning. I. J. Robotic Res. **31**(7), 855–871 (2012)
21. Livingston, S.C., Wolff, E.M., Murray, R.M.: Cross-entropy temporal logic motion planning. In: Proceedings of the 18th International Conference on Hybrid Systems: Computation and Control, HSCC 2015, pp. 269–278 (2015)
22. Box, G.E., Muller, M.E.: A note on the generation of random normal deviates. Ann. Math. Stat. **29**, 610–611 (1958)
23. Hester, T., Stone, P.: Texplore: real-time sample-efficient reinforcement learning for robots. Mach. Learn. **90**(3), 385–429 (2013)
24. Bonet, B., Geffner, H.: Labeled RTDP: Improving the convergence of real-time dynamic programming. In: ICAPS, vol. 3, pp. 12–21 (2003)
25. Karnin, Z., Koren, T., Somekh, O.: Almost optimal exploration in multi-armed bandits. In: Proceedings of the 30th International Conference on Machine Learning (ICML-13), pp. 1238–1246 (2013)
26. Cazenave, T., Pepels, T., Winands, M.H.M., Lanctot, M.: Minimizing simple and cumulative regret in monte-carlo tree search. In: Cazenave, T., Winands, M.H.M., Björnsson, Y. (eds.) CGW 2014. CCIS, vol. 504, pp. 1–15. Springer, Heidelberg (2014)
27. Mansley, C.R., Weinstein, A., Littman, M.L.: Sample-based planning for continuous action markov decision processes. In: Proceedings of the 21st International Conference on Automated Planning and Scheduling, ICAPS (2011)
28. Weinstein, A., Littman, M.L.: Bandit-based planning and learning in continuous-action markov decision processes. In: Proceedings of the 22nd International Conference on Automated Planning and Scheduling, ICAPS (2012)
29. Baier, C., Katoen, J.P., et al.: Principles of Model Checking, vol. 26202649. MIT Press, Cambridge (2008)
30. Wirsing, M., Hölzl, M., Koch, N., Mayer, P. (eds.): Software Engineering for Collective Autonomic Systems: Results of the ASCENS Project. LNCS, vol. 8998. Springer, Heidelberg (2015)
31. Hölzl, M.M., Gabor, T.: Continuous collaboration: A case study on the development of an adaptive cyber-physical system. In: 1st IEEE/ACM International Workshop on Software Engineering for Smart Cyber-Physical Systems, SEsCPS 2015, pp. 19–25 (2015)

Software Component Design with the B Method — A Formalization in Isabelle/HOL

David Déharbe[1]([✉]) and Stephan Merz[2]

[1] UFRN/DIMAp, Natal, RN, Brazil
david@dimap.ufrn.br
[2] Inria, 54600 Villers-lès-Nancy, France
Stephan.Merz@loria.fr

Abstract. This paper presents a formal development of an Isabelle/HOL theory for the behavioral aspects of artifacts produced in the design of software components with the B method. We first provide a formalization of semantic objects such as labelled transition systems and notions of behavior and simulation. We define an interpretation of the B method using such concepts. We also address the issue of component composition in the B method.

Keywords: B-method · Formal semantics · Isabelle/HOL · Simulation

1 Introduction

The B method is an effective, rigorous method to develop software components [1]. There exist tools that support its application, and it is used in industry to produce software components for safety-critical systems.

The B method advocates developing a series of artifacts, starting from an abstract, formal specification of the functional requirements, up to an implementation of this specification, through stepwise refinements. The specification is verified internally for consistency, and may be validated against informal requirements through animation. The specification and the successive refinements are produced manually, and are subject to *a posteriori* verification. In order to systematize the correctness proofs, the B method associates proof obligations with specifications and refinements, and these are automatically generated by the support tools and discharged automatically or interactively by the user. Finally, the implementation produced in the B method is translated to compilable source code (there are code generators for C and Ada, for instance).

Improvements in the application of the B method can be achieved by increasing the degree of automation in the construction of refinements and in the verification activities. The BART project provides a language and a library of refinement rules

This work was partially supported by CNPq grants 308008/2012-0 and 573964/2008-4 (National Institute of Science and Technology for Software Engineering—INES, www.ines.org.br), and STIC/Amsud–CAPES project MISMT.

© Springer International Publishing Switzerland 2016
C. Braga and P.C. Ölveczky (Eds.): FACS 2015, LNCS 9539, pp. 31–47, 2016.
DOI: 10.1007/978-3-319-28934-2_2

that may be applied automatically [2]. However these rules have not been verified, and the resulting artifacts must be submitted to formal verification. Verification of proof obligations also benefits from advancement in automated theorem proving such as the use of SMT solvers [3,4]. One missing step in the verification aspect of the B method is the code generation from the implementation artifacts. In practice, one apprach taken to mitigate risks of errors introduced in the code generators is redundancy: apply multiple code generators and execute the generated components in parallel.

Extending the scope of formal verification in the B method would benefit from having a machine-checkable formalization of the semantics of the B method. Such a formal semantic framework could be applied to prove the correctness of refinement rules, or at least derive proviso conditions that would be simpler to prove than the general-purpose proof obligations applied to refinements, as shown in [5]. Moreover, it could also be the employed to establish a library of verified refactoring rules, such as [6]. Finally, such a semantic framework could be used to demonstrate the correctness of the code generator, assuming that it is extended to include the constructions used in the target programming language.

In this paper, we present a formalization of the behavioral aspects of artefacts of the B method that may be taken as a starting point towards the construction of the formal semantic framework we envision. This formalization is carried out using the proof assistant Isabelle/HOL [7]. We represent the behavior of a (B) software component as a labeled transition system (LTS). We first provide a formalization of LTS, as well as the classic notion of simulation relation between LTSes. Next we formalize the concepts of B specification, refinement and project, based on LTSes as underlying behavioral model. We adapt the notion of simulation so that it matches the concept of refinement in the B method. Finally, we address the composition of components in the B method.

Outline: Section 2 presents the technical background of the paper, namely the B method and formalization in Isabelle/HOL. Section 3 contain a description of the formalization of labeled transition systems and associated concepts: simulation, traces, etc. Then, Sect. 4 formalizes software development in B, relating each type of artifact to its semantic interpretation. Section 5 is devoted to the presentation and formalization of component composition in B. Section 6 concludes the paper, discussing related work and prospective extensions.

2   Background

2.1   The B Method

In the B method [1], an individual project consists in deriving a software system that is consistent with a high-level specification. The derivation follows principled steps of formal system development: specifications are decomposed into (libraries of) modules from which executable programs are eventually obtained. Each module has a specification, called a machine, and its implementation is derived formally by a series of modules called refinements. Such modules may be used to specify additional requirements, to define how abstract data may be encoded using concrete data types, or to define how operations may be implemented algorithmically. From a formal point of view, each module is simulated by the subsequent refinement modules, and this relationship is ensured by discharging specific proof obligations. A refinement is called an implementation when its data is scalar and behavior is described in a procedural style. Implementations may be translated into an imperative programming language such as C.

At every level of the refinement chain, a module describes a state transition system. A module contains variables and instances of other modules; the state space of a module is the compositon of the set of all possible valuations of its variables and the state spaces of its components. A module also contains an initialization clause that establishes the possible initial states. And a module has operations that describe how the system might transition from one state to another state. Each operation has a name, it may have input and output parameters, as well as a precondition, specifying the configurations of state and input parameters values in which the operation is available and guaranteed to terminate.

To illustrate this, Fig. 1 provides a simple B machine of a counter from zero to three. The state of the module is the value of variable `counter`. The invariant provides the type and the range of possible values for this variable. The initialisation specifies two possible initial values for c: either 0 or 3. The operations specify that the counter may always be reset to zero, that it may be incremented only when it has not reached its upper bound. The operation `get` is always available, does not change the state and has a single output parameter which holds the value of c.

Figure 2 contains the graph of the labelled transition system corresponding to the B machine `counter3`. Each node depicts one of the four possible states, and directed edges correspond to transitions between states. They are labelled with events that correspond to the operations active in each state.

```
MACHINE counter3
VARIABLES c
INVARIANT c : INTEGER & c : 0..3
INITIALISATION c :: {0, 3}
OPERATIONS
  zero = c := 0;
  inc = PRE c < 3 THEN c := c + 1 END;
  out <— get = out := c
END
```

Fig. 1. A simple B machine, with one state variable, named c, and three operations (`zero`, `inc` and `get`).

2.2 Formalization in Isabelle/HOL

Isabelle is a logical framework for building deductive systems; we use here Isabelle/HOL, its instantiation for higher-order logic [7]. It provides a language

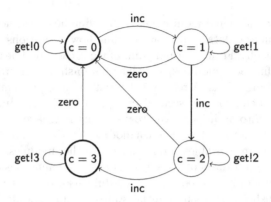

Fig. 2. Labelled transition system of the `counter3` machine. Initial states are drawn with thick lines. Each transition is labelled with the corresponding operation, possibly decorated with parameter values.

combining functional programming and logic that is suitable to develop rigorous formalizations. Isabelle also comes with numerous standard packages and powerful tools for automating reasoning. In particular, Sledgehammer [8] provides access to external proof tools complete with proof reconstruction that is checked by the trusted Isabelle kernel. Formalizations in Isabelle are structured in so-called theories, each theory containing type and function definitions, as well as statements and proofs of properties about the defined entities. Theories and proofs are developed in the Isar [9] language.

Isabelle has an extensible polymorphic type system, similar to functional languages such as ML. Predefined types include booleans and natural numbers, as well as several polymorphic type constructors such as functions, sets, and lists. Type variables are indicated by a quote, as in $'ev$, and function types are written in curried form, as in $'a \Rightarrow 'b \Rightarrow 'c$. Terms can be built using conventional functional programming constructions such as conditionals, local binding and pattern matching. Formulas are built with the usual logic connectives, including quantifiers. Type inference for expressions is automatic, but expressions can be annotated by types for clarity. For example, $e :: E$ specifies that expression e should have type E, which must be an instance of the most general type inferred for e. In the following we introduce the constructions of the language that are used in the presentation of the theories developed in our formalization of the B method.

Our development uses natural numbers, pairs, lists, sets, and options:

- Type *nat* is defined inductively with the constructors 0 and Suc (the successor function).
- Pairs are denoted as (e_1, e_2), and the components may be accessed using the functions fst and snd. If e_1 and e_2 have types E_1 and E_2, then the pair (e_1, e_2) has type $E_1 \times E_2$.
- The type $'a$ *list* represents finite lists with elements of type $'a$; it is defined inductively from the empty list $[]$ and the cons operation $\#$ that prefixes a

list by an element. The standard library contains operators such as *hd* and *tl* (head and tail of a list), @ (concatenation), ! (access by position), *length*, and *map* (constructing a list from a given list by applying a function to every element).

– The theory for sets defines type $'a$ *set* of sets with elements of type $'a$ and contains definition for all the standard operations on sets. Syntax is provided for conventional mathematical notation, e.g. $\{x \cdot x \mod 2 = 0\}$ denotes the set of even numbers. We use the generalized union operator, written $UNION$, of type $'a$ *set set* $\Rightarrow$ $'a$ *set*, that returns the union of its argument sets and the image operation ' :: $('a \Rightarrow 'b) \Rightarrow 'a$ *set* $\Rightarrow 'b$ *set* that is the counterpart of the *map* operation for sets. Also, operator *Collect* yields the set characterized by a given predicate.

– In Isabelle/HOL, all functions must be total. The type $'a$ *option* is handy to formalize partial functions. It has constructors *None* :: $'a$ *option* and *Some* :: $'a \Rightarrow 'a$ *option* to represent either no or some value of type $'a$. Also, operator *the* accesses the value constructed with *Some*.

We also use Isabelle/HOL **record** types. A record is a possibly polymorphic, named type that consists of a series of fields, each field having a name and a type. The field name is also used as a getter function to access the corresponding field in a record value. Record values and patterns can be written as $(\!| fld_1 = val_1, fld_2 = val_2 |\!)$.

Our type definitions are either introduced via **type-synonym** (type abbreviations) or by **record**, in the case of record types. Values, including functional values, are defined either through **definition**, in the case of equational definitions, or **inductive-set**, in the case of inductively defined sets. Such commands, in addition to adding a new binding to the current context, also create theorems for use in subsequent proofs. For instance, an unconditional equational definition gives rise to a theorem expressing the equality between the defined value and the defining expression. (Definitions are not expanded by default in proofs.) Inductive definitions introduce introduction rules corresponding to each clause, as well as theorems for performing case distinction and induction. For notational convenience, a definition may also be accompanied by a syntax declaration, for example for introducing an infix mathematical symbol.

Properties of the entities thus defined are introduced in the form of **lemma**, **theorem** and **corollary** paragraphs (there is no formal distinction between these levels of theorems). Properties are written as $[\![H_1; H_2; \cdots H_n]\!] \Longrightarrow C$ where the H_i are hypotheses and C is the conclusion. An alternative syntax is

assumes H_1 **and** H_2 **and** ... H_n
shows C

In an Isabelle theory, statements of properties are immediately followed by a proof script establishing their validity. In this paper, we have omitted all proof scripts.

3   Formalizing Transition Systems

The specification of a software component in the B formalism describes a labeled transition system (LTS). We therefore start with an encoding of LTSs in Isabelle, which may be of interest independently of the context of the B method.

3.1   Labeled Transition Systems and Their Runs

Our definitions are parameterized by types $'st$ and $'ev$ of states and events. We represent a transition as a record containing a source and a destination state, and an event labeling the transition. An LTS is modeled as a record containing a set of initial states and a set of transitions.

record $('st, 'ev)\ Tr\ =$ **record** $('st, 'ev)\ LTS\ =$
    $src :: 'st$ $init :: 'st\ set$
    $dst :: 'st$ $trans :: ('st, 'ev)\ Tr\ set$
    $lbl :: 'ev$

The auxiliary functions *outgoing* and *accepted-events* compute the set of transitions originating in a given state, and the set of their labels.

definition *outgoing* **where** $outgoing\ l\ s \equiv \{t \in trans\ l\ .\ src\ t = s\}$

definition *accepted-events* **where** $accepted\text{-}events\ l\ s \equiv lbl\ `\ (outgoing\ l\ s)$

The set of reachable states of an LTS l, written *states* l, is defined inductively as the smallest set containing the initial states and the successors of reachable states.

inductive-set *states* **for** $l :: ('st, 'ev)\ LTS$ **where**
    $base : s \in init\ l \Longrightarrow s \in states\ l$
    $|\ step : [\![s \in states\ l;\ t \in outgoing\ l\ s]\!] \Longrightarrow dst\ t \in states\ l$

The alphabet of an LTS is the set of all events that are accepted at some reachable state.

definition *alphabet* **where** $alphabet\ l \equiv UNION\ (states\ l)\ (accepted\text{-}events\ l)$

Runs. We formalize two notions of (finitary) behavior of LTSs. The internal behavior or *run* is an alternating sequence of states and events, starting and ending with a state. In particular, a run consists of at least one state, and the function *append-tr* extends a run by a transition, which is intended to originate at the final state of the run.

record $('st, 'ev)\ Run =$ **definition** *append-tr* **where**
    $trns :: ('st \times 'ev)\ list$ $append\text{-}tr\ run\ t \equiv$
    $fins :: 'st$ $(\!|\ trns = (trns\ run)\ @\ [(fins\ run,\ lbl\ t)],$
                                $fins = dst\ t\ |\!)$

The set of runs of an LTS is defined inductively, starting from the initial states of the LTS, and extending runs by transitions originating at the final state.

inductive-set *runs* **for** $l :: (\prime st, \prime ev)\ LTS$ **where**
   $start : s \in init\ l \Longrightarrow (\!|\ trns = [\,], fins = s\ |\!) \in runs\ l$
  $|\ step :\ [\![\ r \in runs\ l;\ t \in outgoing\ l\ (fins\ r)\ ]\!] \Longrightarrow append\text{-}tr\ r\ t \in runs\ l$

We prove a few lemmas about runs. In particular, every run starts at an initial state of the LTS, and the steps recorded in the run correspond to transitions. Moreover, the reachable states of an LTS are precisely the final states of its runs. The proofs are straightforward by induction on the definition of runs.

lemma *runs-start-initial*:
  assumes $r \in runs\ l$
  shows $(if\ trns\ r = [\,]\ then\ fins\ r\ else\ fst\,(hd\,(trns\ r))) \in init\ l$

lemma *run-steps*:
  assumes $r \in runs\ l$ **and** $i < length\,(trns\ r)$
  shows $(\!|\ src = fst\,(trns\ r\ !\ i),$
              $dst = (if\ Suc\ i < length\,(trns\ r)\ then\ fst\,(trns\ r\ !\ (Suc\ i))$
                    $else\ fins\ r),$
           $lbl = snd\,(trns\ r\ !\ i)\ |\!) \in trans\ l$

lemma *states-runs*: $states\ l\ =\ fins\ `\,(runs\ l)$

Traces. The second, observable notion of behavior is obtained by recording only the successive events that appear in a run. We call this projection a *trace* of the LTS.

type-synonym $\prime ev\ Trace = \prime ev\ list$

definition *trace-of* **where** $trace\text{-}of\ run \equiv map\ snd\ (trns\ run)$

definition *traces* **where** $traces\ l \equiv trace\text{-}of\ `\,(runs\ l)$

3.2 Simulations Between Labeled Transition Systems

Two transition systems l and l' are naturally related by a notion of simulation that ensures that every behavior of l can also be produced by l'. More formally, given a relation between the states of l and l', we say that l is simulated by l' if the two following conditions hold:

– Every initial state of l is related to some initial state of l'.
– Whenever two states s and s' are related and t is an outgoing transition of s then s' has an outgoing transition t' with the same label as t and such that the destination states are related.

The following definitions express these conditions in Isabelle: they lift a relation on states to a relation on transitions, respectively on LTSs. We write $l \preceq l'$ if l is simulated by l' for some relation r. We also sometimes refer to l as the *concrete* and to l' as the *abstract* LTS. Figure 3 illustrates the notion of simulation.

definition *sim-transition* **where**
  $sim\text{-}transition\ r \equiv \{\ (t, t')\ |\ t\ t'\ .\ (src\ t, src\ t') \in r\ \wedge$
  $(dst\ t, dst\ t') \in r \wedge lbl\ t = lbl\ t'\ \}$

definition *simulation* **where**
  $simulation\ r \equiv$
    $\{\ (l, l')\ |\ l\ l'\ .\ (\forall s \in init\ l.\ \exists s' \in init\ l'.\ (s, s') \in r)\ \wedge$
      $(\forall (s, s') \in r.\ \forall t \in outgoing\ l\ s.$
        $\exists t' \in outgoing\ l'\ s'.\ (t, t') \in sim\text{-}transition\ r)\ \}$

definition *simulated* (**infix** $\preceq$) **where**
  $l \preceq l' \equiv \exists r.\ (l, l') \in simulation\ r$

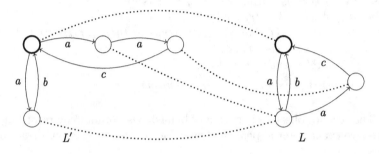

Fig. 3. Example of two LTSs L, L' such that $L' \preceq L$. Dotted lines depicts pairs of states in the simulation relation. Initial states are depicted with a thicker border.

We prove some structural lemmas about simulation: every LTS is simulated by itself through the identity relation on states, and the composition of two simulations is a simulation. It follows that $\preceq$ is reflexive and transitive. All proofs are found automatically by Isabelle after expanding the corresponding definitions.

lemma *simulation-identity*:
  $(Id :: ('st, 'ev)\ LTS\ rel) \subseteq simulation\ (Id :: 'st\ rel)$

lema *simulation-composition*:
  assumes $(l, l') \in simulation\ r$ **and** $(l', l'') \in simulation\ r'$
  shows $(l, l'') \in simulation\ (r\ O\ r')$

lemma *simulates-reflexive*: $l \preceq l$

lemma *simulates-transitive*: $[\![\ l \preceq l';\ l' \preceq l''\ ]\!] \Longrightarrow l \preceq l''$

We now prove that simulation between LTSs gives rise to similar behaviors: every behavior of the simulating LTS corresponds to a behavior of the simulated one. In order to make this idea precise, we first lift a relation on states to a relation on runs.

definition *sim-run* **where**
  $sim\text{-}run\ r \equiv \{\,(run, run') \mid run\ run'\ .$
        $length\,(trns\ run) = length\,(trns\ run') \wedge$
        $(\forall i < length\,(trns\ run).$
          $(fst\,(trns\ run\ !\ i), fst\,(trns\ run'\ !\ i)) \in r \wedge$
          $snd\,(trns\ run\ !\ i) = snd\,(trns\ run'\ !\ i)) \wedge$
        $(fins\ run, fins\ run') \in r\,\}$

By induction on the definition of runs, we now prove that whenever l is simulated by l' then every run of l gives rise to a simulating run of l'.

theorem *sim-run*:
  assumes $(l, l') \in simulation\ r$ **and** $run \in runs\ l$
  shows $\exists run' \in runs\ l'.\ (run, run') \in sim\text{-}run\ r$

Turning to external behavior, it immediately follows that any two similar runs give rise to the same trace. Using the preceding theorem, it follows that the traces of the concrete LTS are a subset of the traces of the abstract one.

lemma *sim-run-trace-eq*:
  assumes $(run, run') \in sim\text{-}run\ r$
  shows $trace\text{-}of\ run = trace\text{-}of\ run'$

theorem *sim-traces*:
  assumes $(l, l') \in simulation\ r$ **and** $tr \in traces\ l$
  shows $tr \in traces\ l'$

corollary *simulated-traces*: $l \preceq l' \implies traces\ l \subseteq traces\ l'$

3.3   A Notion of Simulation Tailored for the B Method

The notion of simulation considered so far requires that for any two related states, every transition of the concrete LTS can be matched by a transition with the same label of the abstract one. In particular, the concrete LTS accepts a subset of the events accepted by the abstract LTS. In the B method, it is required on the contrary that the concrete LTS accepts at least the events accepted by the abstract LTS. Concrete transitions labeled by events that are also accepted by the abstract system must still be matched, but nothing is required of concrete transitions for events that are not accepted by the abstract LTS. This idea is formalized by the following definition.

definition *simulation-B* **where**
  $simulation\text{-}B\ r \equiv$
    $\{\,(l, l') \mid l\ l'\ .\ (\forall s \in init\ l.\ \exists s' \in init\ l'.\ (s, s') \in r) \wedge$
        $(\forall (s, s') \in r.$
          $accepted\text{-}events\ l\ s \supseteq accepted\text{-}events\ l'\ s' \wedge$
          $(\forall t \in outgoing\ l\ s.\ lbl\ t \in accepted\text{-}events\ l'\ s' \longrightarrow$
            $(\exists t' \in outgoing\ l'\ s'.\ (t, t') \in sim\text{-}transition\ r)))\,\}$

definition *simulated-B* (**infix** $\preceq_B$) **where**
  $l \preceq_B l' \equiv \exists r.\ (l, l') \in simulation\text{-}B\ r$

The analogous structural lemmas are proved for this notion of simulation as for the previous one, implying that $\preceq_B$ is again reflexive and transitive. However, runs of the concrete LTS can in general no longer be simulated by runs of the abstract LTS because they may contain events that the abstract LTS does not accept at a given state. The following definition weakens the relation *sim-run*: the abstract run corresponds to a simulating execution of a maximal prefix of the concrete run. We show that whenever l is simulated by l' then a simulating run of l' in this weaker sense can be obtained for every run of l.

definition *sim-B-run* **where**
$sim\text{-}B\text{-}run \; r \; l' \equiv \{\, (run, run') \mid run \; run' \; .$
$\quad length \, (trns \, run') \leq length \, (trns \, run) \; \land$
$\quad (\forall i < length \, (trns \, run').$
$\quad\quad (fst \, (trns \, run \, ! \, i), fst \, (trns \, run' \, ! \, i)) \in r \; \land$
$\quad\quad snd \, (trns \, run \, ! \, i) = snd \, (trns \, run' \, ! \, i)) \; \land$
$\quad\quad (if \; length \, (trns \, run') = length \, (trns \, run)$
$\quad\quad then \; (fins \, run, fins \, run') \in r$
$\quad\quad else \; snd \, (trns \, run \, ! \, (length \, (trns \, run')))$
$\quad\quad\quad \notin accepted\text{-}events \; l' \; (fins \, run')) \, \}$

theorem *sim-B-run*:
assumes $(l, l') \in simulation\text{-}B \; r$ **and** $run \in runs \; l$
shows $\exists run' \in runs \; l'. \, (run, run') \in sim\text{-}B\text{-}run \; r \; l'$

Turning to observable behavior, we introduce a refined notion of a trace that does not only record the events that occur in a run but also which events are accepted at the end of the run.

definition *traces-B* **where**
$traces\text{-}B \; l \equiv \{\, (trace\text{-}of \, r, \; accepted\text{-}events \; l \; (fins \, r)) \mid r \; . \; r \in runs \; l \,\}$

Theorem *sim-B-run* implies that whenever l is simulated by l' then for every (B) trace of l there exists a maximal similar traces of l'.

theorem *sim-traces-B*:
assumes $l \preceq_B l'$ **and** $(tr, acc) \in traces\text{-}B \; l$
shows $\exists (tr', acc') \in traces\text{-}B \; l'.$
$\quad length \; tr' \leq length \; tr \; \land \; (\forall i < length \; tr'. \, tr' \, ! \, i = tr \, ! \, i) \; \land$
$\quad (if \; length \; tr' = length \; tr \; then \; acc' \subseteq acc$
$\quad else \; tr \, ! \, (length \; tr') \notin acc')$

4   Formalizing Development in B

We now turn our attention to the artifacts produced by the application of the B method and associate them to the formal entities we have defined in the preceding section. We address successively B machines (i.e. specifications), refinements, and the development process.

4.1   Specification

The semantics of a B machine identifies it with a labelled transition system, together with an invariant, i.e. a predicate on the states of the LTS.

> **record** $('st, 'ev)$ *B-machine* =
> $lts :: ('st, 'ev)$ *LTS*
> $invariant :: 'st \Rightarrow bool$

This definition of *B-machine* puts no restriction whatsoever on the invariant with respect to the LTS. In contrast, sound B machines are such that all the reachable states of the LTS satisfy the invariant. They are identified by the following predicate:

> **definition** *sound-B-machine* **where**
>   *sound-B-machine* $m \equiv \forall s \in states\,(lts\ m).\ invariant\ m\ s$

The following theorem states two sufficient conditions to establish that a machine is sound: all initial states must satisfy the invariant, and the transition relation must preserve the invariant. These conditions correspond to the standard proof obligations of the B method that express induction on the set of reachable states.

> **theorem** *machine-po*:
>   **assumes** $\bigwedge s.\ s \in init\,(lts\ m) \Longrightarrow invariant\ m\ s$
>   **and** $\bigwedge t.\ [\![\, t \in trans\,(lts\ m);\ invariant\ m\ (src\ t)\,]\!]$
> $\Longrightarrow invariant\ m\ (dst\ t)$
>   **shows**   *sound-B-machine* m

4.2   Refinement

A B refinement is composed of an *abstract* and a *concrete* LTS related by a *gluing invariant*. The gluing invariant is a binary predicate over the states of the abstract LTS and the states of the concrete one; it corresponds to the relation on states considered in Sects. 3.2 and 3.3.

> **record** $('st, 'ev)$ *B-refinement* =
> $abstract :: ('st, 'ev)$ *LTS*
> $concrete :: ('st, 'ev)$ *LTS*
> $invariant :: 'st \times 'st \Rightarrow bool$

As in the previous definitions of simulation, we assume that the two LTSs are defined over the same types of states and events. In practice, we expect the type of states to be a mapping of variable names to values.

A refinement is considered *sound* if the invariant establishes a simulation (in the sense established in Sect. 3.3) of the concrete component by the abstract component.

> **definition** *sound-B-refinement* **where**
>   *sound-B-refinement* $\equiv$
> $(concrete\ r, abstract\ r) \in simulation\text{-}B\,(Collect\,(invariant\ r))$

It then follows that every concrete execution corresponds to some execution of the abstract LTS, and that the former is simulated by the latter.

> **lemma** *refinement-sim*
>   **assumes** *sound-B-refinement r*
>   **shows**   *concrete r $\preceq_B$ abstract r*

We lift the structural properties of simulations to B refinements. First, the trivial refinement of an LTS by itself where the gluing invariant is the identity on states is a sound refinement.

> **definition** *refinement-id* **where**
>   *refinement-id l $\equiv$ (abstract = l, concrete = l, invariant = ($\lambda(s,t).s = t$))*
> **lemma** *refinement-id: sound-B-refinement (refinement-id l)*

Second, we define the composition of two refinements and show that the composition of two refinements is sound, provided that the concrete LTS of the first refinement is the abstract LTS of the second one. Moreover, the composition of refinements admits identity refinements as left and right neutral elements, and it is associative.

> **definition** *refinement-compose* **where**
>   *refinement-compose r r' $\equiv$*
>   *(abstract = abstract r,*
>   *concrete = concrete r',*
>   *invariant = $\lambda p. p \in$ Collect (invariant r') $\circ$ Collect (invariant r))*
> **lemma** *refinement-compose-sound:*
>   **assumes** *sound-B-refinement r* **and**   *sound-B-refinement r'*
>   **and**   *concrete r = abstract r'*
>   **shows**   *sound-B-refinement (refinement-compose r r')*
> **lemma** *refinement-compose-neutral-left :*
>   *refinement-compose (refinement-id (abstract r)) r = r*
> **lemma** *refinement-compose-neutral-right :*
>   *refinement-compose r (refinement-id (concrete r)) = r*
> **lemma** *refinement-compose-associative :*
>   *refinement-compose (refinement-compose r r') r'' =*
>   *refinement-compose r (refinement-compose r' r'')*

4.3   B Development

The development of software components in the B method proceeds by stepwise refinement. We represent this process in a so-called *B design* as a sequence of refinements. The idea is that the abstract LTS of the first refinement is gradually refined into the concrete LTS of the last refinement. Such a design is *sound* if every single refinement is sound and if the concrete LTS of each refinement is the abstract LTS of its successor. By repeated application of lemma *refinement-compose-sound*, it follows that the concrete LTS of the last refinement is simulated by the abstract LTS of the first refinement in the sequence.

type_synonym $('st, 'ev)$ *B-design* $= ('st, 'ev)$ *B-refinement list*

definition *sound-B-design* **where**
  sound-B-design refs $\equiv \forall i < size\ refs.$
    sound-B-refinement $(refs!\,i) \wedge$
    $(Suc\ i < size\ refs \longrightarrow concrete\,(refs!\,i) = abstract\,(refs!\,(Suc\ i)))$

lemma *design-sim*:
  assumes *sound-B-design refs* **and** *refs* $\neq [\,]$
  shows   *concrete*$(last\ refs) \preceq_B abstract\,(hd\ refs)$

Finally, we define a *B development* as consisting of a B machine and a B design. A sound B development consists of a sound B machine and a sound B design such that the abstract LTS of the first refinement in the design is the LTS of the B machine.

record $('st, 'ev)$ *B-development* $=$
  spec   :: $('st, 'ev)$ *B-machine*
  design :: $('st, 'ev)$ *B-design*

definition *sound-B-development* **where**
  sound-B-development dev $\equiv$
    sound-B-machine$(spec\ dev)$
  $\wedge$ *sound-B-design*$(design\ dev)$
  $\wedge$ $(design\ dev \neq [\,] \longrightarrow lts\,(spec\ dev) = abstract\,(hd\,(design\ dev)))$

It follows that in a sound B development, the concrete LTS of the final refinement simulates the initial specification.

theorem *development-sim*:
  assumes *sound-B-development d* **and** *design d* $\neq [\,]$
  shows   *concrete*$(last\,(design\ d)) \preceq_B lts\,(spec\ d)$

5   Component Composition in B

The language B has several mechanisms for composing components:

– The SEES construction allows one component access to definitions found in another component. This modularization mechanism aims at reusing definitions of some module across several components. It is not related to the behavioral aspects explored in this paper.
– The INCLUDES construction makes it possible to use instances of existing components to build a new specification, say machine M. The state of M is a tuple of the variables declared in M and the variables of the imported instances. The imported instances are initialized automatically upon initialization of M. The states of the imported instances are read-only in M, and each operation of M may call at most one operation of each such instance.

- B offers constructions named EXTENDS and PROMOTES that are essentially syntactic sugaring of the INCLUDES construction. A construction named USES provides read access between several instances that are included by the same machine, and provides additional flexibility to build a specification from combinations of INCLUDES components.
- The IMPORTS construction is to B implementations what the INCLUDES is for specifications: existing components may be used as bricks to build implementations. Since B implementations define the body of operations as sequential composition of atomic instructions, they may have multiple calls to operations of imported components.

In the following, we present a formalization of the INCLUDES construction. This formalization is carried out on the semantic objects associated to B components: LTSs and runs. The inclusion of a component C in a component A is represented by a record containing the LTS corresponding to C, a function to project states of A to states C, and a function to map each event of A to at most one event of C.

record $('st, 'ev)$ $Includes$ $=$
$\quad lts :: ('st, 'ev)$ LTS
$\quad sync\text{-}st :: {}'st \Rightarrow {}'st$
$\quad sync\text{-}ev :: {}'ev \Rightarrow {}'ev$ $option$

Next, we express the soundness conditions for such record. With respect to a given LTS A, an $Includes$ record I, with LTS C, is sound when it satisfies two conditions. First, the state projection function π maps every initial state of A to an initial state of C. Next, if t is a transition of A whose event is not mapped to an event in C by the event mapping function σ, then π projects the end states of t to the same C state; if the mapping σ yields an event e of C, then C must contain a transition labeled by e relating the projections of the source and destination states of t.

definition $sound\text{-}includes$ **where**
$\quad sound\text{-}includes\ A\ I \equiv$
$\quad\quad (let\ (C, \pi, \sigma) = (lts\ I, sync\text{-}st\ I, sync\text{-}ev\ I)\ in$
$\quad\quad \pi\,{}^{\backprime}\,(init\ A) \subseteq (init\ C)\ \wedge$
$\quad\quad (\forall t \in trans\ A\,.\,(case\ \sigma(lbl\ t)\ of$
$\quad\quad\quad None \Rightarrow \pi(src\ t) = \pi(dst\ t)$
$\quad\quad\quad |\ Some\ e \Rightarrow (\!|\ src = \pi(src\ t), dst = \pi(dst\ t), lbl = e\ |\!) \in trans\ C)))$

Sound inclusion ensures that the projection of every reachable state of the including LTS is a reachable state of the included LTS.

theorem $includes\text{-}states$:
$\quad$**assumes** $s \in states\ A$ **and** $sound\text{-}includes\ A\ I$
$\quad$**shows** $\quad(sync\text{-}st\ I)\ s \in states\ (lts\ I)$

In order to obtain a similar result for runs, we need to define a relationship between runs of a LTS and behaviors of the included LTS. We first define an auxiliary function *interaction-trns*: given an LTS A, an include record I with a LTS C, and a sequence of state and events corresponding to transitions of A, it filters out those pairs that do not correspond to events in C, and projects the result to states and events in C according to I. The function *interaction* uses *interaction-trns* in order to construct a run of the included LTS C from a run of A.

definition *interaction-trns* **where**
  interaction-trns $A\ I\ seq \equiv$
    $map\ (\lambda(s, e)\ .\ (sync\text{-}st\ I\ s,\ the\,(sync\text{-}ev\ I\ e)))$
      $(filter\ (\lambda(s, e)\ .\ sync\text{-}ev\ I\ e \neq None)\ seq)$

definition *interaction* **where**
  interaction $A\ I\ run \equiv$
    $(\!|\ trns = interaction\text{-}trns\ A\ I\ (trns\ run),$
    $fins = sync\text{-}st\ I\ (fins\ run)\ |\!)$

The soundness result at the level of runs now states that the projection (in the sense produced by *interaction*) of any run of the including LTS is a run of the included LTS. It follows that the projection of any trace of the including LTS to those events that are mapped to an event of the included LTS is a trace of the included LTS.

theorem *interaction-runs*:
  assumes $r \in runs\ A$ **and** $sound\text{-}includes\ A\ I$
  shows $interaction\ A\ I\ r \in runs\ (lts\ I)$

theorem *interaction-traces*:
  assumes $tr \in traces\ A$ **and** $sound\text{-}includes\ A\ I$
  shows $map\ (the \circ sync\text{-}ev\ I)\ (filter\ (\lambda e.\ sync\text{-}ev\ I\ e \neq None)\ tr)$
      $\in traces\ (lts\ included)$

6 Conclusion

This paper presents a formalization of the design of software components using the formal method B. We focus on the concepts that are central to the behavioral semantics of B components, namely labelled transition systems, as well as their internal and external (observable) behavior. An important relation between such entities is that of simulation: we express the classical definition of simulation and we give a variation of simulation that corresponds to B's view of refinement properties between components. All concepts are formally defined in the Isabelle/HOL proof assistant, and related by formally proved theorems. The formalization also addresses B components and the B design process at an abstract level, relating these concepts to the semantic concepts and to simulation. Our formalization also addresses inclusion, i.e. the fundamental mechanism for component composition provided in the B specification language, and characterizes soundness for such component inclusion.

The B method has previously been subject of several formalization efforts addressing either the full B specification language or some aspects of this language. Chartier [10] formalized the language of the B method, also with Isabelle/HOL, with the goal of formally verifying proof obligations and to produce a formally verified proof obligation generator. A similar effort was carried out by Bodeveix et al. [11], but using instead both Coq and PVS as formalization engines. It is noteworthy that their work provides a semantics for the language in terms of state transition systems, and is quite complementary to ours. Dunne [12] produced a mathematical formalization of the generalized substitution language, which was implemented in Isabelle/HOL by Dawson [13]. More recently, Jacquel et al. [14] have used Coq to formalize a proof system for B, therefore providing another rigorous framework to reason about the expression language of B.

In contrast to most previous work, our formalization focuses on the transition system semantics of B and is independent on B's concrete expression language. It would therefore be interesting to specialize the mapping of B artifacts to labelled transition systems as defined in this paper, based on the preexisting work. As a result of such a formalization, we would like to derive a library of sound refinement and refactoring rules for the B method.

References

1. Abrial, J.: The B-book - Assigning Programs to Meanings. Cambridge University Press, New York (2005)
2. Requet, A.: BART: a tool for automatic refinement. In: Börger, E., Butler, M., Bowen, J.P., Boca, P. (eds.) ABZ 2008. LNCS, vol. 5238, p. 345. Springer, Heidelberg (2008)
3. Marché, C., Filliâtre, J.-C., Mentré, D., Asuka, M.: Discharging proof obligations from Atelier B using multiple automated provers. In: Derrick, J., Fitzgerald, J., Gnesi, S., Khurshid, S., Leuschel, M., Reeves, S., Riccobene, E. (eds.) ABZ 2012. LNCS, vol. 7316, pp. 238–251. Springer, Heidelberg (2012)
4. Conchon, S., Iguernelala, M.: Tuning the alt-ergo SMT solver for B proof obligations. In: Ameur, Y., Schewe, K.-D. (eds.) ABZ 2014. LNCS, vol. 8477, pp. 294–297. Springer, Heidelberg (2014)
5. Borba, P., Sampaio, A., Cornélio, M.: A refinement algebra for object-oriented programming. In: Cardelli, L. (ed.) ECOOP 2003. LNCS, vol. 2743, pp. 457–482. Springer, Heidelberg (2003)
6. Cornélio, M., Cavalcanti, A., Sampaio, A.: Sound refactorings. Sci. Comput. Program. **75**(3), 106–133 (2010)
7. Nipkow, T., Paulson, L.C., Wenzel, M.: Isabelle/HOL - A Proof Assistant for Higher-Order Logic. LNCS, vol. 2283. Springer, Heidelberg (2283)
8. Blanchette, J.C., Böhme, S., Paulson, L.C.: Extending sledgehammer with SMT solvers. J. Autom. Reasoning **51**(1), 109–128 (2013)
9. Paulson, L.C., Wenzel, M.: Isabelle/Isar. In: Wiedijk, F. (ed.) The Seventeen Provers of the World. LNCS (LNAI), vol. 3600, pp. 41–49. Springer, Heidelberg (2006)
10. Chartier, P.: Formalisation of B in isabelle/HOL. In: Bert, D. (ed.) B 1998. LNCS, vol. 1393, pp. 66–82. Springer, Heidelberg (1998)
11. Bodeveix, J.P., Filali, M., Muñoz, C.: A formalization of the B-method in Coq and PVS. In: Springer, (ed.) Electronic Proceedings B-User Group Meeting FM 99. LNCS, vol. 1709, pp. 33–49 (1999)

12. Dunne, S.: A theory of generalised substitutions. In: Bert, D., Bowen, J.P., C. Henson, M., Robinson, K. (eds.) B 2002 and ZB 2002. LNCS, vol. 2272, pp. 270–290. Springer, Heidelberg (2002)
13. Dawson, J.E.: Formalising generalised substitutions. In: Schneider, K., Brandt, J. (eds.) TPHOLs 2007. LNCS, vol. 4732, pp. 54–69. Springer, Heidelberg (2007)
14. Jacquel, M., Berkani, K., Delahaye, D., Dubois, C.: Verifying B proof rules using deep embedding and automated theorem proving. Softw. Syst. Model. **14**(1), 101–119 (2015)

Asynchronous Coordination of Stateful Autonomic Managers in the Cloud

Rim Abid, Gwen Salaün$^{(\boxtimes)}$, Noel De Palma, and Soguy Mak-Kare Gueye

University of Grenoble Alpes, Inria, LIG, CNRS, Grenoble, France
rim.abid@inria.fr, Gwen.Salaun@imag.fr

Abstract. Cloud computing is now an omnipresent paradigm in modern programming. Cloud applications usually consist of several software components deployed on remote virtual machines. Managing such applications is a challenging problem because manual administration is no longer realistic for these complex distributed systems. Thus, autonomic computing is a promising solution for monitoring and updating these applications automatically. This is achieved through the automation of administration functions and the use of control loops called autonomic managers. An autonomic manager observes the environment, detects changes, and reconfigures dynamically the application. Multiple autonomic managers can be deployed in the same system and must make consistent decisions. Using them without coordination may lead to inconsistencies and error-prone situations. In this paper, we present our approach for coordinating stateful autonomic managers, which relies on a simple coordination language, new techniques for asynchronous controller synthesis and Java code generation. We used our approach for coordinating real-world cloud applications.

1 Introduction

Autonomic computing [17] is increasingly used to solve complex systems, since it reduces human errors [19]. It has become popular especially in cloud applications where the management is a crucial feature. Autonomic computing is based on the use of autonomic managers [18]. An autonomic manager is built as a control loop. It observes the application execution, ensures a continuous monitoring, and reacts to events and changes by automatically reconfiguring the application. The increasing complexity of cloud applications implies the use of various and heterogeneous autonomic managers, such as self-healing and self-protecting [5], with the objective to reconfigure automatically themselves.

When multiple autonomic managers monitor the same system, they should take globally coherent decisions. Hence, a manager should be aware of decisions of other managers before reacting. When it reacts without taking into account decisions of other managers handling the same application, error-prone situations may occur (*e.g.*, removing a server that will be needed). In order to avoid performance degradation and system consistency problems, and also to limit energy consumption it is necessary to coordinate all autonomic managers.

© Springer International Publishing Switzerland 2016
C. Braga and P.C. Ölveczky (Eds.): FACS 2015, LNCS 9539, pp. 48–65, 2016.
DOI: 10.1007/978-3-319-28934-2_3

In this paper, we present our approach, whose main goal is to synthesize a controller that monitors and orchestrates the reconfiguration operations of the involved managers. The controller also prevents a manager from violating global objectives of the managers. All participants involved in the application interact asynchronously with the controller and messages are stored/consumed into/from FIFO buffers.

More precisely, an autonomic manager is described using a formal model, namely a Labelled Transition System (LTS). We used reaction rules and regular expressions to specify coordination requirements and interaction constraints. As a consequence, each manager is not only able to manage its internal behaviour but also its relationship with other autonomic managers, which is achieved in accordance with the specification of the coordination requirements. As shown in Fig. 1, we propose controller synthesis techniques for asynchronously communicating managers. These techniques rely on an encoding of our inputs (LTS models and coordination requirements) into the LNT process algebra [6]. LNT is one of the input languages of the CADP toolbox [11], a state-of-the-art verification toolbox for concurrent systems. CADP compilers and minimization tools are particularly useful for generating a reduced LTS from the LNT specification. The generated LTS corresponds to all possible executions of the controller. It is worth noting that since we rely on formal techniques and tools, all the verification techniques available in the CADP toolbox can be used for validating the generated controller.

Once we have synthesized the controller LTS, Java code is generated using a code generator we developed. This Java code is finally deployed and used for coordinating real applications. We validated our approach on several variants of a N-tier Web application involving several autonomic managers, such as self-sizing or self-repair managers. We emphasize that our approach covers the whole development process from expression of the requirements to the final implementation and deployment of the solution.

The rest of this paper is structured as follows. In Sect. 2, we introduce our formal model for autonomic managers, the coordination language, and our running example (a multi-tier Web application). In Sect. 3, we present our synthesis techniques that mainly rely on an encoding into process algebra and on LTS

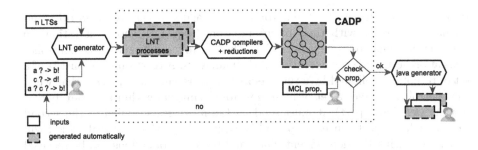

Fig. 1. Overview of our approach

manipulations. Section 4 introduces the code generation techniques for obtaining Java code from controller models. We discuss related work in Sect. 5 and we conclude in Sect. 6.

2 Models

In this section, we first present the abstract model used to represent autonomic managers. In a second step, we introduce reaction rules and regular expressions for specifying how the involved managers are supposed to interact together. Manager models and coordination expressions are used as input to our synthesis techniques (Sect. 3). At the end of this section, we introduce a typical example of distributed cloud application that we use as running example.

2.1 Autonomic Manager

Each autonomic manager is modelled as a Labelled Transition System, which is defined as follows:

Definition 1. *A Labelled Transition System (LTS) is a tuple defined as $LTS = (Q, A, T, q^0)$ where Q is a finite set of states, $A = A^! \cup A^?$ is an alphabet partitioned into a set of send and receive messages, $T \subseteq Q \times A \times Q$ is the transition relation, and q^0 is the initial state.*

We write $m!$ for a send message $m \in A^!$ and $m?$ for a receive message $m \in A^?$. A transition is represented as $q \xrightarrow{l} q' \in T$ where $l \in A$. We assume that managers are deterministic, which can be easily obtained using standard determinization algorithms [16]. Given a set of manager LTSs (Q_i, A_i, T_i, q_i^0), we assume that each message has a unique sender and a unique receiver: $\forall i, j \in 1..n,\ i \neq j$, $A_i^! \cap A_j^! = \emptyset$ and $A_i^? \cap A_j^? = \emptyset$. Furthermore, each message is exchanged between two different managers: $A_i^! \cap A_i^? = \emptyset$ for all i. Uniqueness of messages can be achieved via renaming.

2.2 Coordination Requirements

In order to coordinate multiple autonomic managers, we use reaction rules and regular expressions with their basic operators (sequence, choice, iteration) to describe the behaviour one expects from the controller. The generated controller aims at orchestrating the execution of the managers. A reaction rule consists of a set of receptions followed by a set of emissions. Basically, it expresses that when the controller receives a set of messages from managers within a certain period of time (left hand part), it must send all the messages specified in the second set (right hand part) once the period is expired. Note that the real period will be chosen during the deployment phase and both sets of actions can be received and emitted in any order.

Definition 2. *Given a set of managers* $\{M_1, \ldots, M_n\}$ *with* $M_i = (Q_i, A_i, T_i, q_i^0)$, *a reaction rule* R *is defined as* $a_1, \ldots, a_m \rightarrow b_1, \ldots, b_p$ *where* $a_j \in A_i^?$ *and* $b_k \in A_i^!$ *for* $1 \leqslant j \leqslant m$ *and* $1 \leqslant k \leqslant p$.

The specification of the behaviour one expects from the controller is expressed using a coordination expression.

Definition 3. *A coordination expression* C *is a regular expression over reaction rules* R:

$$C ::= R \mid C_1.C_2 \mid C_1 + C_2 \mid C*$$

where $C_1.C_2$ *is a coordination expression* C_1 *followed by* C_2, $C_1 + C_2$ *is a choice between* C_1 *and* C_2, *and* $C*$ *is a repetition of* C *zero or several times.*

It is worth noting that all participants, namely the autonomic managers and the controller to be generated, communicate asynchronously using message passing via FIFO buffers. Each participant is equipped with one input buffer. Therefore, it consumes messages from its buffer and sends messages to the input buffer of the message recipient. Once generated and added to the system, all managers communicate through the controller, which means that the controller acts as a centralized orchestrator for the whole system.

2.3   Running Example

Our running example is a JEE multi-tier application (Fig. 2) composed of an Apache Web server, a set of replicated Tomcat servers, a MySQL proxy server, and a set of replicated MySQL databases. The Apache server receives incoming requests and distributes them to the replicated Tomcat servers. The Tomcat servers access the database through the MySQL proxy server that distributes fairly the SQL queries to a tier of replicated MySQL databases.

The autonomic manager architecture is based on the **MAPE-K** (Monitor Analyse Plan Execute - Knowledge) reference model [17]. We describe this architecture using several LTS models. First, we model the behaviour of the monitor, analyse, and execute functions of the managers by what we call the application manager (Fig. 3, right), which sends messages when a change occurs in the system and receives messages indicating actual administrative changes to perform on the application. As for the plan functions, we use two models called self-sizing and self-repair managers, resp. The self-sizing manager (Fig. 3, middle) is

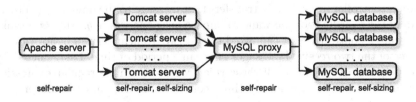

Fig. 2. A multi-tier application

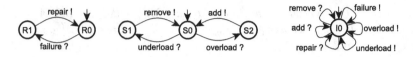

Fig. 3. (left) Self-repair manager LTS, (middle) Self-sizing manager LTS, (right) Application manager LTS

in charge of adapting dynamically the number of replicated servers by sending the message add! (remove!, resp.) to the system when detecting an overload (underload, resp.). The overload (underload, resp.) is detected when the average of the load exceeds (is under, resp.) a maximum (minimum, resp.) threshold. We associate one instance of the self-sizing manager to the Tomcat servers and another instance to the MySQL databases. The self-repair manager (Fig. 3, left) asks the system to repair a failure by creating a new instance of the failed server. We have four instances of the self-repair manager, one per tier.

The absence of coordination between these managers may lead the whole system to some undesired situation such as adding two new servers whereas one was enough as a result of a server failure. More precisely, when the self-repair manager repairs a failure, the other replicated servers receive more requests than before the failure, which causes an overload and therefore the addition of another (unnecessary) server by the self-sizing manager.

We present below an excerpt of the requirements for the controller we want to generate for our running example. These rules ensure that all managers globally satisfy the coordination objectives. Each line presents the actions that can be received by the controller in a period T (left parts of reactions rules). At the end of each period, if the received messages match the left part of one fireable rule, it reacts by emitting the messages appearing in the right part of that rule. All messages are prefixed by the manager name (app stands for the application manager) and suffixed by the name of the tier to which is associated the manager.

```
(   app_failure_apache?    -> repair_failure_apache!                    (❶)
 +  app_overload_tomcat?   -> sizing_overload_tomcat!                   (❷)
 +  app_failure_apache?, app_underload_tomcat?-> repair_failure_apache! (❸)
 +  app_failure_tomcat?, app_overload_tomcat? -> repair_failure_tomcat! (❹)
 +  ...  ) *
```

We distinguish two kinds of rules: (1) those where a unique message appears in the left part of the reaction rule (see, *e.g.*, ❶, ❷). In that case, the corresponding controller immediately transfers that message to the manager; (2) those encoding the coordination we want to impose on managers, *e.g.*, rule ❹ permits to generate a controller that can avoid to add two Tomcat servers by forwarding only one of the two received messages on a same period of time. Last, since there is no specific order between all these rules, we use a simple regular expression where all rules can be fired at any time (combination of + and * operators).

3 Synthesis

In this section, we present our asynchronous controller synthesis techniques, which rely on an encoding of our models and of the coordination requirements into the LNT specification language. From this LNT specification, we can generate the corresponding LTS model using CADP compilers, hiding, and reduction techniques. Validation of the generated controller is also possible using CADP verification tools. This section ends with an illustration of all these techniques on our running example. All the steps presented in this section are fully automated by a tool that we developed in Python. This tool generates the LNT code as well as SVL scripts [11] that are used for invoking CADP exploration and reduction tools, which finally results in the generation of the controller LTS.

3.1 Process Algebra Encoding

The backbone of our solution is an encoding of all managers and of the coordination requirements into the LNT process algebra. The choice of LNT is motivated by several reasons. First, LNT is an expressive behavioural specification language which has a user-friendly syntax and provides expressive operators. Second, LNT is supported by CADP [11], a toolbox that contains optimized state space exploration techniques and verification tools. CADP tools allow to compile the LNT specification into an LTS, which enumerates all the possible executions of the corresponding specification. Third, CADP is a verification toolbox dedicated to asynchronous systems consisting of concurrent processes interacting via message passing. It provides many tools that can be used to make different kinds of analysis, such as model checking.

The behavioural part of the LNT specification language consists of the following constructs: action with input/output parameters, assignment (:=), sequential composition (;), conditional structure (if), loop (loop), parallel composition (par), nondeterministic choice (select), and empty statement (null). Each process defines an alphabet of actions, a list of typed parameters, and a behaviour built using the aforementioned operators. Communication is carried out by rendezvous on actions with bidirectional transmission of multiple values. The parallel composition explicitly declares the set of actions on which processes must synchronize. If the processes evolve independently from one another (interleaving), this set is empty.

In the rest of this section, we successively present the encoding into LNT of the different parts of our system.

Autonomic Manager. An LNT process is generated for each state in the manager LTS. Each process is named using the state identifier. The alphabet of the process contains the set of messages appearing on the LTS transitions. The behaviour of the process encodes all the transitions of the LTS going out from the corresponding state. If there is no such transition, the body of the process is the null statement. If there is a single transition, the body of the process corresponds to the message labelling this transition, followed by a call to the process encoding the target state of the transition. If there is more than one transition, we use the `select` operator. Let us assume that two transitions $q \xrightarrow{l} q'$, $q \xrightarrow{l'} q'' \in T$ have the same source state q. The behaviour of the process encoding q in LNT is `select l; q'[...] [] l'; q'' end select`, where the LNT operator `select` encodes a nondeterministic choice between l and l'.

Since a message name can be used in different autonomic manager LTSs, each message is prefixed with the manager name to avoid further name clashes. We encode emitted messages (received messages, resp.) with a `_EM` (`_REC`, resp.) suffix. These suffixes are necessary because LNT symbols ! and ? are used for the data transfer only. As an example, $m1 \in A^!$ is encoded as $m1\_EM$, and $m2 \in A^?$ is encoded as $m2\_REC$.

Coordination Requirements. The coordination requirements specified using reaction rules and regular expressions correspond to an abstract version of the controller to be generated. These requirements are encoded into an LNT process called *coordination*. The process alphabet is composed of all received and emitted messages appearing in the reaction rules. The body of this process encodes the regular expression of reaction rules. Each reaction rule is translated to LNT separating both sides of the rule using the sequential composition construct (;). In order to make explicit in the controller LTS the logical interval of time that will be chosen in the implementation step and during which the controller receives messages, the left hand part of the reaction rule starts with an action `TBEGIN` and ends with an action `TEND`. The left hand part is translated using the `par` operator without synchronization since all messages can be received in any order. After execution of the `TEND` action, the right hand part of the reaction rule is translated using the parallel composition too, to express that all emissions can be sent in any order. As far as the regular expression is concerned, a sequence (.) of rules is encoded using the sequential composition, a choice (+) between several rules is translated using the `select` construct and an iteration (∗) is encoded using the `loop` operator.

Architecture. In this section, we present how all participants (managers and coordination expression) are composed together. The communication between them is achieved asynchronously. The coordination expression represents an abstract description of the future controller, and all messages must go through this controller, which acts as a centralized orchestrator. Each participant is equipped with an input FIFO buffer. When a participant wants to read a message, it reads the oldest message in its buffer. When a participant sends a message to another participant, it sends the message to the input buffer of that participant. LNT functions are used to describe basic operations on these buffers (*e.g.,* adding and retrieving messages). We present below, an example of function that removes a message from a FIFO buffer (*i.e.,* from the beginning).

```
function remove_MSG (q: TBUFFER): TBUFFER is
  case q in
    var hd: TMessage, tl: TBUFFER in
         nil            -> return nil
       | cons(hd,tl) -> return tl
  end case
end function
```

It is worth noting that our synthesis techniques allow one to choose buffer bounds. One can either decide to fix an arbitrary bound for buffers or to use unbounded buffers. In the first case, the only constraint is that the same buffer bound should be used when deploying the controller, otherwise unexpected behaviours and erroneous situations may occur. In the second case (unbounded buffers), the risk is to attempt to generate a controller whose corresponding state space is infinite [3]. As an intermediate solution, one can use the recent results presented in [2] for identifying whether the interactions between managers with unbounded buffers can be mimicked with bounded buffers. If this is the case, the lower bound returned by these techniques is used as the minimum buffer bound for both synthesis techniques and the deployment of the application.

A buffer in LNT is first encoded using an LNT list and classic operations on it. Then, for the behavioural part, a buffer is encoded using a process with a buffer data type as parameter. This process can receive messages from the other participants, and can synchronize with its own participant when that one wants to read a message. We generate a process encoding each couple (*participant, buffer*) that corresponds to a parallel composition (**par**) of the participant with its buffer. The synchronization set contains messages consumed by the participant from its buffer.

Finally, the whole system (**main** process in LNT, see below) consists of the parallel composition of all these couples. It is worth noting that since autonomic managers communicate via the controller, they evolve independently from one another and are therefore composed using the **par** operator without synchronizations. In contrast, the couple (*coordination, buffer*) must synchronize with all couples (*manager, buffer*) on all emissions from/to the managers, and this is made explicit in the corresponding synchronization set of this parallel composition.

```
process main [message₁:any, ..., messageₙ:any] is
    par messageₚ, ..., messageₖ in
      couple_buffer_coordination [...]
    ||
      par
         couple_buffer_manager₁ [...]
      || . . . ||
         couple_buffer_managerₙ [...]
      end par
    end par
end process
```

3.2   Compilation and Verification

Now that we have encoded our inputs (models and coordination requirements) into LNT, we can use compilers to obtain the LTS corresponding to all behaviours of the LNT specification. In order to keep only the behaviour corresponding to the most permissive controller [26], we need to hide message exchanges corresponding to consumptions of the managers from their buffers and emissions from managers to the coordination expression buffer. All these messages are replaced by internal actions. We use minimization techniques available in CADP for eliminating all internal actions, removing duplicated paths, and determinizing the final LTS. Finally, we preserve only local emissions/receptions from the coordination expression point of view (messages shown in the dashed grey rectangle in Fig. 4). Transitions figuring in the final LTS are labelled with the messages corresponding to the process alphabet of the couple (*coordination, buffer*).

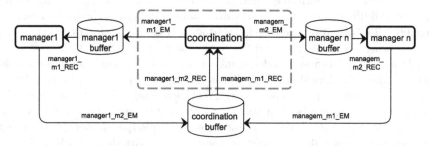

Fig. 4. Exchange of messages between the coordination expression and the managers

Last but not least, let us stress that, since the writing of the coordination expression is achieved manually by a designer, this step of our approach may lead to an error-prone expression. However, we can take advantage of the encoding into LNT to check either the controller LTS (and thus the coordination expression) or the LTS corresponding to the composition of all participants. To do so, one can use the CADP model checker, which takes as input an LTS model and a temporal property specified in MCL [20]. We distinguish two types of properties: (i) those that depend on the application (*e.g.,* the controller must eventually transmit a specific message to a certain manager), (ii) those that do not depend on the application (*e.g.,* checking the absence of deadlock).

3.3   Running Example and Experiments

We present below an example of LNT process encoding the repair manager shown in Fig. 3 and its buffer. This manager synchronizes with its buffer on the `repair_failure_REC` message when this message is available in the buffer. Note that the buffer process (`buffer_repair`) is equipped with a parameter corresponding to the buffer data type, that is the structure where messages are stored, initialized to `nil`.

```
process couple_buffer_repair [repair_failure_REC: any, repair_repair_EM:
any, repair_failure_EM: any] is
  par repair_failure_REC is
    repair_R0 [repair_failure_REC, repair_repair_EM]
  ||
    buffer_repair [repair_failure_EM, ...] (nil)
  end par
end process
```

From the encoded LNT specification obtained when calling the LNT code generator, we use CADP compilers to generate the LTS describing the whole system for our running example (consisting of 194,026,753 states and 743,878,684 transitions). Then, we use hiding and minimization techniques to generate the LTS of the controller (consisting of 28,992,305 states and 46,761,782 transitions). An excerpt of the controller LTS, which focuses on the failure and overload detection in the same period of time, is shown in Fig. 5. We recall that we use specific labels (namely TBEGIN and TEND) for characterizing the messages received during a same period of time. This LTS shows that when the controller receives a failure and an overload message (of a Tomcat server in this example) during a same period, it forwards only the failure message and drops the overload message. In contrast, when the controller receives these two messages in two different periods, it forwards them to the repair and sizing manager, resp.

We show below two examples of liveness properties, the first one is checked on the controller LTS and the second one on the LTS of the whole system:

– The reception of a failure message by the controller is eventually followed by an emission of a repair message

```
[true* .app_failure_tomcat_REC] inev (app_repair_tomcat_EM)
```

– The emission of an overload message by the application manager is eventually followed by an emission of a reparation or addition message by the controller

```
[true* .app_overload_tomcat_EM]
        inev (app_repair_tomcat_EM or app_add_tomcat_EM)
```

This property shows that the overload message is handled by the repair manager when both Tomcat failure and overload occur within a same period of time. Otherwise, it is handled by the sizing manager.

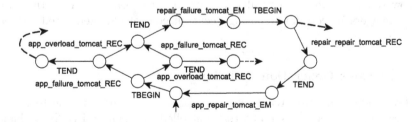

Fig. 5. Excerpt of the controller LTS for the running example

Table 1. Experimental results: LTSs size and synthesis time

Managers	Whole system LTS		Controller LTS		Time
	|states|	|transitions|	|states|	|transitions|	(m:s)
2	2,307	6,284	118	157	0:10
3	103,725	365,845	1,360	2,107	1:15
4	145	267	38	44	0:06
5	10,063,873	39,117,110	17,662	28,003	43:59
6	1,900	4,945	186	285	0:08
10	300,000	1,686,450	1,786	3,471	6:54

Both properties use the macro inev (M), which indicates that a transition labelled with M eventually occurs. This macro is defined as follows:

```
macro inev (M) = mu X .( < true > true and [ not (M) ] X ) end macro
```

Our approach was applied for validation purposes on many illustrative examples of our dataset (managers and coordination requirements). Table 1 summarizes some of our experiments. Each managed application used as input is characterized using the number of managers and the coordination requirements. We give the size of the LTS (states/transitions) of the whole system as well as the controller LTS obtained after minimization (*wrt.* a strong bisimulation relation). The last column gives the overall time to synthesize the controller.

We observe that, for some examples (gray lines), the size of the generated controller LTSs and the time required for generating those LTSs grow importantly when one of the managers exhibit looping behaviours, and particularly cycles with send messages (see, *e.g.*, the 4th example in Table 1). On a wider scale, we note that LTS sizes and generation times increase with the number of managers in parallel (see, *e.g.*, the last line of Table 1).

4   Code Generation and Deployment

We present in this section our Java code generation techniques, which allow to deploy controllers in the context of real-world applications. In particular, we show some experimental results for our running example where the autonomic managers are coordinated using a centralized controller generated with our approach.

4.1   Java Code Generation Techniques

Our Java code generation techniques are based on the use of object-oriented programming. They take as input the controller LTS synthesized beforehand, and automatically generate all java classes, methods, and types necessary for deploying it. The controller LTS is encoded as an instance of a Java class LTS.

This class relies on two classes, namely a class `State` and a class `transition` which represents the transitions between the states. The LTS class also defines an attribute `cstate` representing the current active state in the controller model. This variable is initialized with the LTS initial state. Some Java code is necessary to interface the controller with the running application. We particularly define a method called `react` that takes as input a list of messages received within a period of time and applies successive moves according to the received messages, the current state of the controller, and the behaviour of the generated controller. This method computes the messages that the controller has to send as reaction to these received messages, and updates the current state of the controller.

4.2 Deployment

Our generated Java code can be deployed and applied on concrete applications using the event-based programming paradigm. The period of time described using special actions `TBEGIN` and `TEND` in the controller LTS has to be instantiated with a real value. This period is computed using sampling techniques and implemented using the `sleep` method in Java. The choice of this period cannot be realized during the synthesis phase and is achieved just before deployment. A wrong choice of this period may lead to the reception of these actions in different periods.

The main behaviour of the controller (`run` method) consists of an infinite reactive loop, which successively receives events from the application, computes reactions (messages to be sent by the controller), and encodes these messages as events too. A part of the Java program is dedicated to converting the events raised by the application into the input format of the `react` method, and conversely translates the output of the `react` method into a list of events executed by the system. Each event contains the corresponding message and additional information, for instance a failure event has also as parameter the impacted server and further information (identifier, port, etc.).

4.3 Experiments on Our Running Example

In this section we present some experiments we performed when deploying and running our controller for the multi-tier application introduced previously. To do so, we used a virtualized experimental platform based on Openstack, which consists of six physical machines on which we instantiate virtual machines.

The JEE multi-tier application is initially configured and deployed with a server at each tier, *i.e.*, an Apache Web server, a Tomcat server, a MySQL proxy, and a MySQL database. The initial deployment phase is automated using a dynamic management protocol allowing to connect and start the involved servers and database in the right order [1, 10]. In a second step, we use jmeter to inject increasing load on the Apache server and thus to simulate the clients that send HTTP requests on the managed system. Once we have at least two active Tomcat servers and two MySQL databases, we start simulating failures using a failure injector. When we start injecting failures, we stop augmenting the workload

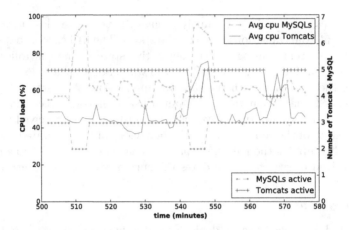

Fig. 6. Tomcat and MySQL failure/overload in a coordinated environment

on the Apache server and keep the same load for the rest of the execution. The failure injector is flexible and can be used for affecting any active server (Apache, Tomcat, MySQL, etc.), any number of times (single failure or multiple failures of the same or of different servers), and at any time (same period of time, different periods of time, etc.). We conducted our experiments on applications with or without controller. We have considered different scenarios with failures of the Apache server and of the MySQL proxy as well as failures/load variation of the Tomcat servers and of the MySQL databases.

Figure 6 shows an excerpt of the system behaviour after 500 min since the application deployment. We observe that, at this moment, the application is composed of five Tomcat servers and three MySQL databases. Figure 6 presents several cases of failure injection. As an example, at minute 508, a failure of a replicated MySQL database causes a workload increase on the other replicated servers. These two actions happen in the same period, but the controller forwards only the failure detection to the repair manager. Accordingly, a single MySQL database is added by the repair manager and the workload returns at once to its average value.

We made several experiments in which we varied the number of failures, the Apache load, and the minimum/maximum thresholds of the Tomcat servers and of the MySQL databases. In all these cases, we observe that the controller succeeds in detecting and correcting the problems while avoiding undesired operations, that is, the unnecessary addition/removal of VMs. Figure 7 shows experimental results obtained with different number of failures. For instance, we see that when injecting 14 failures to our running application, the controller applies 18 reconfiguration operations on the system (instead of 40 without controller), and thus avoids 22 undesired operations.

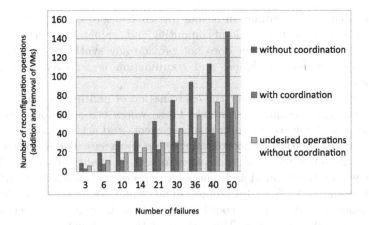

Fig. 7. Number of reconfiguration operations with/without coordination and number of undesired operations avoided by coordination

5 Related Work

Controller synthesis for discrete event systems was originally introduced by Ramadge and Wonham [24,26]. In [26], the authors present a controllable language as a solution for the supervisory of hybrid control systems. This solution generates controllers from a given system called plant and designed as a finite automaton. [24] proposes a supervisor synthesis algorithm, which allows to automatically generate a controller from a plant modelled as a finite automaton and properties to be ensured by the controller. The generated controller permits all possible legal executions. This synthesis approach is based on a classical two-person game approach. These approaches can be characterized as restrictive because they directly influence and impact the controlled system.

In [9], the authors introduce an approach based on contract enforcement and abstraction of components to apply a modular discrete controller synthesis on synchronous programs. These programs are presented by Synchronous Symbolic Transition Systems. The authors integrate this approach in a high-level programming language combining data-flow and automata. Another decentralized supervisory control approach for synchronous reactive systems is presented in [25]. This work is based on finite state machines and computes local controllers that act on the subsystems to ensure a global property. The local controllers are automatically generated and this approach was applied to several examples for validation purposes. This approach allows decentralized control whereas we generate a centralized controller. Moreover, they rely on synchronous systems and synchronous communication semantics, whereas we assume asynchronous systems and communication, meaning that the controllability hypothesis is impossible in our context.

In [22], the authors propose a generic integration model that focuses terms of reciprocal interference. This generic model can be used to manage the synchronization and coordination of multiple control loops, and it was applied to a scenario in the context of cloud computing and evaluated under simulation-based experiments. This paper does not provide any synthesis techniques for coordinating the multiple loops, and coordination is achieved in a rather manual way.

[21] presents a framework for the coordination of multiple autonomic managers in the cloud computing context. These works use a protocol based on synchronous mechanisms and inter-manager events and actions along with synchronization mechanisms for coordinating these managers. The main difference compared with our work is that this paper focuses on quality of service whereas our focus was on behavioural and functional aspects of the system execution.

Other recent works [8,12,13] propose some techniques based on synchronous discrete controller synthesis for coordinating autonomic managers, such as self-repair and self-sizing managers. The communication between the generated controller and the managers is synchronous and uses a synchronous language BZR, which cannot impose a specific order between requirements and contains multiple and complicated operations. This approach uses a background in synchronous systems and languages, whereas our approach assumes that communication is achieved asynchronously.

[7] presents the Aeolus component model and explains how some activities, such as deployment, reconfiguration, and management phases of complex cloud applications, can be automated in this model. Aeolus takes as inputs high-level application designs, user needs, and constraints (*e.g.,* the number of required ports that can be bound to a client port) to provide valid configuration environments. This work presents some similarities with ours, but does not propose solutions for verifying that the constraints are satisfied in the target configurations.

In [4], the authors present an extension of TOSCA (OASIS Topology and Orchestration Specification for Cloud Applications) in order to model the behaviour of component's management operations. More precisely, they specify the order in which the management operations of an instantiated component must be executed. In this work, the authors explain how management protocols are described as finite state machines, where the states and transitions are associated with a set of conditions on the requirements and capabilities of the components.

In [23], the authors introduce AutoMate, a framework for coordinating multiple autonomic components hosted on Grid applications, using high-level rules for their dynamic composition. The rules are executed using a decentralized deductive engine, called RUDDER, and composed of distributed specialized agents. RUDDER deploys the rules and coordinates their execution. It assigns priorities to these rules in order to resolve conflicting decisions between them. However, it uses a manual administration to evaluate and update the interaction rules.

6   Conclusion

In this paper, we propose new controller synthesis techniques to generate a centralized controller that allows to orchestrate a set of autonomic managers.

These managers are modelled as LTSs and the set of coordination requirements is specified using reaction rules and regular expressions. The generated controller communicates with the autonomic managers asynchronously using message passing via FIFO buffers. Our solution for controller synthesis relies on an encoding of our models and of the coordination requirements into the LNT process algebra. From this encoding, an LTS can be generated using CADP compilers, and hiding and reduction techniques. This LTS exhibits all the possible executions of the controller. One can also take advantage of this encoding to validate the generated controller with the CADP verification tools, such as the Evaluator model checker. Indeed, since coordination requirements are written by a human being, they can be erroneous, which results in that case in an erroneous controller as well. Finally, we propose code generation techniques to automatically obtain the Java code corresponding to the controller LTS. We validated our approach with many variants of the multi-tier Web application we used as running example in this paper.

It is worth noting that our approach covers all the development steps from the design of the coordination requirements to the actual deployment of the synthesized controller, which helps to coordinate at runtime real-world applications. In addition, these synthesis techniques can be used to control other applications where components are modelled as LTSs and communicate asynchronously. This is the case in application areas such as Web services, multi-agent systems, or hardware protocols.

A first perspective is to generate distributed controllers instead of a centralized controller. This would permit to preserve the degree of parallelism of the system, where the involved participants could exchange messages without systematically passing through a unique controller. Another perspective aims at applying performance evaluation for the whole system using IMC (Interactive Markov Chain) theory [14, 15].

Acknowledgements. This work has been supported by the OpenCloudware project (2012–2015), which is funded by the French *Fonds national pour la Société Numérique* (FSN), and is supported by *Pôles* Minalogic, Systematic, and SCS.

References

1. De Palma, N., Salaün, G., Bongiovanni, F., Abid, R.: Verification of a dynamic management protocol for cloud applications. In: Van Hung, D., Ogawa, M. (eds.) ATVA 2013. LNCS, vol. 8172, pp. 178–192. Springer, Heidelberg (2013)
2. Basu, S., Bultan, T.: Automatic verification of interactions in asynchronous systems with unbounded buffers. In: Proceedings of ASE 2014, pp. 743–754. ACM (2014)
3. Brand, D., Zafiropulo, P.: On communicating finite-state machines. J. ACM **30**(2), 323–342 (1983)
4. Brogi, A., Canciani, A., Soldani, J., Wang, P.: Modelling the behaviour of management operations in cloud-based applications. In: Proceedings of PNSE 2015, vol. 1372 of CEUR Workshop Proceedings, pp. 191–205 (2015)

5. Buyya, R., Calheiros, R.N., Li, X.: Autonomic cloud computing: open challenges and architectural elements. In: Proceedings of EAIT 2012, pp. 3–10. IEEE Computer Society (2012)
6. Champelovier, D., Clerc, X., Garavel, H., Guerte, Y., Powazny, V., Lang, F., Serwe, W., Smeding, G.: Reference Manual of the LOTOS NT to LOTOS Translator (Version 5.4). INRIA/VASY (2011)
7. Di Cosmo, R., Mauro, J., Zacchiroli, S., Zavattaro, G.: Aeolus: a component model for the cloud. Inf. Comput. **239**, 100–121 (2014)
8. Delaval, G., Gueye, S.M.K., Rutten, E., De Palma, N.: Modular coordination of multiple autonomic managers. In: Proceedings of CBSE 2014, pp. 3–12. ACM (2014)
9. Delaval, G., Marchand, H., Rutten, E.: Contracts for modular discrete controller synthesis. In: Proceedings of LCTES 2010, pp. 57–66. ACM (2010)
10. Etchevers, X., Salaün, G., Boyer, F., Coupaye, T., De Palma, N.: Reliable self-deployment of cloud applications. In: Proceedings of SAC 2014, pp. 1331–1338. ACM (2014)
11. Garavel, H., Lang, F., Mateescu, R., Serwe, W.: CADP 2011: a toolbox for the construction and analysis of distributed processes. STTT **15**(2), 89–107 (2013)
12. Gueye, S.M.K., De Palma, N., Rutten, E., Tchana, A.: Coordinating multiple administration loops using discrete control. SIGOPS Oper. Syst. Rev. **47**(3), 18–25 (2013)
13. Gueye, S.M.K., Rutten, E., Tchana, A.: Discrete control for the coordination of administration loops. In: Proceedings of UCC 2012, pp. 353–358. IEEE Computer Society (2012)
14. Hermanns, H.: Interactive Markov Chains: And The Quest for Quantified Quality. LNCS, vol. 2428. Springer, Heidelberg (2002)
15. Hermanns, H., Katoen, J.P.: Automated Compositional Markov Chain Generation for a Plain-Old Telephone System. Sci. Comput. Program. **36**(1), 97–127 (2000)
16. Hopcroft, J.E., Ullman, J.D.: Introduction to Automata Theory, Languages and Computation. Addison Wesley, Reading (1979)
17. Huebscher, M.C., McCann, J.A.: A Survey of Autonomic Computing Degrees, Models and Applications. ACM Comput. Surv. **40** (2008)
18. Kephart, J.O.: Research Challenges of Autonomic Computing. In: Proceedings of ICSE 2005, pp. 15–22. ACM (2005)
19. Kephart, J.O., Chess, D.M.: The vision of autonomic computing. Computer **36**(1), 41–50 (2003)
20. Thivolle, D., Mateescu, R.: A model checking language for concurrent value-passing systems. In: Cuellar, J., Sere, K. (eds.) FM 2008. LNCS, vol. 5014, pp. 148–164. Springer, Heidelberg (2008)
21. De Oliveira, F.A., Ledoux, T., Sharrock, R.: A framework for the coordination of multiple autonomic managers in cloud environments. In: Proceedings of SASO 2013, pp. 179–188. IEEE (2013)
22. Sharrock, R., Ledoux, T., Alvares de Oliveira Jr., F.: Synchronization of multiple autonomic control loops: application to cloud computing. In: Sirjani, M. (ed.) COORDINATION 2012. LNCS, vol. 7274, pp. 29–43. Springer, Heidelberg (2012)
23. Parashar, M., Liu, H., Li, Z., Matossian, V., Schmidt, C., Zhang, G., Hariri, S.: AutoMate: enabling autonomic applications on the grid. Cluster Comput. **9**(2), 161–174 (2006)
24. Ramadge, P.J.G., Wonham, W.M.: The Control of Discrete Event Systems. Proc. IEEE **77**(1), 81–98 (1989)

25. Seboui, A.B., Hadj-Alouane, N.B., Delaval, G., Rutten, É., Yeddes, M.: An approach for the synthesis of decentralised supervisors for distributed adaptive systems. Int. J. Crit. Comput.-Based Syst. **2**(3/4), 246–265 (2011)

26. Wonham, W.M., Ramadge, P.J.G.: On the supremal controllable sublanguage of a given language. SIAM J. Control Optim. **25**(3), 637–659 (1987)

A Cost/Reward Method for Optimal Infinite Scheduling in Mobile Cloud Computing

Luca Aceto[1], Kim G. Larsen[2], Andrea Morichetta[3]($\boxtimes$),
and Francesco Tiezzi[4]

[1] Reykjavik University, Reykjavik, Iceland
[2] Aalborg University, Aalborg, Denmark
[3] IMT Institute for Advanced Studies Lucca, Lucca, Italy
andrea.morichetta@imtlucca.it
[4] Università di Camerino, Camerino, Italy

Abstract. Computation offloading is a key concept in Mobile Cloud Computing: it concerns the capability of moving application components from a mobile device to the cloud. This technique, in general, improves the efficiency of a system, although sometimes it can lead to a performance degradation. To decide when and what to offload, we propose the use of a method for determining an optimal infinite scheduler, which is able to manage the resource assignment of components with the aim of improving the system efficiency in terms of battery consumption and time. In particular, in this paper we define a cost/reward horizon method for Mobile Cloud Computing systems specified in the language MobiCa. By means of the model checker UPPAAL, we synthesize an optimal infinite scheduler for a given system specification. We assess our approach through a case study, which highlights the importance of a scheduler for reducing energy consumption and improving system performance.

1 Introduction

In the last few years, the ubiquity of the Internet and the increasing use of mobile devices has changed the mobile application market. The majority of these applications are available everywhere at any time with a heavy traffic over the network and a high computation demand. These characteristics require a large amount of resource usage, especially concerning battery lifetime, in limited devices. The current technological constraints have led to the emergence of a new concept called Mobile Cloud Computing (MCC) [1,2]. MCC is a new paradigm given by the combination of mobile devices and cloud infrastructures. This mix exploits the computational power of the cloud and the ubiquity of mobile devices to offer a rich user experience. It relies on the *offloading* concept, that is the possibility of moving the computation away from a mobile device to the cloud.

The evolution of power-saving approaches at hardware level has led to mobile devices that can adapt the speed of their processors. This allows devices to save energy, but it is not powerful enough in case of power hungry applications. Since battery life is the most important feature in mobile devices according to their

© Springer International Publishing Switzerland 2016
C. Braga and P.C. Ölveczky (Eds.): FACS 2015, LNCS 9539, pp. 66–85, 2016.
DOI: 10.1007/978-3-319-28934-2_4

users [3], computation offloading is clearly a cheaper alternative or a valid partner to the hardware solutions to improve performance and efficiency.

Unfortunately, the use of remote infrastructures does not always come without a cost, as sometimes computation offloading may degrade the application's performance. In general, a good rule of thumb is to offload an application component only if the cost of its local execution is greater than the cost for the synchronization of the input and output data plus that of the remote execution. This could be highly influenced by network latency, bandwidth, computational power of the mobile device, and computational requirements of the code to offload. Notably, in the issues discussed above, when we talk about cost we consider both time and the battery energy required to execute the application component. Therefore, in this field it is critical for the developer to assess the cost of the application execution during the development phase, in order to identify the best trade-off between energy consumed and performance.

The decision of whether to offload a given application component can be taken by means of a set of rules, i.e. the so-called *scheduler*. By applying the scheduler rules, we obtain a sequence of offloading choices, called *schedule*, that should allow the system to reach the desired goals while improving performance and reducing battery consumption.

In this paper, we take into consideration schedulers that produce infinite schedules ensuring the satisfaction of a property for infinite runs of the application. This is particularly useful for MCC, where applications are supposed to provide permanent services, or at least to be available for a long period. In particular, considering that our model is equipped with constraints on duration, costs and rewards, are interested in identifying the *optimal* schedulers that permit the achievement of the best result in terms of energy consumption and execution time. In fact, over infinite behaviors, it is possible to recognize a cyclic execution of components that is optimal and is determined by means of the limit ratio between accumulated costs and rewards. Consequently, an optimal scheduler is given by maximizing or minimizing the cost/reward ratio.

We propose here a cost/reward horizon method for MCC systems. We focus on a domain specific language (DSL), called MobiCa [4], that has been devised for modelling and analysing MCC systems. The use of a DSL increases the productivity for non-experts as, due to its high-level of abstraction, it keeps MCC domain concepts independent from the underlying model for the verification. Since the semantics of MobiCa is given in terms of a translation into networks of Timed Automata (TA), we show how the problem of designing and synthesising optimal schedulers can be solved by using the well-known model checker UPPAAL and the cost/reward method. Moreover, our approach also allows the developer of MCC systems to define a custom scheduler and compare its quality vis-a-vis the optimal one. In particular, by performing analysis with the statistical model checker UPPAAL-SMC [5] we are able to precisely quantify how much the custom scheduler differs from the optimal one, to understand if the custom scheduler is more suitable for time or energy optimization, and to simulate its behavior in order to study how it scales as system executions grow longer.

Although the optimal scheduling research field already provides many different techniques, we believe that model checking is an interesting approach for our purposes, due to the flexibility provided by the use of logics for characterizing different system properties and to its capability of performing analysis through optimization techniques already implemented in model verification, which can be fruitfully exploited for designing schedulers for MCC systems.

We illustrate our approach through a simple running example, and show its effectiveness and feasibility by means of a larger case study.

The rest of the paper is structured as follows. Section 2 presents syntax and semantics of the MobiCa language. Section 3 introduces our method for synthesising optimal schedulers for MCC systems, while Sect. 4 illustrates how statistical model checking can be used for evaluating the performance of schedulers. Section 5 shows our approach at work on a navigator case study. Finally, Sect. 6 reports our conclusions and describes future work.

2   The MobiCa Language

In this section we recall syntax and semantics of the MobiCa language [4]. It is designed to model MCC systems and, in particular, permits to specify both the contextual environment where an MCC application will run and its behavior.

2.1   Language Syntax

Table 1 shows the syntax of MobiCa given as BNF grammar. A system in MobiCa is expressed by a set of mobile devices and cloud machines composed in parallel. A typical example of mobile device is a smartphone, a tablet or any kind of device with limited computational and resource capabilities. A *mobile device* $(c, b, n, m) \triangleright \tilde{A}$ consists of a container of applications $\tilde{A}$ (where $\tilde{x}$ denotes a tuple of elements of kind x) and of a tuple of device information (c, b, n, m), which in order denote: computational power (that is the number of instructions executed per second), battery level, network bandwidth and used memory. A *cloud machine* $c \triangleright \tilde{A}$ is also a container of installed applications $\tilde{A}$, but as device information it only specifies the number c of instructions executed per second. An *application A* is organized in components $\tilde{F}$, called 'fragments', whose composition is described by a structure S. A *fragment F* can be a single functionality, a task or an action, derived by partitioning the application in parts. It is described as a name f that uniquely identifies the fragment, the number i of instructions composing it, the amount m of memory required at runtime, the amount s of data to be transferred for synchronization in case of offloading, and finally a boolean value o indicating whether the fragment is designed to be offloadable or not. A *structure* is a collection of terms of the form $f_1 \; Op \; \tilde{f}_2$, where from the source fragment (f_1) on the left of the operator Op the execution can proceed with one or more target fragments $(\tilde{f}_2)$ defined on the right, according to three types of operators:

- *Non-deterministic choice* $(-\!\!-\!\!\rightarrow)$ indicates that the execution will progress from the source fragment to *one* of the target fragments, which is nondeterministically selected.

Table 1. MobiCa syntax

SYSTEMS:	$Sys ::= (c, b, n, m) \triangleright \tilde{A} \mid c \triangleright \tilde{A} \mid Sys_1 \mid Sys_2$
APPLICATIONS:	$A ::= \langle \tilde{F}; S \rangle$
FRAGMENTS:	$F ::= f[i, m, s, o]$
STRUCTURE:	$S ::= f_1 \; Op \; \tilde{f_2} \mid S_1 \,;\, S_2$
OPERATORS:	$Op ::= \longrightarrow \mid \dashrightarrow \mid \longrightarrow\!\!\!\rightarrow$

- *Sequential progress* ($\dashrightarrow$) allows the computation to sequentially progress from the source fragment (on the left of $\dashrightarrow$) to each fragment in the ordered tuple (on the right of $\dashrightarrow$). If the tuple contains more than one fragment, after the execution of each of them the computation should go back to the source fragment.
- *Parallel execution* ($\longrightarrow\!\!\!\rightarrow$) allows the execution to progress from the source fragment to *all* the target ones, by activating their parallel execution.

If we have more operators for the same source fragment, the system will non-deterministically choose among them. Notably, self-loops are disallowed.

Below we show a scenario where an optimal infinite scheduling is necessary for minimizing energy consumption and improving system performance.

Example 1 (A simple application). The example in Fig. 1 is inspired by one from [6] and graphically describes a possible MobiCa application A. The application is composed of three fragments, f_0, f_1 and f_2, connected by means of the non-deterministic operator ($\longrightarrow$) and by the sequential operator ($\dashrightarrow$). Since the application behavior is deterministic in this case, the unique run is composed by an initialization phase $f_0 \rightarrow f_2$, followed by an infinite loop $f_2 \rightarrow f_0 \rightarrow f_2 \rightarrow f_1 \rightarrow f_2$. Each fragment of the sequence, can be executed either on the mobile or in the cloud, with the only requirement of maintaining the data consistent. For consistency we intend that either a fragment is executed on the same location of its predecessor or at a different location only after the result of the predecessor has been synchronized.

Application structure:

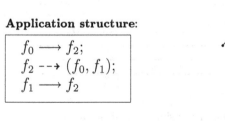

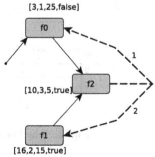

Fig. 1. A simple example of a MobiCa application

In the figure, the fragments are annotated with 4 parameters; in order, we have: the execution time on the mobile device (given by the number of instructions divided by the mobile computation power, i.e. i/c), the execution time on the cloud, the synchronization time of the results on the bus (given by s/n) and a boolean value representing the offloadability of the fragment (a false value indicates that only the local execution is admitted, as in the case of f_0). The graphical notation in Fig. 1 is formalized in terms of the so-called System Graph in Sect. 3 (Definition 1). Notably, the memory parameters introduced in MobiCa are not considered in this particular formalization.

An infinite scheduler for the simple application shown in Fig. 1 should provide a sequence of execution choices for each of the three fragments between the available resources. A schedule is optimal if the total execution time or cost is minimum, considering that the energy consumption per time unit for the mobile device is 5 when it is in use, 1 in the idle state, and 2 for the synchronization.

The Gantt chart in Fig. 2 depicts three possible schedules for the proposed example application. For each of them, we indicate the location of execution between mobile and cloud, and the use of the bus. The values of T and E at the end of the sequence are the time and the energy required by the scheduler for computing a complete loop cycle. In the first schedule, the computation is maintained locally for all fragments; this behavior is reasonable when the network is not available. Another approach might be to maintain the computation locally only for the non-offloadable fragments (in our case only f_0) and to try to move the computation remotely as soon as possible; this allows one to manage the task congestions in the mobile device. The third schedule instead takes into consideration the sequence of offloadable fragments and executes the computation remotely only when the synchronization of data is minimal.   □

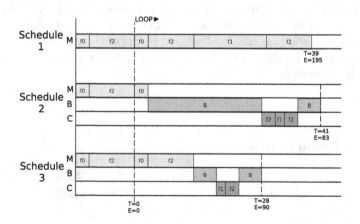

Fig. 2. Schedules for the simple application

2.2   TA-Based Semantics

We describe here the semantics of MobiCa, given in terms of a translation to networks of Timed Automata (TA). Such a semantics can indeed be used to solve the previously described scheduling problems, by resorting to the UPPAAL model checker. We refer the interested reader to [4] for a more complete account of the MobiCa semantics, and to [7] for the presented UPPAAL model.

The translation is divided in two parts: the *passive* part, which focusses on resources, and the *active* one, which focusses on the applications. Thus, the TA corresponding to a given MobiCa system is the composition of the results of the passive and active translations merged together by means of a global declaration. Below we describe the details of the translation in terms of UPPAAL models.

Global declaration. The global declaration consists of all the shared variables used for the synchronization of fragments, clocks for keeping track of time, and variables stating the internal state of the resources. In the global declaration we find also the structure S of the application declared as an adjacency matrix. A structure consists of three $n \times n$ matrices, one for each transition operator, where n is the length of the $\tilde{F}$. Let m_{ij} be the (i,j) entry of a matrix, $m_{ij} \geqslant 1$ if the ith and j^{th} fragments are connected, and 0 otherwise. Notably, the diagonal of each matrix is always zero, as self-loops are not admitted. Table 2 shows the corresponding three adjacency matrices, related to the example shown in Fig. 1. In particular, we have:

($\longrightarrow$): the non-deterministic transition for fragment f_i is activated if row_i has non-zero cells, and the next fragment to be activated is non-deterministically selected in $\{f_j \mid m_{ij} = 1\}$;

($\longrightarrow\!\!\!\!\!\rightarrow$): the parallel transition is similar to the non-deterministic one, with the difference that the fragment f_i activates all the fragments f_j with $m_{ij} = 1$;

($-\!\!-\!\!\rightarrow$): the sequential operator matrix is slightly different from the previous ones, as the values are not only 0 or 1. These values must be interpreted as a sequence defining the order in which the target fragments are activated for each execution of the source fragment. The activation of the sequential operator on a fragment excludes the other operators until the sequence of activation is terminated. In our example, fragment f_2 activates first the execution of f_0 and then the execution of f_1 (see the last row of the matrix at the right-hand side in Table 2).

Fragments. The TA for a generic fragment is depicted in Fig. 3; the template is parametric, so that it is a valid representation for each fragment of the application. The execution of the fragment starts from the initial location where it is waiting for the activation. The activation is managed by the array *activated[]* as

Table 2. Operators translation

$\longrightarrow$	f_0	f_1	f_2
f_0	0	0	1
f_1	0	0	1
f_2	0	0	0

$\longrightarrow\!\!\!\!\!\rightarrow$	f_0	f_1	f_2
f_0	0	0	0
f_1	0	0	0
f_2	0	0	0

$-\!\!-\!\!\rightarrow$	f_0	f_1	f_2
f_0	0	0	0
f_1	0	0	0
f_2	1	2	0

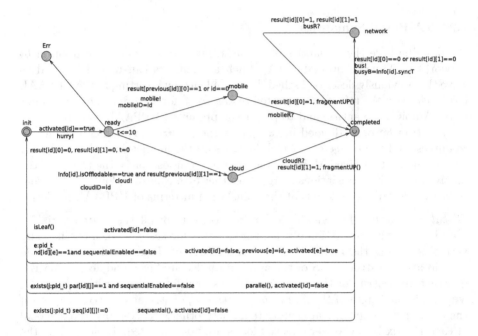

Fig. 3. Fragment translation

follows: whenever the element in the array corresponding to the fragment index becomes *true*, the corresponding fragment can move to the *ready* location. In this latter location, it can continue its execution on the mobile device or the cloud, depending on the evaluation of the guards on the transitions. They state that the fragment can be executed locally only if the the results of the previous fragment are updated locally (*result[previous[id]][0]==1*), or remotely only if they are updated remotely and the fragment is offlodable (*result[previous[id]][1]==1 and Info[id].isOffloadable==true*). When the execution of the fragment is completed, it can proceed towards either the *network* location, in order to synchronize the results locally and remotely (*result[id][0]=1, result[id][1]=1*), or the initial location by following one operator in the structure. Indeed, the use of each operator is rendered as an outgoing transition from the *completed* location to the *init* one; these transitions are concurrent and enabled according to the corresponding adjacency matrix, defined in the global declaration.

Resources. Each kind of resource (i.e., mobile device, cloud and bus) is translated into a specific TA; since these TA are similar, we show here just the one for the mobile device (Fig. 4) and, for the sake of presentation, we describe it in terms of a general resource. A resource can be in the *idle* state,

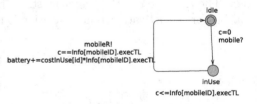

Fig. 4. Mobile translation

waiting for some fragment, or *inUse*, processing the current fragment. When the resource synchronizes with a fragment, it resets the local clock and remains in the *inUse* state until the clock reaches the value corresponding to the occupation time for the current fragment. Before releasing the resource, the battery level of the mobile device is updated according to the permanence time and the energy consumed by the resource. In this model, we assume that no energy is consumed if there is nothing to compute, and the energy power consumed by the cloud during its execution corresponds to the energy used by the mobile in the idle state waiting for the results.

3   Synthesis of Optimal Infinite Schedulers for MCC

In this section, we formalize the notion of optimal infinite scheduler in terms of two cost functions on a System Graph (SG). A SG provides a graphical representation of a MobiCa application, which is useful as an intermediate model between the specification and the resulting network of TA generated by the translation.

Definition 1 (System Graph). *Given an application $\langle \tilde{F}; S \rangle$ installed in a system with a mobile device defined by information (c, b, n, m) and a cloud machine defined by c', its system graph SG is a tuple $\langle N, \longrightarrow, \dashrightarrow, \longrightarrow\!\!\!\!\rightarrow, T, E, O \rangle$ where:*

- $N = \{f \mid f[i, m, s, o] \in \tilde{F}\}$ *is a set of fragment names.*
- $\longrightarrow, \dashrightarrow, \longrightarrow\!\!\!\!\rightarrow \subseteq N \times N$ *are three transition relations defined as $f \longrightarrow f'$ (resp. $f \dashrightarrow f'$, $f \longrightarrow\!\!\!\!\rightarrow f'$) iff $f' \in \tilde{f}$ for some $\tilde{f}$ such that $f \longrightarrow \tilde{f} \in S$ (resp. $f \dashrightarrow \tilde{f} \in S$, $f \longrightarrow\!\!\!\!\rightarrow \tilde{f} \in S$). We use $f \longmapsto f'$ to denote either $f \longrightarrow f'$ or $f \dashrightarrow f'$ or $f \longrightarrow\!\!\!\!\rightarrow f'$.*
- $T : N \times \{M, C, B\} \to \mathbb{N}$ *gives the execution time of a fragment on a resource (where M is the mobile device, C the cloud, and B the bus); given $f[i, m, s, o] \in \tilde{F}$, we have: $T(f, M) = \lfloor i/c \rfloor$, $T(f, C) = \lfloor i/c' \rfloor$, and $T(f, B) = \lfloor s/n \rfloor$.*
- $E : \{M, C, B\} \to \mathbb{N}$ *is the energy, expressed as a natural number, consumed per time unit by the mobile device when a given resource is in use.*
- $O : N \to \{0, 1\}$ *represents the possibility of offloading a fragment (value 1) or not (value 0); given $f[i, m, s, o] \in \tilde{F}$, we have $O(f) = o$.*

Notably, an *SG* is completely derived from the information specified in the corresponding MobiCa system except for the energy function E. Energy consumption information, indeed, is added to that provided by MobiCa specifications in order to enable the specific kind of analysis considered in this work.

A *path* on SG is a finite sequence $\eta = f_0 \longmapsto f_1 \longmapsto \ldots \longmapsto f_k$ $(k \geq 0)$.

Notably, in a path, parallel activations of fragments are interleaved.

Definition 2 (Scheduler). *Given a system graph SG, a scheduler is a partial function $\Theta : N \times Op \times N \to \{0, 1\}^2$ that, given a transition $f \longmapsto f'$ in SG, returns a pair of values $\pi_s, \pi_t \in \{0, 1\}$ which indicate the execution location of the source fragment f and of the target fragment f', respectively, where 0 denotes a local execution and 1 a remote one.*

When a scheduler is applied to a transition of the corresponding SG, it returns information about offloading decisions for the involved fragments. By applying a scheduler Θ to each transition of a sequence of transitions, i.e. a path η, we obtain a *schedule* δ, written $\Theta \cdot \eta = \delta$. A schedule consists of a sequence of triples of the form (f, π, β), each one denoting a fragment f, belonging to the considered path, equipped with its execution location π and the synchronization flag β. Parameters $\pi, \beta \in \{0, 1\}$ indicate the local ($\pi = 0$) and remote ($\pi = 1$) execution and the need ($\beta = 1$) or not ($\beta = 0$) of data synchronization for f. Formally, $\Theta \cdot \eta = \delta$ is defined as follows: for two consecutive fragments f and f' in the path η, there exist in δ two consecutive triples $(f, \pi, \beta) \rightarrowtail (f', \pi', \beta')$ iff $\Theta(f, \rightarrowtail, f') = (\pi_s, \pi_t)$ s.t. $\pi = \pi_s$, $\pi' = \pi_t$ and $\beta = |\pi_s - \pi_t|$. Notice that, as Θ is a partial function, there may be transitions in η that are not in δ; for such transitions the schedule does not provide any information about the offloading strategy to apply, because they are not considered by the scheduler.

Taking inspiration from the approach in [8], we define two cost functions. In particular, we consider the cost of executing a given path in the considered SG using the scheduler, i.e. the cost functions are defined on schedules.

Definition 3 (Time and Energy Costs). *The time and energy costs of a schedule δ for a given $SG = \langle N, \longrightarrow, \dashrightarrow, \longrightarrow, T, E, O \rangle$ are defined as follows:*

$$Time(\delta) = \sum_{(f,\pi,\beta) \in \delta} (\ (1 - \pi) \times T(f, M) \ + \ \pi \times T(f, C) \ + \ \beta \times T(f, B) \ )$$

$$Energy(\delta) = \sum_{(f,\pi,\beta) \in \delta} (\ (1 - \pi) \times T(f, M) \times E(M) \ + \ \pi \times T(f, C) \times E(C) \\ + \ \beta \times T(f, B) \times E(B) \ )$$

The function $Time(\delta)$ calculates the total time required by the schedule δ, i.e. the time for executing a path of SG according to the scheduler that generates δ. For each fragment f in the system, we add the time $T(f, M)$ if the fragment is executed locally ($\pi = 0$), or the time $T(f, C)$ if the fragment is executed remotely ($\pi = 1$). The function considers also the synchronization time $T(f, B)$ if two consecutive fragments are executed at different locations ($\beta = 1$).

The function $Energy(\delta)$ calculates the total energy required to complete the scheduled path. The difference with respect to the previous function is that here the time of permanence of a fragment in a resource is multiplied by the corresponding energy required per time unit.

Relying on the cost functions introduced above, we can have the time-optimal scheduler Θ_T and the energy-optimal scheduler Θ_E for a given SG, which determine the sequence of actions that generates the less costly combination of resources, in terms of $Time(\delta)$ and $Energy(\delta)$ respectively, for a path in SG.

Example 2 (Time and battery costs for the small application). We evaluate here the schedules proposed in Example 1 (Fig. 2) using the cost functions introduced above. Notice that in the calculation we consider only the cyclic part of the application omitting the initialization that is not relevant in terms of an infinite scheduler. Table 3 reports the time and energy consumed for the three schedules calculated according to Definition 3.

Table 3. Time and energy costs of the schedules for the simple application

Sch.	Time	Energy
1	$T_1 = (3 + 10 + 16 + 10) = 39$	$E_1 = (3 + 10 + 16 + 10) \times 5 = 195$
2	$T_2 = (3 + 25 + 3 + 2 + 3 + 5) = 41$	$E_2 = (3 \times 5 + 25 \times 2 + 3 \times 1 + 2 \times 1 + 3 \times 1 + 5 \times 2) = 83$
3	$T_3 = (3 + 10 + 5 + 2 + 3 + 5) = 28$	$E_3 = (3 \times 5 + 10 \times 5 + 5 \times 2 + 2 \times 1 + 3 \times 1 + 5 \times 2) = 90$

Evaluating the results, the time-optimal scheduling for the application is achieved in Schedule 3, that is $(f_0, 0, 0) \rightarrowtail (f_2, 0, 1) \rightarrowtail (f_1, 1, 0) \rightarrowtail (f_2, 1, 1)$, with a total time cost $T_3 = 28$. The offloading choices for achieving such result are formalized in terms of the scheduler (written here using a notation based on triples) $\Theta_T = \{(f_0 \longrightarrow f_2, 0, 0), (f_2 \dashrightarrow f_1, 0, 1), (f_1 \longrightarrow f_2, 1, 1), (f_2 \dashrightarrow f_0, 1, 0)\}$. On the other hand, Schedule 2, that is $(f_0, 0, 1) \rightarrowtail (f_2, 1, 0) \rightarrowtail (f_1, 1, 0) \rightarrowtail (f_2, 1, 1)$, is the energy optimal one, with a total energy consumption $E_2 = 83$. The corresponding scheduler is $\Theta_E = \{(f_0 \longrightarrow f_2, 0, 1), (f_2 \dashrightarrow f_1, 1, 1), (f_1 \longrightarrow f_2, 1, 1), (f_2 \dashrightarrow f_0, 1, 0)\}$. From this example it is clear that there may not be a correspondence between energy and time consumption, since we have different cost results. Hence, defining a scheduler optimized for more resources is not always a simple task.   □

3.1   Cost/Reward Horizon Method

In order to find the optimal scheduler for an application with infinite behavior, as discussed above, we propose a cost/reward horizon method. From the literature [9,10], we know that the optimal ratio is computable for diverging and non-negative rewards systems.

In what follows we first present the basic concepts behind our cost/reward method and then we show how the optimal infinite scheduling problem can be solved using TA and the UPPAAL model checker. The behavior of the application is the starting point for defining an optimal infinite scheduler. It can be described as a set of paths. For each path UPPAAL will generate all possible schedules and will choose the best one according to a specific ratio (clarified below). The chosen schedule is indeed the less costly one and, hence, it can be used to synthesize the rules that compose the optimal scheduler.

Let's start defining the ratio of a finite path η of a SG as follows:

$$Ratio(\eta) = Cost(\eta)/Rewards(\eta)$$

where $Cost()$ and $Rewards()$ are two functions keeping track of the accumulated cost/reward along the path η. Now, we extend this ratio to an infinite path $\gamma = f_0 \rightarrowtail, \dots, \rightarrowtail f_n \rightarrowtail \dots$, with γ_n the finite prefix of length n; the ratio of γ is:

$$Ratio(\gamma) = \lim_{n \to \infty}(Cost(\gamma_n)/Rewards(\gamma_n))$$

An optimal infinite path γ_o is the one with the smallest $Ratio(\gamma)$ among all possible schedules.

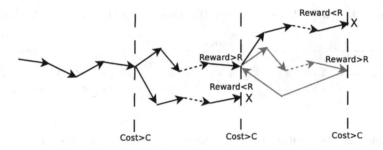

Fig. 5. Cost/reward horizon method

Finding the smallest ratio is not always a tractable problem, but it is possible to improve its tractability reducing the problem to a given horizon. From this new point of view, we want to maximize the reward in a fixed cost window. Notice that, the cost window should be of an appropriate length, in order to complete the execution of at least one application cycle.

This technique can be implemented in UPPAAL considering the query:

$$\texttt{E[]} \quad \texttt{not}\,(f_1.\texttt{Err}, ..., f_n.\texttt{Err})\ \texttt{and}\ (\texttt{Cost} \geq \texttt{C imply Reward} \geq \texttt{R}) \quad (1)$$

This query asks if there exists a trace were the system keeps running without errors and whenever the predefined cost C is reached, the accumulated reward should be at least R (Fig. 5).

For verifying the satisfaction of the above formula, the TA model includes an additional template (Fig. 6) implementing the cost window using the reset mechanisms. It consists of one state and a self-loop transition, where each time the simulation reaches the cost C the transition will reset the accumulated Costs and Rewards.

In this way, the behavior of the application is split in cost windows and in each of them the accumulated rewards should satisfy the formula Reward≥R. Since we are looking for the maximum reward given a predefined cost, for finding the optimal scheduler it is necessary to discover the maximum value of R for which the formula (1) holds. The resulting trace generated by a satisfiable formula has the structure depicted in Fig. 5. The trace starts with some initial actions corresponding to the application start-up and leads to its cyclic behavior.

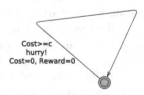

Fig. 6. Reset TA

As shown in the figure, the approach does not consider all possible traces, but only the ones that satisfy the constraints of the query. The candidate schedule is the piece of trace that is highlighted in red, which means that UPPAAL has found a cyclic behavior in the application whose execution satisfies the formula forever. This means that we have found an optimal schedule from which it is possible to derive the set of rules that will generate the optimal scheduler.

3.2   The Horizon Method at Work

In this section we show how the cost/reward horizon method can be applied to MCC systems and, in particular, to the example presented in Fig. 1.

We are interested in finding a time-optimal and/or battery-optimal scheduler. By applying the method presented in Sect. 3.1 to a MCC system, given an infinite path γ, the time- and energy-based ratios become: $r_T = \lim_{n \to \infty}(Time(\gamma_n)/Fragments(\gamma_n))$; $r_E = \lim_{n \to \infty}(Energy(\gamma_n)/Fragments(\gamma_n))$, respectively.

Thus, the accumulated costs are calculated by the functions $Time()$ and $Energy()$ given in Definition 3. The rewards are instead defined by a function $Fragments(): \eta \to \mathbb{N}$ which counts the number of fragments executable in the fixed window. The more fragments we are able to execute with the same amount of time or energy, the better the resources are used.

To find the minimum time-based ratio using the UPPAAL model checker we can ask the system to verify a query of the following form:

```
E[] forall(i:pid_t) not(Fragment(i).Err) and (GlobalTime≥300 imply
                        (fragments>41))
```

In this specific case we want to know if, in a fixed window of 300 units of time, it is always possible to execute 41 fragments. To find the minimum ratio we have to iterate on the number of fragments in the denominator in order to find the maximum number for which the query holds. In our running example, the maximum value that satisfies the query is 41, giving a ratio $300/41 = 7.31$. The resulting trace generated by the presented query results in an execution sequence that can be synthesized as the Schedule 3 shown in Fig. 2.

The query for determining the energy-based ratio is defined as:

```
E[] forall(i:pid_t) not(Fragment(i).Err) and (battery≥900 imply
                  (fragments>43 and battery≤930))
```

In this case, the resulting ratio is $900/43 = 20.93$. thus, the system requires 20.93 units of battery per fragment. Notice that in this query there is an extra constraint defined as an upper bound on the right side of the **imply** keyword. This is because we can have different schedules satisfying the formula, but we consider only the ones that exceed the battery threshold as little as possible. The resulting trace from the energy query gives us the energy optimal schedule, that in this case can be synthesized as the Schedule 2 in Fig. 2.

To assess the truthfulness of the cost/horizon method, we can compare the obtained results with the ones calculated directly in the Gantt chart in Fig. 2. The energy ratio for Schedule 2 on one loop is given by $83/4 = 20.75$. The slight difference in the results is due to the size of the cost window. In the Gantt chart we are considering a window that fits perfectly four fragments and, hence, we do not have any incomplete fragment that affects the final result as in the case of the horizon method, but the approximation is really close to the best case.

4   Evaluating Performance of a Custom Control Strategy

In this section, we present a technique for evaluating the performance of a custom scheduler using the Statistical Model Checking facilities [5,11] provided by UPPAAL (the model checker is called UPPAAL-SMC, or SMC for short).

Let's suppose now that a developer wants to define his own scheduler for an application and to know how much the resulting custom scheduler is close to the optimal one or to calculate some statistics. Possible reasons for customizing a scheduler could be problems in the development phase related to hardware cost or a less quantitative issue, such as security and privacy that force the developer to introduce a static scheduler.

The new personalized scheduler in UPPAAL is modeled as a TA template called Manager. The duty of this manager is to decide on which resource each fragment should be executed. Considering the model presented in Fig. 3, here we do not have anymore the decision in the *ready* location between mobile and cloud transition, but just a transition that is synchronized with the manager. The manager operates as a mediator, between the fragments and the resources. Once the manager receives notice of a new fragment to execute, it decides according to some rules in which resource's waiting list to move it. The resources are modeled following a busy waiting paradigm, where every time the queue is not empty, a new fragment is consumed. Before executing the assigned fragment, the resource checks the execution location of its predecessor; if data synchronization is not required, it just executes the fragment, otherwise it synchronizes the data and then processes it. Once the computation is completed, the resource returns the control back to the executed fragment and passes to the next one.

4.1   A Custom Scheduler

The manager can contain different kinds of rules. One possibility is to define a rule for each fragment or to specify a more general rule that can be applied to the whole application. For example, to execute a fragment remotely when it is offloadable is a very simple rule that a developer can consider to implement in a MCC system.

Figure 7 depicts the manager implementing this custom strategy. In detail, after a fragment is synchronized with the manager, the latter decides to enqueue the fragment on the corresponding waiting list according to the guard `Info[x].isOffloadable`. In this way, if the fragment x is offloadable it is queued locally, otherwise remotely.

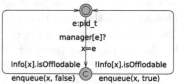

Fig. 7. Manager TA

Looking more closely at the custom scheduler, we notice it realises the same behavior of Schedule 2 in Fig. 2, which we already know to be energy-optimal.

4.2   Evaluation via SMC

As previously said, usually a customized scheduler is defined for reasons related to particular conditions of the environment. Here, we perform some statistical analysis to quantify how much the customized scheduler above is far from the optimal one, in order to have a quantitative measure of any performance loss. In particular, below we present some verification activities and compare the obtained results with the time/energy-optimal scheduling we found in Sect. 3.2.

By evaluating the following queries using the SMC tool, we can determine the expected maximum value for the number of fragments that can be executed in a given temporal window:

`E[time<=300;2000](max:fragments)    E[battery<=900;2000](max:fragments)`

These two queries aim at finding the expected value over 2000 runs in a window of 300 units of time and 900 units of battery, respectively. The results are: 29 fragments for the first query and 41 for the other one. Comparing these results with those of optimal ones, we can clearly see that the scheduler defined by the developer is almost as efficient as the energy-optimal one. Indeed, they differ only for 2 fragments in the energy case. Instead, the performance of the custom scheduler is very far from that of the time-optimal scheduler, as they differ for 14 fragments.

The proposed strategy can be also evaluated to see if it is closer either to the energy-optimal scheduler or to the time-optimal one. This can be achieved by checking if the probability to reach the time-optimal scheduler is greater than the probability to reach the energy-optimal scheduler.

`Pr[time<=300](<>fragments>=43)>=Pr[battery<=900](<> fragments>=41)`

The result of this query is **false** with probability 0.9, meaning that the probability of reaching the energy-optimal scheduler is greater than the one for the time-optimal scheduler.

We can also simulate the system behavior executing the following commands:

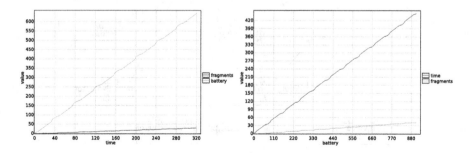

Fig. 8. Simulation results

```
simulate 1[battery<=900]{time,fragments}
```

Their results are shown in Fig. 8. On the left-hand side, we have the number of fragments compared with the consumed battery. On the right-hand side, instead, we have the ratio of executed fragments and required time.

5   Experiments with a Navigator Case Study

In the previous sections we have illustrated the proposed approach by means of a simple application. In this section, we aim at showing the effectiveness and feasibility of the approach by means of a larger case study, drawn from [4], concerning a navigator application. This kind of application is one of the most complex and used in mobile devices. This is an interesting case study for this work from the point of view of its complexity and its strong real-time requirements to be satisfied at runtime. In particular, the greatest challenge for navigation system developers is to provide an application that is able to find the right route, and recalculate it as quickly as possible in case of changes, considering the current traffic condition.

The corresponding MobiCa system is represented in Fig. 9. The system starts when the user inserts the destination in the Configuration panel that consequently activates the Controller. The Controller in turn asks the GPS for the current coordinates and forwards them to the Path calculator. The Path calculator, interacting with the Map and the Traffic evaluator, will provide a possible itinerary. The itinerary is processed by the Navigator, which forwards information to the Navigation Panel. This latter component, with the help of the Voice and Speed Trap Indicator, provides the navigation service to the end user. The Navigator is also responsible for reactivating the Controller in order to check possible updates of the route.

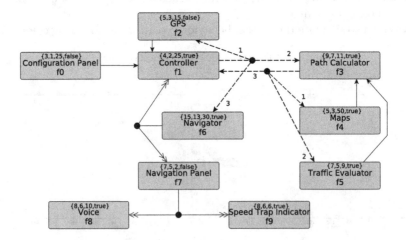

Fig. 9. Navigator case study: MobiCa specification

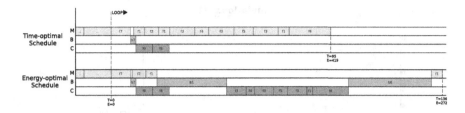

Fig. 10. Navigator case study: optimal schedules

We present now the results obtained using the cost/reward horizon method applied to this case study. The complexity of this example is a good test bed for our method. Notice that the values of the parameters used in the example are generated ad-hoc as a proof of concept. From real life we expect that the developer can determine information about fragment instructions by performing experimentation, statistics or simply studying the complexity in the code. The diagram in Fig. 10 shows the resulting schedules synthesized from the verification of the following queries:

```
E[] forall(i:pid_t) not(Fragment(i).Err)
    and (time≥100 imply (fragments>16 and time<120))
E[] forall(i:pid_t) not(Fragment(i).Err)
    and (battery≥400 imply (fragments>21 and battery<419))
```

The first query defines the time-optimal schedule with respect to a time window of 100 units and with a maximum number of executed fragments equal to 16. The ratio $r_T = 100/16 = 6.25$ was reached keeping the execution local for almost all fragments except for f_8 and f_9, which are executed in parallel remotely.

The opposite behavior is identified in the verification of the second query for the energy-optimal case, where only three fragments are executed locally and all the others remotely. Since the fragments f_7 and f_2 are not offloadable, they are maintained locally together with the fragment f_1. The choice to execute f_1 locally is given by the necessity of the scheduler to wait for a suitable moment to move the computation remotely. Clearly, moving the computation between two non-offloadable fragments is not convenient; furthermore, sometimes it is better to anticipate or postpone the offloading when the data synchronization is minimal or less costly. The ratio of this scheduler is $r_E = 400/21 = 19.05$ with a final energy consumption equal to 272 units per cycle.

The cost/reward horizon method fits MCC systems perfectly. In particular, during the sequential behavior of the application it tries to find the best moment for moving the computation remotely, defining also different strategies according to the role of the fragment. Instead, during parallel behavior, where there are no direct relations between fragments, it tries to exploit the benefit derived by allocating the computation both on the mobile and on the cloud.

As a final evaluation we present the results obtained verifying the custom scheduler described in Sect. 4 on the navigator case study using SMC. Verifying the expected maximum reward using the query E[battery<=400;2000](max:

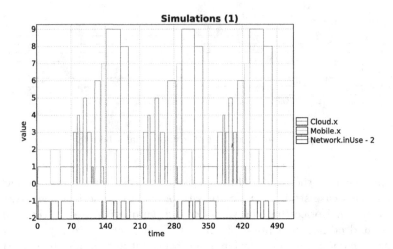

Fig. 11. Navigator case study: fragments execution (Color figure online)

fragments), we obtain a cost energy ratio $r_E = 400/16 = 25$. Even worse is the score obtained by trying to optimize the performance using the query E[time<=100; 2000](max: fragments), which achieves a ratio $r_T = 100/5 = 20$. Thus, comparing the obtained values, it is possible to notice a substantial growth of the ratio for the custom scheduler. Since a higher ratio means a decrease in performance, we can claim that the strategy defined by the developer is not a good approximation of the optimal one. Furthermore, analyzing the results in more detail, we notice that the custom scheduler is very far from the time optimal, with a ratio that is four time larger than the one achieved by the optimal scheduler. Considering instead the energy case, it is possible to reach a ratio of 25 against the 19.05 of the optimal one. Looking at these results, the developer is aware that using his custom scheduler he can achieve a good performance if he is interested in energy optimization, although this is not optimal.

By performing a simulation (we omit the picture due to lack of space), we can see a significant gap between the number of executed fragments and the elapsing of time according to the consumed battery power; there is indeed a symmetric increase of values generated by the cyclic behavior of the application. The plot in Fig. 11, instead, represents a scheduler synthesized using a histogram. Using an appropriate simulation query, which takes into account the fragments in execution on the resources, it is possible to represent each fragment as a column of the same height of its identifier in the specific resource. For the sake of readability, columns referring to cloud (red lines) and mobile (green lines) are depicted on the same level of the graph, while the network columns (blue lines) are reported just below. A peak in the blue line means that the corresponding fragment above requires the synchronization on the bus before its execution.

6   Concluding Remarks

We provide an approach for designing schedulers for MCC systems specified in
MobiCa. Using UPPAAL, and relying on a cost/reward horizon method introduced here, we are able to synthesize an optimal infinite scheduler for a mobile
application. This scheduler defines offloading choices that allow the system to
reach the best results in terms of performance and energy usage.

Related Work. Optimization is a topic that is considered in many application
fields. Also in the MCC literature there is a significant effort on the optimization
of a utility function or specific metrics for the offloading technique. Among the
most significant works, we mention RPF [12], which derives its strategy using the
direct observation of the system. It runs processes alternatively between local
and remote machines in order to determine the best choices. This technique is
not optimized for highly dynamic systems, where the parameters of the resources
change constantly, but it can be a good solution for more static environments.
Another approach based on direct observation is MAUI [8], where information
about the environment is collected and used to formulate the problem as an
optimization problem. The proposed optimization function compares the time
required for executing a process locally against the time for the synchronization
of data plus the remote execution.

The limitations of methods based on the direct observation have been
addressed using the past history. The resulting systems, like Spectra [13],
Chroma [14] and Odessa [15], build a model on past inputs and use it to make
predictions or decisions rather than to observe the current system configuration.

Our approach is similar to the ones mentioned above, with the main difference that we provide a language that describes the system environment. This
language, called MobiCa, was presented for the first time in [4], and here is used
to generate an optimal infinite scheduling using the UPPAAL model checker.
Compared with the other works, we are able to foresee all the possible configurations of the system at design time, by providing a scheduler that is optimal for
a certain interval of parameters. The optimal infinite scheduler is generated using
the cost/reward horizon method implemented with timed automata and solved
verifying a simple query by means of the model checker. The closest related
work, from which we take inspiration for the cost/reward horizon method is presented in [9,10], where a general version of this method was applied to the priced
automata formalism to find the best configuration of the considered system. The
flexibility of this method has permitted to obtain good results in the MCC field,
confirmed also by reasonable performances that are in the order of seconds for
the considered models.

Future Work. There are still several issues which are open for future work. A
possibility would be to extend our work in order to have an automatic procedure
for obtaining the maximum number of fragments in a given time window. Indeed
finding the optimal ratio requires one to consider several computations, that may

become unfeasible in case of high numbers. Thus, a possible idea to optimize the methodology is to develop heuristics that allow one to reach the best result in a faster way. Another aspect to consider is how the proposed approach can be transferred to the technology. A possibility is to include the decision support as part of a middleware that can provide to the developer an optimal scheduler derived through our method. This middleware could be integrated also with the runtime decision support proposed in [4]. Another interesting point of extension is the re-scheduling at runtime. Indeed, a small variation of the environmental parameters can lead to different results in the system optimization leading to an obsolete scheduler. Thus, we need to consider its recalculation at runtime.

Acknowledgements. Luca Aceto has been supported by the projects 'Nominal Structural Operational Semantics' (nr. 141558-051) of the Icelandic Research Fund and 'Formal Methods for the Development and Evaluation of Sustainable Systems', grant under the Programme NILS Science and Sustainability, Priority Sectors Programme of the EEA Grants Framework. Kim G. Larsen is supported by the SENSATION FET project, the Sino-Danish Basic Research Center IDEA4CPS, the Innovation Fund Center DiCyPS and the ERC Advanced Grant LASSO. Andrea Morichetta and Francesco Tiezzi have been supported by the EU projects ASCENS (257414) and QUANTICOL (600708) and by the MIUR PRIN project CINA (2010LHT4KM).

References

1. Fernando, N., Loke, S.W., Rahayu, W.: Mobile cloud computing: a survey. Future Gener. Comput. Syst. **29**(1), 84–106 (2013)
2. Flinn, J.: Cyber foraging: bridging mobile and cloud computing. Synth. Lect. Mob. Pervasive Comput. **7**(2), 1–103 (2012)
3. Kumar, K., Lu, Y.H.: Cloud computing for mobile users: can offloading computation save energy? Computer **43**(4), 51–56 (2010)
4. Aceto, L., Morichetta, A., Tiezzi, F.: Decision support for mobile cloud computingapplications via model checking. In: MobileCloud, vol. 1, pp. 296–302. IEEE (2015)
5. Bulychev et al.: UPPAAL-SMC: statistical model checking for priced timed automata. arXiv preprint arXiv:1207.1272 (2012)
6. Gruian, F., Kuchcinski, K.: Low-energy directed architecture selection and task scheduling for system-level design. In: EUROMICRO, pp. 1296–1302. IEEE (1999)
7. MobiCa, U.: Model. http://www.amorichetta.eu/MobiCa/m_u_model.zip
8. Cuervo, et al.: MAUI: making smartphones last longer with code offload. In: MobiSys, pp. 49–62. ACM (2010)
9. Bouyer, P., Brinksma, E., Larsen, K.G.: Optimal infinite scheduling for multi-priced timed automata. Formal Meth. Syst. Des. **32**(1), 3–23 (2008)
10. Rasmussen, J.I., Larsen, K.G., Subramani, K.: On using priced timed automata to achieve optimal scheduling. Formal Meth. Syst. Des. **29**(1), 97–114 (2006)
11. Larsen, K.G., Mikučionis, M., van Vliet, J., Wang, Z., David, A., Legay, A., Poulsen, D.B.: Statistical model checking for networks of priced timed automata. In: Fahrenberg, U., Tripakis, S. (eds.) FORMATS 2011. LNCS, vol. 6919, pp. 80–96. Springer, Heidelberg (2011)

12. Rudenko, A., Reiher, P., Popek, G.J., Kuenning, G.H.: The remote processing framework for portable computer power saving. In: SAC, pp. 365–372. ACM (1999)
13. Flinn, J., Park, S., Satyanarayanan, M.: Balancing performance, energy, and quality in pervasive computing. In: Distributed Computing Systems, pp. 217–226 (2002)
14. Balan, R.K., Satyanarayanan, M., Park, S.Y., Okoshi, T.: Tactics-based remote execution for mobile computing. In: MobiSys, pp. 273–286. ACM (2003)
15. Ra, M. et al.: Odessa: enabling interactive perception applications on mobile devices. In: MobiSys, pp. 43–56. ACM (2011)

A Contract-Oriented Middleware

Massimo Bartoletti[✉], Tiziana Cimoli, Maurizio Murgia,
Alessandro Sebastian Podda, and Livio Pompianu

Università Degli Studi di Cagliari, Cagliari, Italy
bart@unica.it

Abstract. Developing distributed applications typically requires to integrate new code with legacy third-party services, e.g., e-commerce facilities, maps, etc. These services cannot always be assumed to smoothly collaborate with each other; rather, they live in a "wild" environment where they must compete for resources, and possibly diverge from the expected behaviour if they find it convenient to do so. To overcome these issues, some recent works have proposed to discipline the interaction of mutually distrusting services through *behavioural contracts*. The idea is a dynamic composition, where only those services with *compliant* contracts can establish sessions through which they interact. Compliance between contracts guarantees that, if services behave honestly, they will enjoy safe interactions. We exploit a theory of timed behavioural contracts to formalise, design and implement a message-oriented middleware where distributed services can be dynamically composed, and their interaction monitored to detect contract violations. We show that the middleware allows to reduce the complexity of developing distributed applications, by relieving programmers from the need to explicitly deal with the misbehaviour of external services.

1 Introduction

Modern distributed applications are often composed by loosely-coupled services, which can appear and disappear from the network, and can dynamically discover and invoke other services in order to adapt to changing needs and conditions. These services may be under the governance of different providers (possibly competing among each other), and interact through open networks, where competitors and adversaries can try to exploit their vulnerabilities.

In the setting outlined above, developing trustworthy services and applications can be a quite challenging task: the problem fits within the area of computer security, since we have *adversaries* (in our setting, third-party services), whose exact number and nature is unknown (because of openness and dynamicity). Further, standard analysis techniques from programming languages theory (like e.g., type systems) cannot be applied, since they usually need to inspect the code of the whole application, while under the given assumptions one can only reason about the services under their control.

A possible countermeasure to these issues is to discipline the interaction between services through *contracts*. These are formal descriptions of service

© Springer International Publishing Switzerland 2016
C. Braga and P.C. Ölveczky (Eds.): FACS 2015, LNCS 9539, pp. 86–104, 2016.
DOI: 10.1007/978-3-319-28934-2_5

behaviour, in terms of, e.g., pre/post-conditions and invariants [20], behavioural types [16], etc. Contracts can be used at static or dynamic time to discover and bind Web services, and to guarantee they interact in a protected manner: when a service does not behave as prescribed by its contract, it can be blamed (and punished) for breaching the contract [30]. Although several models and architectures for contract-oriented services have been proposed in the last few years [12, 34, 36], further evidence is needed in order to put this paradigm at work in everyday practice. We also believe that contract-oriented services should be equipped with a formal semantics, in order to make their analysis possible.

Contributions. We formalise, design, implement, and validate a middleware which uses contracts to allow disciplined interactions between mutually distrusting services. The middleware is designed to support different notions of contract, which only need to share some high-level features:

- a *compliance* relation between contracts, which specifies when services conforming to their contracts interact correctly. The middleware guarantees that only services with compliant contracts can interact.
- an *execution monitor*, which checks if the actions done by the services conform to their contracts, and — otherwise — detects which services are *culpable* of a contract violation.

Building upon these basic ingredients, our middleware extends standard message-oriented middleware [4] (MOMs) by allowing services to advertise contracts, establish sessions between services with compliant contracts, and interact through these sessions. The execution monitor guarantees that, whenever a contract is violated, the culprit is sanctioned. Sanctions negatively affect the reputation of a service, and consequently its chances to establish new sessions. We explore several ways to validate our middleware. First, we perform some scalability tests, to measure the execution time of the core primitives as a function of the number of advertised contracts. Second, we develop a distributed application (to solve an RSA factoring challenge [29]), involving a master and a population of workers, some of which do not always respect their contracts. We show that our service selection mechanism allows to automatically marginalize the dishonest services, without requiring the master to explicitly handle their misbehaviour. Third, we use the middleware as a (contract-oriented) communication layer for a real distributed application, i.e. a reservation marketplace where service providers can advertise resources, and clients can reserve them. Resources can be of heterogeneous nature, and their usage protocols are specified by contracts, which are handled by the middleware to guarantee safe interactions.

A public instance of the middleware is accessible from [7], together with all examples and experiments we carried out, and a suite of development tools.

Structure of the Paper. In Sect. 2 we overview the middleware features. In Sect. 3 we introduce a process calculus to specify services. In Sect. 4 we illustrate the main design choices of the middleware, and in Sect. 5 we discuss its architecture; validation is then accomplished in Sect. 6. In Sect. 7 we discuss some related

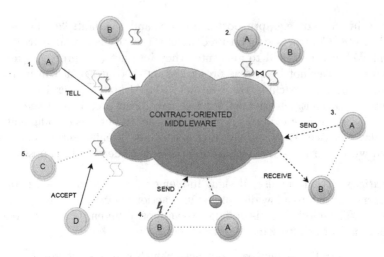

Fig. 1. A schema of the primitive behaviours.

approaches, and in Sect. 8 we conclude. An extended version of the paper, with background and supplementary material, is available in [7].

2   The Middleware at a Glance

Figure 1 illustrates the main features of our middleware. In (1), the participant A advertises its contract to the middleware, making it available to other participants. In (2), the middleware determines that the contracts of A and B are compliant, and then it establishes a session through which the two participants can interact. This interaction consists in sending and receiving messages, similarly to a standard MOM [4]: for instance, in (3) participant A delivers to the middleware a message for B, which can then collect it from the middleware.

Unlike standard MOMs, the interaction happening in each session is monitored by the middleware, which checks whether contracts are respected or not. In particular, the execution monitor verifies that actions can only occur when prescribed by their contracts, and it detects when some expected action is missing. For instance, in (4) the execution monitor has detected an attempt of participant B to do some illegal action. Upon detection of a contract violation, the middleware punishes the culprit, by suitably decreasing its *reputation*. This is a measure of the trustworthiness of a participant in its past interactions: the lower is the reputation, the lower is the probability of being able to establish new sessions with it. The reputation system exploits some of the techniques in [33] to mitigate self-promoting attacks [21].

Item (5) shows another mechanism for establishing sessions: here, the participant C advertises a contract, and D just *accepts* it. Technically, this requires the middleware to construct the *dual* of the contract of C, to associate it with D, and to establish a session between C and D. The interaction happening in this session then proceeds as described previously.

Some simple examples of contract-oriented programs are shown in [7].

3   Specifying Contract-Oriented Services

In this section we introduce TCO$_2$ (for *timed CO$_2$*), a specification language for
contract-oriented services. This is a timed extension of the process calculus in [9],
through which we can specify services interacting through primitives analogous
to those sketched in Sect. 2. Rather than giving a *tour de force* formalization
of the whole middleware behaviour, we focus here on the core functionalities.
Extending the calculus with more advanced features (like e.g. value passing,
exceptions, reputation, etc.) can be done using standard techniques. A more
detailed account of TCO$_2$ is contained in [7].

The formalisation of TCO$_2$ is independent from the chosen contract language,
as we only pivot on a few abstract operators and relations on contracts. In
particular, we assume: (1) a *compliance relation* $\bowtie$, which relates two contracts
whenever their interaction is "correct" [8]; (2) a predicate which says if a contract
admits a compliant one; (3) a function co($\cdot$) that, given a contract p, gives a
contract compliant with p (when this exists); (4) a transition relation $\rightarrow\!\!\!\rightarrow$ between
contract configurations γ, γ', which makes contracts evolve upon actions and time
passing. We denote with $\Gamma_0(\mathsf{A}\!:\!p, \mathsf{B}\!:\!q)$ the initial configuration of an interaction
between A (with contract p) and B (with contract q).

The syntax of TCO$_2$ is defined as follows, where $x, y, \ldots \in \mathcal{V}$ are *variables*,
$s, t, \ldots \in \mathcal{N}$ are *names*, and $u, v, \ldots \in \mathcal{V} \cup \mathcal{N}$. Further, we assume a set of
participants (ranged over by $\mathsf{A}, \mathsf{B}, \ldots$), a set of message labels (ranged over by
$\mathsf{a}, \mathsf{b}, \ldots$), and a set of process names (ranged over by $\mathsf{X}, \mathsf{Y}, \ldots$).

$$S ::= \mathbf{0} \quad\mid\quad \mathsf{A}[P] \quad\mid\quad s[\gamma] \quad\mid\quad (u)S \quad\mid\quad S \mid S \quad\mid\quad \{\downarrow_u p\}_\mathsf{A}$$

$$P ::= \mathbf{0} \quad\mid\quad \mathsf{X}(\boldsymbol{u}) \quad\mid\quad \pi\,.\,P \quad\mid\quad (u)P \quad\mid\quad u \rhd \{\mathsf{a}_i.\,P_i\}_{i\in I}$$

$$\pi ::= \tau \quad\mid\quad \mathtt{tell}\downarrow_u p \quad\mid\quad \mathtt{send}_u\,\mathsf{a} \quad\mid\quad \mathtt{idle}(\delta) \quad\mid\quad \mathtt{accept}(x) \quad\mid\quad \bar{x}y \quad\mid\quad x(y)$$

Systems $S, S', \ldots$ are the parallel composition of *agents* $\mathsf{A}[P]$, *sessions* $s[\gamma]$,
delimited systems $(u)S$, and *latent contracts* $\{\downarrow_u p\}_\mathsf{A}$. The latter represents a
contract p (advertised by A) which has not been stipulated yet; upon stipulation,
the variable u will be instantiated to a fresh session name.

Processes $P, Q, \ldots$ are: prefixed processes $\pi\,.\,P$; branching $u \rhd \{\mathsf{a}_i.\,P_i\}_{i\in I}$,
which behaves as the continuation P_j upon receiving at session u a message
a_j; named processes $\mathsf{X}(\boldsymbol{u})$, used e.g., to specify recursive behaviours[1]; delimited
processes $(u)P$; and the terminated process $\mathbf{0}$.

The *prefix* τ allows to do some internal actions, $\mathtt{tell}\downarrow_u p$ to advertise a
contract p. Intuitively, u is a place-holder for the name of the session where
p will be used. $\mathtt{accept}(x)$ allows to accept the contract received at x, $\mathtt{send}_u\,\mathsf{a}$
to send a message a at session u, and $\mathtt{idle}(\delta)$ to delay by a time $\delta \in \mathbb{R}_{\geq 0}$;
the prefixes $\bar{x}y$ and $x(y)$ allow for the usual channel-based communication à

---

[1] We denote with $\boldsymbol{u}$ a sequence of names/variables, and we assume each X to have a
 unique definition $\mathsf{X}(x_1, \ldots, x_j) \stackrel{\text{def}}{=} P$, with the free vars of P included in $x_1, \ldots, x_j$.

$$\frac{\exists q : p \bowtie q}{\mathsf{A}[\texttt{tell} \downarrow_u p.\, P] \xrightarrow{\texttt{tell}} \mathsf{A}[P] \mid \{\downarrow_u p\}_\mathsf{A}} \qquad [\textsc{Tell}]$$

$$\frac{p \bowtie q \quad \gamma = \varGamma_0(\mathsf{A}:p, \mathsf{B}:q) \quad \sigma = \{s/x, y\} \quad s \text{ fresh}}{(x, y)(S \mid \{\downarrow_x p\}_\mathsf{A} \mid \{\downarrow_y q\}_\mathsf{B}) \xrightarrow{\texttt{fuse}} (s)(S\sigma \mid s[\gamma])} \qquad [\textsc{Fuse}]$$

$$\frac{\gamma = \varGamma_0(\mathsf{A}:\mathsf{co}(q), \mathsf{B}:q) \quad \sigma = \{s/x\} \quad s \text{ fresh}}{(x)(\mathsf{A}[\texttt{accept}(x).\, P] \mid \{\downarrow_x p\}_\mathsf{B} \mid S) \xrightarrow{\texttt{accept}} (s)(\mathsf{A}[P\sigma] \mid s[\gamma] \mid S\sigma)} \qquad [\textsc{Acpt}]$$

$$\frac{\gamma \xrightarrow{\mathsf{A}:!a} \gamma'}{\mathsf{A}[\texttt{send}_s\, a.\, P] \mid s[\gamma] \xrightarrow{\texttt{send}} \mathsf{A}[P] \mid s[\gamma']} \qquad [\textsc{Send}]$$

$$\frac{\gamma \xrightarrow{\mathsf{A}:?a} \gamma' \quad a = a_j}{\mathsf{A}[s \rhd \{a_i.\, P_i\}] \mid s[\gamma] \xrightarrow{\texttt{receive}} \mathsf{A}[P_j] \mid s[\gamma']} \qquad [\textsc{Recv}]$$

$$\frac{\gamma \xrightarrow{\delta} \gamma'}{s[\gamma] \xrightarrow{\delta} s[\gamma']} \; [\textsc{Delay-}\gamma] \qquad \qquad \frac{0 < \delta' \leq \delta}{\mathsf{A}[\texttt{idle}(\delta).\, P] \xrightarrow{\delta'} \mathsf{A}[\texttt{idle}(\delta - \delta').\, P]} \; [\textsc{Idle}]$$

Fig. 2. Reduction semantics of TCO_2 (full set of rules in [7]).

la π-calculus [25]. Note that the primitive `tell` allows process to communicate (when their contracts will be fused), in the absence of any pre-shared name.[2]

The semantics of TCO_2 is summarised in Fig. 2 as a reduction relation between systems. The labels are used to separate urgent actions from non-urgent ones. When an urgent label is enabled, time is not allowed to pass (similarly to the `asap` operator in U-LOTOS [28]). This enforces a fairness property: if an urgent action is enabled, the scheduler can not prevent it by letting time pass. In TCO_2, every discrete action is urgent, except for `fuse`; this formalises the intuition that a session between two compliant contracts can be created at any time by the middleware, independently from the participants' behaviour.

Rule [TELL] adds to the system a latent contract $\{\downarrow_u p\}_\mathsf{A}$, if p admits a compliant contract. Rule [FUSE] searches the system for compliant pairs of latent contracts, i.e. $\{\downarrow_x p\}_\mathsf{A}$ and $\{\downarrow_y q\}_\mathsf{B}$ such that $p \bowtie q$ (and $\mathsf{A} \neq \mathsf{B}$). Then, a fresh session s containing the initial configuration $\gamma = \varGamma_0(\mathsf{A}:p, \mathsf{B}:q)$ is established, and the name s is shared between A and B. Rule [ACPT] allows A to accept a latent contract q, which is passed through the channel x; then, the contract of A at s will be $\mathsf{co}(q)$. Rule [SEND] allows A to send a message $!a$ to the other endpoint of session s. This is only permitted if the contract configuration at s can take a transition on $\mathsf{A} : !a$, whereas messages not conforming to the contract will make A culpable of a violation. Rule [RECV] allows A to receive a message a_j from the other endpoint of s, and to behave like the continuation P_j. Rule [DELAY-γ] allows a session $s[\gamma]$ to idle, if permitted by the contract configuration γ at s (note that idling may make one of the participants culpable). Rule [IDLE]

---

[2] To avoid confusion between "channel-kinded" variables used in input/output prefixes and "session-kinded" variables, we forbid processes which improperly mix them, like e.g. `tell` $\downarrow_y p.y(x)$, where y is used both as a session variable and a channel variable.

is standard [28], and it allows a process to idle for a certain time δ. The other rules for dealing with time (and with the other constructs) are reported in [7].

A simple interaction in TCO_2 is shown in [7].

4 System Design

In this section we show how the interaction paradigm sketched in Sect. 2 (and formalised in Sect. 3) is supported by our middleware, and we illustrate the main design choices.

4.1 Specifying Contracts

Although the design of the middleware is mostly contract-agnostic, in this paper we describe and evaluate *timed session types* [6] (TSTs) as a particular instance of contracts. TSTs extend binary session types [22,35] with clocks and timing constraints, similarly to the way timed automata [2] extend (untimed) finite state automata. We give below a brief overview of TSTs, and we refer to [6] for the full technical development. Clocks $x, y, \ldots$ are variables over $\mathbb{R}_{\geq 0}$, which can be reset, and used within *guards* $g, g', \ldots$. Atomic guards are timing constraints of the form $x \circ d$ or $x - y \circ d$, where $d \in \mathbb{N}$ and $\circ \in \{<, \leq, =, \geq, >\}$, and they can be composed with the boolean connectives $\wedge, \vee, \neg$.

A TST p (Definition 1) describes the behaviour of a single participant involved in an interaction. An *internal choice* $\sum_i ! a_i \{g_i, R_i\} . p_i$ models the fact that its participant wants to do one of the outputs with label a_i in a time window where the guard g_i is true; the clocks in R_i will be reset after the output is performed. An *external choice* $\&_i ? a_i \{g_i, R_i\} . q_i$ models the fact that its participant is available to receive each message a_i at *any instant* within the time window where the guard g_i is true; furthermore, the clocks in R_i will be reset after the input is received. The term 1 denotes *success* (i.e., a terminated interaction). Infinite behaviour can be specified through recursion $\operatorname{rec} X . p$.

Definition 1 (Timed session types [6]). *Timed session types* $p, q, \ldots$ *are terms of the following grammar:*

$$ p ::= 1 \mid \sum_{i \in I} ! a_i \{g_i, R_i\} . p_i \mid \&_{i \in I} ? a_i \{g_i, R_i\} . p_i \mid \operatorname{rec} X . p \mid X $$

where (i) the set I is finite and non-empty, (ii) the labels in internal/external choices are pairwise distinct, (iii) recursion is guarded and considered up-to unfolding. True guards, empty resets, and trailing occurrences of 1 can be omitted.

Message labels are grouped into *contexts*, which can be created and made public through the middleware APIs. Each context defines the labels related to an application domain, and it associates each label with a *type* and a *verification link*. The type (e.g., int, string) is that of the messages exchanged with that label. The verification link is used by the runtime monitor (Sect. 4.4) to delegate the verification of messages to a trusted third party. For instance, the middleware supports Paypal as a verification link for online payments (see Sect. 6.3). The context also specifies the duration of a time unit: the shortest time unit supported by the middleware is that of seconds, which is also the one we use in all the examples in this paper.

4.2 Advertising Contracts

Once a contract has been created, a participant can advertise it to the middleware. At that point, the contract stays *latent* until the middleware finds a *compliant* one, i.e. another latent contract with whom the interaction is guaranteed not to get stuck. When this is found, the middleware creates a *session* between the two participants: the session consists of a private channel name and a *contract configuration*, which keeps track of the state of the contract execution.

The notion of compliance between TSTs (Definition 6 in [6]) is based on a transition system over contract configurations (Definition 5 in [6]). Contract configurations have the form $(p, \nu) \mid (q, \eta)$, where p, q are TSTs, and ν, η are *clock evaluations* (i.e., functions from clocks to $\mathbb{R}_{\geq 0}$); in the initial configuration $\Gamma_0(A : p, B : q)$, the clock evaluations map each clock to 0. Intuitively, p and q are compliant (in symbols, $p \bowtie q$) if, in all reachable configurations, the "required" behaviour of p (i.e., the branches in its internal choice) is "offered" by q in an external choice, while respecting the time constraints.

Example 1. Let $p = ?a\{x \leq 2\}$ & $?b\{x \leq 5\}$, and consider the following TSTs:

$$q_1 = !a\{y \leq 1\} \qquad q_2 = !a\{y \leq 3\} \qquad q_3 = !a\{y \leq 2\} + !c\{y \leq 2\}$$

We have that $p \bowtie q_1$: indeed, q_1 wants to output a within one time unit, and p is available to input a for two time units; compliance follows because the time window for the input includes that for the output.

On the contrary, $p \not\bowtie q_2$, since the time window required by q_2 is larger than the one offered by p.

Finally, $p \not\bowtie q_3$: although the timing constraints for label a match, q_3 can also choose to send c, which is not among the labels offered by p in its external choice.

Deciding Compliance. Compliance between TSTs is decidable (Theorem 1 in [6]). To check if $p \bowtie q$, we use the encoding in [6] to translate p and q into Uppaal timed automata [11], and then we model-check the resulting network for deadlock freedom. This amounts to solve the reachability problem for timed automata, whose theoretical worst-case complexity is exponential (more precisely, the problem is PSPACE-complete [2]). In practice, the overall execution time for compliance checking for the TSTs in our test suite is in the order of milliseconds; e.g., in the experimental setup described in Sect. 6, it takes approximately 20ms to check compliance between the largest TSTs on our hand, i.e. those modelling PayPal Protection for Buyers [1]. Since, however, the execution time of compliance checking is non-negligible, we do not perform an exhaustive search when searching the contract store for compliant pairs of contracts; rather, we use the techniques described in the following paragraphs to reduce the search space.

Compliance Pre-check. When a TST is advertised, the middleware stores in its database the associated timed automaton (which is then computed only once for each TST), and a *digest* of the TST; this digest comprises its context, and one bit which tells whether its top-level operation is an internal or an external choice (up-to unfolding). When looking for a contract compliant with p, the digests are used to rule out (without invoking the Uppaal model checker) some contracts which are surely *not* compliant with p. In particular, we rule out those q belonging to a context different from that of p, and those with the same top-level operator as p (as internal choices can only be compliant with external ones, and *vice versa*). The remaining contracts are potentially compliant with p, and so we restrict the search space to them. The search also takes into account the reputation of the participants who have advertised these contracts, as described in the following paragraph.

Reputation. The middleware assigns to each participant a *reputation*, which measures its ability to respect contracts. Intuitively, the reputation is increased when the participant successfully completes a session, while it is decreased when it is found culpable of a contract violation (more details about the formulation of the reputation system in Sect. 4.4). Reputation is used to sort latent contracts when searching for compliant pairs: the higher the participant's reputation, the higher the probability to establish a session with it. When looking for a contract compliant with p, we first construct the list of contracts potentially compliant with it (sorted by descending reputation). Then, we randomly choose one of them, according to the folded normal probability distribution. This causes contracts with high reputation to be chosen with high probability, while giving some chances also to contracts with low reputation. If the chosen contract is not compliant with p, it is discarded, and the algorithm chooses another one.

Checking the Existence of a Compliant. Not all TSTs admit a compliant one. For instance, no contract can be compliant with $p = \,!a\{y < 7\}.\,?b\{y < 5\}$, because if p outputs a at time 6, the counterpart cannot send b in the required time constraint. A sound and complete decision procedure for the existence of a compliant is developed in [6]. When advertising a contract, we use this procedure to rule out those contracts which do not admit a compliant one.

4.3   Accepting Contracts

As discussed in Sect. 2, a participant A can establish a session with B by accepting one of its contracts, whose identifier has been made public by B. Technically, when A declares to accept a contract p, the middleware constructs the *dual* of p, and assigns it to A. The dual of p is the greatest contract compliant with p, according to the subcontract preorder [6]: intuitively, it is the one whose offers match all of p's requests, and whose requests match all p's offers.

Unlike in the untimed case, the naïve construction of the dual of a TST p (i.e., the one which simply swaps inputs with outputs and internal choices with external ones) does not always produce a compliant TST. For instance, the naïve dual of $p = ?\mathsf{a}\{x \leq 2\}.\,?\mathsf{b}\{x \leq 1\}$ is $q = !\mathsf{a}\{x \leq 2\}.\,!\mathsf{b}\{x \leq 1\}$, which is *not* compliant with p. Indeed, since q can output $!\mathsf{a}$ at any time $1 < \delta \leq 2$, the interaction between p and q can become deadlock, and so they are not compliant.

The dual construction used by the middleware is the one defined in [6], which guarantees to obtain a TST compliant with p, if it exists. Roughly, the construction turns all the internal choices into external ones (without changing guards), and it turns external choices into internal ones, updating the guards to preserve future interactions. For instance, in the example above we obtain the TST $!\mathsf{a}\{x \leq 1\}.\,!\mathsf{b}\{x \leq 1\}$, which is compliant with p.

4.4   Service Interaction and Runtime Monitoring

When a session is established, the participants at the two endpoints can interact by sending and receiving messages. At a more concrete level, sending a message through a session is implemented by posting the message to the middleware, through its RESTful API. The middleware logs the whole interaction history, by recording and timestamping all the messages exchanged in the session. Receiving a message is also implemented by invoking the middleware API; upon a receive request, the middleware inspects the session history to retrieve the first unread message (which is then marked as read). The interaction over the session is asynchronous, as the middleware (similarly to a standard MOM) interprets the session history as two unbounded FIFO buffers containing the messages sent by the two endpoints[3]. However, differently from standard MOMs, our middleware monitors the interaction to verify that contracts are respected.

The runtime monitor processes each message exchanged in a session, by querying the verification link associated to it (to detect whether the message is genuine or not), and by checking that the message is permitted in the current contract configuration. Then, the monitor computes who is in charge of the next move, and, in case of contract violations, it detects which of the two participants is culpable. A participant A can become culpable for different reasons:

1. A sends a message not expected by her contract;
2. A's contract is an internal choice, but A loses time until all the branches become unfeasible (i.e., the time constraints are no longer satisfiable);
3. A sends some action at a valid time, but the trusted third party (associated to the action by the verification link) rejects it. For instance, this can happen if A tries to send a fake payment, but Paypal does not certify it.

The monitor guarantees that, in all possible states of the interaction, only one of the participants can be in charge of the next action; if no one is in charge nor culpable, then both participants have reached success (Lemma 3 in [6]).

---

[3] Asynchronous communication is possible despite TSTs having a synchronous semantics, as the middleware is delegated to receive messages on behalf of the recipient.

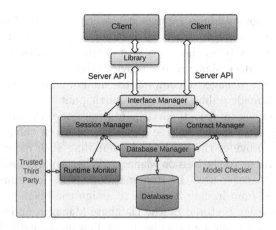

Fig. 3. A diagram of the middleware architecture.

Once a session terminates (either succesfully or not), the reputation of the involved participants is updated. If the session terminates successfully, then the reputation of both participants is increased; otherwise, the reputation of the culpable participant is decreased, while the other participant's reputation is increased. Further, we make participants consume reputation points each time they enter in session, and we use the *fading memories* technique of [33] to calculate the reputation value without recording the whole history of interactions. We weight recent negative behavior more than old positive behaviour, in order to mitigate *self-promoting attacks*, where a malicious participant tries to gain reputation by running successful sessions with himself or with some accomplices [21].

5   System Architecture

The middleware is a Java RESTful Web service; the primitives described in Sect. 4 are organised in components, as shown in Fig. 3. We have adopted a 3-tier architecture, consisting of a presentation layer, a business logic layer, and a data storage layer. The Interface Manager, which is the only component in the presentation layer, offers APIs to query the middleware, through HTTP POST requests. APIs can be accessed through language-specific libraries, which allow for an object-oriented programming style (see Appendix A in [7]). The data storage layer comprises a relational DB and a Database Manager, which takes care of handling queries, managing the cache, and modelling the data used in the other layers. The business logic layer manages contracts and sessions. More specifically, the Contract Manager performs the contract validation, advertisement (as in Sect. 4.2), and accept requests (Sect. 4.3); the Session Manager establishes sessions, by allowing clients to send and receive messages, managing the session history, and querying the Runtime Monitor to detect contract violations.

A client advertises a contract p with the tellContract API of the Interface Manager, encoding the required data in the JSON data exchange format.

The Interface Manager validates p, then it asks the Contract Manager to store it and to find a compliant contract, as outlined in Sect. 4.2. If no latent contracts are compliant with p, then p is kept latent, otherwise a new session is established. The Interface Manager also provides the acceptContract API, which requires the Contract Manager to compute the dual of a latent contract q, whose identifier has been made public by another participant.

When a session is established, participants can query the middleware to get the current time, to send and receive messages, to check culpability, etc. The Interface Manager provides the methods for handling such requests, delegating the internal operations to the Session Manager. When a participant sends a message, the Session Manager uses the Runtime Monitor to determine whether the action is permitted (and in case it is not, to assign the blame). If the action is permitted, the message is stored by the Database Manager, and then forwarded to the other participant upon a receive. To verify a message, the Runtime Monitor can invoke a trusted third party: if the verification fails, the action is rejected (so, our monitor implements *truncation*, in the terminology of [24]).

6 Validation

In this section we validate our middleware, mainly focussing on the aspects related to system scalability (Sect. 6.1), and to the effectiveness of the reputation system to rule out services not respecting contracts (Sect. 6.2). We also discuss how the middleware has been exploited to implement a large software system for managing online reservations (Sect. 6.3).

We carry out our experiments using a public instance of the middleware, accessible from the Web at co2.unica.it. The instance is a Web service running in a dedicated cloud server, equipped with a quad-core Intel Xeon CPU @ 2.27 GHz, 16 GB of RAM and a 50 GB SSD hard drive; the server runs Ubuntu 14.04 LTS, with Apache Tomcat and Oracle MySQL. Clients are tested in standard desktop PCs and laptops, while the multi-threaded simulations are executed in a high-level desktop configuration, with an octa-core Intel Core i7 @ 4.00 GHz and 16 Gb of memory, running Microsoft Windows 7 and Oracle JRE 1.7.

6.1 Scalability

In this section we assess the scalability of our middleware. We start by benchmarking the tell primitive, which triggers a search for compliant pairs of TSTs in the contract store. This is the most computationally expensive operation in the middleware: although the heuristics discussed in Sect. 4.2 allow for limiting the number of calls to the Uppaal model checker, the execution time of a tell could be non-negligible for a high number of latent contracts. So, we measure the execution time of tell p as a function of the number of TSTs in the contract store, and of the number of latent TSTs compliant with p.

Our second experiment concerns the performance of the runtime monitor. As described in Sect. 4.4, this component processes all the messages exchanged in

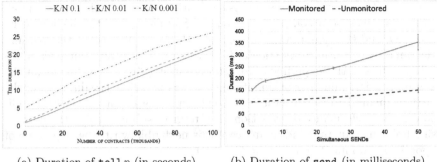

(a) Duration of `tell p` (in seconds).   (b) Duration of `send` (in milliseconds).

Fig. 4. Results of the scalability tests. In (a), K is the number of contracts compliant with p, and N is the total number of contracts.

sessions, to check if contracts are respected. Potentially, this could introduce a relevant computational overhead, so we measure the execution time of **send** in case the runtime monitor is turned on, or off. Note that, while the duration of **tell** does not affect the interaction between the participants once a session is established, a slowdown of the **send** can make an otherwise-honest participant culpable for not respecting some deadline. So, it is important that the overhead of the runtime monitor is negligible, w.r.t. the time scale of temporal constraints.

We build our scalability tests upon the discrete-event simulator DESMO-J [18], and the statistical model-checker MultiVeStA [32]. In particular, we use DESMO-J to define a single instance of the simulation, and MultiVeStA to run sequences of simulations until reaching a given confidence interval.

Tell. We test the execution time of `tell p` as a function of the number N of contracts stored in the middleware. The contract p used in our experiments is a simplified version of the Paypal Protection for Buyers (Example 1 in [6]). We assume that, among the N contracts, only $K \ll N$ are compliant with p, while the remaining $N - K$ are not, but they still pass the pre-check discussed in Sect. 4.2 (so, we are considering a worst-case scenario, because in the average case we expect that only a fraction of the contracts would pass the pre-check). We populate the contract store by choosing at each step whether to insert a contract compliant with p or a non-compliant one, according to a random weighted probability. Then, with DESMO-J we execute `tell p`, and we measure its execution time. MultiVeStA makes DESMO-J execute this simulation for several times, each time collecting the new **tell** duration and updating the average and the standard deviation; the simulations stop when the average fits into the confidence interval.

The results of our experiments are shown in Fig. 4. As we can see, the **tell** duration grows linearly with N, and it increases by a constant when the percentage K/N of contracts compliant with p decreases; note that the slope of the curves does not seem to be significantly affected by K/N.

Runtime Monitor. The goal of this experiment is to quantify how the execution of a large number of simultaneous **send** affects the performance of the middleware. To achieve this goal, we use a multi-threaded simulation, where all the threads advertise a contract with an internal sum, wait the session to be established, and then simultaneously perform the send. We repeat the measure of the send duration until its standard deviation fits into the confidence interval. The results of this experiment are reported in Fig. 4b, which shows that the execution of a large number of simultaneous sends penalizes the duration of the request, compared to the situation where the runtime monitor is switched off. However, the performance degradation seem to grow sub-linearly in the number of simultaneous requests, and in any case it is negligible w.r.t. the time scale of temporal constraints (1 time unit = 1 second).

6.2   A Distributed Experiment: RSA Cracking

Consider a service (hereafter referred to as *master*, or just M) who wants to solve a cryptographic problem by exploiting the computational resources of external nodes (hereafter called *workers*, or W) distributed over the network. In particular, M wants to crack a set of public RSA keys, in order to get the corresponding private keys. However, the master does not know the network structure (i.e., how many workers are available, where they are located, and how they are connected), and it does not have any pre-shared channel for communicating with them. Furthermore, the master does not trust the workers: they are not bound to run any particular cracking algorithm, they can return wrong/incomplete results, or they can fail to answer within the expected deadline.

To cope with these issues, the master exploits our middleware to automatically discover and invoke suitable workers. For each public key in its set, the master spawns a process which advertises the contract:

$$p_M = \text{!pubkey}\{;x\}.\,(\text{?confirm}\{x < 15\}.\,\text{?result}\{x < 90\}.\,\text{!pay1xbt}\{x < 120\}$$
$$\&\ \text{?abort}\{x < 15\})$$

Here, M is promising to send a public key (pubkey); doing so triggers a reset of the clock x. Then, the worker has 15 seconds to either confirm that he will carry on the task, or abort (e.g., if the key is considered too strong). If the worker confirms, it must return the corresponding result (a private key) within 90 seconds since the public key was sent (the correctness of the result is checked by a trusted third party,[4] specified by the context of p_W); finally, M rewards the worker with 1 bitcoin (pay1xbt). At runtime, the master behaves as prescribed by its contract; if the worker accepts the public key and it returns the corresponding private key, then M removes that public key from the list; otherwise, it advertises another instance of p_M, and when the session is established it sends the same public key to another worker.

The advantage offered by the middleware in terms of code succinctness is clear, as the search of workers, the establishment of sessions, and the runtime

---

[4] Note that verifying the correctness of private keys has a polynomial complexity in the number of bits of the public key, while the problem of cracking RSA keys is considered to be exponentially hard.

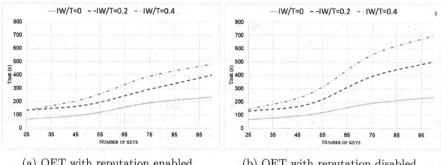

(a) OET with reputation enabled.   (b) OET with reputation disabled.

Fig. 5. Overall Execution Time as a function of the number of keys to be broken. *IW* is the number of inefficient workers, and *T* is the total number of workers.

monitoring is completely transparent to programmers. So, we assess below the reputation system implemented in the middleware (Sects. 4.2 and 4.4). In particular, we measure the time taken by the master for cracking all the public keys in its list (*Overall Execution Time, OET*). We do this in two configurations of the middleware: the one where the reputation system is turned on, and the one where it is turned off. Our conjecture is that turning the reputation system on will reduce the OET, because it increases the probability of establishing sessions with *honest* workers which produce correct results while respecting deadlines.

In our experiments, we assume that workers are drawn from two different classes: those using an efficient cracking algorithm, which always return the correct result within the deadline; and those using an inefficient algorithm, which sometimes may miss the deadline, because the computation takes too long. We also assume that the number of public keys is bigger than the number of workers, so each of them may receive many keys to break. Each worker iteratively advertises its contract (the dual of p_M), then waits for a public key, runs the cracking algorithm, and finally return the private key to the master.

The results of our experiment are shown in Fig. 5, where we measure the OET as a function of the number of keys to be broken, and of the ratio between efficient and inefficient workers. The solid curve is identical in the two figures, since the reputation system does not affect the selection of workers when there are only efficient ones. In the dashed curve and in the dot-dashed one the percentage of inefficient workers grows (to 20 % and 40 %, respectively), and we see that the OET grows accordingly when the reputation system is turned off. This is because the reputation system penalizes inefficient workers, by reducing the probability they can establish sessions with the master.

6.3 Case Study: A Contract-Oriented Reservation Marketplace

To test the effectiveness and versatility of our middleware for the development of real distributed applications, we have exploited it as a *contract layer* in a software infrastructure for online reservations [5]. The infrastructure acts as a marketplace wherein service providers make available their resources, which can then be searched, reserved, and used by clients. These reservations can be of arbitrary nature, as the infrastructure features an abstract model of resources, which can be suitably instantiated by service providers. The infrastructure has been tested with various instances of providers, offering e.g. car sharing facilities, medical appointments, and hotel accommodations.

The reservation marketplace adds a search layer to that of the middleware: clients can search among the resources, and when they find a suitable one they can `accept` its contract. Contracts are constructed by service providers through a GUI, starting from a template and then selecting among various options and parameters. For instance, a simple contract for a service provider is the following:

$$p = \text{?pay}\{t < d_{pay}\}.\,\text{?details}\{t < d_{pay} + 60, t\}.\,p' \quad \& \quad \text{?cancel}\{t \leq d_{cc}\}$$
$$p' = \text{rec}\,X.\,\big(\text{?feedback}\{t < d_{fb}\} \quad \& \quad \text{?cancel}\{t < d_{cc}\}.\,\text{!refund}\{t \leq d_{rf}\} \quad \& \quad p''\big)$$
$$p'' = \text{?move}\{t < d_{mv}\}.\,\big(\text{!ok}\{t < d_{ok}\}.\,\text{?feedback}\{t < d_{fb}\} + \text{!no}\{t < d_{no}\}.\,X\big)$$

The provider waits for a `payment` and some `details` about the reservation; then, it gives the client a choice among three actions: accept the reservation (and leave a `feedback`), `cancel` it (which involves a `refund`), or `move` it to another date. Moving reservations is not always permitted (e.g., because the new date is not available), so when the provider notifies `no`, it allows the client to try again.

Contracts are enforced by the runtime monitor of the middleware, which delegates the verification of `payment`s and `refund`s to PayPal. Clients and providers can check the state of their contracts through the GUI, which at any time also highlights the permitted actions and their deadlines.

7   Related Work

Our middleware builds upon CO_2 [9,10], a core calculus for contract-oriented computing; in particular, the middleware implements all the main primitives of CO_2 (`tell`, `send`, `receive`), and it introduces new concepts, like e.g. the `accept` primitive, time constraints, and reputation.

From the theoretical viewpoint, the idea of constraint-based interactions has been investigated in other process calculi, e.g. Concurrent Constraint Programming (CCP [31]), and cc-pi [17], albeit the kind of interactions they induce is quite different from ours. In CCP, there is a global constraint store through which processes can interact by telling/asking constraints. In cc-pi, interaction is a mix of name communication à la π-calculus [25] and `tell` à la CCP (which is used to put constraints on names). E.g., $\bar{x}\langle z \rangle$ and $y\langle w \rangle$ can synchronise iff the constraint store entails $x = y$; when this happens, the equality $z = w$ is added to the store, unless making it inconsistent. In cc-pi consistency plays a crucial role: `tell`s *restricts* the future interactions with other processes, since adding constraints can lead to more inconsistencies; by contrast, in our middleware telling a contract *enables* interaction with other services, so consistency is immaterial.

The notion of time in behavioural contracts has been studied in [15], which addresses a timed extension of multi-party asynchronous session types [23];

however, the goals of [15] are quite different from ours. The approach pursued in [15] is top-down: a *global type* (specifying the overall communication protocol of a set of services, and satisfying some safety properties, e.g. deadlock-freedom) is projected into a set of *local types*; then, a composition of services preserves the properties of the global type if each service type-checks against the associated local type. Our middleware fosters a different approach to service composition: a distributed application is built bottom-up, by advertising contracts to delegate work to external (unknown and untrusted) services. Both our approach and [15,27] use runtime monitoring to detect contract violations and assign the blame; additionally, in our middleware these data are exploited as an automatic source of information for the reputation system. Another formalism for communication protocols with time constraints is proposed in [19], where live sequence charts are extended with a global clock. The approaches in [15,19] cannot be directly used in our middleware, because they do not provide algorithms to decide compliance, or to construct a contract compliant with a given one.

From the application viewpoint, several works have investigated the problem of *service selection* in open dynamic environments [3,26,37,38]. This problem consists in matching client requests with service offers, in a way that, among the services respecting the given functional constraints, the one which maximises some *non-functional* constraints is selected. These non-functional constraints are often based on quality of service (QoS) metrics, e.g. cost, reputation, guaranteed throughput or availability, etc. The selection mechanism featured by our middleware does not search for the "best" contract compliant with a given one (actually, typical compliance relations in behavioural contracts are qualitative, rather than quantitative); the only QoS parameter we take into account is the reputation of services (see Sect. 4.2). In [3,38] clients can require a sequence of tasks together with a set of non-functional constraints, and the goal is to find an assignment of tasks to services which optimises all the given constraints. There are two main differences between these approaches and ours. First, unlike behavioural contracts, tasks are considered as atomic activities, not requiring any interaction between clients and services. Second, unlike ours, these approaches do not consider the possibility that a service may not fulfil the required task.

In the work [26], a service selection mechanism is implemented where functional constraints can be required in addition to QoS constraints: the first are described in a web service ontology, while the others are defined as requested and offered ranges of basic QoS attributes. A runtime monitor and a reputation system are also implemented, which, similarly to ours, help to marginalise those services which do not respect the advertised QoS constraints. Some kinds of QoS constraints cannot be verified by the service broker, so their verification is delegated to clients. This can be easily exploited by malicious participants to carry on *slandering attacks* to the reputation system [21]: an attacker could destroy another participant's reputation by involving it in many sessions, and each time declare that the required QoS constraints have been violated. In our middleware there is no need to assume participants trusted, as the verification of contracts is delegated to the middleware itself and to trusted third parties.

8   Conclusions

We have explored a new application domain for behavioural contracts, i.e. their use as interaction protocols in MOMs. In particular, we have developed a middleware where services can advertise contracts (in the form of timed session types, TSTs), and interact through sessions, which are created only between services with compliant contracts. To implement the middleware primitives, we have exploited much of the theory of TSTs in [6]: in particular, a decidable notion of compliance between TSTs, a decidable procedure to detect when a TST admits a compliant one (and, if so, to construct it), and a decidable runtime monitoring.

We have validated our middleware through a series of experiments. The scalability tests (Sect. 6.1) seem to suggest that the performance of middleware is acceptable for up to $100K$ latent contracts. However, we feel that good performance can be obtained also for larger contract stores, for two reasons. First, in our experiments we have considered the pessimistic scenario where *all* latent contracts in the store are potentially compliant with a newly advertised one. Second, the current prototype of the middleware is sequential and centralised: parallelising the instances of the compliance checker, or distributing those of the middleware, would result in a performance boost. The experiments about the reputation system (Sect. 6.2) show that the middleware can relieve developers from dealing with misbehaviour of external services, and still obtain efficient distributed applications, which dynamically reconfigure themselves to foster the interaction among trustworthy services.

Although in this paper we have focussed on TSTs, the middleware only makes mild assumptions about the nature of contracts, e.g., that their observable actions are **send** and **receive**, and that they feature some notion of compliance with a sound (but not necessarily complete) verification algorithm. Hence, with minor efforts it would be possible to extend the middleware to support other contract models. For instance, communicating timed automata [14] (which are timed automata with unbounded communication channels) would allow for multi-party sessions, while session types with assertions [13], would allow for an explicit specification of the constraints among the values exchanged in sessions.

Besides the issues related to the expressiveness of contracts and to the scalability of their primitives (e.g., service binding and composition, runtime monitoring, *etc.*), we believe that also security issues should be taken into account: indeed, attackers could make a service sanctioned by exploiting discrepancies between its contracts and its actual behaviour. These mismatches are not always easy to spot (see e.g. the online bookstore example in Appendix A.4 in [7]); analysis techniques are therefore needed to ensure that a service will not be susceptible to this kind of attacks.

Acknowledgments. The authors thank Maria Grazia Patteri, Mirko Joshua Mascia and Stefano Lande for their assistance in setting up the evalution and the case studies, and Alceste Scalas for the discussion about Java APIs. This work is partially supported by Aut. Reg. of Sardinia grants L.R.7/2007 CRP-17285 (TRICS), P.I.A. 2010 ("Social Glue"), P.O.R. F.S.E. Operational Programme of the Aut. Reg. of Sardinia, EU Social

Fund 2007-13 – Axis IV Human Resources, Objective l.3, Line of Activity l.3.1), by MIUR PRIN 2010-11 project "Security Horizons", and by EU COST Action IC1201 "Behavioural Types for Reliable Large-Scale Software Systems" (BETTY).

References

1. PayPal buyer protection. https://www.paypal.com/us/webapps/mpp/ua/useragreement-full#13. Accessed 8 July 2015
2. Alur, R., Dill, D.L.: A theory of timed automata. Theor. Comput. Sci. **126**(2), 183–235 (1994)
3. Ardagna, D., Pernici, B.: Adaptive service composition in flexible processes. IEEE Trans. Software Eng. **33**(6), 369–384 (2007)
4. Banavar, G., Chandra, T., Strom, R.E., Sturman, D.: A case for message oriented middleware. In: Jayanti, P. (ed.) DISC 1999. LNCS, vol. 1693, pp. 1–17. Springer, Heidelberg (1999)
5. Bartoletti, M., Cimoli, T., Murgia, M., Patteri, M.G., Mascia, M.J., Podda, A.S., Pompianu, L., COREserve: a contract-oriented reservation marketplace (2015). http://coreserve.unica.it
6. Bartoletti, M., Cimoli, T., Murgia, M., Podda, A.S., Pompianu, L.: Compliance and subtyping in timed session types. In: Graf, S., Viswanathan, M. (eds.) Formal Techniques for Distributed Objects, Components, and Systems. LNCS, vol. 9039, pp. 161–177. Springer, Heidelberg (2015)
7. Bartoletti, M., Cimoli,T., Murgia, M., Podda, A.S., Pompianu, L.: A contract-oriented middleware (2015). http://co2.unica.it
8. Bartoletti, M., Cimoli, T., Zunino, R.: Compliance in behavioural contracts: a brief survey. In: Kahramanogullari, O., et al. (eds.) Degano Festschrift. LNCS, vol. 9465, pp. 103–121. Springer, Heidelberg (2015). doi:10.1007/978-3-319-25527-9_9
9. Bartoletti, M., Tuosto, E., Zunino, R.: Contract-oriented computing in CO_2. Sci. Ann. Comp. Sci. **22**(1), 5–60 (2012)
10. Bartoletti, M., Zunino, R.: A calculus of contracting processes. In: LICS (2010)
11. Behrmann, G., David, A., Larsen, K.G.: A tutorial on UPPAAL. In: Bernardo, M., Corradini, F. (eds.) SFM-RT 2004. LNCS, vol. 3185, pp. 200–236. Springer, Heidelberg (2004)
12. Rueß, H., Schätz, B., Blech, J.O., Falcone, Y.: Behavioral specification based run-time monitors for OSGi services. In: Margaria, T., Steffen, B. (eds.) ISoLA 2012, Part I. LNCS, vol. 7609, pp. 405–419. Springer, Heidelberg (2012)
13. Tuosto, E., Bocchi, L., Yoshida, N., Honda, K.: A theory of design-by-contract for distributed multiparty interactions. In: Gastin, P., Laroussinie, F. (eds.) CONCUR 2010. LNCS, vol. 6269, pp. 162–176. Springer, Heidelberg (2010)
14. Bocchi, L., Lange, J., Yoshida, N.: Meeting deadlines together. In: CONCUR (2015, to appear)
15. Yang, W., Yoshida, N., Bocchi, L.: Timed multiparty session types. In: Baldan, P., Gorla, D. (eds.) CONCUR 2014. LNCS, vol. 8704, pp. 419–434. Springer, Heidelberg (2014)
16. Brogi, A., Canal, C., Pimentel, E.: Behavioural types for service integration: achievements and challenges. ENTCS **180**(2), 41–54 (2007)
17. Buscemi, M.G., Montanari, U.: CC-Pi: a constraint-based language for specifying service level agreements. In: De Nicola, R. (ed.) ESOP 2007. LNCS, vol. 4421, pp. 18–32. Springer, Heidelberg (2007)

18. Göbel, J., Joschko, P., Koors, A., Page, B.: The discrete event simulation framework DESMO-J: review, comparison to other frameworks and latest development. In: Proceedings of ECMS, pp. 100–109 (2013)

19. Harel, D., Marelly, R.: Playing with time: on the specification and execution of time-enriched LSCs. In: MASCOTS, pp. 193–202 (2002)

20. Heckel, R., Lohmann, M.: Towards contract-based testing of Web services. Electr. Notes Theor. Comput. Sci. **116**, 145–156 (2005)

21. Hoffman, K.J., Zage, D., Nita-Rotaru, C.: A survey of attack and defense techniques for reputation systems. ACM Comput. Surv. **42**(1), 1:1–1:31 (2009)

22. Honda, K., Vasconcelos, V.T., Kubo, M.: Language primitives and type discipline for structured communication-based programming. In: Hankin, C. (ed.) ESOP 1998. LNCS, vol. 1381, pp. 122–138. Springer, Heidelberg (1998)

23. Honda, K., Yoshida, N., Carbone, M.: Multiparty asynchronous session types. In: POPL (2008)

24. Ligatti, J., Bauer, L., Walker, D.: Run-time enforcement of nonsafety policies. ACM Trans. Inf. Syst. Secur. **12**(3), 19:1–19:41 (2009)

25. Milner, R., Parrow, P., Walker, D.: A calculus of mobile processes. I and II. Inf. Comput. **100**(1), 1–77 (1992)

26. Mukhija, A., Dingwall-Smith, A., Rosenblum, D.: QoS-aware service composition in Dino. In: ECOWS, pp. 3–12 (2007)

27. Neykova, R., Bocchi, L., Yoshida, N.: Timed runtime monitoring for multiparty conversations. In: BEAT, pp. 19–26 (2014)

28. Larsen, K.G., Skou, A.: An overview and synthesis on timed process algebras. In: Larsen, K.G., Skou, A. (eds.) CAV 1991. LNCS, vol. 575, pp. 376–398. Springer, Heidelberg (1992)

29. Rivest, R.L., Shamir, A., Adleman, L.: A method for obtaining digital signatures and public-key cryptosystems. Commun. ACM **21**(2), 120–126 (1978)

30. Sahai, A., Machiraju, V., Sayal, M., van Moorsel, A.P.A., Casati, F.: Automated SLA monitoring for Web services. In: DSOM, pp. 28–41 (2002)

31. Saraswat, V.A., Rinard, M.C.: Concurrent constraint programming. In: POPL, pp. 232–245 (1990)

32. Sebastio, S., Vandin, A.: MultiVeStA: statistical model checking for discrete event simulators. In: Proceedings of ValueTools, pp. 310–315 (2013)

33. Srivatsa, M., Xiong, L., Liu, L.: TrustGuard: countering vulnerabilities in reputation management for decentralized overlay networks. In: WWW, pp. 422–431 (2005)

34. Strunk, A.: QoS-aware service composition: a survey. In: ECOWS, pp. 67–74. IEEE (2010)

35. Takeuchi, K., Honda, K., Kubo, M.: An interaction-based language and its typing system. In: Halatsis, C., Philokyprou, G., Maritsas, D., Theodoridis, S. (eds.) PARLE 1994. LNCS, vol. 817, pp. 398–413. Springer, Heidelberg (1994)

36. Tuosto, E.: Contract-oriented services. In: Beek, M.H., Lohmann, N. (eds.) WS-FM 2012. LNCS, vol. 7843, pp. 16–29. Springer, Heidelberg (2013)

37. Yu, T., Zhang, Y., Lin, K.-J.: Efficient algorithms for Web services selection with end-to-end QoS constraints. ACM Trans. Web **1**(1), 6 (2007)

38. Zeng, L., Benatallah, B., Ngu, A.H., Dumas, M., Kalagnanam, J., Chang, H.: QoS-aware middleware for Web services composition. IEEE Trans. Software Eng. **30**(5), 311–327 (2004)

A Robust Framework for Securing Composed Web Services

Najah Ben Said[1], Takoua Abdellatif[3],
Saddek Bensalem[1], and Marius Bozga[2]([⊠])

[1] University Grenoble Alpes, VERIMAG, 38000 Grenoble, France
[2] CNRS, VERIMAG, 38000 Grenoble, France
marius.bozga@imag.fr
[3] Tunisia Polytechnic School, University of Carthage, Tunis, Tunisia

Abstract. This paper proposes a framework that automatically checks and configures data security in Web Services starting from high level business requirements. We consider *BPEL*-based composed Web Services. *BPEL* processes and initial security parameters are represented as component-based models labeled with security annotations. These models are formal and enable automated analysis and synthesis of security configurations, under the guidance of the service designer. The security property considered is the non-interference. The overall approach is practical since security is defined separately from functional processes and automatically verified. We illustrate its utility to solve intricate security problems using a smart grid application.

Keywords: Component-based systems · Information flow security · Non-interference · Dependency flow graph · Automated verification

1 Introduction

With the expansion of Web Services (WS) [1] deployed on the enterprise servers, cloud infrastructures and mobile devices, Web Service composition is currently a widely used technique to build complex Internet and enterprise applications. Orchestration languages like *BPEL* [2] allow rapidly developing composed WS by defining a set of activities binding sophisticated services. Nevertheless, advanced security skills and tools are required to ensure critical information security. Indeed, it is important to track data flow and prevent illicit data access by unauthorized services and networks; this task can be challenging when the service is complex or when the composition is hierarchical (the service is composition of composed services and atomic services). For example, a classical travel organization WS has to keep a client's destination secret as messages are exchanged between different services like travel agency services and the payment service.

The research leading to these results has received funding from the European Community's Seventh Framework Programme [FP7/2007-2013] under grant agreement ICT-318772 (D-MILS).

C. Braga and P.C. Ölveczky (Eds.): FACS 2015, LNCS 9539, pp. 105–122, 2016.
DOI: 10.1007/978-3-319-28934-2_6

Each piece of information depending on the destination, like ticket price, can lead to the secret disclosure if it is not protected. WS security standards [3,4] provide information flow security solutions for point-to-point inter-service communication but fall short in ensuring end-to-end information flow security in composed services. Furthermore, the *BPEL* language does not state any rules on how to properly apply security mechanisms to services. Generally, developers manually set up their system security configuration parameters which can be tedious and error-prone.

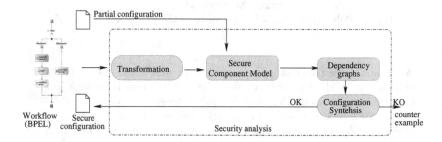

Fig. 1. Information flow analysis overview with component-based model

Information flow control, particularly the non-interference [5] property check, is an alternative, more robust, approach than applying access control for point to point communication. Indeed, it allows tracking information propagation in the entire system and prevents secret or confidential information from being publicly released. Information flow control relies on annotating system data with specific levels of security and uses specific methods for checking non-interference, that is, absence of leakage between different levels. Nonetheless, providing annotations and establishing their correctness are equally difficult, especially for distributed implementations, where only code is available and no higher-level abstractions exist to give a better view and easier way of correction.

In this paper, we propose a robust tool assisting a designer ensuring end-to-end information flow security in WS composition. Figure 1 shows a workflow overview of this tool. The service designer describes in *BPEL* his process and defines partial security constraints in a configuration file. The constraints are expressed as authorization rights, that is, a list of services owners and authorized readers for a subset of critical data. The *BPEL* process and the configuration information are then automatically transformed into a component-based framework. This framework was first adapted to abstract distributed WS orchestration to a component-based model where all Web services are transformed into atomic components communicating through interactions by sending and receiving variables and second, to synthesize security configuration for total system variables with respect to security constraints by considering all implicit and explicit data dependencies in the system. The calculated configuration is optimal that is only data that need to be protected is configured as critical and its security level is minimal. It is indeed, very important to reduce the security processing overhead like cryptography encryption and decryption, signature calculation, certificate verification, etc. In case a total configuration file is generated by the tool, the system information flow is then considered non-interferent with respect to initially defined configuration. Otherwise, the system is interferent and system designer has to re-define the input initial configuration. As a security advisor, automated configuration synthesis allows designers, developers and administrators to focus on functional constraints and be confident that their secret data is protected and people privacy respected. The proposed framework is based on a formal compositional security model. It is implemented and tested on a smart grid application. This application shows the practical usage of our tool since only basic security skills are required and WS standards are respected.

The paper is structured as follows. Section 2 presents the functional and security aspects of the adopted component-based framework. In Sect. 3, we present a practical compositional approach to synthesize security configurations in component-based system models. In Sect. 4, we apply this approach to Web Service orchestration. We consider a transformation from *BPEL* orchestration language to the component-based framework and we present the adopted security annotation model and the tool implementation. In Sect. 5, we provide a use-case as illustrative example. Finally, Sect. 6 discusses the related work and Sect. 7 concludes and presents some lines for future work.

2   Component-Based Model

In the scope of this work, we consider systems composed of atomic components interacting through point-to-point communications. Atomic components are in form of finite automata extended with data. Communication is synchronous and directed between one sender and one receiving component. Regarding security, we consider transitive information flow policies expressed on system variables and we focus on non-interference properties.

The proposed model is general enough to deal with information flow security from a practical point of view for commonly used programming languages and/or modeling frameworks such as *BPEL*. Nevertheless, it should be mentioned that this model is actually a strict subset of the *secureBIP* component model previously introduced in [6,7]. The latter considers additional coordination mechanisms through multiparty interactions as well as different definitions of non-interference. For the sake of readability we recall hereafter the key concepts and we re-formulate the key results which are useful in our precise context, on the restricted subset considered.

2.1   Preliminaries

Let $\mathbb{D} = \{D_j\}_{j \in \mathcal{J}}$ be a universal set of data domains (or data types) including the Boolean domain $\mathbb{D}_{Bool} = \{true, false\}$. Let $\mathbb{E}xpr$ be an universal set of operators, that is, functions of the form $op : \times_{i=1}^{m} D_{j_i} \to D_{j_0}$, where $m \geq 0$,

$D_{j_i} \in \mathbb{D}$ for all $i = 0, m$. We consider typed variables $x : D$ where x denotes the name of the variable and $D \triangleq dom(x) \in \mathbb{D}$ its domain of values. We define expressions e as either (i) constant values $u \in \cup_j D_j$, (ii) variables $x : D$ or (iii) composed expressions $op(e_1, ..., e_m)$ constructed by applying operators op on sub-expressions $e_1, ..., e_m$ such that, their number and their domains match exactly the domain of op. We denote by $use(e)$ the set of variables occurring in expression e and by $\mathbb{E}xpr[X]$ the set of expressions constructed from a set of variables X and operators in $\mathbb{E}xpr$. We denote by $\mathbb{A}sgn[X]$ the set of assignments to variables in X, that is, any subset $\{(x_i, e_i)\}_{i \in I} \subseteq X \times \mathbb{E}xpr[X]$ where $(x_i)_{i \in I}$ are all distinct. An assignment (x, e) is denoted by $x := e$.

Given a set of variables X, we define valuations V of X as functions $V : X \rightarrow \cup_{j \in J} D_j$ which assign values to variables, such that moreover, $V(x) \in dom(x)$, for all $x \in X$. We denote by $V[u/x]$ the valuation where variable x has assigned value u and any other variable has assigned the same values as in V. For a subset $Y \subseteq X$, we denote by $V_{|Y}$ the restriction of V to variables in Y.

Given an expression $e \in \mathbb{E}xpr[X]$ and a valuation V on X we denote by $e(V)$ the value obtained by evaluating the expression according to values of X on the valuation V. Moreover, given an assignment $a \in \mathbb{A}sgn[X]$ and a valuation V of X we denote by $a(V)$ the new valuation V' obtained by executing a on V, formally $V'(x) = e(V)$ iff $x := e \in a$ and $V'(x) = V(x)$ otherwise.

2.2   Operational Model

An atomic component B is a tuple (Q, P, X, T) where Q is a set of states, X is a set of local variables, P is a set of ports (or action names) and T is a set of transitions. We distinguish respectively input ports $P^{in} \subseteq P$ and output ports $P^{out} \subseteq P$ and we assume they are disjoint, $P^{in} \cap P^{out} = \emptyset$. Every input or output port $p \in P^{in} \cup P^{out}$ is associated to a unique variable $var(p) \in X$. Every transition $t \in T$ is a tuple (q, p, g, a, q') where $q \triangleq src(t), q' \triangleq dst(t) \in Q$ are respectively the source and the target states, $p \triangleq port(t) \in P$ is a port, $g \triangleq guard(t) \in \mathbb{E}xpr[X]$ is the enabling condition and $a \triangleq asgn(t) \in \mathbb{A}sgn[X]$ is the assignment of t.

In our model, atomic components have exclusive access on their variables. Interactions between components take place only through explicit input/output binary connectors. A connector defines a static communication channel from one output port p^{out} of a sender component B to an input port p^{in} in a receiver component $B' \neq B$. The connector is denoted by the tuple (p^{out}, p^{in}). Intuitively, when communication takes place, the value of $var(p^{out})$ is assigned to $var(p^{in})$.

Figure 2 provides examples of atomic components. The *Producer* component contains two states l_1 and l_2 and one output port *out*. The transition labelled with port *produce* takes place only if the guard $[w \leq 3]$ is true. Then, the variable x is updated by executing the assignment $x := 3x + 1$.

We denote by $\Gamma(B_1, ..., B_n)$ the composition of a set of atomic components $B_i = (Q_i, X_i, P_i, T_i)_{i=1,n}$ through a set of connectors Γ. For the sake of simplicity, we tacitly assume that every input and output port of every B_i is used in exactly one connector in Γ. The operational semantics of a composition is defined

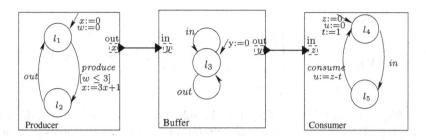

Fig. 2. A *Producer-Buffer-Consumer* example

as a labelled transition system $(\mathcal{Q}, \mathcal{A}, \rightarrow)$ where states correspond to system configurations and transitions to internal steps or communication through connectors. A system configuration $\langle \boldsymbol{q}, \boldsymbol{V} \rangle$ in $\mathcal{Q}$ where $\boldsymbol{q} = (q_1, ..., q_n)$, $\boldsymbol{V} = (V_1, ..., V_n)$ is obtained from component configurations (q_i, V_i) where $q_i \in Q_i$ and V_i is a valuation of X_i, for all $i = 1, n$. The set of labels $\mathcal{A}$ is defined as $\Gamma \cup \{\tau\}$, that is, either communication on connectors or internal action (τ). The set of transitions $\rightarrow \subseteq \mathcal{Q} \times \mathcal{A} \times \mathcal{Q}$ between configurations are defined by the following two rules:

$$
\text{INTER} \frac{\begin{array}{c} (q_i, p_i, g_i, a_i, q_i') \in T_i \quad p_i \notin P_i^{in} \cup P_i^{out} \\ g_i(V_i) = true \quad V_i' = a_i(V_i) \quad \forall k \neq i. \ (q_k', V_k') = (q_k, V_k) \end{array}}{\langle (q_1, ..., q_n), (V_1, ..., V_n) \rangle \xrightarrow{\tau} \langle (q_1', ..., q_n'), (V_1', ..., V_n') \rangle}
$$

$$
\text{COMM} \frac{\begin{array}{c} (p_i^{out}, p_j^{in}) \in \Gamma \quad (q_i, p_i^{out}, g_i, a_i, q_i') \in T_i \quad (q_j, p_j^{in}, g_j, a_j, q_j') \in T_j \\ g_i(V_i) = g_j(V_j) = true \quad u = V_i(var(p_i^{out})) \quad V_i' = a_i(V_i) \\ V_j' = a_j(V_j[u/var(p_j^{in})]) \quad \forall k \neq i, j. \ (q_k', V_k') = (q_k, V_k) \end{array}}{\langle (q_1, ..., q_n), (V_1, ..., V_n) \rangle \xrightarrow{p_i^{out} p_j^{in}} \langle (q_1', ..., q_n'), (V_1', ..., V_n') \rangle}
$$

The system evolves either by performing asynchronously an internal step of some component B_i (INTER rule) or by performing a synchronous communication between two components B_i, B_j involving respectively ports p_i^{out}, p_j^{in} related by a connector in Γ (COMM rule). Transitions are executed only if guards are evaluated to *true* in the current configuration. As usual, next configurations are obtained by taking into account variable assignments and communication.

A run ρ of the system $\Gamma(B_1, ..., B_n)$ is a finite sequence $\langle \boldsymbol{q}_0, \boldsymbol{V}_0 \rangle \ \alpha_1 \ \langle \boldsymbol{q}_1, \boldsymbol{V}_1 \rangle$ $\alpha_2 \ ... \ \alpha_\ell \ \langle \boldsymbol{q}_\ell, \boldsymbol{V}_\ell \rangle$ where $\langle \boldsymbol{q}_{k-1}, \boldsymbol{V}_{k-1} \rangle \xrightarrow{\alpha_k} \langle \boldsymbol{q}_k, \boldsymbol{V}_k \rangle$ for all $k = 1, \ell$. The set of all runs starting from a configuration $\langle \boldsymbol{q}_0, \boldsymbol{V}_0 \rangle$ are denoted by $Runs\langle \boldsymbol{q}_0, \boldsymbol{V}_0 \rangle$.

Finally, for a run ρ and a subset of variables $Y \subseteq \cup_{i=1}^n X_i$ we denote by $tr(\rho, Y)$ the trace of ρ with respect to Y. Traces represent what is actually observable from a trace by having access to variables in Y. They are inductively defined for runs as follows:

$$tr(\langle \boldsymbol{q}, \boldsymbol{V} \rangle, Y) = \langle \boldsymbol{q}, \boldsymbol{V}_{|Y} \rangle$$

$$tr(\langle \boldsymbol{q}, \boldsymbol{V} \rangle) \, \alpha \, \rho', Y) = \begin{cases} tr(\rho', Y) \\ \quad \text{if } \alpha = \tau \text{ and } tr(\rho', Y) \text{ starts with } \langle \boldsymbol{q}, \boldsymbol{V}_{|Y} \rangle \\ \langle \boldsymbol{q}, \boldsymbol{V}_{|Y} \rangle \, \alpha \, tr(\rho', Y) \\ \quad \text{otherwise} \end{cases}$$

where $\boldsymbol{V}_{|Y}$ denotes $(V_{1|Y_1}, ..., V_{n|Y_n})$ for $Y_i = Y \cap X_i$, for all $i = 1, n$. Finally, for a trace $tr(\rho, Y)$ we define the set $Enable(tr(\rho, Y))$ of configurations which are enabling the same trace on alternative runs, formally:

$$Enable(tr(\rho, Y)) = \{ \, \langle \boldsymbol{q}_0, \boldsymbol{V}_0 \rangle \mid \exists \rho' \in Runs\langle \boldsymbol{q}_0, \boldsymbol{V}_0 \rangle, \, tr(\rho, Y) = tr(\rho', Y) \, \}$$

2.3 Security Model

We consider transitive information flow policies expressed on system variables and we focus on the non-interference properties. We restrict ourselves to confidentiality and we ensure that no illegal flow of information exists between variables having incompatible security levels.

Formally, we represent security domains as finite lattices $(\mathbb{S}, \leq)$ where $\mathbb{S}$ denotes the security levels and $\leq$ the *flows to* relation. For a level s, we denote by $[-, s]$ (resp. by $[s, -]$) the set of levels allowed to flow into (resp. from) s. Moreover, for any subset $S \subseteq \mathbb{S}$, we denote by $\sqcup S$ (resp. $\sqcap S$) the unique least upper (resp. greatest lower) bound of S according to $\leq$.

Let $\Gamma(B_1, ..., B_n)$ be a system and let $X = \cup_{i=1}^{n} X_i$ (resp. $P = \cup_{i=1}^{n} P_i$) be the set of all components variables (resp. ports). A security annotation on variables is a function $\sigma : X \to \mathbb{S}$ which associates security levels to variables. We denote by $\sigma^{-1} : 2^{\mathbb{S}} \to 2^X$ the pre-image of σ, defined as $\sigma^{-1}(S) = \{x \in X \mid \sigma(x) \in S\}$, for all $S \subseteq \mathbb{S}$. For any s, define $Y_s = \sigma^{-1}([-, s])$, the set of variables having security levels at most s. For a security level s, we denote by $\approx_s$ the indistinguishability relation on configurations at level s defined by $\langle \boldsymbol{q}_1, \boldsymbol{V}_1 \rangle \approx_s \langle \boldsymbol{q}_2, \boldsymbol{V}_2 \rangle$ iff $\boldsymbol{q}_1 = \boldsymbol{q}_2$ and $\boldsymbol{V}_{1|Y_s} = \boldsymbol{V}_{2|Y_s}$. That is, configurations are identical on control states and up to variables with security levels at most s. For a set of configurations $C \subseteq \mathcal{Q}$, we denote by $[\![C]\!]_s = \{c' \in \mathcal{Q} \mid \exists c \in C. \ c' \approx_s c\}$. We are now ready to define the security criterion for an annotated system.

Definition 1. *A security annotation σ is secure for a system $\Gamma(B_1, ..., B_n)$ and initial configurations Init iff $\forall s \in \mathbb{S}. \ \forall \langle \boldsymbol{q}_0, \boldsymbol{V}_0 \rangle \in Init. \ \forall \rho \in Runs\langle \boldsymbol{q}_0, \boldsymbol{V}_0 \rangle$*

$$Enable(tr(\rho, Y_s)) = [\![Enable(tr(\rho, Y_s))]\!]_s$$

Intuitively, the definition states that for any security level s, no additional information is obtained by observing traces with respect to variables Y_s behind the equivalence $\approx_s$. Or, any two indistinguishable initial states enable precisely the same set of traces with respect to Y_s. If this would not be the case for let say, $(\boldsymbol{q}_0, \boldsymbol{V}_0) \approx_s (\boldsymbol{q}_0, \boldsymbol{V}_0')$, then one could find a run $\rho_0 \in Runs\langle \boldsymbol{q}_0, \boldsymbol{V}_0 \rangle$ such that no run $\rho' \in Runs\langle \boldsymbol{q}_0, \boldsymbol{V}_0' \rangle$ had the same trace with respect to Y_s. But then, this means $(\boldsymbol{q}_0, \boldsymbol{V}_0) \in Enable(tr(\rho_0, Y_s))$ whereas $(\boldsymbol{q}_0, \boldsymbol{V}'_0) \notin Enable(tr(\rho_0, Y_s))$. and consequently $Enable(tr(\rho, Y_s)) \subsetneqq [\![Enable(tr(\rho, Y_s))]\!]_s$.

The following proposition defines static conditions ensuring that a security annotation on variables is secure for a system.

Proposition 1. *A security annotation σ is secure for a system $\Gamma(B_1, ..., B_n)$ with an arbitrary non-empty set of initial configurations Init whenever*

- *all local transitions t in components B_i are* sequentially consistent
  $\forall(x := e) \in asgn(t). \; \forall y \in use(e) \cup use(guard(t)). \; \sigma(y){\le}\sigma(x)$
- *all components B_i are* port deterministic *i.e., for all transitions t_1, t_2*
  $src(t_1) = src(t_2) \; \wedge \; port(t_1) = port(t_2) \; \Rightarrow \; guard(t_1) \wedge guard(t_2) \equiv false$

and moreover, there exists a security annotation on ports $\varsigma : P \rightarrow \mathbb{S}$ such that:

- *ports of all* causal *local transitions t_1, t_2 have increasing levels of security*
  $dst(t_1) = src(t_2) \; \Rightarrow \; \varsigma(port(t_1)){\le}\varsigma(port(t_2))$
- *ports of all* conflicting *local transitions t_1, t_2 have the same level of security*
  $src(t_1) = src(t_2) \; \Rightarrow \; \varsigma(port(t_1)) = \varsigma(port(t_2))$
- *variables and ports are consistently annotated on all local transitions t*
  $\forall(x := e) \in asgn(t). \; \forall y \in use(guard(t)). \; \sigma(y){\le}\varsigma(port(t)){\le}\sigma(x)$
- *variables and ports are consistently annotated on connectors*
  $\forall(p^{out}p^{in}) \in \Gamma. \; \sigma(var(p^{out})){\le}\varsigma(p^{out}) = \varsigma(p^{in}){\le}\sigma(var(p^{in}))$

Proof (Sketch). It can be shown that the conditions above imply the *unwinding conditions* of [8] for indistinguishability $\approx_s$ at security level s. In turn, unwinding conditions are guaranteeing non-interference and therefore security as defined in Definition 1. A detailed proof is available in [6,7] for a slightly more general component-based model allowing multiparty interactions between components.

3   Configuration Synthesis

The configuration synthesis problem is defined as follows. Given a partial security annotation of a system, extend it towards a complete annotation which is provable secure according to Proposition 1, or show that no such annotation actually exists. We assume that system components are port deterministic.

We rely on flow dependency graphs as an intermediate artifact for solving this problem. For every component $B_i = (Q_i, X_i, P_i, T_i)$, we define the flow dependency graph $\mathcal{G}_i = (N_i, \hookrightarrow_i)$ where the set of vertices $N_i = X_i \cup P_i$ contains the ports and variables of B_i and edges $\hookrightarrow_i \subseteq N_i \times N_i$ correspond to flow dependencies required by Proposition 1 and are defined below, for every $x, y \in X_i, p, r \in P_i$:

$y \hookrightarrow_i x$	iff	$\exists t \in T_i. \; x := e \in asgn(t), \; y \in use(e) \cup use(guard(t))$
$p \hookrightarrow_i x$	iff	$\exists t \in T_i. \; x := e \in asgn(t), \; p = port(t) \bigvee p \in P_i^{in}, x = var(p)$
$y \hookrightarrow_i p$	iff	$\exists t \in T_i. \; y \in use(guard(t)), p = port(t) \bigvee p \in P_i^{out}, y = var(p)$
$p \hookrightarrow_i r$	iff	$\exists t, t' \in T_i. \; p = port(t), r = port(t'), (dst(t) = src(t') \vee src(t) = src(t'))$

Using flow dependency graphs, the configuration synthesis problem is formally rephrased as follows:

- Given system $\Gamma(B_1, ..., B_n)$, partial annotation $\sigma_0 : X \to \mathbb{S} \cup \{\bot\}$
- Find complete annotation $\zeta : X \cup P \to \mathbb{S}$ such that
  (C1) (initial annotation) $\forall x \in X. \ \sigma_0(x) \neq \bot \implies \zeta(x) = \sigma_0(x)$
  (C2) (flow preservation) $\forall i = 1, n. \ \forall x, y \in P_i \cup X_i. \ x \hookrightarrow_i y \implies \zeta(x) \leq \zeta(y)$
  (C3) (connector consistency) $\forall \gamma = (p^{out} p^{in}) \in \Gamma. \ \zeta(p^{out}) = \zeta(p^{in})$

If a complete annotation ζ exists and satisfies the conditions (C1-C3) above, then the system $\Gamma(B_1, ..., B_n)$ is provable secure for $\sigma = \zeta_{|X}$ and $\varsigma = \zeta_{|P}$, which are respectively the projections of ζ to variables X and ports P. That is, all conditions required by Proposition 1 on annotation of ports and variables within components are captured by dependency graphs $(\mathcal{G}_i)_{i=1,n}$ and satisfied according to (C2). Connectors are consistently annotated according to (C3). Moreover, the initial annotation is preserved by (C1).

An iterative algorithm to compute the complete annotation ζ is depicted as Algorithm 1 below. If the algorithm terminates without detecting inconsistencies, then ζ is the less restrictive annotation satisfying conditions (C1-C3). If an inconsistency is detected, then no solution exists. In this case, the initial annotation is inconsistent with respect to the information flow within the system.

Algorithm 1. Annotation Synthesis

---

1 $\zeta(n) \leftarrow \begin{cases} \sigma_0(n) \text{ if } n \in X, \sigma_0(n) \neq \bot \\ \sqcap \mathbb{S} \quad \text{otherwise} \end{cases}$ ▷ initialization

2 $BList \leftarrow \{B_i\}_{i=1,n}$ ▷ inter-component outer loop

3 **while** $BList \neq \emptyset$ **do**

4      $choose\text{-}and\text{-}remove(BList, B_i)$

5      $nList \leftarrow X_i \cup P_i$ ▷ intra component inner loop for $\mathcal{G}_i$

6   **while** $nList \neq \emptyset$ **do**

7         $choose\text{-}and\text{-}remove(nList, n_i)$

8         $s_i \leftarrow \sqcup \{\zeta(n) \mid n \hookrightarrow_i n_i\}$ ▷ recompute security level of n_i

9   **if** $\zeta(n_i) \leq s_i$ and $s_i \neq \zeta(n_i)$ **then**

10   **if** $n_i \in X_i$ and $\sigma_0(n_i) \neq \bot$ and $\sigma_0(n_i) \leq s_i$ **then**

11   **stop**   ▷ inconsistency detected

12           $\zeta(n_i) \leftarrow s_i$ ▷ update and propagate change within $\mathcal{G}_i$

13           $nList \leftarrow nList \cup \{n \mid n_i \hookrightarrow_i n\}$

14   **foreach** $p_i \in P_i^{out} \cup P_i^{in}$ **do**

15         $find \ p_j \in P_j^{out} \cup P_j^{in}$ with $(p_i p_j) \in \Gamma$ or $(p_j p_i) \in \Gamma$

16   **if** $\zeta(p_i) \neq \zeta(p_j)$ **then**

17           $\zeta(p_j) \leftarrow \zeta(p_i)$ ▷ update and propagate change across connectors

18           $BList \leftarrow BList \cup \{B_j\}$

Initially, all system variables are either annotated by security levels given from system designer σ_0 if it exist or a default level that correspond to the lowest security level ($\sqcap \mathbb{S}$) in the lattice (line 1). The algorithm visits iteratively all components (lines 2–18). For every component B_i, it propagates forward the current annotation ζ within the flow graph $\mathcal{G}_i$ (lines 3–13). The security level $\zeta(n_i)$ of every node n_i is eventually increased to become more restrictive than the levels of its predecessors (lines 8–13). An inconsistency is reported if the security level increases for an initially annotated variable (lines 10–11). Any change triggers recomputation of successors nodes of n_i (lines 12–13). Finally, once the annotation within $\mathcal{G}_i$ is computed, any change on security levels on input/output ports is propagated to connected ports (lines 14–18). After this propagation step, any pair of connected ports has again the same security level. As for variables, notice that annotations for connected ports can only increase: any increase due to propagation within a component is immediately propagated to the connected port. The involved components need to be revisited again (line 18). Notice that both while loops are guaranteed to terminate as the number of annotation changes is bounded for every node. That is, the security level can only be increased finitely many times in a bounded lattice $(\mathbb{S}, \leq)$.

Proposition 2. *Algorithm 1 solves the configuration synthesis problem.*

Proof. Initially, the annotation ζ is defined to satisfy initial annotation condition (C1). It equally satisfies connector consistency (C3) but not necessarily flow preservation (C2). The algorithm propagates this annotation along the flow graphs, without changing the initially annotated variables. Intra-component propagation makes flow preservation (C2) hold for the component but may actually destroy (C3). On the contrary, the propagation across connectors re-establish (C3) but may destroy (C2) for connected components. At termination, no annotation changes are possible/needed, hence, the final annotation ζ satisfies both flow preservation condition (C2) but and connector consistency (C3).

As an example, we apply Algorithm 1 to the Producer-Buffer-Consumer presented in Fig. 2 with initial annotation $\{x \mapsto M, z \mapsto H\}$, for security levels L(ow), M(edium) and H(igh), such that $L \leq M \leq H$. The three flow dependency graphs and their dependencies through connectors are depicted in Fig. 3. For this initial labelling, the algorithm succeeds to generate a complete annotation for variables $\{x \mapsto M, w \mapsto L, y \mapsto M, z \mapsto H, t \mapsto L, u \mapsto H\}$ and all ports are mapped to M. If however we add to the initial configuration a label to the guard variable w, $\{w \mapsto H\}$, Algorithm 1 detects an inconsistency at the *Producer* component and an illicit flow from the w variable to y variable through port *produce* is reported to the user.

4 Application to Web Services

In this section, we apply the synthesis approach to generate secure configurations of WS applications. We consider a composition of *BPEL* and elementary services annotated using the decentralized label security model (DLM) [9]. We briefly present how such WS compositions are represented in the component-based model and we show how the DLM annotations are used in the *BPEL* context.

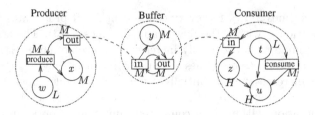

Fig. 3. Dependency graphs of Producer-Buffer-Consumer from Fig. 2

4.1 The BPEL Composition

BPEL provides structuring mechanisms to compose several WS into a new one. We particularly focus on *BPEL4WS* [10] processes which compose services from activities, that are either (1) *basic* such as receive, reply, invoke, assign, throw, exist, or (2) *structured* such as sequence, if, while, repeatuntil, pick, flow.

The representation of *BPEL* processes in our component model is structural, that is, the structure of the source *BPEL* model is preserved in the target model. More precisely, a process is represented as an atomic component where the behavior encompasses all its basic and structured activities. All process variables are added to the atomic component. Basic activities such as ⟨*receive...*/⟩, ⟨*reply...*/⟩, ⟨*invoke...*/⟩ are translated into specific transitions triggered by respectively *Receive_** and *Reply_** ports. Their corresponding variables are implicitly attached to the above ports. The ⟨*assign...*/⟩ activity is translated as an internal transition that executes the corresponding assignment.

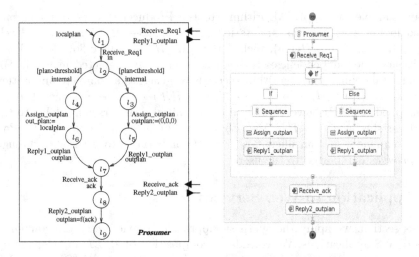

Fig. 4. Atomic component representation of a *BPEL* process

Structured activities define the overall control flow of transitions in the atomic component, in the usual way. In particular, transition guards are extracted from $\langle if..., while..., repeatuntil.../\rangle$ and $\langle pick.../\rangle$ activities. As a restriction, the parallel execution of activities within a $\langle flow.../\rangle$ is not supported. In this case, their execution is made sequential in an arbitrary order.

Finally, we define the connectors and the composition of the atomic components by using the *PartnerLinks* defined for *BPEL* processes. Every $\langle invoke.../\rangle$, $\langle receive.../\rangle$ and $\langle reply.../\rangle$, $\langle receive.../\rangle$ interaction defined over partner links is translated to a connector relating the corresponding components and their respective ports. Let us notice that processes may interact through partner links with external WS, that is, developed in other languages than *BPEL* (such as Java, C, etc.). In this case, these WS are represented as atomic components with an implicit behaviour, for arbitrarily sending and receiving data through their connected ports.

Similar translations have been already defined in the literature [11]. As the above translation is structural the resulting model remains comprehensive for the WS designer. The representation relies basically on adapting reusable and composable model components that directly maps processes with limited numbers of execution steps. Despite that, some features in *BPEL* language are not considered such as fault/event handling and scopes. Security errors that can be generated by these aspects are not in the scope of this paper.

4.2   Decentralized Label Model

The decentralized label model (DLM) [9] provides a universal labeling scheme where security labels (or levels) are expressed using set of policies. A confidentiality label L contains (1) an owner set, denoted $O(L)$, that are principals representing the originating sources of the information, and (2) contains for each owner $o \in O(L)$ a set of readers, denoted $R(L,o)$, representing principals to whom the owner o is willing to release the information. The association of an owner o and a set of readers $R(o)$ defines a policy. Principals are ordered using an *acts_for* partial order relation (denoted $\prec$) which is a delegation mechanism that enables a principal to pass his rights to another principal (e.g., $o_1 \prec o_2$ states that o_2 can act for o_1). A security domain is defined over the set of confidentiality labels by using a *flows to* relation defined as follows:

$$L_1 \leq L_2 \equiv \forall o_1 \in O(L_1).\ \forall o_2 \in O(L_2).\ o_1 \prec o_2\ \wedge$$
$$\forall r_1 \in R(L_1, o_1).\ \exists r_2 \in R(L_2, o_2).\ r_1 \prec r_2$$

The intuition behind the *flows to* relation $\leq$ above is that *(1)* the information can only flow from one owner o_1 to either the same or a more powerful owner o_2 where o_2 can act for o_1 and *(2)* the readers allowed by $R(L_2, o)$ must be a subset of the readers allowed by $R(L_1, o)$ where we consider that the readers allowed by a policy include not only the principals explicitly mentioned but also the principals able to act for them.

In our setting for *BPEL* WS composition, the principals used to define the *acts_for* relation and the security domain are obtained from *BPEL* partner links that correspond to WS URI. That is, principals can be either BPEL processes or atomic WS in some primitive language.

The designer expresses his security policy by tagging *BPEL* variables using DLM labels. The security domain and these annotations are then transposed as such on the component-based model. For example, a confidentiality label *L*: {*Prosumer:SMG*} assigned to the variable *outplan* in the *Prosumer* process presented in Fig. 4 (right side) is used directly, as it is, for the *outplan* variable in *Prosumer* atomic component obtained by translation (left side).

4.3   Implementation

The configuration synthesis algorithm described in Sect. 3 is implemented and available for download at http://www-verimag.imag.fr/~bensaid/secureBIP/. The user provides the WS composition in *BPEL* and a configuration file (.xml) that contains an *acts_for* relation defining authorities for different processes and the DLM annotations for some process variables. An example of a configuration file is provided in the Appendix. In a first step, the *BPEL* composition is structurally transformed into a component-based model representation in *BIP* [12]. The transformation extends an already existing translation of *BPEL* to BIP developed in [11] to study functional aspects. In a second step, the synthesis tool takes as input the system model (.bip) and the configuration file (.xml), builds the dependency graphs of components and runs the synthesis algorithm to produce the complete configuration.

5   Use-Case: Smart Grid Application

To illustrate the use of our framework we consider a simplified model of a smart grid system [13] managed through Internet network using WS. Smart grid systems usually interconect a number of cooperating *prosumers*, (that is, *pro*-ducers and con-*sumers*) of electricity on the same shared infrastructure. In principle, every prosumer is able to produce, store and consume energy within the grid. However, its use of the grid has to be negotiated in advance (e.g., on a daily basis) in order to adapt to external conditions (e.g., weather conditions, day-to-day demands,...) as well as to maintain the behaviour of the grid in some optimal parameters (e.g., no peak consumption). Smart grids are subject to requirements related to safety and security e.g., the power consumption/production of a prosumer must remain secret as it actually may reveal sensitive information.

In our WS model of the smart grid, the system consists of a finite number of prosumer processes, Pr_i, communicating with a *smart grid* process, *SMG*. Initially, each Pr_i sends its consumption and production plan, (P_i, C_i, B_i), for the next day to the grid. Production P_i, consumption C_i and (storage) battery B_i are expressed using energy units (integer) where $0 \preceq P_i \preceq 2, -3 \preceq C_i \preceq 0$ and $-1 \preceq B_i \preceq 1$. The *SMG* validates the plans received by checking that the overall energy flow through the grid implied by these plans does not exceed the power line capacity. This check measures the consumption exceed acknowledgment,

ack, compared to a bound, that is, $ack=0$ if the $-1 \preceq \sum_{i=1}^{n}(P_i + C_i + B_i) \preceq 4$, otherwise, it returns the difference between the sum of the plans and the consumption bounds. The SMG sends back to each Pr_i an ack_i to negotiate updating its own plan, where $ack = \sum_{i=1}^{n} ack_i$. The negotiation terminates when $ack=0$ meaning that the energy flow on the grid does not exceed the line capacity. Figure 5 shows the system overview with two prosumers that exchange queries with the smart grid.

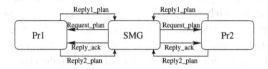

Fig. 5. Smart grid application overview

The information flow security requirements that we emphasize here consist first, on ensuring the confidentiality of energy consumption plan for each Pr_i, (which can reveal sensitive competitive information such as its production capacity) and second, ensuring that no prosumer is able to deduce the consumption plan of any other prosumer by observing the received ack information. For instance, consider two prosumers such that one of them, Pr_1, sends an extreme consumption plan $(0, -3, -1)$ to the SMG while the second, Pr_2, sends $(0, -3, 0)$ as a consumption plan. The SMG first calculates the acknowledgment message that is $ack=3$ then sends $ack_1=1$, $ack_2=2$ messages to respectively Pr_1 and Pr_2. Assume now that Pr_2 sends back a new consumption plan $(1, -2, 1)$ and gets back $ack_2=0$. By only observing other $ack1$ message sent to Pr_1, the Pr_2 can deduce that the consumption plan of Pr_1 is equal to $(0,-3,-1)$. The translation of Pr_1 process is given in Fig. 4 while the translation of the SMG process is given in the appendix.

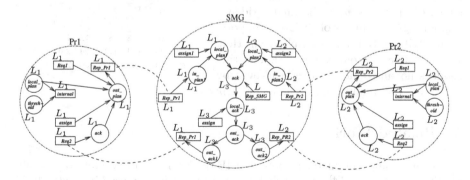

Fig. 6. Generated dependency graphs (fragments).

For applying our approach to check system security, the designer introduces initially his partial security policy by tagging intuitively some variables that he considers sensitive in system model with security annotations. He also provides an *acts_for* diagram for all model components where he gives authorities to some of them to act for others. In this system the *SMG* component can only acts for both Pr_1 and Pr_2. To ensure confidentiality of prosumers plan, the system administrator annotates *out_plan*1 with $L_1 = \{Pr_1 : SMG\}$ label and *out_plan*2 with $L_2 = \{Pr_2 : SMG\}$ label. Obviously, $L_1 \not\leq L_2$ and $L_2 \not\leq L_1$ are indicating that both prosumers represent separate security domains that can only communicate with the *SMG* component. Then, the tool automatically generates the dependency graph of the transformed smart grid system. Presented in Fig. 6, the dependency graph is build over ports (rectangles) and data variables (circles) locally at each atomic component(big circles), where arrows intra-circles represent dependencies between ports and data in the same atomic component while arrow inter-circles represent inter-components dependencies. The application of Algorithm 1 to the system dependency graph detects an illegal information flow in the system and generates an error in the *out_plan* node for both prosumers. Indeed, the label propagation in the system creates at *ack* node of the *SMG* component a new label $L_3 = L_1 \sqcup L_2$. Obviously, label $L_3 = \{Pr_1 : SMG; Pr_2 : SMG\}$ is more restrictive than both labels L_1 and L_2. Since the *ack* node depends on *out_ack*1 in Pr_1 and *out_ack*2 in Pr_2, then it is labelled with L_3 in both prosumers which causes security level inconsistency at *out_plan* nodes. Algorithm 1 generates an inconsistent security level error between both *out_plan* and *ack* nodes. Here, the system designer has to redefine the initial configuration, for instance, by given more privilege to prosumers to act for *SMG* component and enforce variable *ack* to higher security level $L_3 = \{SMG : SMG\}$. In this case, and with the authority that each prosumer gain, flow can go from L_3 to L_1 and L_2.

As an evaluation of the compositional approach performance, Table 1 presents some experiments over configuration time t for different variation of the number of prosumer components, n, in the smart grid system for a given number of variables X, ports P and with initial labels number, σ_0. Here we can notice that our configuration synthesis does not introduce an overhead even by increasing the number of system components.

Table 1. Model size and configuration time (in s) for smart grid application with one initial security label by each prosumer.

n	P	X	σ_0	t
4	26	24	3	1.82
13	98	87	12	1.94
25	194	171	24	2.01
101	802	703	100	2.82

6   Related Work

There are many commercial tools like IBMs XML Security Gateway XS40, application servers [14] and Web Service Enhancements for Microsoft .NET (WSE) [15] that provide GUI to help users configure and verify WS security but the user has to learn about standard WS-Security syntax and options.

In [16], authors propose a high-level GUI for configuring WS security with a business-policy-oriented view. It models the messaging with customers and business partners, lists various threats, and presents best-practice security patterns against these threats. A user can select among proposed generated basic patterns according to the business policies, and then apply them to the messaging model. The result of the pattern application is, afterwards, described in the Web Services Security Policy Language (WS-Security Policy). None of these tools handle the non-interference property like we do. Regarding formal models for non-interference in WS, in [17], authors present WS data flows as extensions of the Petri-net model and in [18], non-interference has been formalized for Petri-nets. Nevertheless, these solutions have some drawbacks which are mainly that data and resource description is manual and can be therefore error prone. Later on, the same authors propose the IFAudit tool that represents data flow as *propagation graphs* generated from workflow's log data. The propagation graphs are analyzed against the security policies.

Distinct security models are proposed in [19] where authors propose a classification of security-aware WS. They list a set of works classified in information flow category. Nevertheless, these works are restricted to verification rather than security configuration synthesis. Here we propose a practical automated verification method for transformed model of composed *BPEL* WS, based on formally proved security conditions. In [20], the authors deal with chained services and security is checked with a notion of back check procedure and pass-on certificate. It is not clear how to apply this solution to WS orchestration workflows and how to handle implicit interference. A recent work extends *BPEL*-orchestra engine [21] to handle IFC security. This work is inspired from SEWSEC framework [22] by adopting the distributed security label to annotate information. Nevertheless, instead of using abstractions like PDG, this annotation is set inside the *BPEL* code. Code annotation requires security skills, does not separate functional and security concerns and induces development overhead.

Finally, our work is related to information flow security in component-based systems. In contrast to [23] where authors verify security in a component-based model by annotating the system ADL (Architecture Description Language) and tracking information flow at intra- and inter-components separately, this work provides a sound model with formal proofs guaranteeing system non-interference. Besides, and compared to our previous work [6] where we adopted a more general component-based model to build secure distributed systems, here we propose a simpler message-based send-receive model suitable to model applications with web-style primitives and communications like BPEL-based composed WS and we propose not only a security verification but also a practical solution for security configuration synthesis.

7   Conclusion and Future Work

In this paper, we propose a component-based approach to assist system designers to analyze and enforce information flow security in WS compositions.

We implemented a compositional synthesis algorithm that propagates labels and generates secure system configurations starting from partial configurations.

As future work, we plan to extend this work in several directions. First, we are seeking for less restrictive syntactic conditions for establishing non-interference. In particular, we believe that a finer control flow analysis using for instance dominance analysis [24] can provide finer dependencies amongst variables and ports. Second, we are working on relaxing the non-interference property and introducing declassification mechanisms to our model. Declassification has been studied for sequential interactive programs with inputs and outputs [25], nevertheless, its extension to distributed concurrent component-based models such as Web Services is less understood.

Appendix

Figure 7 shows a transformation of the *SMG* process of the smart grid system given as *BPEL* workflow, into an atomic component. The behavior of the atomic component represents the activities given in the *BPEL* process.

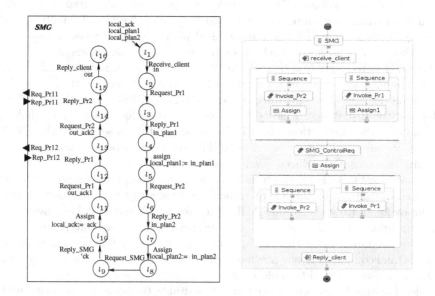

Fig. 7. Translation of the *SMG* component

The designer input configuration file includes an *acts_for* relation as well as some annotated variables. Here we presented an example of a configuration file of the smart grid system. In this xml file we define ⟨*authority/*⟩ to different system components representing the *acts_for* relation. Moreover, we specify by ⟨*var_config/*⟩ the annotations of variables from different atomic components (processes).

```xml
<?xml version="1.0"?>
<config>
  <acts_for>
    <authority>SMG: Prosumer1, Prosumer2, Prosumer3</authority>
  </acts_for>
  <var_config>
    <variable var="outplan" process="Prosumer1"
      label="Prosumer1:SMG"></variable>
    <variable var="outplan" process="Prosumer2"
      label="Prosumer2:SMG"></variable>
    <variable var="outplan" process="Prosumer3"
      label="Prosumer3:SMG"></variable>
  </var_config>
</config>
```

References

1. Walsh, A.: UDDI, SOAP, and WSDL: The Web Services Specification Reference Book. Prentice Hall, Upper Saddle River (2002)
2. Juric, M.B.: Business Process Execution Language for Web Services BPEL and BPEL4WS, 2nd edn. Packt Publishing, Birmingham (2006)
3. Damiani, E., di Vimercati, S.D.C., Paraboschi, S., Samarati, P.: Securing SOAP e-services. Int. J. Inf. Secur. **1**(2), 100–115 (2002)
4. Della-Libera, G., Gudgin, M., Hallam-Baker, P., Hondo, M., Granqvist, H., Kaler, C., Maruyama, H., McIntosh, M., Nadalin, A., Nagaratnam, N., Philpott, R., Prafullchandra, H., Shewchuk, J., Walter, D., Zolfonoon, R.: Web services security policy language (WS-SECURITYPOLICY). Technical report (2005)
5. Goguen, J.A., Meseguer, J.: Security policies and security models. In: IEEE Symposium on Security and Privacy, pp. 11–20 (1982)
6. Bozga, M., Ben Said, N., Abdellatif, T., Bensalem, S.: Model-driven information flow security for component-based systems. In: Bensalem, S., Lakhneck, Y., Legay, A. (eds.) From Programs to Systems. LNCS, vol. 8415, pp. 1–20. Springer, Heidelberg (2014)
7. Ben Said, N., Abdellatif, T., Bensalem, S., Bozga, M.: Model-driven information flow security for component-based systems. Technical report TR-2013-7, VER-IMAG. http://www-verimag.imag.fr/TR/TR-2013-7.pdf
8. Rushby, J.: Noninterference, transitivity, and channel-control security policies. Technical report CSL-92-2, SRI International (1992)
9. Myers, A.C., Liskov, B.: Protecting privacy using the decentralized label model. ACM Trans. Softw. Eng. Methodol. **9**, 410–442 (2000)
10. Andrews, T., Curbera, F., Dholakia, H., Goland, Y., Klein, J., Leymann, F., Liu, K., Roller, D., Smith, D., Thatte, S., Trickovic, I., Weerawarana, S.: BPEL4WS, Business Process Execution Language for Web Services Version 1.1. IBM (2003)
11. Stachtiari, E., Mentis, A., Katsaros, P.: Rigorous analysis of service composability by embedding WS-BPEL into the BIP component framework. In: 2012 IEEE 19th International Conference on Web Services, pp. 319–326 (2012)
12. Basu, A., Bensalem, S., Bozga, M., Combaz, J., Jaber, M., Nguyen, T.H., Sifakis, J.: Rigorous component-based design using the BIP framework. IEEE Softw. **28**(3), 41–48 (2011). Special Edition - Software Components beyond Programming - from Routines to Services
13. Koss, D., Sellmayr, F., Bauereiss, S., Bytschkow, D., Gupta, P., Schaetz, B.: Establishing a smart grid node architecture and demonstrator in an office environment using the SOA approach. In: First International Workshop on Software Engineering Challenges for the Smart Grid, SE4SG, pp. 8–14 (2012)

14. Corporation., I.B.M.: Using BPEL processes in WebSphere Business Integration Server Foundation. IBM, International Technical Support Organization (2004)
15. Microsoft Development network. http://msdn.microsoft.com/
16. Tatsubori, M., Imamura, T., Nakamura, Y.: Best-practice patterns and tool support for configuring secure web services messaging. In: IEEE International Conference on Web Services (ICWS 2004), pp. 244–251 (2004)
17. Busi, N., Gorrieri, R.: A survey on non-interference with petri nets. In: Desel, J., Reisig, W., Rozenberg, G. (eds.) Lectures on Concurrency and Petri Nets. LNCS, vol. 3098, pp. 328–344. Springer, Heidelberg (2004)
18. Busi, N., Gorrieri, R.: Structural non-interference in elementary and trace nets. Math. Struct. Comput. Sci. **19**(6), 1065–1090 (2009)
19. Movahednejad, H., Ibrahim, S.B., Sharifi, M., Selamat, H.B., Tabatabaei, S.G.H.: Security-aware web service composition approaches: State-of-the-art. In: 13th International Conference on Information Integration and Web-based Applications and Services, iiWAS 2011, pp. 112–121. ACM (2011)
20. She, W., Yen, I., Thuraisingham, B.M.: Enhancing security modeling for web services using delegation and pass-on. Int. J. Web Service Res. **7**(1), 1–21 (2010)
21. Demongeot, T., Totel, E., Traon, Y.L.: Preventing data leakage in service orchestration. In: 7th International Conference on Information Assurance and Security, IAS 2011, pp. 122–127 (2011)
22. Zorgati, H., Abdellatif, T.: Sewsec:a secure web service composer using information flow control. In: Sixth International Conference on Risks and Security of Internet and Systems, CRiSIS 2011, pp. 62–69 (2011)
23. Abdellatif, T., Sfaxi, L., Robbana, R., Lakhnech, Y.: Automating information flow control in component-based distributed systems. In: 14th International ACM Sigsoft Symposium on Component Based Software Engineering, CBSE 2011, pp. 73–82. ACM (2011)
24. Reinhartz-Berger, I., Sturm, A., Clark, T., Cohen, S., Bettin, J. (eds.): Domain Engineering, Product Lines, Languages, and Conceptual Models. Springer, New York (2013)
25. Askarov, A., Sabelfeld, A.: Tight enforcement of information-release policies for dynamic languages. In: 22nd IEEE Computer Security Foundations Symposium, CSF 2009, pp. 43–59 (2009)

Combinatory Synthesis of Classes
Using Feature Grammars

Jan Bessai[1]([⊠]), Boris Düdder[1], George T. Heineman[2], and Jakob Rehof[1]

[1] Technical University of Dortmund, Dortmund, Germany
{jan.bessai,boris.duedder,jakob.rehof}@tu-dortmund.de
[2] Worcester Polytechnic Institute, Worcester, USA
heineman@cs.wpi.edu

Abstract. We describe a method for automatically transforming feature grammars into type-specifications which are subsequently used to synthesize a code-generator for a product of a given feature selection. Feature models are assumed to be given in the form of feature grammars with constraints, and we present a generic type-theoretic representation of such grammars. Our synthesis method is based on an extension of previous work in combinatory logic synthesis, where semantic types can be superimposed onto native APIs to specify a repository of components as well as synthesis goals. In our case, semantic types correspond to feature selections. We use an encoding of boolean logic in intersection types, which allows us to directly represent logical formulas expressing complex feature selection constraints. The novelty of our approach is the possibility to perform retrieval, selection and composition of products in a unified form, without sacrificing modularity. In contrast to constraint based methods, multiple selections of a single feature can coexist.

Keywords: Feature models · Program synthesis · Type theory · Combinatory logic · Feature grammar

1 Introduction

Feature models are a hierarchical representation of all products of a software product line (SPL) which can be distinguished by a set of features. A selection of features leads to a product configuration. Selections are required to satisfy imposed constraints, e.g., exclusive choices between features. Various equivalent representations of feature models exist. Most prominently, feature diagrams have been introduced by Czarnecki [15]. Feature grammars are a widely known alternative that avoids graphical representation issues in large systems [6,24]. Based on ideas on product line validation by Mannion [26], a representation as propositional formulas has been independently suggested by Batory [6] and Benavides, Trinidat and Ruiz [10]. The validity of feature selections w.r.t. constraints can be obtained automatically in the two last representations, e.g., by using truth maintenance systems. These approaches can only automatically solve the problem how to select features, but not the problem how to combine them into a

© Springer International Publishing Switzerland 2016
C. Braga and P.C. Ölveczky (Eds.): FACS 2015, LNCS 9539, pp. 123–140, 2016.
DOI: 10.1007/978-3-319-28934-2_7

product. The latter problem is easy to solve with annotation-based techniques, where all features are implemented in a single code-base [2]. However, as discussed in [2] annotation-based approaches bear several disadvantages because of their lack of modularity. Our approach solves both problems - selection and composition - in the presence of a component-orientented code-base.

An algorithm for combinatory logic synthesis [12,21] is used to compose features guided by hierarchy information obtained from feature models. During composition, types ensure that semantic constraints on selections are observed. Connecting the domain specific problem space and the implementation specific solution space via types, the process results in a composition specification suitable for product code generation. The synthesis algorithm is based on the type inhabitation problem: given a type environment Γ representing a feature model and a type τ representing an (incomplete) feature selection, can we generate a valid composition specification e that is composable from features in Γ and satisfies the selection τ, noted as $\Gamma \vdash e : \tau$? As soon as a feature model and code generators for each single feature are given, this leads to an automated process, directly presenting the user with all valid and ready to execute product choices on the input of her individual feature requirements.

The paper is structured as follows. Feature models and their representations are discussed in Sect. 2, and feature grammars (our chosen representation) are defined by a meta-grammar which is illustrated by an example in Sect. 2.1. In Sect. 3, the theoretical background of the translation into type environments and of the synthesis problem are highlighted. The translation from feature grammars is presented in detail, including a soundness proof, in Sect. 4. The translation, synthesis and interpretation are applied to an example depicting resulting code in Sect. 5. In Sect. 6 we discuss related work. Section 7 concludes the paper.

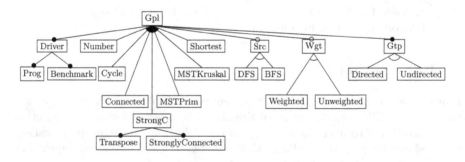

Fig. 1. Feature diagram for the GPL example

The contributions of this paper are: a translation of feature models given as features grammars to type environments, the encoding of constraints as semantic types, the synthesis and interpretation of composition specifications as program code of products (possibly including feature replications), and an application of translation and synthesis to an example.

2   Feature Models

A feature model is a representation of all products of a software product line (SPL). Components of feature models are features and constraints organizing them hierarchically. An instance or member of a feature model is a single product, i.e. a combination of features satisfying the imposed constraints. We describe members using feature configurations, specifying which features are selected (feature selection) and how they are organized wrt. to each other. There are at least three equivalent ways of specifying feature models. Classically, annotated feature diagrams are used as a visual specification [15,25]. According to [24] feature diagrams are a visual representation of feature grammars. In both approaches constraints are represented as propositional formulas. This insight led to the idea of representing features as well as their hierarchy as propositional formulas [6,10]. Standard constraints on features are naturally expressible by logical connectives: Features that are mandatory ($\Leftrightarrow$), features that are optional ($\Rightarrow$), subfeatures (children) ($\wedge$), alternative subfeatures ($\oplus$), repeated subfeatures ($\vee$), and mutually exclusive features (NAND). This unified representation lends itself to automating feature selection with constraint solvers. However, it does not provide organizational information needed for a construction specification of the resulting product. Grammars can provide such information and therefore they are used in practical code generation tools like GenVoca [8] and AHEAD [5]. We follow this line of work in our approach towards directly constructing feature configurations and products from grammars.

2.1   Grammars and GPL Example

Batory [6] explains the stepwise conversion of feature diagrams into feature grammars, following the ideas presented in [24]. We follow the standard example of a Graph Product Line (GPL) as presented in [6], allowing for a comparison between diagrams, grammars and later our approach.

Figure 1 shows the GPL example as a feature diagram. We see that a Graph Product Line (Gpl) requires a driver consisting of a main procedure (Prog) together with a benchmark. It can include at least one of the algorithms Number, Cycle, Connected, StrongC, MSTPrim, MSTKruskal and Shortest. Their details are given in [6]. A Gpl also includes an optional traversal strategy (DFS or BFS), an optional weight specification and a mandatory specification for directed or undirected graphs. Batory [6] explains how to transform the diagram of Fig. 1 into the grammar shown in Fig. 2. This grammar includes a production for each feature and explicitly names productions (not visible in the diagram), e.g., MainGpl. The grammar also adds constraints, which are imposed on the product line by semantic requirements, e.g., minimum spanning trees are only meaningful in weighted graphs. Table 1 assigns a numbered feature vector entry to each terminal, non-terminal and pattern name of the grammar. We subsume these extra-grammatical constraints as the constraint GLOBAL(ψ). It is defined as the conjunction of the constraints listed in the rightmost column of Table 1.

```
Gpl     : Driver Alg+ [Src] [Wgt] Gtp :: MainGpl;
Gtp     : Directed | Undirected;
Wgt     : Weighted | Unweighted;
Src     : DFS | BFS;
Alg     : Number | Connected | Cycle | MSTPrim | MSTKruskal | Shortest
          | Transpose StronglyConnected :: StrongC;
Driver : Prog Benchmark :: DriverProg;

%% // constraints
Number implies Src;
Connected implies Undirected and Src;
StrongC implies Directed and DFS;
Cycle implies DFS;
MSTKruskal or MSTPrim implies Undirected and Weighted;
MSTKruskal or MSTPrim implies not (MSTKruskal and MSTPrim);
Shortest implies Directed and Weighted;
```

Fig. 2. Feature Grammar and constraints for the GPL example [6]

Table 1. Feature Vector entries and constraints

F	Feature Name	In GLOBAL(ψ)	F	Feature Name	In GLOBAL(ψ)
ϕ_0	Directed		ϕ_{12}	Strongly Connected	
ϕ_1	Undirected		ϕ_{13}	Cycle	$\phi_{13} \Rightarrow \phi_6$
ϕ_2	Gtp		ϕ_{14}	MSTPrim	$\phi_{14} \vee \phi_{15} \Rightarrow \phi_1 \wedge \phi_3$
ϕ_3	Weighted		ϕ_{15}	MSTKruskal	$\phi_{14} \vee \phi_{15} \Rightarrow \neg(\phi_{14} \wedge \phi_{15})$
ϕ_4	Unweighted		ϕ_{16}	Shortest	$\phi_{16} \Rightarrow \phi_0 \wedge \phi_3$
ϕ_5	Wgt		ϕ_{17}	Alg	
ϕ_6	DFS		ϕ_{18}	Driver	
ϕ_7	BFS		ϕ_{19}	Prog	
ϕ_8	Src		ϕ_{20}	Benchmark	
ϕ_9	Number	$\phi_9 \Rightarrow \phi_8$	ϕ_{21}	MainGpl	
ϕ_{10}	Connected	$\phi_{10} \Rightarrow \phi_1 \wedge \phi_8$	ϕ_{22}	StrongC	$\phi_{22} \Rightarrow \phi_0 \wedge \phi_6$
ϕ_{11}	Transpose		ϕ_{23}	DriverProg	

We use the GPL example to demonstrate our approach, which will be formalized in Sect. 4. The main idea is to turn the grammar representation into combinators that build valid parse trees. For the Gpl production we take the pattern MainGpl as the combinator name and turn each right hand side of the production into a parameter. Types of iterated non-terminal parameters are wrapped by **List** and types of optional basic terms are wrapped by **Opt**. Other types just correspond to the name of the non-terminal. Non-optional terminals are omitted, because they are constant and thereby do not constitute relevant parameters. The resulting type encodes a tree (sentence) rooted in MainGpl. Note that parameters are separated by $\rightarrow$, i.e., the combinator is written as a higher order function in curried form (e.g. $(A \times B) \rightarrow C \cong A \rightarrow (B \rightarrow C)$).

MainGpl : $Driver \rightarrow \textbf{List}(Alg) \rightarrow \textbf{Opt}(Src) \rightarrow \textbf{Opt}(Wgt) \rightarrow Gtp \rightarrow MainGpl$

Given that each parse tree node is linked to source code implementing the corresponding feature, we can identify the combinator specification with a code generator interface type. A synthesis algorithm can construct a valid program by providing valid arguments to all parameters. Values of type *MainGpl* are feature configurations, as exemplified in Fig. 3. Up to this point, however, the construction is limited to feature grammars without additional constraints. We can include them by refining types, adding a vector $\mathbf{F}(\varphi)$ of features present in each parameter and the result.

$$\texttt{MainGpl} : Driver \cap \mathbf{F}(\varphi_1) \to \mathbf{List}(Alg) \cap \mathbf{F}(\varphi_2) \to \mathbf{Opt}(Src) \cap \mathbf{F}(\varphi_3) \to$$
$$\mathbf{Opt}(Wgt) \cap \mathbf{F}(\varphi_4) \to Gtp \cap \mathbf{F}(\varphi_5) \to MainGpl \cap \mathbf{F}(\psi)$$

We read a constraint like $Driver \cap \mathbf{F}(\varphi_1)$ as requiring an argument that is of both types $Driver$ and $\mathbf{F}(\varphi_1)$. Each variable φ, ψ is substituted by a type representing a feature selection. In the present form, features of arguments and results are not yet linked. The link can be established by adding a constraint on how to substitute variables:

$$\texttt{MainGpl} : \mathrm{OR}(\varphi_1, \varphi_2, \psi_1), \mathrm{OR}(\varphi_3, \psi_1, \psi_2), \mathrm{OR}(\varphi_4, \psi_2, \psi_3), \mathrm{OR}(\varphi_5, \psi_3, \psi) \Rightarrow$$
$$Driver \cap \mathbf{F}(\varphi_1) \to \mathbf{List}(Alg) \cap \mathbf{F}(\varphi_2) \to \mathbf{Opt}(Src) \cap \mathbf{F}(\varphi_3) \to$$
$$\mathbf{Opt}(Wgt) \cap \mathbf{F}(\varphi_4) \to Gtp \cap \mathbf{F}(\varphi_5) \to MainGpl \cap \mathbf{F}(\psi)$$

The constraint $\mathrm{OR}(\varphi_1, \varphi_2, \psi_1)$ can be read as ψ_1 being substitutable by the result of a componentwise disjunction of feature selections φ_1 and φ_2. All subsequent constraints have to be satisfied in conjunction. Finally, valid substitutions for ψ are constrained to include all feature selections of all arguments. We read $C(\boldsymbol{\alpha}) \Rightarrow \tau$ as τ being qualified by the constraint $C(\boldsymbol{\alpha})$, where $\boldsymbol{\alpha}$ is a vector of variables that might occur in τ. The present formulation still lacks the selection of features Gpl and $MainGpl$. We can add them introducing predicates $\mathrm{SET}_{Gpl}(\psi_4, \psi_5)$ and $\mathrm{SET}_{MainGpl}(\psi_5, \psi)$, which allow all substitutions in which Gpl (respectively $MainGpl$) are selected in ψ_5 (ψ). Additionally, a constraint $\mathrm{GLOBAL}(\psi)$ ensures that global constraints are satisfied.

$$\texttt{MainGpl} : \mathrm{GLOBAL}(\psi), \mathrm{OR}(\varphi_1, \varphi_2, \psi_1), \mathrm{OR}(\varphi_3, \psi_1, \psi_2),$$
$$\mathrm{OR}(\varphi_4, \psi_2, \psi_3), \mathrm{OR}(\varphi_5, \psi_3, \psi_4)$$
$$\mathrm{SET}_{Gpl}(\psi_4, \psi_5), \mathrm{SET}_{MainGpl}(\psi_5, \psi) \Rightarrow$$
$$Driver \cap \mathbf{F}(\varphi_1) \to \mathbf{List}(Alg) \cap \mathbf{F}(\varphi_2) \to$$
$$\mathbf{Opt}(Src) \cap \mathbf{F}(\varphi_3) \to \mathbf{Opt}(Wgt) \cap \mathbf{F}(\varphi_4) \to$$
$$Gtp \cap \mathbf{F}(\varphi_5) \to MainGpl \cap \mathbf{F}(\psi)$$

$$\texttt{MainGpl DriverProg (add}_{\texttt{Alg}} \texttt{ (singleton}_{\texttt{Alg}} \texttt{ Cycle) Number)}$$
$$\texttt{(some}_{\texttt{Src}}\texttt{DFS) (none}_{\texttt{Gtp}}\texttt{) Undirected.}$$

Fig. 3. Example for a combinatory term (inhabitant) representing a feature configuration of the GPL example

To formalize the presented translation in Sect. 4, we need a more detailed understanding of the type system.

3   Intersection Types

Sentences of feature grammars can be represented by *combinatory terms*. Such terms are formed by application of combinators from a *repository* Γ mapping combinator names D to their associated types τ.

Definition 1. *(Combinatory Term)*

$$E, E' ::= \text{D} \mid (E\ E'), \text{D} \in dom(\Gamma)$$

Application is left-associative and we omit unnecessary parenthesis when possible. An example for a combinatory term is shown in Fig. 3. Types of combinators are formed according to the grammar given in Definition 2.

Definition 2 *(Intersection Types)*. *The set* $\mathbb{T}_\mathbb{C}$ *is given by:*

$$\mathbb{T}_\mathbb{C} \ni \sigma, \tau, \ldots, \tau_n ::= \alpha \mid \omega \mid \tau_1 \to \tau_2 \mid \tau_1 \cap \tau_2 \mid c(\tau_1, \ldots, \tau_n)$$

α *ranges over type variables and* c *over polyadic type constructors* $\mathbb{C}$. *We identify nullary constructors with constants and omit empty parameter brackets.*

Examples for type constructors with non-empty arguments are $\mathbf{F}(\varphi)$, $\mathbf{List}(\sigma)$ and $\mathbf{Opt}(\sigma)$, marking feature vectors of type φ and lists or optionals of type σ.

For our type-system $\mathbb{T}_\mathbb{C}$ we choose the subtyping rules of the **BCD** intersection type system [4] and extend them to encompass covariant constructors. Additionally, different constructors may be related by a customizable relation $\mathcal{R}$ on their names. The extended rules are given in Table 2 with the original rules in the upper part and the extension in the last three rows. We define equality $\sigma = \tau$ on types as the transitive symmetric closure of $\leq$, i.e. $\sigma \leq \tau$ and $\tau \leq \sigma$.

Types are assigned to combinatory terms according to the rules (Var), $(\to E)$, $(\leq)$ and $(\cap)$ defined in Definition 3.

Definition 3. *(Type Assignment in* $\mathbb{T}_\mathbb{C}$*)*

$$\frac{\text{Substitution } S}{\Gamma, \text{D} : \tau \vdash \text{D} : S(\tau)}\ (Var) \qquad\qquad \frac{\Gamma \vdash E : \sigma \qquad \sigma \leq \tau}{\Gamma \vdash E : \tau}\ (\leq)$$

$$\frac{\Gamma \vdash E : \sigma \to \tau \qquad \Gamma \vdash E' : \sigma}{\Gamma \vdash EE' : \tau}\ (\to E) \qquad \frac{\Gamma \vdash E : \sigma \quad \Gamma \vdash E : \tau}{\Gamma \vdash E : \sigma \cap \tau}\ (\cap)$$

Given a repository Δ with constraints, we can reencode it to a repository Γ, where constraints are encoded by intersection types.

Table 2. Subtyping rules of $\mathbb{T}_C$ based on **BCD** [4]

Description	Rule
Subtyping is a preorder	$\sigma \leq \sigma$
	if $\sigma_1 \leq \sigma_2$ and $\sigma_2 \leq \sigma_3$ then $\sigma_1 \leq \sigma_3$
ω is the greatest type	$\sigma \leq \omega$
Functions computing ω equal ω	$\omega \leq \omega \rightarrow \omega$
Intersection acts as meet	$\sigma \cap \tau \leq \sigma \qquad \sigma \cap \tau \leq \tau$
	if $\sigma \leq \tau_1$ and $\sigma \leq \tau_2$ then $\sigma \leq \tau_1 \cap \tau_2$
Intersection distributes over function targets	$(\sigma \rightarrow \tau_1) \cap (\sigma \rightarrow \tau_2) \leq \sigma \rightarrow \tau_1 \cap \tau_2$
Functions are co- and contravariant	if $\sigma_2 \leq \sigma_1$ and $\tau_1 \leq \tau_2$ then $\sigma_1 \rightarrow \tau_1 \leq \sigma_2 \rightarrow \tau_2$
Constructors are covariant	if $\tau_1 \leq \tau_1', \ldots, \tau_n \leq \tau_n'$ then $c(\tau_1, \ldots, \tau_n) \leq c(\tau_1', \ldots, \tau_n')$
Custom subtype relation on constructor names	if $\mathcal{R}(c, c')$ then $c(\tau_1, \ldots, \tau_n) \leq c'(\tau_1, \ldots, \tau_n)$

Definition 4. *(Constraint Elimination)*

$$\frac{D : C_1(\boldsymbol{\alpha}_1), \ldots, C_n(\boldsymbol{\alpha}_n) \Rightarrow \tau \in \Delta \quad \mathbf{S} = \{Substitution\ S \mid \bigwedge_{i=1}^{n} C_i(S(\boldsymbol{\alpha}_i))\}}{D : \bigcap_{S \in \mathbf{S}} S(\tau) \in \Gamma} (C\ E)$$

An example for a type-derivation is shown in Fig. 4, where we assume $\Delta = \{$Shopper $: FavoriteColor(\alpha) \Rightarrow Item \cap \alpha \rightarrow Shopper \cap Happy$, Shoes $: Item \cap \alpha\}$. First Δ is translated into $\Gamma = \{$Shopper $: Item \cap b \cap r \rightarrow Shopper \cap Happy$, Shoes $: Item \cap \alpha\}$ using the $(C\ E)$-rule, satisfying the constraint $FavoriteColor$, which limits α to be substituted only by $b \cap r$ (blue and red). In the derivation, combinator Shoes is instantiated twice, with $Item \cap r$ and $Item \cap b$. Resulting types for Shoes are intersected applying the $(\cap)$-rule.

$$\frac{\Gamma \vdash \text{Shopper} : Item \cap b \cap r \rightarrow Shopper \cap Happy \quad \dfrac{\dfrac{S(\alpha) = b}{\Gamma \vdash \text{Shoes} : Item \cap b} \quad \dfrac{S(\alpha) = r}{\Gamma \vdash \text{Shoes} : Item \cap r}}{\Gamma \vdash \text{Shoes} : Item \cap b \cap r}(\rightarrow E)}{\dfrac{\Gamma \vdash \text{Shopper Shoes} : Shopper \cap Happy}{\Gamma \vdash \text{Shopper Shoes} : Happy}(\leq)}$$

Fig. 4. Example type-derivation for a happy shopper

Now **Shopper** can be applied to **Shoes** using $(\to E)$. Finally, the resulting happy shopper can be upcast to a value of type *Happy*, by one application of $(\le)$.

For feature vectors **F** we define constraints operating on vectors (constructed by $\times$) of truth-values. We use t for true and f for false. An example feature vector is $F(\times(t, f))$.

Predicate	Semantic	Example
$\mathrm{OR}(\varphi, \psi, \psi')$	ψ' is the bitwise or of φ and ψ	$\mathrm{OR}(\times(t, f), \times(f, t), \times(t, t))$
$\mathrm{SET}_{X_n}(\varphi, \psi)$	The bit corresponding to feature X_n is set to true	$\mathrm{SET}_{X_2}(\times(t, f), \times(t, t))$
$\mathrm{ONLY}_{a_n}(\varphi)$	Only the bit corresponding to feature a_n is set to true	$\mathrm{ONLY}_{a_2}(\times(f, t, f))$
$\mathrm{EMPTY}(\varphi)$	All bits of φ are set to false	$\mathrm{EMPTY}(\times(f, f, f))$

The table above lists all defined constraints. The OR constraint restricts its third argument to be the bitwise or of the first and the second argument. SET_{X_i} constraints are parameterized over a feature X_i. They copy their first argument and set the bit corresponding to X_i to true. Similarly, ONLY_{a_n} sets all bits except the bit corresponding to a_n to false and the bit for a_n to true. EMPTY forces all bits of its argument to be false. Note that $\mathrm{ONLY}_{a_n}(\psi)$ is syntactic sugar for $\mathrm{EMPTY}(\varphi), \mathrm{SET}_{a_n}(\varphi, \psi)$.

4   Feature Grammar Translation

Feature Grammars are a formalized graphics-neutral representation of feature models [6,24]. Their meta-grammar can be summarized by the following productions:

$$P \to \emptyset \mid P, X : patterns$$
$$patterns \to pattern \text{ `::' } Pat \mid pattern \text{ `::' } Pat \text{ `|' } patterns$$
$$pattern, p \to optbasicterm+$$
$$optbasicterm, t \to basicterm \mid \text{ `[' } basicterm \text{ `]'}$$
$$basicterm, b \to a \mid ref$$
$$ref \to X \mid X \text{ `+'}$$

Here, X is a placeholder for non-terminal symbols, *Pat* a placeholder for pattern names and a for terminal symbols. The start symbol for the meta-grammar is P, which forms sets of productions of feature grammars. Each production assigns patterns to a non-terminal. Each pattern is named and consists of at least one, possibly optional (indicated by '[ ]'), basic term. Basic terms are terminals or references. References are either a single non-terminal or a non-terminal with a +, which marks the non-terminal as repeatable. An instance of this meta-grammar is given in the GPL example from Fig. 2, where pattern names for productions using exactly one terminal are omitted. Reduction rules to build sentences of a given feature grammar can be formalized[1]. We write the (multi-step) reduction starting at the production $X : patterns$ in the context of the production set P to the sentence $s \in \Sigma^*$ as $X : patterns@P \longrightarrow^* s$.

We can now formalize the translation exemplified in Sect. 2.1. The translation relation $\Longrightarrow$ presented in Fig. 6 (last page) operates on productions and translates them to a tuple $(\mathcal{R}; \Delta)$, where $\mathcal{R}$ is a subtype relation on constructor names and Δ is a repository of typed combinators (cf. Sect. 3).

Rule (T) creates a combinator for a production consisting of a single terminal symbol a. The combinator is named after the pattern name Pat. Since terminals encode constants, it does not take any parameters. Its result is an instance of the type for trees rooted in the pattern name Pat. Further, the feature vector $\mathbf{F}(\psi')$ is constrained to include only the features corresponding to the terminal a, the left-hand side non-terminal X, and the pattern name Pat. Names for type variables φ, ψ, ψ' are chosen fresh to avoid name conflicts when combining translation results. The extension of the subtype relation will become clear when considering the next rule for non-terminal symbols.

Rule (NT) is constructed in an analogous fashion. It operates on productions including a single non-terminal symbol Y. In contrast to rule (T), the non-terminal is not constant, therefore the resulting combinator is parameterized over a type for trees rooted in sentences derived from the non-terminal Y. This also explains why the subtype relation is extended by $Pat \leq X$ in each step: types for trees rooted in Pat are subtypes of X, since all of them may be used in places where sentences derived from X are required.

Both **Rule (PT)** and **Rule (PNT)** operate on patterns consisting of multiple optional basic terms. In their premises the first and remaining pattern components are translated recursively, where in rule (PT) the first component is a terminal symbol and in rule (PNT) the first component is a reference. Constraints are collected by conjoining them and computing the bitwise or of their results. Disjunction of results ensures that features required to satisfy constraints on sub-components remain effective. Special care is taken to update the result type, which needs to include the feature vector parameterized over the disjunctive result. To this end, the target ψ_3 feature vector of the remaining pattern components is extracted by **tgt** and updated by a substitution with the fresh variable ψ_4, restricted to contain the result of the bitwise or of ψ_2 and ψ_3. Considering the non-terminal case (PNT), advantages of the curried types become obvious, since they avoid having to extract and update the arguments of the type of the remaining pattern components τ.

Rule (CH) translates choices between patterns, by recursively translating each subpattern and joining results.

Rule (LI) translates repeated non-terminal symbols $Y+$. The resulting combinator for the production is constructed by lifting the parameter of the combinator for the non-repeated non-terminal symbol Y to a list. Two additional combinators are added for constructing non-empty lists. Combinator $\mathtt{singleton}_Y$

---

[1] Details available in the technical appendix at http://www-seal.cs.tu-dortmund.de/seal/downloads/papers/facs15.zip.

takes a value of type Y and returns a singleton list containing just the argument value. Combinator add_Y takes a value of type Y and prepends it to its second argument, which is a non-empty list of values of type Y. Features effective in any of the list constituents remain effective, due to the use of OR.

Both **Rule (OPT)** and **Rule (OPNT)** translate optional basic terms. They again distinguish between terminal and non-terminal symbols, constructing their combinators recursively. The resulting combinator for each production is parameterized over the type corresponding to the basic term lifted to be optional. Optionals are of type $\mathbf{Opt}(\sigma)$. They are constructed via newly created combinators some_σ and none_σ, reflecting the presence or absence of the optional value. The some_a combinator for terminal symbols again omits its parameter, since it is constant.

Figure 5 shows the result of applying the formal translation $\Longrightarrow$ to the GPL example from Fig. 2. Note that some redundant SET constraints are produced, due to the genericity of the translation. Automatic elimination of redundant constraints can be achieved, but is purely a matter of optimization and is not discussed in this paper. The GLOBAL constraint is added to the combinator translation of the start symbol $MainGpl$.

In contrast to preexisting solutions which employ constraint solvers to find valid feature selections, in combinatory logic terms can occur multiple times in a solution. This distinction results from the generation of combinatory terms in tree form instead of computing valuations. Constraints in our system are solved for each sub-tree. Global constraints are met considering the presence of all features in the tree, using the disjunction of feature vectors from all subtrees.

4.1 Translation Result

Applying the constraint elimination rule $(C\ E)$ to the result $(\mathcal{R};\Delta)$ of our translation, $(\mathcal{R};\Gamma)$ can be used as input for a type inhabitation algorithm. Type inhabitation is the problem of enumerating combinatory terms E (inhabitants) that satisfy a given goal type τ. We abbreviate the problem by $\Gamma \vdash?\ :\ \tau$. In our scenario, such an inhabitant can be seen as a valid feature configuration based on the feature selection specified in its type τ, which consists of the type of a non-terminal X or pattern-name Pat and a feature vector $\mathbf{F}(\varphi)$. Values of type X correspond to sentences derived from the grammar non-terminal X (i.e. trees rooted in Pat). The notion of correspondence has been exemplified in the example presented in Fig. 3 and is formalized in Lemma 3. By Lemma 4 inhabitation can be used to obtain all feature configurations. Theorem 1 (soundness) combines both of these properties. Lemmas 1 and 2 ensure that the translation is computable in finite time and produces unique results. We used Ott [29] to formalize the translation and extract code[2] for the automated theorem-prover Coq [11].

---

[2] Also available in the aforementioned technical appendix: http://www-seal.cs. tu-dortmund.de/seal/downloads/papers/facs15.zip.

$\Delta = \{$

MainGpl :$\text{GLOBAL}(\psi_{14}), \text{SET}_{Gpl}(\varphi_1, \psi_1), \text{SET}_{MainGpl}(\psi_1, \psi_2),$

   $\qquad \text{SET}_{Gpl}(\varphi_2, \psi_3), \text{SET}_{MainGpl}(\psi_3, \psi_4),$

   $\qquad \text{SET}_{Gpl}(\varphi_3, \psi_5), \text{SET}_{MainGpl}(\psi_5, \psi_6),$

   $\qquad \text{SET}_{Gpl}(\varphi_4, \psi_7), \text{SET}_{MainGpl}(\psi_7, \psi_8),$

   $\qquad \text{SET}_{Gpl}(\varphi_5, \psi_9), \text{SET}_{MainGpl}(\psi_9, \psi_{10}),$

   $\qquad \text{OR}(\psi_2, \psi_4, \psi_{11}), \text{OR}(\psi_{11}, \psi_6, \psi_{12}), \text{OR}(\psi_{12}, \psi_8, \psi_{13}), \text{OR}(\psi_{13}, \psi_{10}, \psi_{14}) \Rightarrow$

   $\qquad Driver \cap \mathbf{F}(\varphi_1) \to \mathbf{List}(Alg) \cap \mathbf{F}(\varphi_2) \to$

   $\qquad \mathbf{Opt}(Src) \cap \mathbf{F}(\varphi_3) \to \mathbf{Opt}(Wgt) \cap \mathbf{F}(\varphi_4) \to Gtp \cap F(\varphi_5) \to MainGpl \cap \mathbf{F}(\psi_{14})$

add$_{\text{Alg}}$:$Or(\psi_1, \psi_2, \psi_3) \Rightarrow Alg \cap \mathbf{F}(\psi_1) \to \mathbf{List}(Alg) \cap \mathbf{F}(\psi_2) \to \mathbf{List}(Alg) \cap \mathbf{F}(\psi_3)$

singleton$_{\text{Alg}}$:$Alg \cap \mathbf{F}(\psi_1) \to \mathbf{List}(Alg) \cap \mathbf{F}(\psi_1)$

some$_{\text{Src}}$:$Src \cap \mathbf{F}(\varphi) \to \mathbf{Opt}(Src) \cap \mathbf{F}(\varphi)$

none$_{\text{Src}}$:$\text{EMPTY}(\varphi) \Rightarrow \mathbf{Opt}(Src) \cap \mathbf{F}(\varphi)$

some$_{\text{Wgt}}$:$Wgt \cap \mathbf{F}(\varphi) \to \mathbf{Opt}(Wgt) \cap \mathbf{F}(\varphi)$

none$_{\text{Wgt}}$:$\text{EMPTY}(\varphi) \Rightarrow \mathbf{Opt}(Wgt) \cap \mathbf{F}(\varphi)$

DriverProg :$\text{ONLY}_{Prog}(\varphi_1), \text{SET}_{Driver}(\varphi_1, \psi_1), \text{SET}_{DriverProg}(\psi_1, \psi2), \text{ONLY}_{Benchmark}(\varphi_2),$

   $\qquad \text{SET}_{Driver}(\varphi_2, \psi_3), \text{SET}_{DriverProg}(\psi_3, \psi_4), \text{OR}(\psi_2, \psi_4, \psi_5) \Rightarrow DriverProg \cap \mathbf{F}(\psi_5)$

Number :$\text{ONLY}_{Number}(\varphi), \text{SET}_{Alg}(\varphi, \psi), \text{SET}_{Number}(\psi, \psi') \Rightarrow Number \cap \mathbf{F}(\psi')$

Connected :$\text{ONLY}_{Connected}(\varphi), \text{SET}_{Alg}(\varphi, \psi), \text{SET}_{Connected}(\psi, \psi') \Rightarrow Connected \cap \mathbf{F}(\psi')$

Cycle :$\text{ONLY}_{Cycle}(\varphi), \text{SET}_{Alg}(\varphi, \psi), \text{SET}_{Cycle}(\psi, \psi') \Rightarrow Cycle \cap \mathbf{F}(\psi')$

StrongC :$\text{ONLY}_{Transpose}(\varphi_1), \text{SET}_{Alg}(\varphi_1, \psi_1), \text{SET}_{StrongC}(\psi_1, \psi_2), \text{ONLY}_{StronglyConnected}(\varphi_2),$

   $\qquad \text{SET}_{Alg}(\varphi_2, \psi_3), \text{SET}_{StrongC}(\psi_3, \psi_4), \text{OR}(\psi_2, \psi_4, \psi_5) \Rightarrow StrongC \cap \mathbf{F}(\psi_5)$

MSTPrim :$\text{ONLY}_{MSTPrim}(\varphi), \text{SET}_{Alg}(\varphi, \psi), \text{SET}_{MSTPrim}(\psi, \psi') \Rightarrow MSTPrim \cap \mathbf{F}(\psi')$

MSTKruskal :$\text{ONLY}_{MSTKruskal}(\varphi), \text{SET}_{Alg}(\varphi, \psi), \text{SET}_{MSTKruskal}(\psi, \psi') \Rightarrow MSTKruskal \cap \mathbf{F}(\psi')$

Shortest :$\text{ONLY}_{Cycle}(\varphi), \text{SET}_{Alg}(\varphi, \psi), \text{SET}_{Shortest}(\psi, \psi') \Rightarrow Shortest \cap \mathbf{F}(\psi')$

DFS :$\text{ONLY}_{DFS}(\varphi), \text{SET}_{Src}(\varphi, \psi), \text{SET}_{DFS}(\psi, \psi') \Rightarrow DFS \cap \mathbf{F}(\psi')$

BFS :$\text{ONLY}_{BFS}(\varphi), \text{SET}_{Src}(\varphi, \psi), \text{SET}_{BFS}(\psi, \psi') \Rightarrow BFS \cap \mathbf{F}(\psi')$

Weighted :$\text{ONLY}_{Weighted}(\varphi), \text{SET}_{Wgt}(\varphi, \psi), \text{SET}_{Weighted}(\psi, \psi') \Rightarrow Weighted \cap \mathbf{F}(\psi')$

Unweighted :$\text{ONLY}_{Unweighted}(\varphi), \text{SET}_{Wgt}(\varphi, \psi), \text{SET}_{Unweighted}(\psi, \psi') \Rightarrow Unweighted \cap \mathbf{F}(\psi')$

Directed :$\text{ONLY}_{Directed}(\varphi), \text{SET}_{Gtp}(\varphi, \psi), \text{SET}_{Directed}(\psi, \psi') \Rightarrow Directed \cap \mathbf{F}(\psi')$

Undirected :$\text{ONLY}_{Undirected}(\varphi), \text{SET}_{Gtp}(\varphi, \psi), \text{SET}_{Undirected}(\psi, \psi') \Rightarrow Undirected \cap \mathbf{F}(\psi')$

   $\}$

$\mathcal{R} = \{ MainGpl \le Gpl, Directed \le Gtp, Undirected \le Gtp, Weighted \le Wgt,$
$\quad Unweighted \le Wgt, BFS \le Src, DFS \le Src, Number \le Alg,$
$\quad Connected \le Alg, Cycle \le Alg, MSTPrim \le Alg, MSTKruskal \le Alg,$
$\quad Shortest \le Alg, StrongC \le Alg, DriverProg \le Driver \}$

Fig. 5. GPL-Example repository and subtyping relation

Lemma 1. *(Translation Confluence)*
For all productions $X : patterns$, if $X : patterns \Longrightarrow \mathcal{R}_1, \Delta_1$ and
$X : patterns \Longrightarrow \mathcal{R}_2, \Delta_2$, then $\mathcal{R}_1 = \mathcal{R}_2$ and $\Delta_1 = \Delta_2$.

Proof. By induction on the possible translations, where in each case only one translation is applicable.

Lemma 2. *(Translation Computability)*
The translation relation $\Longrightarrow$ is computable.

Proof. For all productions $X : patterns$ only one translation step $\Longrightarrow$ can be applied. Premises of each translation rule only contain structurally smaller productions to be translated. By Lemma 1, translations in premises have uniquely determined results.

Lemma 3. *(Translation Correctness)*
Let P be a fixed set of productions and Δ and $\mathcal{R}$ be obtained by the union of each Δ_i and $\mathcal{R}_i$, st. $X_i : patterns_i \in P$ and $X_i : patterns_i \Longrightarrow \mathcal{R}_i; \Delta_i$. Let Γ be obtained from Δ by applying (C E). There exists a translation function $[\![\_]\!] : E \to \Sigma^*$, st.

$$\text{if } \Gamma \vdash M : X, \text{ then } X : patterns@P \longrightarrow^* [\![M]\!].$$

Proof. $[\![\_]\!]$ fills in terminal symbols and unpacks lists as well as optionals. The applicative shape of combinatory terms already matches the structure of sentences. The side condition holds by induction over possible shapes of M and typing rules.

Lemma 4. *(Translation Completeness)*
Let P be a fixed set of productions and Δ and $\mathcal{R}$ be obtained by the union of each Δ_i and $\mathcal{R}_i$, st. $X_i : patterns_i \in P$ and $X_i : patterns_i \Longrightarrow \mathcal{R}_i; \Delta_i$. Let Γ be obtained from Δ by applying (C E). There exists a translation function $[\![\_]\!]^{-1} : \Sigma^* \to E$, st.

$$\text{if } X : patterns@P \longrightarrow^* s, \text{ then } \Gamma \vdash [\![s]\!]^{-1} : X.$$

Proof. $[\![\_]\!]^{-1}$ discards terminal symbols and packs lists as well as optionals. The structure of sentences already matches the applicative shape of combinatory terms. The side condition holds by induction over possible shapes of *patterns* and derivable sentences.

Theorem 1. *(Translation Soundness)*
The translation is sound with respect to $\longrightarrow^*$ and $\vdash$.

Proof. Direct consequence of Lemmas 3 and 4.

The inhabitant can be interpreted as a construction specification for a product specified by a feature configuration. In contrast to feature selections, usually provided by constraint-solvers, this configuration also provides order information. In the next section we see how the typed combinators forming inhabitants can be implemented as code generation functions, maintaining a tight correspondence to grammar rules.

5   Experiments

Type inhabitation can be performed by an algorithm implemented in the (CL)S framework [12]. Since all constraints considered in our context have finitely many solutions, we may precompute them (e.g. using an SMT solver [28] like Z3 [18]). Precomputed function tables can be encoded as intersection types [4] by $(C\ E)$. In the following example we consider a global constraint in which a selection of feature X forces the selection of feature a, while the grammar only states that a is optional. We translate the grammar and constraints into a repository Δ and postprocess it to a repository Γ, where each function table entry is inserted via intersection. The translation can be produced automatically by application of the rules (Var) and ($\cap$).

$$\text{GLOBAL}(\times(\phi_a, \phi_P, \phi_X)) \text{ iff } \phi_X \text{ implies } \phi_a$$

$$X : [a] :: P \Longrightarrow \{P \leq X\};$$

$$\{\quad P : \text{SET}_X(\varphi, \psi), \text{SET}_P(\psi, \psi') \Rightarrow \mathbf{Opt}(a) \cap \mathbf{F}(\varphi) \to P \cap \mathbf{F}(\psi'),$$
$$\text{some}_a : \text{ONLY}_a \Rightarrow \mathbf{Opt}(a) \cap \mathbf{F}(\varphi), \ \dots \}$$

$$\Delta = \{\quad P : \text{GLOBAL}(\psi'), \text{SET}_X(\varphi, \psi), \text{SET}_P(\psi, \psi') \Rightarrow$$
$$\mathbf{Opt}(a) \cap \mathbf{F}(\varphi) \to P \cap \mathbf{F}(\psi'),$$
$$\text{some}_a : \text{ONLY}_a \Rightarrow \mathbf{Opt}(a) \cap \mathbf{F}(\varphi), \ \dots \}$$

$$\Gamma = \{\quad P : (\mathbf{Opt}(a) \cap \mathbf{F}(\times(f,f,f)) \to P \cap \mathbf{F}(\times(t,t,t))$$
$$\cap(\mathbf{Opt}(a) \cap \mathbf{F}(\times(f,f,t)) \to P \cap \mathbf{F}(\times(t,t,t))$$
$$\cap(\mathbf{Opt}(a) \cap \mathbf{F}(\times(f,t,f)) \to P \cap \mathbf{F}(\times(t,t,t))$$
$$\cap(\mathbf{Opt}(a) \cap \mathbf{F}(\times(f,t,t)) \to P \cap \mathbf{F}(\times(t,t,t))$$
$$\cap(\mathbf{Opt}(a) \cap \mathbf{F}(\times(t,f,f)) \to P \cap \mathbf{F}(\times(t,t,t))$$
$$\cap \dots ,$$
$$\text{some}_a : \mathbf{Opt}(a) \cap \mathbf{F}(\times(t,f,f)), \ \dots \}$$

We have assigned a Haskell implementation to each of the generated combinators for the GPL example (cf. Fig. 5). A functional datatype is assigned to each type for non-terminal symbols. This datatype serves as a domain model for a code generator building Java ASTs[3]. It is presented in Listing 1.1. The toplevel type *Gpl* is a Java compilation unit, i.e. the AST of a full .java file. Implementation types of combinators are direct translations of the types present in the repository, e.g., `mainGpl :: Driver -> [Alg] -> Maybe Src -> Maybe Wgt -> Gtp -> Gpl`. The result of the code generation is a Java program that implements a product configuration built on top of the preexisting Java graph library JGraphT[4]. Only necessary features are selected from the library and a customized minimal interface is exposed, hiding genericity for unselected features and implementing benchmark code. Listing 1.2 depicts an excerpt of the

---

[3] http://github.com/vincenthz/language-java.

[4] http://jgrapht.org/.

generated Java code for a product. The top-level feature `MainGpl` is translated
to a class containing member functions for each selected algorithm and a main
method for the benchmark driver program. Combinator implementations, which
the interested reader may find included in the technical appendix, are straightforward AST constructions and manipulations. It is noteworthy that any language
capable of building and pretty-printing ASTs or supporting string templating
could have been used. Here, we chose Haskell for its support of Java ASTs and
the direct mapping from combinator types to code generator types.

```
type Gpl = CompilationUnit
data Gtp = Directed | Undirected
data Wgt = Weighted | Unweighted
data Src = DFS | BFS
data Alg = Number | Connected | Cycle | StrongC
         | MSTPrim | MSTKruskal | Shortest
data Driver = DriverProg
```

Listing 1.1. Domain Model of a code generator for the GPL example

```
import java.util.Iterator;
...
import org.jgrapht.traverse.DepthFirstIterator;
...
public class MainGpl <V> {
  private ListenableUndirectedWeightedGraph<V,DefaultWeightedEdge> graph;
  public DepthFirstIterator<V, DefaultWeightedEdge> getIterator() {...}
  public MainGpl() { ... }
  public MainGpl(
    ListenableUndirectedWeightedGraph<V, DefaultWeightedEdge> graph) {...}
  public Map<V, Integer> number() {...}
  public Set<DefaultWeightedEdge> mstKruskal() {...}
  public static void main (String[] args) {...}
}
```

Listing 1.2. Excerpt of a generated product of the GPL example

The product generated in Listing 1.2 has been generated by the inhabitation
question $\Gamma \vdash ? : Gpl \cap \mathbf{F}(\sigma)$, where σ is the type of a feature vector $\times(\phi_0, \ldots, \phi_{23})$
in which ϕ_9 (Number) and ϕ_{15} (MSTKruskal) is set to t. Unspecified features
are set to the least upper bound of t and f, which is the greatest element ω.
The inhabitation algorithm is free to select or deselect features obeying the
constraints, e.g., $\mathbf{F}(\times(f,t)) \leq \mathbf{F}(\times(\omega,t))$ and $\mathbf{F}(\times(t,t)) \leq \mathbf{F}(\times(\omega,t))$ are both
valid. The resulting inhabitants are all combinatory terms representing valid
feature configurations including the selected features. For the question above,
(CL)S automatically synthesizes an inhabitant:

$$\text{MainGpl DriverProg (add}_{Alg}\text{ Number (singleton}_{Alg}\text{ MSTKruskal))}$$

$$(\text{some}_{Src}\text{ DFS) (some}_{Wgt}\text{ Weighted) Undirected}$$

This inhabitant can be directly mapped to the Haskell implementation

$$\text{mainGpl DriverProg (Number : [MSTKruskal])}$$

$$(\mathbf{Just}\text{ DFS) (}\mathbf{Just}\text{ Weighted) Undirected}$$

Execution of this function yields a value of type *CompilationUnit*, the pretty
printing of which generates Listing 1.2. There are more inhabitants, for example
selecting breadth first search (BFS) instead of depth first search (DFS). (CL)S
generates all these inhabitants iteratively on demand growing in the number of
included features, allowing a user selection of the desired products.

$$\boxed{X : patterns \implies \mathcal{R}; \Delta}$$

$$\frac{fresh(\varphi) \qquad fresh(\psi) \qquad fresh(\psi')}{X : a :: Pat \implies \{Pat \leq X\}; \{Pat : \text{ONLY}_a(\varphi), \text{SET}_X(\varphi, \psi), \text{SET}_{Pat}(\psi, \psi') \Rightarrow Pat \cap \mathbf{F}(\psi')\}} \text{(T)}$$

$$\frac{fresh(\varphi) \qquad fresh(\psi) \qquad fresh(\psi')}{X : Y :: Pat \implies \{Pat \leq X\};} \text{(NT)}$$
$$\{Pat : \text{SET}_X(\varphi, \psi), \text{SET}_{Pat}(\psi, \psi') \Rightarrow Y \cap \mathbf{F}(\varphi) \to Pat \cap \mathbf{F}(\psi')\}$$

$$\frac{\begin{array}{l} X : t :: Pat \implies \mathcal{R}_1; \{Pat : \text{ONLY}_a(\varphi), \text{SET}_X(\varphi, \psi_1), \text{SET}_{Pat}(\psi_1, \psi_2) \Rightarrow Pat \cap \mathbf{F}(\psi_2)\} \\ X : p :: Pat \implies \mathcal{R}_2; \Delta_2, Pat : pr \Rightarrow \tau \\ \mathbf{tgt}\,(pr) = \psi_3 \\ fresh(\psi_4) \end{array}}{X : t\,p :: Pat \implies \{Pat \leq X\}; \Delta_2 \cup} \text{(PT)}$$
$$\{Pat : \text{ONLY}_a(\varphi), \text{SET}_X(\varphi, \psi_1), \text{SET}_{Pat}(\psi_1, \psi_2), pr, \text{OR}(\psi_2, \psi_3, \psi_4) \Rightarrow [\psi_3 := \psi_4]\,\tau\}$$

$$\frac{\begin{array}{l} X : t :: Pat \implies \mathcal{R}_1; \Delta_1, Pat : \text{SET}_X(\varphi, \psi_1), \text{SET}_{Pat}(\psi_1, \psi_2) \Rightarrow \sigma \cap \mathbf{F}(\varphi) \to Pat \cap \mathbf{F}(\psi_2) \\ X : p :: Pat \implies \mathcal{R}_2; \Delta_2, Pat : pr \Rightarrow \tau \\ \mathbf{tgt}\,(pr) = \psi_3 \\ fresh(\psi_4) \end{array}}{X : t\,p :: Pat \implies \{Pat \leq X\}; \Delta_1 \cup \Delta_2 \cup} \text{(PNT)}$$
$$\{Pat : \text{SET}_X(\varphi, \psi_1), \text{SET}_{Pat}(\psi_1, \psi_2), pr, \text{OR}(\psi_2, \psi_3, \psi_4) \Rightarrow \sigma \cap \mathbf{F}(\varphi) \to [\psi_3 := \psi_4]\,\tau\}$$

$$\frac{\begin{array}{c} X : p :: Pat \implies \mathcal{R}_1; \Delta_1 \\ X : patterns \implies \mathcal{R}_2; \Delta_2 \end{array}}{X : p :: Pat | patterns \implies \mathcal{R}_1 \cup \mathcal{R}_2; \Delta_1 \cup \Delta_2} \text{(CH)}$$

$$\frac{X : Y :: Pat \implies \mathcal{R}; \{Pat : \text{SET}_X(\varphi, \psi), \text{SET}_{Pat}(\psi, \psi') \Rightarrow Y \cap \mathbf{F}(\varphi) \to Pat \cap \mathbf{F}(\psi')\}}{X : Y+ :: Pat \implies \{Pat \leq X\};} \begin{array}{ccc} fresh(\psi_1) & fresh(\psi_2) & fresh(\psi_3) \end{array} \text{(LI)}$$
$$\{Pat : \text{SET}_X(\varphi, \psi), \text{SET}_{Pat}(\psi, \psi') \Rightarrow \mathbf{List}(Y) \cap \mathbf{F}(\varphi) \to Pat \cap \mathbf{F}(\psi')\} \cup$$
$$\{\mathbf{add}_Y : \text{OR}(\psi_1, \psi_2, \psi_3) \Rightarrow Y \cap \mathbf{F}(\psi_1) \to \mathbf{List}(Y) \cap \mathbf{F}(\psi_2) \to \mathbf{List}(Y) \cap \mathbf{F}(\psi_3)\} \cup$$
$$\{\mathbf{singleton}_Y : Y \cap \mathbf{F}(\psi_1) \to \mathbf{List}(Y) \cap \mathbf{F}(\psi_1)\}$$

$$\frac{X : a :: Pat \implies \{Pat \leq X\}; \{Pat : \text{ONLY}_a(\varphi), \text{SET}_X(\varphi, \psi), \text{SET}_{Pat}(\psi, \psi') \Rightarrow Pat \cap \mathbf{F}(\psi')\}}{X : [a] :: Pat \implies \{Pat \leq X\};} \text{(OPT)}$$
$$\{Pat : \text{SET}_X(\varphi, \psi), \text{SET}_{Pat}(\psi, \psi') \Rightarrow \mathbf{Opt}(a) \cap \mathbf{F}(\varphi) \to Pat \cap \mathbf{F}(\psi')\} \cup$$
$$\{\mathbf{some}_a : \text{ONLY}_a(\varphi) \Rightarrow \mathbf{Opt}(a) \cap \mathbf{F}(\varphi)\} \cup$$
$$\{\mathbf{none}_a : \text{EMPTY}(\varphi) \Rightarrow \mathbf{Opt}(a) \cap \mathbf{F}(\varphi)\}$$

$$\frac{\begin{array}{l} X : ref :: Pat \implies \{Pat \leq X\}; \Delta \cup \\ \quad \{Pat : \text{SET}_X(\varphi, \psi), \text{SET}_{Pat}(\psi, \psi') \Rightarrow \sigma \cap \mathbf{F}(\varphi) \to Pat \cap \mathbf{F}(\psi')\} \end{array}}{X : [ref] :: Pat \implies \{Pat \leq X\}; \Delta \cup} \text{(OPNT)}$$
$$\{Pat : \text{SET}_X(\varphi, \psi), \text{SET}_{Pat}(\psi, \psi') \Rightarrow \mathbf{Opt}(\sigma) \cap \mathbf{F}(\varphi) \to Pat \cap \mathbf{F}(\psi')\} \cup$$
$$\{\mathbf{some}_\sigma : \sigma \cap \mathbf{F}(\varphi) \to \mathbf{Opt}(\sigma) \cap \mathbf{F}(\varphi)\} \cup$$
$$\{\mathbf{none}_\sigma : \text{EMPTY}(\varphi) \Rightarrow \mathbf{Opt}(\sigma) \cap \mathbf{F}(\varphi)\}$$

Fig. 6. Translation rules from grammar productions to type-environments

6 Related Work

The book on Feature-Oriented Software Product Lines [2] provides a detailed overview and useful starting point on the subject. A broader overview is given in [3]. For a specific review of the automated analysis and formal treatment of feature models we refer the interested reader to [9]. The line of work we follow is mainly concerned with automatic synthesis of feature configurations [20]. Starting with the insight that feature models can be represented as propositional formulas [6,10,26], various techniques have been employed to synthesize feature selections. They are mostly characterized by the choice of the underlying logic truth maintenance system. Classically, SAT solving techniques have been used [6,10,27]. Another important class of approaches is based on unification [14,22]. It allows for flexible definition of user-defined constraints in a Turing-complete programming language (Prolog). However, structural information about solutions cannot be provided by the preexisting systems, which is why type inhabitation plays an important role in our approach. It is not only helpful for constructing products, but also allows for feature replication. Similar to Gen-Voca [7], we focus on grammars, but aim to directly use them for synthesis and code generation. This is possible by identifying grammar productions with code generator interfaces. As of the state of this contribution code generators and their compositions are well-typed wrt. to their implementation language (e.g. Haskell), but not wrt. to the generated target language. There is an ongoing effort to study the type-safe composition of product line code in object-oriented languages [19,30]. The use of type inhabitation to generate object-oriented code has been studied in [23] for auto-completion features of IDEs. Intersection type inhabitation has been used to synthesize mixin composition chains [13]. The further exploration of the role of staging [17] in type-inhabitation driven composition of object-oriented code [12] is a goal for future research.

The line of work presented in [1,16] also performs synthesis, but with the goal of extracting feature models from logic specifications. Via the connection between diagrams and grammars it might be possible to pipeline these approaches, in order to use a logic feature specification as a starting point instead of a grammar. There are however more direct ways to connect logic and type inhabitation via the curry-howard isomorphism [31]. We chose not to take this path in order to keep the close connection between code generator APIs and the problem space as modeled by the feature diagram. More research would be necessary to obtain this connection in a direct logic based encoding.

7 Conclusion

We presented a method for automatically transforming feature models into type-specifications for synthesizing code-generators. Such a synthesized code-generator produces a product of a given partial feature selection obeying feature constraints. Feature models are given in the form of feature grammars with constraints. Such grammars are shown to be representable in a generic type-theoretic representation. Combinatory logic synthesis is used to synthesize composition specifications. Constraints on specifications are encoded as semantic types. Using (CL)S we could demonstrate the applicability of our approach and exemplified it for an implementation of a Graph Product Line.

References

1. Andersen, N., Czarnecki, K., She, S., Wasowski, A.: Efficient synthesis of feature models. In: SPLC 2012, pp. 106–115. ACM (2012)
2. Apel, S., Batory, D., Kästner, C., Saake, G.: Feature-Oriented Software Product Lines. Springer, Heidelberg (2013)
3. Apel, S., Kästner, C.: An overview of feature-oriented software development. J. Object Technol. 8(5), 49–84 (2009)
4. Barendregt, H., Coppo, M., Dezani-Ciancaglini, M.: A filter lambda model and the completeness of type assignment. J. Symbolic Logic 48(4), 931–940 (1983)
5. Batory, D.: Feature-oriented programming and the AHEAD tool suite. In: ICSE 2004, pp. 702–703. IEEE Computer Society (2004)
6. Batory, D.: Feature models, grammars, and propositional formulas. In: Obbink, H., Pohl, K. (eds.) SPLC 2005. LNCS, vol. 3714, pp. 7–20. Springer, Heidelberg (2005)
7. Batory, D., Geraci, B.J.: Composition validation and subjectivity in GenVoca generators. IEEE Trans. Softw. Eng. 23(2), 67–82 (1997)
8. Batory, D., Singhal, V., Thomas, J., Dasari, S., Geraci, B., Sirkin, M.: The GenVoca model of software-system generators. IEEE Softw. 11(5), 89–94 (1994)
9. Benavides, D., Segura, S., Ruiz-Cortés, A.: Automated analysis of feature models 20 years later: a literature review. Inf. Syst. 35(6), 615–636 (2010)
10. Benavides, D., Trinidad, P., Ruiz-Cortés, A.: Automated reasoning on feature models. In: Pastor, Ó., Falcão e Cunha, J. (eds.) CAiSE 2005. LNCS, vol. 3520, pp. 491–503. Springer, Heidelberg (2005)
11. Bertot, Y., Castéran, P.: Interactive Theorem Proving and Program Development. Springer Science & Business Media, Heidelberg (2004)
12. Bessai, J., Rehof, J., Düdder, B., Martens, M., Dudenhefner, A.: Combinatory logic synthesizer. In: Margaria, T., Steffen, B. (eds.) ISoLA 2014, Part I. LNCS, vol. 8802, pp. 26–40. Springer, Heidelberg (2014)
13. Bessai, J., Dudenhefner, A., Duedder, B., De'Liguoro, U., Chen, T.C., Rehof, J.: Mixin Composition synthesis Based on Intersection Types. In: TLCA 2015 (2015), (to appear)
14. Beuche, D.: Composition and Construction of Embedded Software Families. Ph.D. thesis, Otto-von-Guericke-Universität Magdeburg, Universitätsbibliothek (2003)
15. Czarnecki, K., Eisenecker, U.W.: Generative Programming: Methods, Tools, and Applications. ACM Press/Addison-Wesley Publishing Co., New York (2000)
16. Czarnecki, K., Wasowski, A.: Feature diagrams and logics: there and back again. In: SPLC 2007, pp. 23–34. IEEE (2007)
17. Davies, R., Pfenning, F.: A modal analysis of staged computation. J. ACM 48(3), 555–604 (2001)
18. de Moura, L., Bjørner, N.S.: Z3: an efficient SMT solver. In: Ramakrishnan, C.R., Rehof, J. (eds.) TACAS 2008. LNCS, vol. 4963, pp. 337–340. Springer, Heidelberg (2008)

19. Delaware, B., Cook, W., Batory, D.: A machine-checked model of safe composition. In: FOAL 2009, pp. 31–35. ACM (2009)
20. Düdder, B., Heineman, G.T., Hoxha, A., Rehof, J.: Towards migrating object-oriented frameworks to enable synthesis of product line members. In: Proceedings of SPLC 2015 (2015), (to appear)
21. Düdder, B., Martens, M., Rehof, J., Urzyczyn, P.: Bounded Combinatory Logic. In: CSL 2012. LIPIcs, vol. 16, pp. 243–258, Schloss Dagstuhl (2012)
22. Eichberg, M., Klose, K., Mitschke, R., Mezini, M.: Component composition using feature models. In: Grunske, L., Reussner, R., Plasil, L. (eds.) CBSE 2010. LNCS, vol. 6092, pp. 200–215. Springer, Heidelberg (2010)
23. Gvero, T., Kuncak, V., Kuraj, I., Piskac, R.: On Fast Code Completion using Type Inhabitation. Technical report, École polytechnique fédérale de Lausanne (2012)
24. de Jonge, M., Visser, J.: Grammars as feature diagrams. In: ICSR7 Workshop on Generative Programming, pp. 23–24 (2002)
25. Kang, K.C., Cohen, S.G., Hess, J.A., Novak, W.E., Peterson, A.S.: Feature-oriented domain analysis (FODA) feasibility study. Technical report, DTIC Document (1990)
26. Mannion, M.: Using first-order logic for product line model validation. In: Chastek, G.J. (ed.) SPLC 2002. LNCS, vol. 2379, p. 176. Springer, Heidelberg (2002)
27. Neubauer, J., Steffen, B., Margaria, T.: Higher-order process modeling: product-lining, variability modeling and beyond. In: Semantics, Abstract Interpretation, and Reasoning about Programs: Essays Dedicated to David A. Schmidt. EPTCS, vol. 129, pp. 259–283 (2013)
28. Nieuwenhuis, R., Oliveras, A., Tinelli, C.: Solving SAT and SAT modulo theories: from an abstract Davis-Putnam-Logemann-Loveland Procedure to DPLL(T). J. ACM **53**(6), 937–977 (2006)
29. Sewell, P., Nardelli, F.Z., Owens, S., Peskine, G., Ridge, T., Sarkar, S., Strniša, R.: Ott: Effective tool support for the working semanticist. J. Funct. Program. **20**(01), 71–122 (2010)
30. Thaker, S., Batory, D., Kitchin, D., Cook, W.: Safe composition of product lines. In: GPCE 2007, pp. 95–104. ACM (2007)
31. Venneri, B.: Intersection types as logical formulae. J. Logic Comput. **4**(2), 109–124 (1994)

Towards Modular Verification of Threaded Concurrent Executable Code Generated from DSL Models

Dragan Bošnački[1]([✉]), Mark van den Brand[1], Joost Gabriels[1], Bart Jacobs[2],
Ruurd Kuiper[1], Sybren Roede[1], Anton Wijs[1], and Dan Zhang[1]

[1] Eindhoven University of Technology, Eindhoven, The Netherlands
dragan@win.tue.nl
[2] KU Leuven, Leuven, Belgium

Abstract. An important problem in Model Driven Engineering is maintaining the correctness of a specification under model transformations. We consider this issue for a framework that implements the transformation chain from the modeling language SLCO to Java. In particular, we verify the generic part of the last transformation step to Java code, involving change in granularity, focusing on the implementation of SLCO communication channels. To this end we use a parameterized modular approach; we apply a novel proof schema that supports fine grained concurrency and procedure-modularity, and use the separation logic based tool VeriFast. Our results show that such tool-assisted formal verification can be a viable addition to traditional techniques, supporting object orientation, concurrency via threads, and parameterized verification.

1 Introduction

Model-Driven Software Engineering (MDSE) [18] is a methodology that recently gained popularity as a method for efficient software development. Constructing a model enables the developer to deal with difficult aspects at a higher and less complex level of abstraction. Transformations are used to create new models, source code, test scripts and other artifacts. By shifting the focus from the code to the model, MDSE allows to tackle defects in the software already in the modeling phase. Resolving errors in the early stages of the software development process reduces the costs and increases the reliability of the end product.

An important question is whether transformations are correct. Various types of correctness are relevant for model transformations, such as type correctness and correspondence correctness [22]. In earlier work, we have addressed how to determine that model-to-model transformations preserve functional properties [28–30]. In this paper, we focus on checking that model-to-code transformations preserve the behavioural semantics of the model [22]: If we have proven

R. Kuiper, A. Wijs and D. Zhang—This work was done with financial support from the China Scholarship Council (CSC), the Netherlands Organisation for Scientific Research (NWO), and ARTEMIS Joint Undertaking project EMC2 (grant agreement 621429).

© Springer International Publishing Switzerland 2016
C. Braga and P.C. Ölveczky (Eds.): FACS 2015, LNCS 9539, pp. 141–160, 2016.
DOI: 10.1007/978-3-319-28934-2_8

that certain functional properties hold in a model, such as the absence of data races or deadlocks, how can we ensure that those properties still hold in the generated source code?

Specifically, we focus on models of systems consisting of concurrent, interacting components, and wish to transform those models into multi-threaded software. For compositional models, an Object Oriented (OO) implementation language seems a natural choice, since it allows us to map components to objects. We have chosen Java. The modelling language we use is called SLCO (Simple Language of Communicating Objects) [1]. SLCO models consist of components that communicate through channels. Each component is described in terms of a finite number of concurrently operating state machines that can share variables. After a chain of transformations of SLCO models, in which incrementally more concrete information about the specified system can be added, multi-threaded Java code should be generated based on the last SLCO model, in which each SLCO state machine is mapped to its own thread.

SLCO has a coarse granularity that supports thinking about concurrency at a convenient high level of abstraction. On the other hand, the generated code implements concurrency through multi-threading, with a level of granularity that is much more fine-grained. This approach facilitates the development of correct, well-performing, complex software. However, the code generation step is challenging to implement, since the transition from coarse to fine-grained concurrency needs to be done in a way that correct and well-performing software can be generated.

Our approach to setting up the model-to-code transformation step is to identify the concepts in SLCO that are model independent on the one hand, and model dependent on the other. The model independent concepts can be transformed to Java once, and from that moment on referred to in all code generated from specific SLCO models. An example of a model independent SLCO concept is the communication channel, while state machines are model dependent concepts, since their structure differs from one model to another.

For the specification of the behaviour of Java objects, we opt for using separation logic [23], since it allows us to specify behaviour in a way independent of the implementation language. We require concurrency, so we actually work with the version of separation logic with fractional permissions. Full verification of semantics preservation of model-to-code transformations then involves establishing that these specifications correspond with the semantics of the corresponding SLCO constructs. For this to be possible, we require a modular approach, in which the specification of constructs can be used for the verification of code in which those constructs play a role.

As a first step, in this paper, we focus on how to formally specify the behaviour of model independent concepts, such that modular verification of code using those concepts is possible. In fact, using such specifications allows the verification of code without relying on the actual implementation of the model independent concepts, thereby truly realising a modular way of working. Our aim is to show that modular verification of model-to-code transformations of multi-component systems is necessary and feasible, and we demonstrate how this can be concretely done.

The model independent concepts are implemented in what we refer to as *generic code*. To verify this code, a theorem proving approach is called for, because the generic code contains parameters that only get concrete values when used in specific code derived from particular input models. Furthermore, since the generic code has fine-grained concurrency, we require procedure-modularity, and we use the approach from [16] that supports this. Tool-wise, we require a verification tool that supports OO code, concurrency and separation logic with fractional permissions, leading to the choice of VeriFast [15]. A procedure-modular approach can be achieved by using ghost code and abstract predicates.

Contributions. First of all, we introduce a new modular specification schema to specify the behaviour of modelling constructs in a setting where (1) fine-grained parallelism is used, and (2) the environment is general, i.e., we do not need to know anything about the environment to specify the constructs. Compared to earlier work, our schema allows a better abstraction from the implementation details of the methods being specified.

We demonstrate our approach by specifying and verifying a representative part of the generic code, namely the communication channel. This shows the feasibility of the approach, but also that judicious choices of implementation language, specification language, verification approach and tooling are required.

As mentioned in [22], proving correctness of a program is not as complex as proving correctness of a transformation that produces programs. By making a distinction between generic and specific code, the complexity of proving the correctness of model-to-code transformations can be lowered. Generic code can largely be treated as any other program, apart from the fact that it raises new concerns regarding the larger program context in which code constructs can be placed; these concerns are covered in this paper. As a result, the remaining proof obligations for the transformation as a whole can be simplified; once we turn our attention to the specific code, we can directly use the specifications of the generic code constructs. With respect to related work (Sect. 6), this is a novel way to address the correctness of model-to-code transformations.

Section 2 introduces SLCO and explains how SLCO models are transformed to Java code. Section 3 explains the essentials of separation logic. In Sect. 4, the new modular specification schema is described, and in Sect. 5 it is demonstrated how to apply the schema to specify and verify a Java implementation of the SLCO channel datatype using VeriFast. Section 6 discusses related work, and Sect. 7 contains our conclusions and pointers to future work.

2   SLCO and Its Transformation to Java

In SLCO, systems consisting of concurrent, communicating components can be described using an intuitive graphical syntax. The components are instances of classes, and connected by asynchronous channels, over which they send and receive signals. They are connected to the channels via their ports.

The behaviour of a component is specified using a finite number of state machines, such as in Fig. 1, where two components are defined (the two main rectangles). The parallel execution of those machines is formalised in the form of interleaving semantics. Variables either belong to the whole component or an individual state machine. The variables

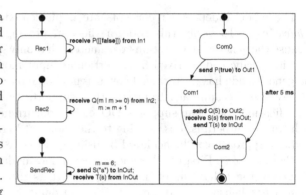

Fig. 1. Behaviour diagram of an SLCO model

that belong to a component are accessible by all state machines that are part of the component (for instance, variable m in the left component of Fig. 1). Each transition has a source and target state, and a list of statements that are executed when the transition is fired. A transition can be fired if it is enabled, and it is enabled if the first of the associated statements is enabled. If a transition is fired but subsequent statements are blocked, the transition blocks until they become enabled. SLCO supports a variety of statement types. For communication between components, there are statements for sending and receiving signals over channels. The statement **send** $T(s)$ **to** *InOut*, for instance, sends a signal named T with a single argument s via port *InOut*. Its counterpart **receive** $T(s)$ **from** *InOut* receives a signal named T from port *InOut* and stores the value of the argument in variable s. A send statement is enabled if the buffer of the channel is not full, and a receive statement is enabled if there is a message in the buffer.

Statements such as **receive** $P([[\textbf{false}]])$ **from** *In1* offer a form of conditional signal reception. Only those signals whose argument is equal to **false** will be accepted. Another example is the statement **receive** $Q(m \mid m \geq 0)$ **from** *In2*, which only accepts those signals whose argument is greater than or equal to 0. For the above statements to be enabled, there must be a message available in the channel buffer satisfying the conditions.

Boolean expressions, such as $m{==}6$, denote statements that are enabled iff the expression holds. Time is incorporated by means of delay statements. For example, the statement **after** 5 **ms** blocks until 5 ms have passed since the moment the source state was entered. Assignment statements, such as $m := m + 1$, are used to assign values to variables. They are always enabled.

Our approach to derive executable code from an SLCO model is as shown in the activity diagram of Fig. 2: generic code constructs are used for the basic elements in SLCO, i.e., for channels (synchronous and asynchronous), states, transitions, and a mechanism to move between states by performing transitions. A model-to-code transformation takes an SLCO model as input and produces

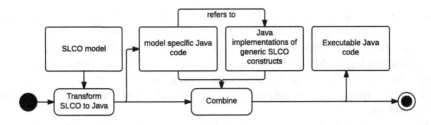

Fig. 2. Activity diagram of the transformation process from SLCO to Java

model specific Java code that refers to the generic constructs as output. There is a one-to-one mapping between SLCO state machines and Java threads. Finally, this specific code is combined with the generic code to obtain a complete, executable implementation that should behave as the SLCO model specifies.

3 Separation Logic

Separation logic [20,23] builds upon Hoare logic [13] and in the context of concurrent programs also on the Owicki-Gries method [21].

We assume a Java-like OO programming language that supports aliasing and references: allocation and deallocation of heap addresses (memory cells), as well as assignments to and from a heap memory cell. The main motivation behind the separation logic is to describe in a succinct way the state of the heap during program execution.

A separation logic assertion is interpreted on a program state (s, h), where s and h are a store and a heap, respectively. The store is a function mapping program variables to values and the heap is a partial map from pairs of object IDs and object fields to values. A value is either an object or a constant. To capture the heap related aspects, separation logic extends the syntax and semantics of the assertional part of Hoare logic. Separation logic adds heap operators (expressions) to the usual first order assertions of Hoare logic. The basic heap expressions are **emp**, i.e., the empty heap, satisfied by states having a heap with no entries, and $E \mapsto F$ (read as "E points to F"), i.e., a singleton heap, satisfied by a state with a heap consisting of only one entry at address E with content F. For instance, $o.x \mapsto v$ means that field x of object o has value v. Two heap expressions H_1 and H_2 corresponding to heaps h_1 and h_2, respectively, can be combined using the *separating conjunction operator* $*$, provided h_1 and h_2 have disjoint address domains. Expression $H_1 * H_2$ corresponds to the (disjoint) union $h_1 \uplus h_2$ of the heaps. Note that H_1 and H_2 describe two separate parts of the heap, h_1 and h_2, respectively. In contrast, the standard conjunction $p_1 \wedge p_2$, where p_1 and p_2 are separation logic formulae, corresponds to the whole heap satisfying both p_1 and p_2. Because of the domain disjointness requirement, the separation logic formula $(o.f \mapsto 10) * (o.f \mapsto 10)$ evaluates to **false**, whereas $(o.f \mapsto 10 \wedge o.f \mapsto 10)$ is equivalent to $(o.f \mapsto 10)$.

Like in Hoare logic, the triple $\{P\}C\{Q\}$, where C is a (segment of) a program and P and Q are assertions describing its pre- and post-condition, respectively, only concerns partial correctness; termination of C needs to be proven separately.

Separation logic adds to the standard rules (axioms) of the Hoare framework axioms for each of the new statements - allocation, deallocation, and assignments involving the heap cells. An important characteristic of separation logic is *tight interpretation*.

In some cases it is needed to embed a precise specification of a program segment C into a more general context. A specific axiom that allows this by enlarging the specification of a program segment C with an assertion R describing a disjoint heap segment which is not modified by any statement in C, is the *frame rule*:[1]

$$\frac{\{P\}\ C\ \{Q\}}{\{P * R\}\ C\ \{Q * R\}}$$

In a concurrent setting, the programming language is extended with a `fork` statement, allowing to run program components in separate threads. For synchronized access to global objects, semaphores are added, together with the corresponding methods `acquire` and `release`.

The Owicki-Gries method extends the Hoare approach to concurrent programs preserving modularity. The first idea is to capture component behavior with non-shared ghost variables enabling separate proofs of concurrent components (for more on ghost variables, see Sect. 4). The second idea is to link shared resource and ghost variable values through an invariant that holds outside critical regions [21]. A resource A is a set of heap locations, and I_A is its associated invariant. The crucial idea is that each component may update or access these locations only within critical regions [11,14] in which the component has exclusive access to the locations. Although I_A may be violated within the critical region, it is guaranteed to hold at the beginning and at the end of the critical region. This is reflected in the rules for `acquire` and `release`:

$$\{\mathbf{emp}\}\mathtt{s.acquire()}\{I_A(s)\}$$

$$\{I_A(s)\}\mathtt{s.release()}\{\mathbf{emp}\}$$

The above described approach allows compositional verification. Each method m belonging to a class C is verified as a sequential program considering the invariants as extra constraints. Class C is considered verified when all its methods are verified. Since the program can be seen as a combination of classes and declarations, the whole program is verified when all its classes are verified.

One of the central concepts in concurrent separation logic is *ownership*. Due to tight interpretation, separation logic assertions can describe precisely the heap "footprint" of a given program C, i.e., the parts of the heap which C is allowed

---

[1] Here we disregard the usual side condition of the frame rule, since we assume a Java-like programming language not supporting global variables.

to use. Let l be a program component location and E a heap address. The component owns address E at location l iff E is contained in a heap corresponding to an assertion H which is true at location l. If $E \mapsto F$ is part of the heap corresponding to H, then this can be seen as an informal *permission* [5] for the verified component to read, write or dispose of the contents of the heap cell at address E.

Partial permissions are introduced to allow shared ownership of variables. Ownership is split into a number of fractional permissions, each of which only allows read only access. Expression $E \mapsto F$ denotes permission 1, i.e., exclusive ownership, whereas a fractional permission is expressed as $[z]E \mapsto F$ with $0 < z < 1$. Expression $[1]E \mapsto F$ is equivalent to $E \mapsto F$. Permissions can be split and merged during a proof. For instance, two fractional permissions can be merged according to the following rule: $[z]E \mapsto F * [z']E \mapsto F$, where $z + z' \leq 1$, implies $[z + z']E \mapsto F$. One acquires full ownership (and therefore write access) in case $z + z' = 1$. The split rule is analogous.

We use fractional permissions to enforce the syntactic rules and side conditions of Owicki-Gries on the use of the (global) real and ghost variables. For instance, by acquiring a semaphore, a component acquires the semaphore invariant. The semaphore invariant provides full permission to change the real variables and the ghost variables associated with the component. A component always holds a fraction of the permission for its ghost variables, thereby ruling out that other components change them. When releasing the semaphore, the component also releases the acquired (partial) ownerships.

4   Modular Specification Schema

Our aim is to specify modelling constructs and verify the implementation of those constructs in a modular way, meaning that each construct and its implementation should be independently specifiable and verifiable. The benefits of a modular approach are (1) that it will scale better than a monolithic approach and (2) that once a construct has been specified, we can abstract away its implementation details when verifying properties of the system.

It is crucial that implementations of constructs do not need to be verified again when their context changes. Because of this, and the fine-grained nature of the generic code, standard methods like Owicki-Gries do not suffice. In [16], a modular specification schema was proposed to solve this problem. In this section, we introduce an improved version of this modular approach which, compared to [16], provides a better abstraction from the implementation of the verified method.

As already mentioned, the Java methods in our transformation framework implement fine-grained parallelism. This means that each method may acquire and release access to multiple critical regions (CR) during its execution, instead of following a coarse-grained approach in which the complete method is executed in one big CR. As CRs tend to form performance bottlenecks in software, a fine-grained approach tends to decrease the level of dependency between threads in a multi-threaded system, and thereby increase the overall performance.

In order to verify methods with fine-grained parallelism, so-called *ghost code* must be inserted as part of the annotations. To see how this mechanism of code insertion works, we consider a method m belonging to a class C instantiated in an object o. We want to give a specification of m in the form of a standard Hoare logic triple $\{P\}o.m\{Q\}$. Under fine-grained parallelism one cannot formulate P and Q in terms of the actual fields determining the state of o. For instance, consider method send(msg, G) that sends a message msg to a channel queue q (q is a field of C), as in Listing 1. At line 8, the piece of code G given as a parameter to send is inserted.

Listing 1. A fine-grained **send** operation

```
1  class C
2      queue q
3      semaphore s
4      method send(msg,G)
5      begin
6          s.acquire()
7          q := q + msg
8          G
9          s.release()
10     end
```

In a concurrent setting, multiple threads may send messages to the queue of a single instance of C. In that case, q may be changed by some other send call between the call to send(b) leaving the CR protecting q (line 9) and send(b) returning the control to the calling client program (line 10). We cannot claim that once send(a) is finished, the new content of q is q+a, where + indicates concatenation. This is analogous to Owicki-Gries, where global variables altered by multiple modules cannot be used directly to specify a module.[2]

To resolve this, ghost variables (also called logical or auxiliary variables) are added to the program. Ghost variables are write-only, i.e., the instrumented program can change them, but not read them. Hence, they do not change the control flow of the program and are only auxiliary verification devices. Each ghost variable is owned by a particular process, and only this process can potentially change its content. To illustrate the use of ghost variables, let us assume that send is used by a client program as shown in Listing 2.

Listing 2. A client using the **send** method.

```
1  o := New C()
2  o.send(a) || o.send(b)
```

Suppose we want to prove that if in the beginning of the program $len(q) = 0$ holds, where len gives the length of the queue, then at the end, $len(q) = 2$. We specify the two instances of send by introducing ghost variables y and z to capture the local effect on the length of q in the left and right method call, respectively. Resource invariant $I_A \equiv len(q) = y + z$ captures how these local effects relate to the global resource. Now we can specify send(a) with $\{y = 0\}$send(a)$\{y = 1\}$ and send(b) with $\{z = 0\}$send(b)$\{z = 1\}$. Finally, we define

---

[2] In the classical Owicki-Gries framework this is directly forbidden by the interplay of the syntactic rules of the usage of the global variable and the side conditions of the axioms for CR and parallel composition.

$G \equiv y := 1$ for $\mathsf{send}(a)$ and $G \equiv z := 1$ for $\mathsf{send}(b)$, to update y and z, respectively, at line 8 in Listing 1 when send is executed.

With verification axioms similar to Owicki-Gries, it can be proved that these assertions indeed confirm the correctness of the client property. In particular, the conjunction of the postconditions of $\mathsf{send}(a)$ and $\mathsf{send}(b)$, and I_A, i.e., $y = 1 \wedge z = 1 \wedge len(\mathsf{q}) = y + z$, implies the desired client postcondition $len(\mathsf{q}) = 2$.

Passing corresponding ghost codes G to instances of m allows for abstraction and parallelism, but it does not make the approach modular. Each context and/or property likely requires different ghost variables, and hence different P, Q, I_A, and G. Suppose that we want to verify a property about the content of q using a function cnt mapping the queue content to a set of messages. Specifically, we want to prove that if in the beginning, $cnt(\mathsf{q}) = \emptyset$, then at the end, $cnt(\mathsf{q}) = \{\mathsf{a}, \mathsf{b}\}$. In this case, our ghost variables range over sets of messages, and the specifications must be adjusted accordingly, i.e., $\{y = \emptyset\}\mathsf{send}(a)\{y = \{\mathsf{a}\}\}$, $\{z = \emptyset\}\mathsf{send}(b)\{z = \{\mathsf{b}\}\}$, $I_A \equiv cnt(\mathsf{q}) = y \cup z$, and $G \equiv y := \{\mathsf{a}\}$ and $G \equiv z := \{\mathsf{b}\}$ for $\mathsf{send}(a)$ and $\mathsf{send}(b)$, respectively. Even if we had a library of predicate sets and ghost code blocks, in general we would not be able to cover all possible contexts in which the generic code, i.e., m, could be used.

Greater generality can be achieved by a schema along the lines of [16] in which P, Q, I_A, and G are parameters of the specification of m. The schema imposes some constraints on these parameters which become proof obligations when verifying code involving m. Under these constraints, m needs to be verified only once. For each new context, the client only needs to verify that the contraints hold. We propose a new modular specification schema (MSS) that allows further abstraction from the implementation details of m, by supporting parameterization based on CRs. Unlike in [16], the semaphores that implement the CR as well as the names of the fields that determine the state of the object (s and q, resp., in the send example) remain absent from the specification. As a result one retains the flexibility of the OO approach. For example, if the implementation of the CR is changed such that locks are used instead of semaphores, the specification can remain the same.

We proceed by giving the intuition behind the MSS. We first establish the relationships between the parameters P, Q, I_A, and G, that need to hold in order for the specification to be correct. Later we lift these relationships to the level of the whole method m to formulate the MSS.

Listing 3. A semaphore based implementation of a CR

```
 1 {P}
 2 s.acquire()
 3 {IA(s) * P}
 4 {O(v) * I(v) * P}
 5 C
 6 {O(post(v)) * I(v) * P}
 7 G
 8 {O(post(v)) * I(post(v)) * Q}
 9 {IA(s) * Q}
10 s.release()
11 {Q}
```

Assume that the body of m consists of only a single CR implemented by using semaphore s. The CR is of the form $s.acquire()$ C $s.release()$ as given in Listing 3. Without loss of generality, let us assume that the CR protects a single field f of an instance o of class C. Field f can be changed only within the CR.

When establishing the relationships, we are guided by the correctness requirements for the annotation of Listing 3 in the familiar Hoare logic/Owicki-Gries style. The validity of P and Q at lines 1 and 11, respectively, implies that $I_A(s)*P$ and $I_A(s)*Q$ hold at lines 3 and 9, respectively (we write $I_A(s)$ instead of just I_A to emphasize that it is associated with s). This follows from the rules from Sect. 3 (for acquire and release combined with the frame rule), and the fact that P and Q do not refer to s and hence involve parts of the heap disjoint from the parts affected by acquire and release. This is analogous to the proof rule for the CR in Owicki-Gries.

To capture the environment constraints, next to ghost variables, $I_A(s)$ may also depend on $o.f$. To avoid directly referring to f and thereby making the approach modular, we introduce a so-called *payload invariant* I, parameterized with a ghost variable v. In the example of Listing 2, $I_A(s) \equiv len(q) = y + z$ would be substituted by $I(v) \equiv len(v) = y + z$. To link the actual field f with its ghost counterpart v we use predicate $O(v)$ (for the earlier send example, we could define $O(v) \equiv q = v$). $O(v)$ is an abstract predicate local to o that is not visible for the client. By defining $I_A(s) = \exists v.O(v) * I(v)$, we circumvent the need to refer to $o.f$ in the client invariant.

Line 4 in Listing 3 is obtained by substituting $O(v) * I(v)$ for $I_A(s)$ at line 3. Since C affects only actual variables, P holds also in the postcondition of C at line 6. However, since the actual variables have changed while ghost variable v remains the same, predicate O holds only for an adjusted value of v given by $post(v)$. In our example, $post(v) \equiv len(v) + 1$. G only affects y and z, so after G, $O(post(v))$ remains valid. So, in order to recover the invariant I_A, G at line 7 should be chosen such that it modifies the ghost variables occurring in $I(v)$ and P in such a way that $I(post(v))$ becomes **true** and P is transformed to Q (line 8). Proving that G indeed has this property remains a proof obligation for the client program calling m and as such becomes a premise of our schema. It is easy to check that this constraint is satisfied by all instances of send in the running example for both client properties. Finally, line 9 follows directly from line 8 by the definition of $I_A(s)$.

The Modular Specification Schema. By summarizing the constraints on the various elements of the annotation, and lifting them to the level of method m, we obtain the MSS:

$$\frac{\forall v \bullet \{P * I(v)\}\ G\ \{Q(res(v)) * I(post(v))\}}{\{\exists v \bullet O(v) * [\pi]o.A(I(v)) * P\}\ r := o.m(G)\ \{\exists v \bullet O(v) * [\pi]o.A(I(v)) * Q(r)\}}$$

For simplicity, we assume that m has no parameters besides G. However, additional parameters can be captured in the usual way for procedure verification rules in Hoare logic. We also assume that m returns a result $res(v)$ immediately after leaving the CR, that is assigned to variable r. In general, Q depends on r. Both $res(v)$ and $post(v)$ are fixed by the supplier of m.

Predicate A links semaphore s with the payload invariant I. Both A and O are abstract predicates in the sense that the client does not need to know their definition since they are local to o. For the send example, A would state that there is a semaphore s that is properly initialized and it associates to A a semaphore invariant $I_A(\mathbf{s})$ (formed using $I(v)$ as described earlier). These implementation details, including s, are hence not visible to the client calling m. Finally, π is an arbitrary fraction denoting a fractional permission for A.

Note that MSS is not an axiom or a proof rule of separation logic, since for any correct module it can be derived from other axioms and rules. The correctness of MSS can be verified using the annotation in Listing 3.

MSS can be seen as a means to divide the proof obligations between the client and the supplier of m. The schema is implicitly universally quantified over P, Q, I, and G. Note that $post$ and res are fixed by the supplier and that they implicitly define the effect of C on o.f in a sequential environment. On the other hand, the client is free to use any predicates P, Q, I, and G satisfying the premise of MSS. For any such predicates, the supplier guarantees that the implementation of m satisfies the triple in the consequent of MSS.

The premise of MSS $\forall v.\{P * I(v)\}\ G\ \{Q(res(v)) * I(post(v))\}$ is analogous to the premise of the Owicki-Gries CR axiom $\{P * I_A(\mathbf{s})\}\ C\ \{Q(\mathbf{r}) * I_A(\mathbf{s})\}$. MSS, however, shifts the verification from the actual code C and invariant I_A to the ghost code G and the payload invariant I. Although C does not appear in MSS, its specification is reflected in v, $post(v)$ and $res(v)$. Although G has to reflect all important aspects of each call of o.m, the method is still to a great extent modular since the implementation and verification of the program text of $o.m$ remains completely independent of the call of o.m which is invoked.

The soundness of the modular schema follows from the same arguments presented in [16].

5   Specifying and Verifying the SLCO Channel

In this section we present the specification and verification of an essential part of the generic code for our SLCO-to-Java transformation, namely the communication channel. We specify the channel for use in a generic, multi-threaded environment. Using VeriFast, we verify the absence of race conditions and deadlocks, and show how to prove properties of clients using the channel.

SLCO models use asynchronous non-blocking lossless channels that can hold a predefined maximum number of messages. The channel datastructure provides two operations, send and receive, to add and remove messages. It has a FIFO structure, i.e., messages are added to the end and removed from the front of a queue. Provided that the client program invoking a channel operation has exclusive access to the channel, the specification of the operations is as follows. The send operation has one parameter msg, the message that is being sent. If the contents of the channel is q and it is not full when send is started, then after execution of **send** the contents of the channel is q + msg, where + denotes concatenation of sequences of messages. Furthermore, **send** returns a Boolean result indicating whether or not the operation was successful; if the channel is already full when **send** is started, **false** is returned. Whenever **receive** is started and the channel has contents msg + q, then the channel's new contents after execution of **receive**, provided that any provided conditions hold, is q, and message msg is returned as a result. If the channel is empty when **receive** starts executing, then **receive** is blocked until it succeeds to remove a message. Since the channel is used in a multi-threaded environment, adding and removing messages should be done atomically.

We illustrate our modular approach described in Sect. 4 on the **send** method of the channel implementation. In VeriFast, each Java source code file being verified is linked to a specification file only containing (abstract) predicates and specifications of Java methods and ghost functions. The VeriFast specification of the method following MSS is given in Listing 4. (The complete specification and annotated implementation files will become part of the Java examples set in the standard distribution of VeriFast.)

Listing 4. Part of the channel specification

```
1  public final class Channel {
2      // ...
3
4      boolean send(String msg)
5      /*@
6      requires
7          [?pi]A(?I) &*&
8          is_G_S(?G, this, I, msg, ?P, ?Q) &*& P();
9      @*/
10     /*@
11     ensures
12         [pi]A(I) &*& Q(result);
13     @*/
14     // ...
15 }
```

The VeriFast specific text, i.e., specifications and ghost variable declarations, is inside special comments delimited by @. The pre- and postconditions that form the contract are denoted by the keywords **requires** and **ensures**, respectively. Component predicates of the pre- and postcondition are glued by the separating conjunction operator denoted by &*&. Predicates A, I, P, and Q correspond to their namesakes in the MSS, whereas the assertion is_G_S implements the passing of the ghost code G into the method. Both [?pi] and [pi] correspond to the fractional permission $[\pi]$. The question mark ? in front of a variable means that the value of the variable is recorded and that all later occurrences of that variable in the contract must be equal to the first occurrence. For instance, in Listing 4, the value of the fractional permission pi in the precondition must be the same as the one in the postcondition (as also required in the MSS).

Predicates P, Q and is_G_S are left undefined and are supposed to be provided by the client. More precisely, a *lemma function* G is supplied by the client based on which VeriFast automatically creates the predicate is_G_S. A VeriFast lemma function is a method without side effects which helps the verification engine.

The contract of a lemma function corresponds to a theorem, its body to the proof, and a lemma function call to an application of the theorem. Listing 5 contains the specification of G that corresponds to the ghost statement block G.

Note that the specification of G in Listing 5 corresponds to the premise of MSS, where $post(v)$ specifies that if $res = \mathbf{true}$, msg has been added to the channel, and otherwise it has not (line 4).

Listing 5. A lemma function specifying the ghost statement block G

```
1  /*@
2  typedef lemma void G(Channel c, predicate(list<Object>, int) I,
       String msg, predicate() P, predicate(boolean) Q)(boolean res);
3     requires P() &*& I(?items, ?qms);
4     ensures Q(res) &*& I(res ? append(items, cons(msg, nil)) :
          items, qms);
5  @*/
```

Method send is part of the class Channel (Listing 6), implementing the SLCO channel construct. Class Channel contains three fields: the list itemList implementing the FIFO queue, semaphore s that is used to implement access to the CR within the operations, and queueMaxSize defining the maximum channel capacity. For verification purposes we add the ghost field inv which is used to keep track of the invariant.

Semaphore invariant I_A, corresponding to I_A in Sect. 4, is given at lines 3–4 in Listing 6. The invariant is defined by means of a predicate constructor parameterized with the payload invariant I. Corresponding to the definition of I_A, in I_A, it is checked that for ghost variables items and qms, i.e., the contents of the item list and the maximum number of messages, respectively, I holds. The question mark ? is used to record the value of the variable following it, for use later on in the predicate. Operator $\mapsto$ is written in VeriFast as |->, and the expression of the form [f] denotes fractional ownership with fraction f. When $f = 1$, the fractions are omitted, and an arbitrary fraction is denoted as [_].

Listing 6. A specification of the Channel class

```
1
2  /*@
3  predicate_ctor I_A(Channel channel, predicate(list<Object>, int) I)
       () =
4     channel.O(?items, ?qms) &*& I(items, qms);
5  @*/
6
7  public final class Channel {
8     List itemList;
9     Semaphore s;
10    int queueMaxSize;
11    //@ inv inv;
12    //@ predicate O(list<Object> items, int qms) = this.itemList |->
          ?itemList &*& itemList.List(items) &*& this.queueMaxSize
          |-> qms &*& length(items) <= qms;
13    //@ predicate A(predicate(list<Object>, int) I) = ... &*& s |->
          ?sem &*& [_]sem.Semaphore(I_A(this, I));
14 }
```

In predicate O (line 12), as explained earlier, the links are established between ghost variables and fields. Its first conjunct channel.itemList |-> ?itemList implies exclusive ownership of the field `itemList` and at the same time that the value of `itemList` is recorded for later use in the contract. Expression `itemList.List(items)` states the fact that `itemList` is a list with elements `items`. The final conjunct links `queueMaxSize` to ghost variable `qms`.

We use the VeriFast ownership concept to implement syntactic restrictions on the variables. In particular, we need to ensure that the fields like `itemList` can be modified only in the CR implemented by semaphore `s` and that the ghost variables are modified exclusively by at most one method, in this case `send`.

Predicate A is given at line 13 in Listing 6. Like its MSS counterpart A, it is parameterized with the payload invariant I (corresponding to I in MSS). Besides some auxiliary conjuncts, it has two conjuncts to associate I_A with `s`, the first of which is parameterized with the payload invariant and the object itself.

Listing 7. The annotation of the Channel **send** method

```
1  public final class Channel {
2      // ...
3      public boolean send(String msg)
4      /*@ requires ... ensures ... @*/
5      {
6          //@ open [pi]A(I);
7          //@ s.makeHandle();
8          s.acquire();
9          //@ open I_A(this, I)();
10
11         boolean result = itemList.size() < queueMaxSize;
12         if (result)
13             itemList.add(msg);
14
15         //@ G(result);
16         //@ length_append(items, cons(msg, nil));
17         //@ close I_A(this, I)();
18         s.release();
19         //@ close [pi]A(I);
20         return result;
21     }
22     // ...
23 }
```

Listing 8. Client program specification

```
1  public class Program {
2      //@ static int sendCount;
3      //@ static int receiveCount;
4      public static int messageMaxCount; // k
5
6      public static void main(String[] args)
7      //@ requires class_init_token(Program.class) &*&
                     Program_messageMaxCount(?mmc) &*& 0 < mmc;
8      //@ ensures Program_messageMaxCount(mmc) &*& [_]
                    Program_sendCount(?sc) &*& [_]Program_receiveCount(?rc) &*&
                    mmc == sc &*& mmc == rc;
9      {
10         // ...
11     }
12 }
```

Listing 7 contains the **send** method with its corresponding full annotation that further facilitates verification. Since VeriFast does not automatically unfold predicate definitions, ghost statement **open** is used to do this, i.e., to replace the predicate with its definition. In this way the heap chunks of the definition are made visible to the verifier. The opposite effect is achieved by `close` which replaces heap chunks with the corresponding predicate definition. At line 6 predicate `A` is unfolded to obtain the predicates needed for acquiring `s`. After the acquisition of the semaphore also its invariant `I_A` is opened at line 9 to get access to the heap chunks related to `itemList` and `queueMaxSize`.

The code segment at lines 11–13 corresponds to C in the MSS, and affects the "real" variables. The code at lines 15–17 is ghost code. The lemma function performing the updates of the ghost variables is called at line 15. Annotation of the `receive` method can be done in an analogous way.

Class `Channel` annotated as in Listing 7 is verifiable against its specification in VeriFast. This means that it is free of deadlocks and race conditions. Those requirements are not explicitly specified, but are always checked when VeriFast tries to verify code. The class is now ready to be used by client programs to verify specific properties, using the pre- and postconditions and the payload invariant.

Listing 9. SenderThread class specification

```
1  class SenderThread implements Runnable {
2      //@ predicate pre() = this.c |-> ?c &*& [_]c.A(I) &*& [_]
              Program_sendCount(0) &*& [_]Program_messageMaxCount(?mmc)
              &*& 0 < mmc;
3      //@ predicate post() = this.c |-> ?c &*& [_]c.A(I) &*& [_]
              Program_messageMaxCount(?mmc) &*& [_]Program_sendCount(?sc)
              &*& mmc == sc;
4
5      Channel c;
6      ...
7
8      public void run()
9      //@ requires pre();
10     //@ ensures post();
11     {
12         for (i = 0; i < Program.messageMaxCount; i++)
13         {
14             for (;;) {
15             /*@
16                 predicate P() = [1/2]Program_sendCount(i) &*& [1/3]
                      Program_messageMaxCount(mmc);
17                 predicate Q(boolean r) = [1/2]Program_sendCount(r ? i
                      + 1 : i) &*& [1/3]Program_messageMaxCount(mmc);
18                 lemma void ghost_send(boolean r)
19                     requires ... ensures ...
20                 {
21                     open P();
22                     ...
23                 }
24             @*/
25             //@ produce_lemma_function_pointer_chunk(ghost_send) : G_S
                   (c, I, m, P, Q)(r) { call(); };
26             //@ close P();
27             boolean success = this.c.send("message");
28             //@ open Q(success);
29             }
30         }
31         //@ close post();
32     }
33 }
```

Next, we discuss how the property 'if k messages are sent over the channel, k messages will be received' can be specified for a program using the channel via one sending and one receiving thread. First, of all, Listing 8 specifies the client program we use. In the `main` method (lines 6 and onwards), an instance of the channel is created, and a sending and a receiving thread are started, one sending k, i.e. `messageMaxCount`, messages, and the other one trying to receive them. To specify the property, we introduce two new ghost variables for counting the number of messages (lines 2 and 3). In the precondition of `main`, we require that the class has been properly initialized (conjunct 1 at line 7), link the `messageMaxCount` variable to the ghost variable `mmc`, and have an additional requirement that it is at least equal to 1. In the post-condition, we link `sendCount` and `receiveCount` respectively to `sc` and `rc`, and require that they are both equal to `mmc` (line 8).

To determine that the post-condition holds, we need to specify the thread sending the messages. In Listing 9, at lines 2 and 3, its pre- and post-condition are specified. In the `run` method, the messages are sent. For the `send` call at line 27, we need to provide ghost code `G_S`. This is done in lemma `ghost_send`, where the ghost variables are updated. This lemma is linked to the call at line 25. The pre- and post-condition of `send` are specified as two predicates, `P` and `Q`, see lines 16 and 17.

VeriFast was able to verify the code against its specification, meaning that the property holds. Besides the environment with two threads, we were also able to consider an environment consisting of multiple senders and receivers, to verify that no conflicts can arise in such a setting.

6   Related Work

Much work has been done and continues to be done on the verification of model transformations. For an overview of the field, see [22]. Here, we mention some relevant work that also focusses on (1) model-to-code transformations, (2) formal verification of correctness using theorem provers, and (3) correctness as the preservation of behavioural semantics. The latter seems to be the most relevant interpretation of correctness mentioned in [22], as it addresses behavioural aspects, in our case, for example, race and deadlock freedom of communication channels, both in SLCO and the Java implementation.

Amphion [2] is a tool to generate code from models of space geometry problems. It uses a theorem prover automatically, hiding the details from the user, to create Fortran source code that is correct by construction. Besides addressing a different type of models, they do not separately consider the generic code constructs used. We, on the other hand, have yet to prove correctness of our entire transformation method. It would be interesting to see if their approach is to some degree applicable for us.

In [24], the QVT language and transformations are formalised for use with the KIV theorem prover, to verify Java code generators for security properties and syntactic correctness. Their approach is operational, but scalability is still a serious issue. We wonder whether a split similar to ours of the proof obligations for generic and specific code would improve the scalability.

Other techniques address very similar issues, but work strictly indirectly, i.e., they focus on code generated from a concrete model as opposed to transformations that produce code. We mention some works here, since our work can to some extent also be considered as indirect (one condition for directness given in [22] is that the transformation rules are formalised, which we have not done yet). Blech [4] verifies semantics preservation of a statechart-to-Java transformation using Isabelle/HOL. In [9,10], annotations are generated together with code to assist automatic theorem proving. The latter is a very interesting approach that we may consider for the analysis of our specific code.

An approach to generate Java code from Communicating Sequential Processes (CSP) specifications is described in [27]. The authors describe how they have verified that a CSP model of their implementation of a channel semantically corresponds with a simpler CSP model describing the desired functionality of that channel. First of all, by working from a model describing the implementation, as opposed to the implementation itself, one still needs to prove that the model corresponds exactly with the implementation to establish that the implementation itself is correct. Second of all, it seems that a fully modular verification approach in the way we wish to have it is not completely possible; for instance, although it would be possible to use their simpler CSP model of a channel within detailed implementation-level CSP models of systems using channels, one could not abstract away the functionality of a channel to the same extent as when using separation logic if one would like to prove a functional property referring to communication, but not expressing how the communication itself should proceed.

Regarding theorem proving, to the best of our knowledge the approach in [16] was the first one supporting fully general modular specification and verification of fine-grained concurrent modules and their clients. Compared to the schema in [16], the MSS we propose imposes conditions on the ghost code instead of the actual code, and abstracts away the implementation of the protected object better than [16] does, thereby improving the modular nature of the approach.

An approach comparable to [16] appears in [26] where a new separation logic is presented with concurrent abstract predicates. Furthermore, in [25] they have applied their approach to prove correctness of some synchronisation primitives of the Joins concurrent C# library. As far as we know, the authors do not intend to eventually use their approach to verify model transformations. It remains to be investigated whether theirs can be used for that as well.

Another viable option to verify model-to-code transformations seems to be the use of software model checking techniques, in which a formalization of a program is checked against an automaton capturing a specification [7,17]. However, it remains to be investigated whether one can verify implementations of modelling constructs for general environments as we have done here.

The Java Modelling Language (JML) is a behavioural interface specification language for Java. An advantage of JML over separation logic is that Java expressions can be used. Several verification tools have been developed that use JML as a specification language [6]. The extended static checker for Java (ESC/Java2) [8], for instance, was one of the first of such tools. However, it is not designed to prove full functional correctness, but rather find common programming errors, and hence it is not suitable for our task. Krakatoa [19] and the Key tool [3], on the other hand, are program verifiers that may be used by us as alternatives to VeriFast. To which extent this is possible remains to be investigated.

Adding ownership types [12,33] to Java is a very effective technique to verify that Java threads always access data correctly, i.e. for which they have acquired the proper access rights. Such a technique offers an alternative way to verify that our channel implementation is always correctly accessed. However, it cannot be used to verify arbitrary functional properties that may rely on ownership, but express more than that, such as that some desired behaviour is guaranteed to always eventually happen. On the other hand, with separation logic, one can express and verify such properties as well.

7   Conclusions

We introduced an MDSE approach where generated code is separated into a generic and a model specific part. We presented an application of a modular approach for the verification of fine grained concurrent code in this context using the VeriFast tool. This paper showed the ideas behind and the feasibility of such an approach. With its support of parameterized verification, concurrency via threads, object-oriented code, and fast verification results, VeriFast was up to the task - though an experienced user is required. This underlines the relevance of the idea of re-using generic code that has to be verified only once.

We introduced a novel module specification schema which improves the modularity of the VeriFast approach. Although the schema was originally developed having in mind separation logic and VeriFast, it can be straightforwardly adapted for the standard Owicki-Gries method (assuming extensions with modules) or similar formalisms for concurrent verification.

Finally, using theorem provers to verify the correctness of code still requires considerable expert knowledge. We observe that by using model-to-code transformations, experts can focus on proving correctness of those transformations, thereby relieving developers from the burden to prove that code derived from specific models is correct.

In future work, we plan to address liveness issues, both in the framework and as regards verification, and we plan to address verification of the complete model-to-code transformation, i.e., not only that the used generic code constructs are correct, but that it is guaranteed that the complete executable code is always correct. This is quite challenging, since SLCO also supports the timing of actions. SLCO models with timing can be formally verified by first discretising the timing [31]. Other relevant challenges and ideas are reported in [32].

Acknowledgments. We would like to thank Suzana Andova for the discussions in the early phases of the work described in this paper.

References

1. van Amstel, M., van den Brand, M., Engelen, L.: An exercise in iterative domain-specific language design. In: EVOL/IWPSE. pp. 48–57. ACM (2010)
2. Baalen, J.V., Robinson, P., Lowry, M., Pressburger, T.: Explaining synthesized software. In: ASE. pp. 240–248. IEEE (1998)
3. Beckert, B., Hähnle, R., Schmitt, P. (eds.): Verification of Object-Oriented Software. LNCS (LNAI), vol. 4334. Springer, Heidelberg (2007)
4. Blech, J., Glesner, S., Leitner, J.: Formal verification of java code generation from UML models. In: Fujaba Days, pp. 49–56 (2005)
5. Bornat, R., Calcagno, C., O'Hearn, P., Parkinson, M.: Permission accounting in separation logic. ACM SIGPLAN Not. **40**(1), 259–270 (2005)
6. Burdy, L., Cheon, Y., Cok, D., Ernst, M., Kiniry, J., Leavens, G., Leino, K., Poll, E.: An overview of JML tools and applications. STTT **7**(3), 212–232 (2005)
7. Chaki, S., Clarke, E., Groce, A., Jha, S., Veith, H.: Modular verification of software components in C. In: ICSE, pp. 385–395. IEEE (2003)
8. Leavens, G.T., Poll, E., Kiniry, J.R., Chalin, P.: Beyond assertions: advanced specification and verification with JML and ESC/Java2. In: de Boer, F.S., Bonsangue, M.M., Graf, S., de Roever, W.-P. (eds.) FMCO 2005. LNCS, vol. 4111, pp. 342–363. Springer, Heidelberg (2006)
9. Denney, E., Fischer, B.: Generating customized verifiers for automatically generated code. In: GPCE, pp. 77–88. ACM (2008)
10. Denney, E., Fischer, B., Schumann, J., Richardson, J.: Automatic certification of kalman filters for reliable code generation. In: IEEE Aerospace Conference. pp. 1–10. IEEE (2005)
11. Dijkstra, E.W.: Cooperating sequential processes. In: Brinch Hansen, P. (ed.) The Origin of Concurrent Programming. From Semaphores to Remote Procedure Calls, pp. 65–138. Springer, New York (2002)
12. Fogelberg, C., Potanin, A., Noble, J.: Ownership meets java. In: IWACO, pp. 30–33 (2007)
13. Hoare, C.: An axiomatic basis for computer programming. Commun. ACM **12**(10), 576–580 (1969)
14. Hoare, C.A.R.: Towards a Theory of Parallel Programming. In: Brinch Hansen, P. (ed.) The Origin of Concurrent Programming. From Semaphores to Remote Procedure Calls, pp. 231–244. Springer, New York (2002)
15. Jacobs, B.: VeriFast website. people.cs.kuleuven.be/~bart.jacobs/verifast/ (2012)
16. Jacobs, B., Piessens, F.: Expressive modular fine-grained concurrency specification. In: POPL, pp. 271–282. ACM (2011)
17. Jhala, R., Majumdar, R.: Software model checking. ACM Comput. Surv. **41**(4), 21:1–21:54 (2009)
18. Kleppe, A., Warmer, J., Bast, W.: MDA Explained: The Model Driven Architecture(TM): Practice and Promise. Addison-Wesley Professional, Boston (2005)
19. Marché, C., Paulin-Mohring, C., Urbain, X.: The krakatoa tool for certification of java/javacard programs annotated in JML. J. Logic Algebraic Program. **58**(1–2), 89–106 (2004)
20. O'Hearn, P.W., Reynolds, J.C., Yang, H.: Local reasoning about programs that alter data structures. In: Fribourg, L. (ed.) CSL 2001 and EACSL 2001. LNCS, vol. 2142, pp. 1–19. Springer, Heidelberg (2001)
21. Owicki, S., Gries, D.: Verifying properties of parallel programs: an axiomatic approach. Commun. ACM **19**(5), 279–285 (1976)

22. Rahim, L., Whittle, J.: A survey of approaches for verifying model transformations. Softw. Syst. Model. **14**(2), 1003–1028 (2015)

23. Reynolds, J.: Separation logic: a logic for shared mutable data structures. In: LICS, pp. 55–74. IEEE (2002)

24. Stenzel, K., Reif, W., Moebius, N.: Formal verification of QVT transformations for code generation. In: Whittle, J., Clark, T., Kühne, T. (eds.) MODELS 2011. LNCS, vol. 6981, pp. 533–547. Springer, Heidelberg (2011)

25. Svendsen, K., Birkedal, L., Parkinson, M.: Joins: a case study in modular specification of a concurrent reentrant higher-order library. In: Castagna, G. (ed.) ECOOP 2013. LNCS, vol. 7920, pp. 327–351. Springer, Heidelberg (2013)

26. Parkinson, M., Birkedal, L., Svendsen, K.: Modular reasoning about separation of concurrent data structures. In: Felleisen, M., Gardner, P. (eds.) ESOP 2013. LNCS, vol. 7792, pp. 169–188. Springer, Heidelberg (2013)

27. Welch, P., Martin, J.: Formal analysis of concurrent java systems. In: CPA, pp. 275–301. IOS Press (2000)

28. Wijs, A.: Define, verify, refine: correct composition and transformation of concurrent system semantics. In: Fiadeiro, J.L., Liu, Z., Xue, J. (eds.) FACS 2013. LNCS, vol. 8348, pp. 348–368. Springer, Heidelberg (2014)

29. Wijs, A., Engelen, L.: Efficient property preservation checking of model refinements. In: Piterman, N., Smolka, S.A. (eds.) TACAS 2013 (ETAPS 2013). LNCS, vol. 7795, pp. 565–579. Springer, Heidelberg (2013)

30. Engelen, L., Wijs, A.: REFINER: towards formal verification of model transformations. In: Badger, J.M., Rozier, K.Y. (eds.) NFM 2014. LNCS, vol. 8430, pp. 258–263. Springer, Heidelberg (2014)

31. Wijs, A.: Achieving discrete relative timing with untimed process algebra. In: ICECCS, pp. 35–44. IEEE (2007)

32. Zhang, D., Bošnački, D., van den Brand, M., Engelen, L., Huizing, C., Kuiper, R., Wijs, A.: Towards verified java code generation from concurrent state machines. In: AMT, CEUR Workshop Proceedings, vol. 1277, pp. 64–69 (2014). CEUR-WS.org

33. Zibin, Y., Potanin, A., Li, P., Ali, M., Ernst, M.: Ownership and immutability in generic java. In: OOPSLA. ACM SIGPLAN Notices, vol. 45, pp. 598–617. ACM (2010)

An Operational Semantics of BPMN Collaboration

Flavio Corradini, Andrea Polini, Barbara Re$^{(\boxtimes)}$, and Francesco Tiezzi

School of Science and Technology, University of Camerino, Camerino, Italy
{flavio.corradini,andrea.polini,barbara.re,francesco.tiezzi}@unicam.it

Abstract. In the last years we are observing a growing interest in formalising the execution semantics of business process modelling languages that, despite their lack of formal characterisation, are widely adopted in industry and academia. In this paper, we focus on the OMG standard BPMN 2.0. Specifically, we provide a direct formalisation of its operational semantics in terms of Labelled Transition Systems (LTS). This approach permits both to avoid possible miss-interpretations due to the usage of the natural language in the specification of the standard, and to overcome issues due to the mapping of BPMN to other formal languages, which are equipped with their own semantics. In addition, it paves the way for the use of consolidated formal reasoning techniques based on LTS (e.g., model checking). Our operational semantics is given for a relevant subset of BPMN elements focusing on the capability to model collaborations among organisations via message exchange. Moreover, one of its distinctive aspects is the suitability to model business processes with arbitrary topology. This allows designers to freely specify their processes according to the reality without the need of defining well-structured models. We illustrate our approach through a simple, yet realistic, running example about commercial transactions.

Keywords: Business process modelling · BPMN collaboration · Operational semantics

1 Introduction

Organisations, such as big companies or public administrations, nowadays operate in complex and volatile contexts, that ask for prompt reactions to emerging changes in order to maintain competitiveness and efficiency. To answer to such a need, in the last years a lot of effort has been put in the definition of modelling languages and tools permitting to represent and reason on different perspectives of such organisations. Among the others, Business Process (BP) modeling is certainly the activity that received the most attention, given its relevance in the reflection and definition of strategies for the alignment of introduced IT systems and business activities. A BP is described as *"a collection of related and*

This research has been partially founded by EU project LearnPAd (GA:619583) and by the Project MIUR PRIN CINA (2010LHT4KM).

C. Braga and P.C. Ölveczky (Eds.): FACS 2015, LNCS 9539, pp. 161–180, 2016.
DOI: 10.1007/978-3-319-28934-2_9

structured activities undertaken by one or more organisations in order to pursue some particular goal. Within an organisation a BP results in the provisioning of services or in the production of goods for internal or external stakeholders. Moreover BPs are often interrelated since the execution of a BP often results in the activation of related BPs within the same or other organisations" [1]. In deriving a BP model many different information and perspectives of an organisation can be captured [2]. Among the others we focus on: information related to the activities to be performed (function perspective), who should perform them (organisation perspective), when they should be performed and how they are organised in a flow (behaviour perspective). Many different languages and graphical notations have been proposed to represent BP models with differences both in the possibility to express aspects related to the perspectives, and in the level of formality used to define the elements composing the notation. BPMN 2.0[1], which has been standardised by OMG [3], is currently acquiring a clear predominance, among the various proposal, due to its intuitive graphical notation, the wide acceptance by industry and academia, and the support provided by a wide spectrum of modelling tools[2].

BPMN's success comes from its versatility and capability to represent BPs with different levels of detail and for different purposes. The notation acquired, at first, acceptance within business analysts and operators, who use it to design BP models. Successively, it has been more and more adopted by IT specialists to lead the development and settlement of IT systems supporting the execution of a BP model. Among the various characteristics of the notation, particularly interesting is the possibility to model a *collaboration* of different organisations exchanging messages and cooperating to reach a shared business goal. Collaboration diagrams are indeed the focus of our work since they contains enough information to assess the alignment of participants behavior, and the message flow specified to permit successful cooperations. If from the point of view of the notation the inter-organisation message exchange could seem a simple graphical element, its impact is absolutely relevant. When a modelling notation is used in a homogeneous context, such as a single organisation, the precise definition of the meaning of the various elements constituting the notation can be sometime avoided. Nevertheless, mutual understanding is possible thanks to the direct communications among the involved stakeholders, and from the emergence of established and accepted practices. This is not the case when two or more organisations are involved. In particular, in order to correctly collaborate, the involved organisations have to share the same understanding of communication mechanisms. Moreover, when a BP model includes the specification of collaborations among more organisations, it becomes fundamental that they can rely on a shared understanding of the model. In the last years, a relevant effort has been devoted by the research community to provide a formal semantics to the BPMN notation (we refer to Sect. 5 for an overview of major contributions

---

[1] We use BPMN or BPMN 2.0 interchangeably to refer to version 2.0 of the notation.

[2] BPMN is currently supported by 75 tools (see http://www.bpmn.org for a detailed list).

on this side). Indeed, in defining the notation, OMG did not intend to provide a rigorous semantics for the various graphical elements; instead the meaning is given using natural language descriptions, permitting a wider adoption of the notation in different contexts. The use of formal tools to define the semantics of the various elements, and hence of a BP model, is relevant in order to enable automatic analysis activities that allow the designers to check if the BP satisfies desired properties or not. This aspect seems to be even more relevant when organisations get in contact with each other and need to analyse the impact of collaborative actions. Consider for instance the merging of two companies, in which there is not a common understanding of the models, and then the importance of analysis activities run to get a better understanding on the impact of the integration, and to discover flaws in the collaboration resulting from the possible integration.

In this paper, we intend to contribute to such a research effort aiming at providing a precise characterisation of BPMN elements with a special emphasis on communication within collaboration diagrams. This is mainly motivated by the need of achieving inter-organisation correctness, which is still a challenge [4]. More specifically, the contribution of the paper is a novel formalisation that provides an operational semantics to BPMN in the SOS style [5] by relying on the notion of Labeled Transition System (LTS). The major benefits of our semantics are as follows:

- it is a native semantics, rather than a mapping to other formalisms (equipped with their own semantics) like most of the proposals in the literature (see Sect. 5);
- it provides a compositional approach based on LTS, which paves the way for the use of consolidated analysis techniques and related software tools (see Sect. 6);
- it is suitable to model business processes with arbitrary topology, without imposing syntactical restrictions to the modeler, such as *well-structuredness* [6] (which, e.g., imposes gateways in a process to form single-entry-single-exit fragments) typically required by other proposals (see Sect. 5);
- besides core elements, such as tasks, gateways, etc., it takes into account collaborations and message exchange, which are overlooked by other formalisations.

The rest of the paper is organised as follows. Section 2 reports some background material on BPMN 2.0. Sections 3 and 4 introduce BPMN syntax and operational semantics we propose. Section 5 presents a detailed comparison of our approach with the related ones available in the literature. Finally, Sect. 6 closes the paper with some conclusions and opportunities for future work.

2   Background Notions on BPMN 2.0

The focus of this section is not a complete presentation of the standard, but a discussion of the main concepts of BPMN we use in the following. These concepts

Fig. 1. Considered BPMN 2.0 elements.

are briefly described below and reported in Fig. 1. **Pools** are used to represent a participant or an organisation involved in the collaboration, and provide details on internal process specifications and related elements. Pools are drawn as rectangles. **Events** are used to represent something that can happen. An event can be a *Start Event*, representing the point in which the process starts, while an *End Event* is raised when the process terminates. Events are drawn as circles. **Tasks** are used to represent a specific work to perform within a process. Tasks are drawn as rectangles with rounded corners. **Gateways** are used to manage the flow of a process both for parallel activities and choices. Gateways are drawn as diamonds and act as either join nodes or split nodes. Different types of gateways are available, and we report here the most used ones. A *XOR gateway* gives the possibility to describe choices both in input (joining) and output (splitting); it is activated each time the gateway is reached and, when executed, it activates exactly one outgoing edge. An *AND gateway* enables a parallel flow execution: when used to split the sequence flow, all outgoing branches are activated simultaneously; when it joins parallel branches, it waits for all incoming branches to complete before triggering the outgoing flow. An *OR gateway* gives the possibility to select an arbitrary number of outgoing edges each time it is reached; all active incoming branches must complete before joining. Notably, even if XOR and OR splitting gateways may have guard conditions in their outgoing sequence flows. In this work we do not consider such possibility, as conditions have a significant role only when actual input values are taken into account, while our aim is to enable the verification of all possible flows of a process, and not only those triggered by specific input values. Finally, **Connecting Edges** are used to connect process elements in the same or different pools. Sequence flow is used to specify the internal flow of the process, thus ordering events, activities and gateways in the same pool, while message flow is a dashed connector used to visualise communication flows between organisations.

We introduce here a BPMN collaboration specification used throughout the paper as a running example.

Running Example (1/3). Figure 2 shows an example of BPMN process which combines the activities of a buyer organisation and a reseller one that have to interact in the market in order to complete a commercial transaction. After the buyer organisation analyses the market, it places its order by sending the *order* message to the reseller. Then, the buyer forks into two parallel paths by means of the AND gateway G1. The upper path receives the *invoice* from the reseller and settles it; in parallel the lower path receives the products from the reseller. Finally, the two flows of the buyer synchronise at the AND gateway G2

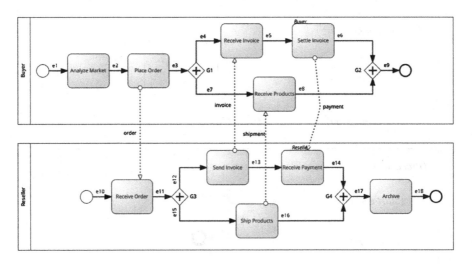

Fig. 2. Buyer-Reseller example (source [7] p. 223).

and the buyer stops its activities. This exchange of messages is supported by
the behaviour of the reseller that, after receiving the order, forks its behaviour
into two parallel paths using the AND gateway G3. In the upper path, the
reseller sends the *invoice* and receives the *payment*, while in the bottom one it
performs the *shipment* of the ordered products. Finally, the flows of the reseller
synchronise at the AND gateway G4 and the process of the reseller ends after
the order is archived.   □

It is worth noticing that we focus on the control flow and interacting aspects of
business processes. This is mainly motivated by the need of keeping the semantics
of the considered language rigorous but still manageable. Therefore, we intentionally left out other aspects, including timed events, data objects, sub-processing,
error handling, and multiple instances. Instead, other aspects of BPMN can be
easily rendered with our syntax, such as intermediate message events that can
be reconducted to tasks with an incoming message flow. Anyway, we do not
consider this restriction on the syntax as a major limitation, because we focus
on the BPMN constructs most used in practice (indeed, even if the BPMN specification is quite wide, only less than 20 % of its vocabulary is used regularly in
designing BP models [8]).

3   BNF Syntax

The syntax of BPMN 2.0 is given in [3] by a metamodel in classical UML-style.
In this section we provide an alternative syntax, in BNF-style, that is more
suitable for defining a formal operational semantics.

The syntax is defined by grammar productions of the form $N ::= A_1 \mid \ldots \mid A_n$, where N is a non-terminal symbol and alternatives $A_1, \ldots, A_n$ are compositions of terminal and non-terminal symbols. In particular, in the grammar

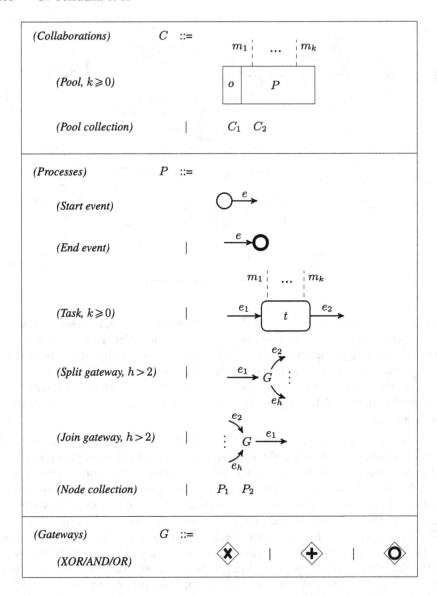

Fig. 3. BPMN SyntaxBPMN syntax

in Fig. 3, the non-terminal symbols are C, P and G, representing *collaborations*, *processes* and *gateways*, respectively, while the terminal symbols are the typical graphical elements of a BPMN model, i.e. pools, events, tasks, gateways, and edges.

Intuitively, a BPMN collaboration model is rendered in our syntax as a collection of pools, where message edges can connect different pools. Each pool contains a process, defined as a collection of nodes, with incoming and/or outgoing sequence edges. Such nodes are events, tasks and (XOR/AND/OR) gateways. Notably, to obtain a compositional definition, each (message/sequence) edge is divided in two parts: the part outgoing from the source node and the part incoming into the target node. In fact, a term of the syntax can be straightforwardly obtained from a BPMN model by decomposing the collaboration in collection of pools, processes in collection of nodes, and edges in two parts.

We use the following disjoint sets of names: the set of *organisation* names (ranged over by o), the set of *message* names (ranged over by m), the set of *edge* names (ranged over by e), and the set of *task* names (ranged over by t). As a matter of notation, we use edges of the form $\_ \overset{m}{\_\_} \_$ to denote edges of the form $\text{---}\overset{m}{\text{---}}$ either incoming into or outgoing from pools/tasks.

We only consider specifications that are *well-defined*, in the sense that they comply with the following four syntactic constraints:

- Distinct pools (resp. tasks) have different pool (resp. task) names.
- In a collaboration, for each message edge labelled by m outgoing from a pool, there exists only one corresponding message edge labelled by m incoming into another pool, and vice versa.
- For each incoming (resp. outgoing) message edge labelled by m at pool level, there exists only one corresponding incoming (resp. outgoing) message edge labelled by m at the level of the process within the pool.
- In a process, for each sequence edge labelled by e outgoing from a node, there exists only one corresponding sequence edge labelled by e incoming into another node, and vice versa.

Well-definedness could be easily checked through a standard (and trivial) static analysis; more practically, the rationale is that each term of the language can be easily derived from a BPMN model whose only constraint is to have (pool, task, edge) unique names.

Notably, in this work we do not consider specifications using the OR join gateway, because formalising its semantics is a tricky task (see, e.g., [9–11]) that would make our formalisation much more complicated and, hence, out of focus.

Running Example (2/3). The BPMN model presented in Sect. 2 is expressed in our syntax as the following collaboration:

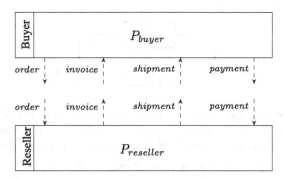

where (an excerpt of) process P_{buyer} is defined as follows:

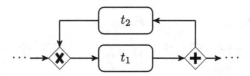

and process $P_{reseller}$ is defined in a similar way.   □

4   Operational Semantics

We give the semantics of BPMN in terms of *marked collaborations*, i.e. collections of pools equipped with a marking. A *marking* is a distribution of tokens over pool message edges and process elements that indicate message arrivals and the process nodes that are active or not in a given step of the execution. This resembles the notions of token and marking in Petri Nets; this is not surprising as such formalism has strongly inspired the workflow constructs of BPMN. Similarly to the token-passing semantics in [12,13], our tokens move along the syntax constructs, acting as sort of program counters.

For the sake of presentation, the operational semantics of BPMN is defined over an enriched syntax, w.r.t. the one given in Sect. 3, where pools' message edges are marked (i.e., labelled) by message tokens ⊠, while processes' edges, events and tasks are marked by workflow tokens •. As a matter of notation, the presence of a number of message (resp. workflow) tokens in the same place is represented by means of one token of the form $B\,n$ (resp. $•\,n$), where $n \in \mathbb{N}_0$ is the token multiplicity. The initial marking of a collaboration assigns a single workflow token to the start events of the process of each pool in the collaboration. Notably, in this work we only consider business processes instantiated with single instances. In fact, dealing with multiple instances in presence of message interactions would require to properly deliver each message to its appropriate instance; this would add complexity to our formal treatment, which we want to avoid in order to keep it as easy to understand as possible. On the other hand, the use of tokens with multiplicity is necessary also with single instances, e.g. due to the behaviour of the combined use of AND and XOR gateways as in the following piece of BPMN model:

Formally, the operational semantics of marked collaborations is defined in the SOS style by relying on the notion of Labeled Transition System (LTS). The labeled transition relation of the LTS defining the semantics of collaborations, at pool layer, is induced by the inference rules in Fig. 4. We write $C \xmapsto{\;l\;} C'$ to mean that "collaboration C can perform a transition labeled by l and become C' in doing so". Transition labels are generated by the following production rule:

$$(Labels) \qquad l \ ::= \quad o : \alpha \quad | \quad o_1 \to o_2 : m$$

The meaning of labels is as follows: $o : \alpha$ denotes an action α peformed by the process instance of organisation o, while $o_1 \to o_2 : m$ denotes the exchange of a message m from organisation o_1 to o_2. The definition of the above relation relies on an auxiliary transition relation defining the semantics of process instances and induced by the inference rules in Figs. 5, 6, and 7. We write $P \overset{\alpha}{\longmapsto} P'$ to mean that "process P can perform a transition labeled by α and become P' in doing so". The labels used by this auxiliary transition relation are generated by the following production rules:

$$(Actions) \qquad \alpha \ ::= \quad \tau \quad | \quad !m \quad | \quad ?m$$
$$(Internal\ actions) \qquad \tau \ ::= \quad enabled\ t \quad | \quad completed\ t \quad | \quad (-\tilde{e}_1, +\tilde{e}_2)$$

where notation $\tilde{e}$ indicates a set of edges. The meaning of labels is as follows: τ denotes an action internal to the process, while $!m$ and $?m$ denote send and receive actions, respectively. The meaning of internal actions is as follows: $enabled\ t$ and $completed\ t$ denote the start and completion of the execution of task t, respectively; the pair $(-\tilde{e}_1, +\tilde{e}_2)$ denotes movement of workflow tokens in the process graph, in particular one token is removed from each edge in $\tilde{e}_1$ and one is added to each edge in $\tilde{e}_2$ (whenever one of the two sets of edges is empty, its field is omitted from the pair).

We now briefly comment the rules in Fig. 4. The first three rules allow a single pool, representing organisation o, to evolve according to the evolution of its enclosed process P. In particular, if P performs an internal action (rule *Internal*), a sending action (rule *Send*) or a receiving action (rule *Receive*), the pool performs the corresponding action at collaboration layer, i.e. the label is enriched with the name o of the organisation performing the action. Notably, rule *Receive* can be applied only if there is at least one ($n > 0$) message m queued in the corresponding message edge of the pool; of course, a message token is consumed by this transition. Instead, when an organisation o_1 indicates the willingness to send a message m (represented by a transition labelled by $o_1 : !m$), such message is properly delivered to the receiving organisation o_2 by applying rule *Deliver*. The resulting transition, labelled by $o_1 \to o_2 : m$, has the effect of increasing in the pool of o_2 the number of message tokens queued in the message edge labelled by m. If organisation o_2 does not have a message edge labelled by m, i.e. o_2 is not supposed to receive message m, no interaction between o_1 and o_2 takes place and label $o_1 : !m$ is propagated (rule *Skip*). It is worth noticing that, as prescribed by the BPMN 2.0 specification, inter-organisation communication is *asynchronous*: the sending action is not blocking, while the receiving one is blocking when there is no message token to consume. The two *Interleaving* rules permit to interleave the execution of actions performed by pools of the same collaboration, so that if a part of a larger collaboration evolves, the whole collaboration evolves accordingly. Interleaving is disallowed in case of a sending

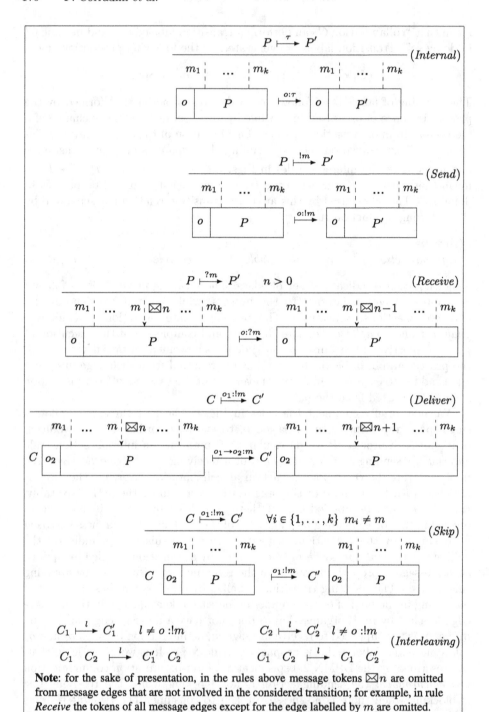

Fig. 4. BPMN operational semantics: collaboration layer.

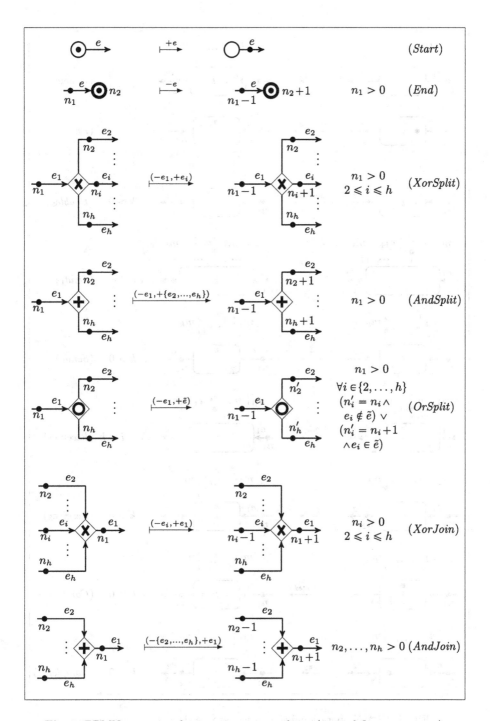

Fig. 5. BPMN operational semantics: process layer (control flow constructs).

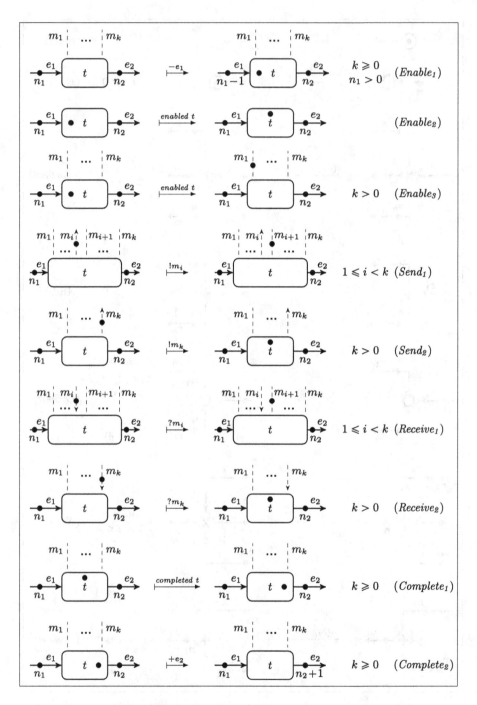

Fig. 6. BPMN operational semantics: process layer (task constructs).

$$\frac{P_1 \xmapsto{(-\tilde{e}_1, +\tilde{e}_2)} P_1'}{P_1 \ P_2 \xmapsto{(-\tilde{e}_1, +\tilde{e}_2)} P_1' \ P_2 \pm_{\tilde{e}_1, \tilde{e}_2}} \qquad \frac{P_2 \xmapsto{(-\tilde{e}_1, +\tilde{e}_2)} P_2'}{P_1 \ P_2 \xmapsto{(-\tilde{e}_1, +\tilde{e}_2)} P_1 \pm_{\tilde{e}_1, \tilde{e}_2} \ P_2'}$$

$$\frac{P_1 \xmapsto{\alpha} P_1' \quad \alpha \neq (-\tilde{e}_1, +\tilde{e}_2)}{P_1 \ P_2 \xmapsto{\alpha} P_1' \ P_2} \qquad \frac{P_2 \xmapsto{\alpha} P_2' \quad \alpha \neq (-\tilde{e}_1, +\tilde{e}_2)}{P_1 \ P_2 \xmapsto{\alpha} P_1 \ P_2'}$$

Fig. 7. BPMN operational semantics: process layer (node collection).

action, in order to force the use of rules *Deliver* and *Skip* for synchronising the sending pool with the receiving one. In fact, labels of the form $o_1 :\!!m$ are never exhibited by a well-defined collaboration (see Sect. 3), as they are just auxiliary labels used for properly, and compositionally, inferring transitions labelled by $o_1 \rightarrow o_2 : m$.

Rules in Fig. 5 deal with control flow constructs, i.e. events and gateways. All these rules are axioms (i.e., they have no premises) producing transition labels of the form $(-\tilde{e}_1, +\tilde{e}_2)$. This means that the effect of these rules is simply changing the marking of the process, i.e. moving workflow tokens among edges. For example, the effect of the rule *AndSplit* is to consume a token from the incoming edge e_1 of the AND gateway and to add a token to each outgoing edge e_i, with $2 \leq i \leq h$. The propagation of marking updates to other nodes of the process is dealt with by the interleaving rules in Fig. 7 (see comments below).

Rules in Fig. 6 are axioms devoted to the evolution of tasks. When a task is enabled (rule $Enable_1$), a token from its incoming edge is consumed and is placed on the left of the task name to indicate the starting status of the task. Notably, a task can be activated only when no token is placed inside the task rectangle or on its message edges; this means that parallel executions of the same task are not allowed. The fact that a task t is enabled is notified by applying either rule $Enable_2$ or $Enable_3$, depending on the presence of message edges. When a message edge is marked by a token, the corresponding sending or receiving action is performed; moreover the token is moved to the next edge (rules $Send_1$ or $Receive_1$) or on the top of the task name (rules $Send_2$ or $Receive_2$). Notice that the order of message edges is relevant for the execution: messages are processed from left to right. This permits disambiguating the semantics of tasks in case of multiple message edges. Finally, when all messages are processed, the completion of the task execution is notified (rule $Complete_1$) and the number of tokens on the outgoing edge is increased by one (rule $Complete_2$).

The last group of rules, shown in Fig. 7, deal with interleaving of process node evolutions. The first two rules are applied when the evolution involves a change in the marking of process edges, while the second two are applied in the other cases. In particular, the former rules relies on the marking updating function $P \pm_{\tilde{e}_1, \tilde{e}_2}$, which returns a process obtained from P by unmarking (resp. marking) edges in $\tilde{e}_1$ (resp. $\tilde{e}_2$). Formally, this function is inductively defined on the structure of process P, by also relying on the following auxiliary function:

$$n \pm^e_{\tilde{e}_1,\tilde{e}_2} = \begin{cases} n-1 & \text{if } e \in \tilde{e}_1 \\ n+1 & \text{if } e \in \tilde{e}_2 \\ n & \text{otherwise} \end{cases}$$

Notably, in the above definition we exploit the fact that, since self-loop are not admitted in a process, it holds $\tilde{e}_1 \cap \tilde{e}_2 = \emptyset$. In each base case of the inductive definition of the marking updating function, we simply apply the auxiliary function to the multiplicity of all tokens that mark an edge of the process node. We report below few significant cases of the definition (the others are similar):

$$(P_1 \quad P_2) \pm_{\tilde{e}_1,\tilde{e}_2} = P_1 \pm_{\tilde{e}_1,\tilde{e}_2} \quad P_2 \pm_{\tilde{e}_1,\tilde{e}_2}$$

$$\overset{e}{\underset{n_1}{\longrightarrow}} \odot n_2 \pm_{\tilde{e}_1,\tilde{e}_2} = \overset{e}{\underset{n_1 \pm^e_{\tilde{e}_1,\tilde{e}_2}}{\longrightarrow}} \odot n_2$$

Running Example (3/3). We describe here the semantics of the BPMN model informally introduced in Sect. 2 and fomalised in Sect. 3. The initial state of the execution is represented by the collaboration in Fig. 8(a), where the start events of the processes of the two organisations are marked by a workflow token each. Thus, the execution of both processes can start and, as a possible evolution, after few computational steps the status of the collaboration becomes the one shown in Fig. 8(b). In such a configuration, according to the position of the two tokens, the buyer is performing the *Analize Market* task, while the reseller is already waiting for the order from the buyer. After other few steps, the collaboration status becomes the one in Fig. 8(c), where the buyer has completed the *Analize Market* task and sent the *order* message to the reseller (as indicated by the message token ⊠ queued in the corresponding incoming message edge of the reseller's pool). Now, the reseller can consume the message and resume its computation. Finally, after further steps, the collaboration reaches the final configuration in Fig. 8(d), where two workflow tokens mark the final events of the two processes.   □

5   Related Work

Much effort has been devoted to the formalisation of BPMN. Here we refer to the most relevant attempts: we first consider the other direct formalisations available in the literature, then we discuss some mappings from BPMN to well-known formalisms.

With regard to direct formalisations, we refer to Van Gorp and Dijkman [14], Christiansen et al. [9], El-Saber and Boronat [15], and Borger and Thalheim [16].

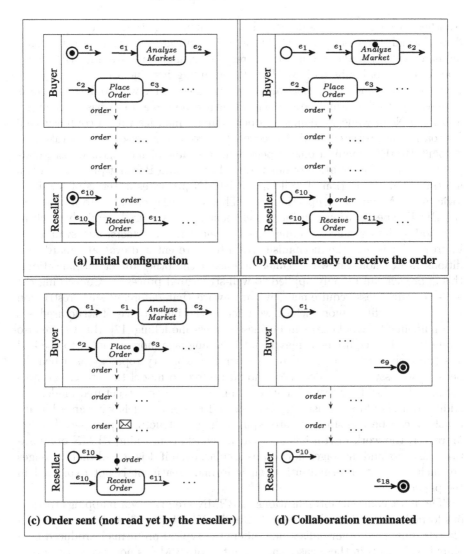

Fig. 8. Semantics of the running example: an excerpt

Among them, our contribution was mainly inspired by the one presented in [14]. They propose a BPMN 2.0 formalisation based on in-place graph transformation rules; these rules are defined to be passed as input to the GrGen.NET tool, and are documented visually using BPMN syntax. With respect to our work, the used formalisation techniques are different, since we provide an operational semantics in terms of LTS. This allows us to apply verification techniques based on transition labels, as e.g. model checking of properties expressed as formulae of action-based temporal logic. This gives us the possibility to be tool interdependent rather than be constrained to tools specific for graph transformation rules.

Another interesting work is described in [9], where Christiansen et al. propose a direct formalisation of the BPMN 2.0 Beta 1 Specification using algorithms based on incrementally updated data structures. The semantics is given for BPMNinc, that is a minimal subset of BPMN 2.0 containing just inclusive and exclusive gateways, start and end events, and sequence flows. This work differs from ours with respect to the formalisation method, as it proposes a token-based semantics à la Petri Nets, while we define an operational semantics with a compositional approach à la process calculi. Moreover, the work in [9] also lacks to take into account BPMN organisational aspects and the flow of messages, whose treatment is a main contribution of our work. El-Saber and Boronat proposed in [15] a formal characterisation of well-formed BPMN processes in terms of rewriting logic, using Maude as supporting tool. This formalisation refers to a subset of the BPMN specification considering elements that are used regularly, such as flow nodes, data elements, connecting flow elements, artefacts, and swimlanes. Interesting it is also the mechanism given to represent and evaluate guard conditions in decision gateways. Differently from the other direct formalisations, this approach can be only applied to well-structured processes. Concerning the well-structuredness requirement, we are aware that enforcing such restriction may have benefits, among which we refer to the importance of structuredness as a guideline to avoid errors in business process modelling [17]. But we are also aware that this requirement may result in a language more complex to use and less expressive [18]. We therefore consider the arbitrary topology as a benefit, because we assume that designers should be free to model the process according to the reality they feel without needing to define well-structured models. In addition, it should be considered that not all process models with an arbitrary topology can be transformed into equivalent well-structured processes [19,20]. Moreover, the work in [15] has another drawback, concerning BPMN organisational aspects and messages flow. In particular, even if it is stated that messages are included in the formalisation, their formal treatment is not explained in the paper.

The most common formalisations of BPMN are given via mappings to various formalisms, such as Petri Nets [6,21–25], YAWL [26,27] and process calculi [28–34]. This kind of formalisations suffers the typical problems introduced by a mapping. In fact, in these cases the semantics of BPMN is not given in terms of features and constructs of the language, but in terms of low-level details of their encodings. This makes the verification of BPMN models less effective, because the verification results refer to the low-level implementation of the models and may be difficult to be interpreted at BPMN level. Moreover, no formal proof of the correctness of these encodings with respect to a native semantics of BPMN is provided.

Regarding the mapping from BPMN to Petri Nets, the one proposed by Dijkman et al. in [6] is probably the most relevant contribution. It enables the use of standard tools for process analysis, such as soundness of BPMN models. However, differently from our approach, even if the mapping deals with messages, it does not properly consider multiple organisation scenarios, and does not provide information to the analysis phase regarding who are the participants involved in the exchange of messages.

Other relevant mappings are those from BPMN to YAWL, a language with a strictly defined execution semantics inspired by Petri Nets. Among the proposed mappings, we would like to mention the ones by Ye and Song [26] and Dumas et al. [27]. The former is defined under the well-formedness assumption, which instead we do not rely on. Moreover, although messages are taken into account in the mapping, pools and lanes are not considered; thus it is not possible to identify who is the sender and who is the receiver in the communication. This results in the lack of capability to introduce verification at message level considering the involved organisations. The latter mapping, instead, formalises a very small portion of BPMN elements. In particular, limitations about pools and messages are similar to the previous approach: pools are treated as separate business processes, while messages flow is not covered by the mapping.

Process calculi has been also considered as means for formalising BPMN. Among the others, Wong and Gibbons presented in [29] a translation from a subset of BPMN process diagrams, under the assumption of well-formedness, to a CSP-like language based on Z notation. This enables the introduction of formal verification to check properties like consistency and compatibility. Even if messages have been omitted in the formalisation presented in [29], their treatment is discussed in [28]. Messages are also considered by Arbab et al. in [30], where the main BPMN modeling primitives are represented by means of the coordination language Reo. Differently from the other mappings, this one considers a significantly larger set of BPMN elements. Prandi et al., instead, defined in [31] a semantics in term of a mapping from BPMN to the process calculus COWS, which has been specifically devised for modelling service-oriented systems. Last but not least, also π-calculus was taken as target language of mapping by Hutchison et al. [32] and Puhlmann [33]. Even if our proposal differs from the above ones, as it is a direct semantics rather than a mapping, it has drawn inspiration from those based on process calculi for the use of a compositional approach in the SOS style.

6   Concluding Remarks

The lack of a shared, well-established, comprehensive formal semantics for BPMN was the main driver of our work. This is also a critical point of the specification considering the wide adoption of the language both from the industry and research community. In this paper, we present an operational semantics in terms of LTS. We focus on the collaboration capability supported by message exchange. The proposed semantics enables designers to freely specify their processes with an arbitrary topology supporting the adherence to the standard, without the requirement of defining well-structured models.

The proposed formalisation allows one to verify properties on the model using consolidated formal reasoning techniques based on LTS. For instance, by expressing such properties by means of temporal logic, we can check, e.g., if *after* the enabling of a given task it can be *eventually* completed or not. More in general, we can verify, e.g., if *for all* possible executions all processes involved in a collaboration successfully terminates. This is quite relevant also with reference to the message exchange as, although communication is asynchronous, message receiving is blocking. We intend to investigate verification of such kind of properties in the near future. We plan to achieve this by implementing our semantics in Maude[3] that allows to render operational rules of the semantics in terms of rewriting rules. This enables the (automatic or interactive) exploration of the evolutions of BPMN models, and it permits to exploit the rich analysis tool set provided by Maude. Even if we consider the use of Maude the most promising approach for our purposes, we plan to also investigate other approaches, such as [35,36]. Moreover, we intend to develop a tool chain integrating the verification environment with a BPMN modelling environment, such as Eclipse BPMN Modeller[4]. This will offer the possibility of going back and forth between the modelling environment and the verification one, by e.g. graphically visualising on the BPMN model the feedbacks of the verification.

We also aim at extending our formalisation to model more BPMN elements, such as data objects, sub-processing, and error handling. In particular, we intend to focus on tricky issues concerning multiple instances of the same process and OR join gateway. Last but not least, we plan to prove some consistency properties of our operational semantics ensuring, e.g., that some syntactic constraints are preserved along the evolution of marked collaborations.

References

1. Lindsay, A., Downs, D., Lunn, K.: Business processes - attempts to find a definition. Inf. Softw. Technol. **45**(15), 1015–1019 (2003)
2. Reichert, M., Weber, B.: Enabling Flexibility in Process-Aware Information Systems: Challenges, Methods, Technologies. Springer, Heidelberg (2012)
3. OMG: Business Process Model and Notation (BPMN v2.0), Normative document, Jan 2011
4. Breu, R., Dustdar, S., Eder, J., Huemer, C., Kappel, G., Köpke, J., Langer, P., Mangler, J., Mendling, J., Neumann, G., Rinderle-Ma, S., Schulte, S., Sobernig, S., Weber, B.: Towards living inter-organizational processes. In: CBI, pp. 363–366. IEEE (2013)
5. Plotkin, G.: A structural approach to operational semantics. J. Log. Algebr. Program. **60–61**, 17–139 (2004)
6. Dijkman, R.M., Dumas, M., Ouyang, C.: Semantics and analysis of business process models in BPMN. Inf. Softw. Technol. **50**(12), 1281–1294 (2008)
7. Weske, M.: Business Process Management. Springer, Heidelberg (2012)
8. Recker, Jan, Muehlen, M.Z.: How much language is enough? theoretical and practical use of the business process modeling notation. In: Bellahsène, Z., Léonard, M. (eds.) CAiSE 2008. LNCS, vol. 5074, pp. 465–479. Springer, Heidelberg (2008)
9. Christiansen, D.R., Carbone, M., Hildebrandt, T.T.: Formal semantics and implementation of BPMN 2.0 inclusive gateways. In: WSFM, pp. 146–160 (2011)

---

[3] http://maude.cs.illinois.edu/.
[4] http://www.eclipse.org/bpmn2-modeler/.

10. Wilmsmann, G., Völzer, H., Gfeller, B.: Faster or-join enactment for BPMN 2.0. In: Dijkman, R., Hofstetter, J., Koehler, J. (eds.) BPMN 2011. LNBIP, vol. 95, pp. 31–43. Springer, Heidelberg (2011)
11. Dumas, M., Grosskopf, A., Hettel, T., Wynn, M.T.: Semantics of standard process models with OR-joins. In: Tari, Z., Meersman, R. (eds.) OTM 2007, Part I. LNCS, vol. 4803, pp. 41–58. Springer, Heidelberg (2007)
12. Sinot, F.-R.: Call-by-name and call-by-value as token-passing interaction nets. In: Urzyczyn, P. (ed.) TLCA 2005. LNCS, vol. 3461, pp. 386–400. Springer, Heidelberg (2005)
13. Kirchner, F., Sinot, F.: Rule-based operational semantics for an imperative language. Electr. Notes Theor. Comput. Sci. **174**(1), 35–47 (2007)
14. Van Gorp, P., Dijkman, R.: A visual token-based formalization of BPMN 2.0 based on in-place transformations. Inf. Softw. Technol. **55**(2), 365–394 (2013)
15. El-Saber, N., Boronat, A.: BPMN formalization and verification using maude. In: BM-FA, pp. 1–12. ACM Press (2014)
16. Thalheim, B., Börger, E.: A method for verifiable and validatable business process modeling. In: Börger, E., Cisternino, A. (eds.) Advances in Software Engineering. LNCS, vol. 5316, pp. 59–115. Springer, Heidelberg (2008)
17. Laue, R., Mendling, J.: The impact of structuredness on error probability of process models. In: Kaschek, R., Kop, C., Steinberger, C., Fliedl, G. (eds.) Information Systems and e-Business Technologies. Lecture Notes in Business Information Processing, vol. 5, pp. 585–590. Springer, Heidelberg (2008)
18. Kiepuszewski, B., ter Hofstede, A.H.M., Bussler, C.J.: On structured workflow modelling. In: Wangler, B., Bergman, L.D. (eds.) CAiSE 2000. LNCS, vol. 1789, p. 431. Springer, Heidelberg (2000)
19. Polyvyanyy, A., Garcuelos, L., Dumas, M.: Structuring acyclic process models. Inf. Syst. **37**(6), 518–538 (2012)
20. Polyvyanyy, A., Garcia-Banuelos, L., Fahland, D., Weske, M.: Maximal structuring of acyclic process models. Comput. J. **57**(1), 12–35 (2014)
21. Huai, W., Liu, X., Sun, H.: Towards trustworthy composite service through business process model verification. In: UIC/ATC, pp. 422–427. IEEE (2010)
22. Koniewski, R., Dzielinski, A., Amborski, K.: Use of petri nets and business processes management notation in modelling and simulation of multimodal logistics chains. In: ECMS, pp. 99–102 (2006)
23. Ramadan, M., Elmongui, H.G., Hassan, R.: BPMN formalisation using coloured petri nets. In: SEA (2011)
24. Awad, A., Decker, G., Lohmann, N.: Diagnosing and repairing data anomalies in process models. In: Rinderle-Ma, S., Sadiq, S., Leymann, F. (eds.) Business Process Management Workshops. LNBIP, vol. 43, pp. 5–16. Springer, Heidelberg (2010)
25. Corradini, F., Polini, A., Re, B.: Inter-organizational business process verification in public administration. Bus. Process Manag. J. **21**(5), 1040–1065 (2015)
26. Ye, J., Song, W.: Transformation of BPMN diagrams to YAWL nets. J. Softw. **5**(4), 396–404 (2010)
27. Dijkman, R., Decker, G., García-Bañuelos, L., Dumas, M.: Transforming BPMN diagrams into YAWL nets. In: Dumas, M., Reichert, M., Shan, M.-C. (eds.) BPM 2008. LNCS, vol. 5240, pp. 386–389. Springer, Heidelberg (2008)
28. Wong, P.Y., Gibbons, J.: Formalisations and applications of BPMN. Sci. Comput. Program. **76**(8), 633–650 (2011)
29. Gibbons, J., Wong, P.Y.H.: A process semantics for BPMN. In: Liu, S., Araki, K. (eds.) ICFEM 2008. LNCS, vol. 5256, pp. 355–374. Springer, Heidelberg (2008)

30. Arbab, F., Kokash, N., Meng, S.: Towards using reo for compliance-aware business process modeling. In: Margaria, T., Steffen, B. (eds.) Leveraging Applications of Formal Methods, Verification and Validation. CCIS, vol. 17, pp. 108–123. Springer, Heidelberg (2008)

31. Quaglia, P., Zannone, N., Prandi, D.: Formal analysis of BPMN via a translation into COWS. In: Lea, D., Zavattaro, G. (eds.) COORDINATION 2008. LNCS, vol. 5052, pp. 249–263. Springer, Heidelberg (2008)

32. Weske, M., Puhlmann, F.: Investigations on soundness regarding lazy activities. In: Dustdar, S., Fiadeiro, J.L., Sheth, A.P. (eds.) BPM 2006. LNCS, vol. 4102, pp. 145–160. Springer, Heidelberg (2006)

33. Puhlmann, F.: Soundness verification of business processes specified in the Pi-calculus. In: Meersman, R., Tari, Z. (eds.) OTM 2007, Part I. LNCS, vol. 4803, pp. 6–23. Springer, Heidelberg (2007)

34. Corradini, F., Polini, A., Polzonetti, A., Re, B.: Business processes verification for e-government service delivery. Inf. Syst. Manag. **27**(4), 293–308 (2010)

35. Lucanu, D., Şerbănuţă, T.F., Roşu, G.: $\mathbb{K}$ framework distilled. In: Durán, F. (ed.) WRLA 2012. LNCS, vol. 7571, pp. 31–53. Springer, Heidelberg (2012)

36. Rosu, G., Stefanescu, A.: Matching logic: a new program verification approach. In: ICSE, pp. 868–871. ACM (2011)

k-Bisimulation: A Bisimulation for Measuring the Dissimilarity Between Processes

Giuseppe De Ruvo[1]([✉]), Giuseppe Lettieri[2], Domenico Martino[1],
Antonella Santone[1], and Gigliola Vaglini[2]

[1] Department of Engineering, University of Sannio, Benevento, Italy
{gderuvo,santone}@unisannio.it, martinodomenico88@gmail.com
[2] Department of Information Engineering, University of Pisa, Pisa, Italy
{g.lettieri,g.vaglini}@ing.unipi.it

Abstract. We propose to use bisimulation to quantify dissimilarity between processes: in this case we speak of k-bisimulation. Two processes p and q, whose semantics is given through transition systems, are k-bisimilar if they differ from at most k moves, where k is a natural number. Roughly speaking, the k-bisimulation captures the extension of the dissimilarity between p and q when they are neither strong nor weak equivalent. The importance of the formal concept of k-bisimulation can be seen in several application fields, such as clone detection, process mining, business-IT alignment. We propose several heuristics in order to efficiently check such a bisimulation. The approach can be applied to different specification languages (CCS, LOTOS, CSP) provided that the language semantics is based on the notion of transition system. We have implemented a prototype tool and we have conducted experiments on well-known systems for a proof of concept of our methodology.

1 Introduction and Motivation

Equivalence checking is important in many fields including formal verification, temporal logic, set theory, XML indexing, clone detection, game theory, etc. In essence, the problem is: given the description of two systems, are the behaviors of these systems equivalent with respect to some notion of equivalence? A classical application example is that in which one system describes the implementation, and another one describes the specification. There are many different points of view that can be taken in defining equivalence of systems. The different types of equivalence proposed in literature can be organized, as described in [14], into the linear-time/branching-time spectrum. Moreover, we can consider as equivalence checking problems cases where we have to decide some general relation between systems, not necessarily equivalence. For example, in the field of the process mining a main point is the so-called *conformance checking* that aims at the detection of inconsistencies between a predefined process model and an execution log, and their quantification by the formation of metrics. It is particularly interesting whether the model describes the observed process in a suitable way, i.e., its appropriateness. Appropriateness tries to capture the idea of Occam's

© Springer International Publishing Switzerland 2016
C. Braga and P.C. Ölveczky (Eds.): FACS 2015, LNCS 9539, pp. 181–198, 2016.
DOI: 10.1007/978-3-319-28934-2_10

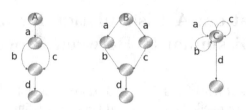

Fig. 1. Three non bisimilar processes

razor, i.e., *one should not increase, beyond what is necessary, the number of entities required to explain anything.*

Milner [19] introduced in the concurrency theory the notion of bisimulation to support the definition of equivalence for transition systems. Moreover, he defined the notion of observational equivalence for his Calculus of Communicating Systems (CCS) and thus for transition systems. Formal verification environments such as Concurrency Workbench of the New Century [7] and CADP [13] incorporate bisimulation checkers in their tool sets: in this area the notion was primarily used to minimize the state space of the system representation. Many works have be done in this direction, [25] is just an example.

In this paper, we present the k-bisimulation that is a bisimulation aiming at the observational equivalence between processes when some moves are hidden. The importance of a formal concept of the k-bisimulation can be highlighted in several application fields, such as clone detection, process mining, business-IT alignment, wiki design and even malware analysis. We propose different heuristics in order to efficiently check such a bisimulation. The approach can be applied to various specification languages (CCS [19], LOTOS [3], CSP [16]) provided that the language semantics is based on the notion of transition systems. We have implemented a prototype tool and we have conducted experiments on five popular systems for a proof of concept of our methodology. Clearly, it is not very interesting to apply k-bisimulation when two systems have a vastly different structure and then the number of moves to hide is very near to the total number of moves of the two systems. Nevertheless it is possible, even if the value of k is not too high, to have a relevant difference between the number of moves to be hidden in a system and the number hidden in the second one. Consequently, in order to test our methodology we use small values of k and try to show that the proposed method works well when processes are very similar.

Considering again the process mining context, the appropriateness relation between systems can be divided into structural and behavioral appropriateness; both these characteristics are well captured by the concept of bisimulation as can be seen by examining the transition systems in Fig. 1. Processes A, B and C include the same computation set, but the process A can be more appropriate than B and C, because C allows more computations (it is less structurally appropriate than A) and B is less compact (it is less behaviorally appropriate) than A. Bisimulation distinguishes the three processes; k-bisimulation gives a measure of their dissimilarity. As a first hint of the meaning of the k-bisimulation, we anticipate that when considering A and C, we can see that they are 3-bisimilar; while A and B are 2-bisimilar. Thus, if A is the predefined process model and B and C are possible real processes retrieved from the log, the model describes B with better appropriateness than C.

2   Preliminaries

Process algebras can be used to describe both implementations of processes and specifications of their expected behaviors. Therefore, they support the so-called single language approach to process theory, that is, the approach in which a single language is used to describe both actual processes and their specifications. An important ingredient of these languages is therefore a notion of behavioral equivalence. The well-known Milner's weak equivalence describes how an action of a process can be matched by a sequence of actions from another one when considering the same "observational content" (i.e., ignoring internal actions, also called silent transitions and represented by a special action τ); weak equivalence is based on the concept of bisimulation and then gives a very meaningful semantics to processes. To develop our method in a specification language independent way, we assume a set of processes Δ, a set of actions Θ and a function σ that maps each $p \in \Delta$ to a finite set $\{(p, \alpha_1, p_1), \ldots, (p, \alpha_n, p_n)\} \subseteq \Delta \times \Theta \times \Delta$. The existence of $(p, \alpha, p') \in \sigma(p)$ means that p can perform the action α and transform into the process p'; we can also express this capability as $p \xrightarrow{\alpha} p'$; we assume the existence of the special action $\tau \in \Theta$. From now on, the *transition system* of p, namely $\mathcal{S}(p)$, is the smallest sub-set of $\Delta \times \Theta \times \Delta$ such that:

1. $\sigma(p) \subseteq \mathcal{S}(p)$, and
2. whenever $(p', \alpha, p'') \in \mathcal{S}(p)$, it is $\sigma(p'') \subseteq \mathcal{S}(p)$ too.

We say also that each $(q, \alpha, q') \subseteq \mathcal{S}(p)$ is a *transition* of the transition system and α is the action labelling the transition, that q, q' are states of the transition system.

Now we give the definition of weak equivalence [19] in our context: the following transition relation, based on σ, permits to ignore silent transitions.

Let p and q be processes in Δ: $p \Longrightarrow q$ holds if and only if[1] there is a (possibly empty) sequence of silent transitions leading from p to q. If the sequence is empty, then $p = q$. For each action α, it is $p \xRightarrow{\alpha} q$ iff processes p' and q' exist such that: $p \xRightarrow{\epsilon} p' \xrightarrow{\alpha} q' \xRightarrow{\epsilon} q$. Thus, $p \xRightarrow{\alpha} q$ holds if p can reach q by performing an α action, possibly preceded and followed by sequences of τ actions. For each action α, $\widehat{\alpha}$ stands for ϵ if $\alpha = \tau$, and for α otherwise.

Definition 1 *(Weak Equivalence). Let p and q be two processes.*

– *A weak bisimulation, $\mathcal{B}$, is a binary relation on Δ such that $p \mathcal{B} q$ implies:*
   (i) $p \xrightarrow{\alpha} p'$ implies $\exists q'$ such that $q \xRightarrow{\widehat{\alpha}} q'$ with $p' \mathcal{B} q'$; and

---

[1] We use iff thereafter.

(ii) $q \xrightarrow{\alpha} q'$ *implies* $\exists p'$ *such that* $p \xRightarrow{\widehat{\alpha}} p'$ *with* $p' \mathcal{B} q'$
- *p and q are weakly equivalent ($p \approx q$) iff there exists a weak bisimulation $\mathcal{B}$ containing the pair (p, q).*

Note that we use the notation of $\approx$ equivalently for processes and for transition systems.

3   The *k*-Bisimulation

Defining the similarity, or distance, between mathematical objects in some class is generally an important undertaking, and there is no exception in process algebra setting. Inspired by the Hamming and Levenshtein distance [12,15], we propose a new bisimulation for processes defined in the process algebra context, the *k*-bisimulation, which, to the best of our knowledge, has never been defined before. In information theory, the Levenshtein distance between two strings is the number of modifications needed to transform a string into the other, whilst the Hamming's distance refers to strings of equal length and measures the number of positions with corresponding different symbols. When we switch in the process algebra setting, the *k*-bisimulation measures the minimum number of transitions of two transition systems to be relabelled in order to make the two processes equivalent. It is well known that a large number of graph similarity measures have been proposed in literature, as, for example, the edit distance [28]. The overall idea of a graph distance is to define the dissimilarity of two graphs by the minimum amount of distortion that is needed to transform one graph into another. Traditionally, the computation of a graph distance is carried out by means of a tree search algorithm which explores the space of all possible mappings of the nodes and edges of the first graph to the nodes and edges of the second graph, performing several heavy graph operations, like edge-insertion, edge-deletion, node-insertion, node-deletion. Using all these transformations we could reach strong equivalence between processes. The aim is to obtain equivalence in a simpler way and at a lower cost, so we try to reach weak equivalence instead. Consequently, the only transformation we perform is the setting of the labels of some transitions to τ. *k*-bisimulation captures the dissimilarity between p and q when they are not weak equivalent. In fact, given a natural number k and two processes p and q, we say that p and q are *k*-bisimilar if they differ from at most k moves.

Note that the use of bisimulation allows us to obtain a measure of dissimilarity that includes an evaluation of the structure of the two processes (even if not so accurate as when using branching equivalence [14]) and not only of the sequences of performed moves. We start from the definition of *k*-relabelled transition system.

Definition 2 (*k*-relabelled Transition System). *Let k be a natural number and r a process, $\mathcal{T}^k(r)$ is the set of the transition systems obtained relabeling by τ at most k transitions of the standard transition system of r (denoted in the following $\mathcal{S}(r)$).*

The notion of k-bisimulation is as follows.

Definition 3 (k-**bisimulation**). *Two processes p and q are k-bisimilar ($p \approx_k q$) iff there exist a natural number k and two transition systems, $t' \in \mathcal{T}^k(p)$ and $t'' \in \mathcal{T}^k(q)$, such that $t' \approx t''$.*

For example, in Fig. 2, the process p and q are 1-bisimilar. In fact, it is sufficient to relabel only one move of the process q, i.e., the transition $q \xrightarrow{a} q_1$ becomes $q \xrightarrow{\tau} q_1$.

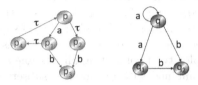

Fig. 2. Example of two transition systems not weak bisimilar

The following theorem holds, stating that if p and q are i-bisimilar then they are also j-bisimilar, for each $j > i$. Roughly speaking, given a measure k of the minimum level of dissimilarity between two processes, the same processes can be made more dissimilar by changing into τ any two equal actions for transitions, one in a process and one in the other.

Theorem 1. *Let p and q be two processes and i, j two natural numbers such that $j \geq i$.*

$$p \approx_i q \quad implies \quad p \approx_j q$$

Proof. Straightforward by Definition 3.

Obviously, when $k = 0$, $\mathcal{T}^0(p) = \{\mathcal{S}(p)\}$ for any process p, then 0-bisimulation between p and q coincides with the weak bisimulation (or with the strong bisimulation in absence of τ labels in the standard transition systems of p and q), which is an equivalence relation. It is worth noting that, on the contrary, the k-bisimulation is not in general an equivalence relation: in fact, it is easy to see that $\approx_k$ is reflexive and symmetric, but non transitive. As an example, consider the set of processes $\Delta = \{p, p_1, p_2, q, q_1, q_2, r, r_1, r_2\}$; the set of actions $\Theta = \{a, b, c, d\}$; and the function σ such that:

$$p \xrightarrow{a} p_1 \xrightarrow{b} p_2; \qquad q \xrightarrow{c} q_1 \xrightarrow{b} q_2; \qquad r \xrightarrow{c} r_1 \xrightarrow{d} r_2$$

It turns out that: $p \approx_1 q$, $q \approx_1 r$, while $p \not\approx_1 r$.

Nevertheless, it is possible to prove that k-bisimulation establishes a *distance* between processes since the triangle inequality holds (as in the example above). Resuming, several simple upper and lower bounds can be set for the dissimilarity between processes measured by the k-bisimulation:

- k is at least the maximum size of the sets (one for each process) of different actions of the transitions of the two processes;
- k is at most the size of the biggest between the sets of transitions of the two processes;
- k can be equal to zero iff if the processes are weak equivalent (or strong equivalent in absence of τ labels).

4   Computing k-Bisimulation

Suppose that we want to check whether $p \approx_k q$. A naive algorithm exhaustively substitutes all subsets consisting of at most k labels in the transition system of p with τ (the same for q) and, for each combination of substitutions, checks the weak equivalence between the transformed processes. It is easy to see that such algorithm has the complexity of computing all possible subsets containing 0 to k transitions of $\mathcal{S}(p)$ combined with all possible subsets of transitions of $\mathcal{S}(q)$ plus, for each combination, the cost of computing the weak equivalence. More formally, the maximum number of attempts is given as follows:

Definition 4 (Maximum Number of Attempts). *Let p and q be two processes. The maximum number of attempts to compute whether $p \approx_k q$ is:*

$$\left[\sum_{i=0}^{\min(k,n)} \binom{n}{i} \right] \left[\sum_{i=0}^{\min(k,m)} \binom{m}{i} \right] \tag{1}$$

where n is the number of transitions in $\mathcal{S}(p)$ labelled with actions different to τ, m is the number of transitions in $\mathcal{S}(q)$ labelled with actions different to τ, and $\binom{a}{b}$ is the binomial coefficient indexed by a and b.

Thus, exhaustive algorithms cannot be applied in the case of large graphs. We suggest the use of some heuristics for k-bisimulation checking; obviously, computing a heuristic function can be costly too. Notwithstanding, heuristics should be designed with care, otherwise the overhead introduced by the heuristics could waste the advantages it should provide.

Such heuristics comes out by the intuition that some combinations (i.e., some transitions which belong both to $T^k(p)$ and $T^k(q)$) have a higher probability than others to be the final solution. In this way, we reduce the cost of computing weak equivalence since we explore only subsets of transitions. Therefore, if the solution exists we can find it with lesser effort - compared with the effort required by the naive algorithm itself that explores all the possible attempts given by Definition 4.

In the following subsections, we present four heuristics to efficiently compute the k-bisimulation. Based on the aforementioned intuition, we consecutively apply our heuristics, i.e., when a heuristic is not able to establish that two transitions systems are k-bisimilar, we proceed by applying another one.

Before introducing the heuristics, we have to verify whether p and q cannot be k-bisimilar. Given the set of transitions of $\mathcal{S}(p)$ and $\mathcal{S}(q)$, we call, respectively, L_p and L_q the set of actions different from τ labelling transitions in such sets. The following theorem holds stating the condition of the non-existence of k-bisimilarity.

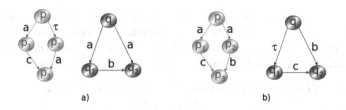

Fig. 3. *k*-bisimilar processes

Theorem 2 (Non-existence of *k*-bisimilarity). *Let p and q two processes. p and q cannot be k-bisimilar when:*

$$k < \underbrace{\max\{|L_p - (L_p \cap L_q)|, |L_q - (L_p \cap L_q)|\}}_{max\_value} \qquad (2)$$

Proof. Straightforward by Definition 3.

4.1 Preliminary Step: Sort Based Step

The first step is based on comparing the sets of the visible actions that the processes can perform. If p and q are not k-bisimilar, the primary cause is the existence of actions that p can perform and q cannot (or vice versa). Theorem 2 suggests that the transitions to be relabelled are all those having actions not in the set $L_p \cap L_q$. Accordingly, the "sort based" step operates as follows.

Definition 5 (Sort Based Step). *Let $\mathcal{S}(p)$ and $\mathcal{S}(q)$ be two transition systems. We define:*

$$N = \{(r, \alpha, r') \in \mathcal{S}(p) \mid \alpha \notin L_q\}; \qquad M = \{(s, \alpha, s') \in \mathcal{S}(q) \mid \alpha \notin L_p\}.$$

Roughly speaking, the sort based step sets to τ all the actions which belong to set L_p, but which do not belong to the set L_q (and vice versa). We apply once the weak equivalence after simultaneously setting to τ all such actions. If the processes are weak equivalent then they also are k-bisimilar. After applying the sort based step, the number of actions set to τ is different for the two transition systems: for $\mathcal{S}(p)$ that number is $k_p = k - |N|$ (i.e., we decrement k of the number of actions set to τ in $\mathcal{S}(p)$), while for $\mathcal{S}(q)$ that number is $k_q = k - |M|$ (i.e., we decrement k of the number of actions set to τ in $\mathcal{S}(q)$).

For instance, let us consider the transition systems of Fig. 3a. In order to make p and q k-bisimilar for some k, it is necessary to change into τ at least the action c in p, and the action b in q. In this case, it is $p \approx_1 q$ with lower bound $k = 1$. For the transition systems of Fig. 3b, the two processes are 2-bisimilar since two labels in p must be changed. Clearly, this heuristics is not useful when $L_p = L_q$.

After this first necessary step, we define several heuristic functions that, given $\mathcal{S}(p)$ and $\mathcal{S}(q)$, return two subsets of transitions N of $\mathcal{S}(p)$ and M of $\mathcal{S}(q)$.

These subsets are used to reduce the number of possible attempts stated by the Definition 4, since we assume that the probability of relabeling to τ an action of the triples in N and M is higher than that of relabeling any other triple.

More formally, an heuristic function is generically defined as:

Definition 6 (Heuristic Function h). *Let T_1 and T_2 be two transition systems, $h(T_1, T_2) = \langle N, M \rangle$, where $N \subseteq T_1$ and $M \subseteq T_2$.*

All the actions of triples which belong to $N \cup M$ represent all the possible candidates to be set to τ. Thus, we first consider all the combinations given by Definition 4 where n (resp. m) is the size of the set N (resp. M) returned by the heuristic function. For each combination, we apply weak equivalence checking. Note that, even if applying all the heuristic functions defined in the following section, we do not necessarily succeed in deciding the k-bisimulation, we may have to explore all the possible remaining configurations. Now we are ready to introduce the first heuristics.

4.2   Counterexample Based Heuristics

When we perform equivalence checking, formal verification tools return a counterexample when the result of the equivalence is false. Typically, counterexamples are modelled as transition systems and specify the actions that one process can carry out in a state while the other one in the corresponding state cannot, we call θ the set of these actions; the "counterexample based" heuristics is built upon θ.

Definition 7 (Counterexample Based Heuristics h_1). *Let $\mathcal{S}(p)$ and $\mathcal{S}(q)$ be two transition systems.*

- *Check whether $\mathcal{S}(p) \approx \mathcal{S}(q)$. Let C be the counterexample returned and θ the set of actions occurring in C such that one process can carry out it in a state while the other one cannot when reached the corresponding state.*
- *$h_1(\mathcal{S}(p), \mathcal{S}(q)) = \langle N, M \rangle$, where*

$$N = \{ (r, \alpha, r') \in \mathcal{S}(p) \mid \alpha \in \theta \}; \quad M = \{ (r, \alpha, r') \in \mathcal{S}(q) \mid \alpha \in \theta \}.$$

The Counterexample based heuristics uses the result of weak equivalence checking between the initial processes and creates two subsets of transitions N of $\mathcal{S}(p)$ and M of $\mathcal{S}(q)$ based on the generated counterexample. For example, from the counterexample returned by CADP [13] we can easily individuate θ, since the terminal states of the diagnostic have additional "error" outgoing transitions with labels, for example, of the form "Present in p: α"(or "Absent in p: α"), indicating that the action α cannot be matched by the other process q. Consider again the processes q e p in Fig. 2, the "counterexample based" heuristic based on CADP [13] builds $\theta = \{a\}$. In fact, after reaching q_1 through $q \xrightarrow{\alpha} q_1$, q_1 can perform only the action b, while each state reachable from p using $\xRightarrow{\hat{\alpha}}$ can perform also the action a besides b. Accordingly, we create the subsets $N = \{(p, a, p_1)\}$ and $M = \{(q, a, q_1), (q, a, q)\}$.

4.3   Different Behaviour Based Heuristics

This heuristics works by analysing the behaviour of the states of the transition systems. Let s be a state of a transition system, $\mathcal{O}(s)$ denotes the set of actions labelling ingoing and outgoing transitions of s. More precisely:

Definition 8 ($\mathcal{O}(s)$). *Let s be a process in Δ and T its labelled transition system.*

$$\mathcal{O}(s) = \langle S_1, S_2 \rangle \qquad where:$$
$$S_1 = \{\, \alpha \mid (r, \alpha, r') \in T \ and \ r' = s, \ \alpha \neq \tau \,\};$$
$$S_2 = \{\, \alpha \mid (r, \alpha, r') \in T \ and \ r = s, \ \alpha \neq \tau \,\}.$$

Roughly speaking, S_1 (resp. S_2) is the set of all ingoing (resp. outgoing) actions labelling transitions of the state s. We can say that two states, s and s', have a "similar behaviour" when $\mathcal{O}(s) = \mathcal{O}(s')$. Thus, the heuristics looks for states that have not a similar behaviour considering all the transitions of $\mathcal{S}(p)$ and $\mathcal{S}(q)$. The "different behaviour based" heuristics operates as follows.

Definition 9 (Different Behaviour Based Heuristics h_2). *Let $\mathcal{S}(p)$ and $\mathcal{S}(q)$ be two transition systems. First, we define the sets X and Y as follows:*

$$X = \{\, x \text{ state of } \mathcal{S}(p) \mid \forall y \text{ state of } \mathcal{S}(q) \text{ it holds that } \mathcal{O}(x) \neq \mathcal{O}(y) \,\};$$
$$Y = \{\, y \text{ state of } \mathcal{S}(q) \mid \forall x \text{ state of } \mathcal{S}(p) \text{ it holds that } \mathcal{O}(y) \neq \mathcal{O}(x) \,\}.$$

Now, we define N and M:

$$N = \{\, (r, \alpha, r') \in \mathcal{S}(p), \ (r', \alpha, r) \in \mathcal{S}(p) \mid r \in X \,\};$$
$$M = \{\, (s, \alpha, s') \in \mathcal{S}(q), \ (s', \alpha, s) \in \mathcal{S}(q) \mid s \in Y \,\}.$$

Thus, $h_2(\mathcal{S}(p), \mathcal{S}(q)) = \langle N, M \rangle$.

The "different behaviour based" heuristics creates $\mathcal{O}(s)$ (resp. $\mathcal{O}(s')$) for each state of $\mathcal{S}(p)$ (resp. $\mathcal{S}(q)$). Then, it collects (in the sets X and Y) all states s in a transition system for which there does not exist a state s' in the other transition system with a similar behaviour ($\mathcal{O}(s) = \mathcal{O}(s')$) creating two subsets of transitions N of $\mathcal{S}(p)$ and M of $\mathcal{S}(q)$. For example, let us consider again the processes q e p in Fig. 2. The sets of $\mathcal{O}(s)$ for the transition system of p and q are:

$$\mathcal{O}(p) = \langle \varnothing, \{a\} \rangle \qquad\qquad \mathcal{O}(q) = \langle \{a\}, \{a, b\} \rangle$$
$$\mathcal{O}(p_1) = \langle \{a\}, \{b\} \rangle \qquad\qquad \mathcal{O}(q_1) = \langle \{a\}, \{b\} \rangle$$
$$\mathcal{O}(p_2) = \langle \{\varnothing, \{b\} \rangle \qquad\qquad \mathcal{O}(q_2) = \langle \{b\}, \varnothing \rangle$$
$$\mathcal{O}(p_3) = \langle \{b\}, \varnothing \rangle$$
$$\mathcal{O}(p_4) = \langle \varnothing, \varnothing \rangle \,.$$

It turns out that: $X = \{p, p_2, p_4\}$, while $Y = \{q\}$. Thus, we create the following two subsets M and N as explained above:

$$N = \{(p, a, p_1), (p_2, b, p_3)\}; \qquad M = \{(q, a, q), (q, a, q_1), (q, b, q_2)\}.$$

4.4   Jaccard Based Heuristics

The following heuristic can be used only when we want to check the k-bisimilarity between two processes with $k = 1$. It employs the information gained by the "different behaviour based" heuristic and exploits the dissimilarity between processes calculated by means of the Jaccard index [17]. The latter is defined as follows:

Definition 10 (Jaccard index). *Let A and B be two sets, then:*

$$J(A, B) = \frac{|A \cap B|}{|A \cup B|} \tag{3}$$

where $0 \leq J(A, B) \leq 1$.

We use the following notation. If $s \in \Delta$ and $\mathcal{O}(s) = \langle A, B \rangle$, with $\mathcal{O}'(s)$ we denote the set $A \cup B$. The heuristic operates as follows:

Definition 11 (Jaccard based heuristics h_3). *Let $\mathcal{S}(p)$ and $\mathcal{S}(q)$ be two transition systems. First, we define the sets X and Y as done for the Different behaviour based heuristic.*

$$X = \{\, x \text{ state of } \mathcal{S}(p) \mid \forall y \text{ state of } \mathcal{S}(q) \text{ it holds that } \mathcal{O}(x) \neq \mathcal{O}(y) \,\};$$
$$Y = \{\, y \text{ state of } \mathcal{S}(q) \mid \forall x \text{ state of } \mathcal{S}(p) \text{ it holds that } \mathcal{O}(y) \neq \mathcal{O}(x) \,\}.$$

Then,

$$S = \{\, (s_1, s_2) \mid s_1 \in X, \ s_2 \in Y \text{ and } J(\mathcal{O}'(s_1), \mathcal{O}'(s_2)) \geq 0.5 \,\};$$
$$N = \{\, (r, \alpha, r') \in \mathcal{S}(p), \ (r', \alpha, r) \in \mathcal{S}(p) \mid \exists (r, s) \in S \,\};$$
$$M = \{\, (s, \alpha, s') \in \mathcal{S}(q), \ (s', \alpha, s) \in \mathcal{S}(q) \mid \exists (r, s) \in S \,\}.$$

Thus, $h_3(\mathcal{S}(p), \mathcal{S}(q)) = \langle N, M \rangle$.

Roughly speaking, the Jaccard based heuristics creates two subsets of transitions N of $\mathcal{S}(p)$ based on X and M of $\mathcal{S}(q)$ based on Y. After that, it computes S which considers the Jaccard index $J(A, B) \geq 0.5$. In fact, if $J(A, B) < 0.5$ the processes are not 1-bisimilar, since it must be $k \geq 1$.

For example, let consider the processes q and p in Fig. 4. The states where $\mathcal{O}(s) \neq \mathcal{O}(s')$ are p_3 and p_6 belonging to $\mathcal{S}(p)$ and q_3 and q_6 belonging to $\mathcal{S}(q)$, i.e., $X = \{p_3, p_6\}$ and $Y = \{q_3, q_6\}$. It turns out that

$$\mathcal{O}'(p_3) = \{d, c\},$$
$$\mathcal{O}'(p_6) = \{c, a\},$$
$$\mathcal{O}'(q_3) = \{d\} \quad \text{and}$$
$$\mathcal{O}'(q_6) = \{a, d\}.$$

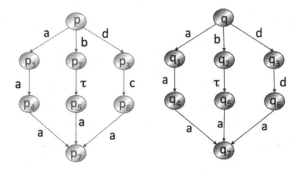

Fig. 4. 1-bisimilar processes

The Jaccard similarities for these states are

$$J(p_3, q_3) = 0.5,$$
$$J(p_3, q_6) = 0.33,$$
$$J(p_6, q_3) = 0.33,$$
$$J(p_6, q_6) = 0.$$

Then, $S = \{(p_3, q_3)\}$.

Thus, we only have to consider the states p_3 and q_3 and build the two subsets $N = \{(p, d, p_3), (p_3, c, p_6)\}$ and $M = \{(q, d, q_3), (q_3, d, q_6)\}$.

4.5 Action Occurrence Based Heuristics

The last heuristics is based on the number of transitions labelled with the same action belonging to a transition system $\mathcal{S}(p)$ compared to another transition system $\mathcal{S}(q)$. The "action occurrence based" heuristics operates as follows.

Definition 12 (Action occurrence based heuristics h_4). *Let $\mathcal{S}(p)$ and $\mathcal{S}(q)$ be two transition systems.*

– for each $\alpha \in L_p$, n_α is the number of transitions $(r, \alpha, r') \in \mathcal{S}(p)$;
– for each $\alpha \in L_q$, m_α is the number of transitions $(s, \alpha, s') \in \mathcal{S}(q)$.

We define N and M as follows:

$$N = \{ (r, \alpha, r') \in \mathcal{S}(p) \mid n_\alpha \neq m_\alpha \};$$
$$M = \{ (s, \alpha, s') \in \mathcal{S}(q) \mid n_\alpha \neq m_\alpha \}.$$

Thus, $h_4(\mathcal{S}(p), \mathcal{S}(q)) = \langle N, M \rangle$.

Roughly speaking, the action occurrence based heuristic compares the number of transitions labelled with an action α of a process with the number of transitions labelled with the same action α of the other process. Then, it creates the two subsets of transitions N of $\mathcal{S}(p)$ and M of $\mathcal{S}(q)$ based on the result of the previous comparison.

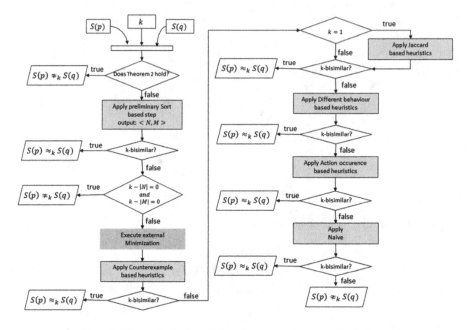

Fig. 5. Flow chart describing the core of our methodology

For instance, let consider the processes p and q in Fig. 3b. The first process contains: 2 times a and once for either b or c. Thus, $n_a = 2$ and $n_b = n_c = 1$. Whilst the second one yet contains once either b or c, so $n_b = n_c = 1$. Thus, we create two subsets $N = \{(p, a, p_a), (p, a, p_2)\}$ and $M = \varnothing$.

4.6   How the Heuristics Are Applied

All the heuristics are independent each other and we may choose any order. To efficiently figure out if two processes are k-bisimilar, we need to apply the presented heuristics in a precise order, as shown in Fig. 5. Based on empirical evaluation, we figured out such a order. We apply the next heuristics only when the previous one is not able to establish that two processes are k-bisimilar. Of course, when we consider a new heuristics we avoid to call the weak equivalence checker on the previous already explored space of solutions.

Before deciding the order of the application of each heuristic function, several experiments were run with different combinations and the presented order gave the best results.

Thus, Fig. 5 constitutes the core of our methodology. We called it "k-btH", i.e., k-bisimulation through Heuristics. Each heuristics re-applies weak equivalence checking starting from $k = 1$ until the desired k.

The process starts with two transition systems, i.e., $\mathcal{S}(p)$ and $\mathcal{S}(q)$ and the natural number k. First we verify whether the Theorem 2 holds. In this case the processes are not k-bisimilar. Conversely, if the Theorem 2 does not hold we apply the preliminary "Sort based" step setting to τ all the transitions which belong to a process, but which do not belong to the other one (and vice versa). If the processes are not yet k-bisimilar, the workflow proceeds only if we can set to τ further actions either in $\mathcal{S}(p)$ or in $\mathcal{S}(q)$, applying the external minimization of the processes. Successively the "Counterexample based" heuristic is executed. In case the latter is not able to figure out the k-bisimilarity, we apply the "Jaccard based" heuristics only if $k = 1$. We keep applying the heuristics "Different behaviour based", and "Action occurrence based" until either the processes are k-bisimilar or we apply the "brute force" way, i.e., the "Naive" algorithm, which constitutes the last chance to check k-bisimilarity and it also is the most inefficient way to do it. In fact, the "Naive" algorithm explores all the possible remaining configurations. Notwithstanding, such an algorithm has not been implemented strictly following Definition 4. Some optimizations have been introduced in order to further improve the calculation of the k-bisimulation. For example, we empirically noticed that it is better to examine first the configurations with $i = 0$, for both processes and then for $i = 1$ and so on.

5   Application Fields of the k-Bisimulation

The concept of the k-bisimulation has, in our knowledge, never been proposed before, but it can be usefully employed in several application fields. In the following we analyse in more detail the application of the k-bisimulation in five different fields.

5.1   Clone Detection

Reusing code fragments by copying and pasting with minor modifications is customary in software development. As a result, software systems often contain sections of code that are similar, i.e., code clones. Clone detection [24] has been recognized as an important issue in software analysis and it is an active field of research. In [9] the authors presented the design and implementation of CD-Form (Clone Detector based on FORmal Methods), a tool targeted at the detection of Type-2 clones. CD-Form is based on the analysis of the Java bytecode that is transformed into CCS processes, which are checked for equivalence. The more suitable application field for the k-bisimulation is the detection of Type-3 clones, where the minimum k gives a measure of the effort to obtain a clone of maximal length. Clearly, there are other existing measures of Type-3 clone similarity. However, the use of the k-bisimulation can be useful in the CD-Form tool that is valuable also in different contexts.

5.2   Process Mining

Process mining is a process management technique that allows the analysis of business processes using the event logs. The basic idea is to extract knowledge from event logs recorded by the company information system to retrieve the model of the performed process and to compare this model against the required behavior for that type of company. Techniques and tools are defined and several algorithms have been developed to reconstruct causality from a set of sequences of events [2], as for example the α-algorithm [1]. k-bisimulation can be used to evaluate the outputs of different algorithms and to compare how closely related they are to the real processes [20].

5.3   Business-IT Alignment

Business organizations have become heavily dependent on information technology (IT) services. The process of alignment is defined as the mutual synchronization of business goals and IT services [27]. The alignment between business objectives and the IT requirements, maintained over time, is crucial to the success of an enterprise [8]. Thus, there is a need to elaborate and evaluate models, techniques and methodologies supporting the detection and understanding of misalignment between business and technological objectives. Recent surveys, however, concluded that in most companies IT is not aligned with business strategy, therefore this is still a prominent area of concern. Process mining techniques, aiming at discovering a process model from the log, can be usefully employed for this purpose. k-bisimulation can help to evaluate the misalignment between a predefined process model and the software system that should realize that process in a company.

5.4   Wiki Design

Wikis are becoming a new work tool in enterprises and are widely spreading everywhere. Indeed, it is important to consider the design and evolution of a wiki. The k-bisimulation may be exploited to obtain a starting point to design a wiki or a wiki category, i.e., a set of pages regarding a specific topic, looking for similar structures [11].

5.5   Malware Analysis

Software that aims to produce damaging intent is defined as malicious code (or malware). Malware analysis is the process of understanding the behavior and purpose of a sample (such as a virus, worm, or Trojan horse), in order to develop effective detection techniques and tools. Since malware is rare to change even after a sequence of syntactic code transformations, researchers have investigated behaviour-based techniques [21]. We claim that after formal modelling a malware, the k-bisimulation may constitute a building block to figure out even subtle differences between malicious and non-malicious behaviours.

6   Experimental Results

In this section we discuss experimental results conducted on six well known systems with increasing number of actions and states: **Demos_13_A1** and

Table 1. Experimental results on six well known systems

	Case Study (transitions, states)	Maximum number of attempts: Definition 4	$k-$btH	Naive Algorithm
k=1	**Demos_13_A1** (32, 16)	1055	5	352
	Demos_13_B2 (48, 27)	991	11	744
	2 Philosophers (138, 74)	6319	85	6241
	Diva (418, 213)	99854	142	98590
	CM-ASE (1749, 926)	1763531	36	1143355
	CRAIL (17362, 3616)	130564901	7	1005488
k=2	**Demos_13_A1** (32, 16)	231580	1748	197593
	Demos_13_B2 (48, 27)	279313	5	273350
	2 Philosophers (138, 74)	9988761	34	3240
	Diva (418, 213)	2477102672	1829	39058
	CM-ASE (1749, 926)	777558453953	3618	930804953

Demos_13_B2[2] from CADP [13]; **2-philosophers**: the popular dining philosophers problem with a size of 2 [4]; **Diva**: a Video on Demand distributed application developed at the University of Naples, called *DIstributed Video Architecture* (DiVA), and it can be operated both in a WAN or a LAN scenario (a CCS specification can be found in [18]); **CM-ASE**: Context Management Application Service Element (CM-ASE) - a model of the Application Layer of the Aeronautical Telecommunications Network, developed by Gurov and Kapron[3]; **Railway system (Crail)**: the system specification given in [4]. This system describes the British Rail's Solid State Interlocking which is devoted "to adjust, at the request of the signal operator, the setting of signal and points in the railway to permit the safe passage of trains". Note that in Table 1, the number of transitions of all the case studies include the τ actions.

---

[2] http://cadp.inria.fr/demos.html.
[3] http://webhome.cs.uvic.ca/~bmkapron/ccs.html.

We have implemented a prototype Java tool and employed the popular CADP [13] toolbox as equivalence checker and external minimizator tool, for the purpose of computing the k-bisimulation on the aforementioned systems.

In Table 1 we compare the performance of our methodology "k-btH" - k-bisimulation through Heuristics - against the direct application of the Maximum number of attempts, given in Definition 4 and "Naive Algorithm" as described in Sect. 4.6. For performance we do not intend execution time, but the number of attempts to figure out whether the processes are k-bisimilar.

We checked the k-bisimulation with $k = 1$ and $k = 2$, since it is useful only when two processes are very similar. Furthermore, in order to test our methodology for each case study we obtained the two processes to compare to randomly modifying each one. In other words, we modified each process randomly changing at most one action or two actions (using actions in the sort of the process) respectively for $k = 1$ and $k = 2$. The percentage of reduction was over 90 % in all the experiments and in some case very near to 100 %, whilst the execution time was maximum 10 min. It is worth noting that the k-bisimulation is useful especially when the two processes are very similar. Thus, in order to test our methodology we check the k-bisimulation with small values of k. Clearly, it is not very interesting to apply k-bisimulation when the systems have a vastly different structure. Therefore, the proposed method works well for processes that are very similar and no advantage is obtained when the systems are not k-bisimilar.

7   Conclusion and Related Work

We have presented a methodology to quantify dissimilarities between processes based on the concept of k-bisimulation. The latter takes into account the extension of the unlikeness between two given processes. In order to efficiently compute the k-bisimulation, we have proposed several heuristics and a workflow to properly apply them. Moreover, we have implemented a prototype tool for the purpose of testing our methodology, obtaining very good results on six well knowns systems. The application of such bisimulation may involve different contexts from clone detection to process mining and malware analysis.

In the last few years we can find in the literature different notions of distance between processes that try to quantify "how far away" is a process to be related with some other with respect to a certain semantics. Most of them base their definitions on the (bi)simulation game that characterizes (bi)simulations between processes [5,6]. These distances have a local character since only one of the successors of each state is taken into account in their computation.

Moreover, these approaches cannot synthesize a system that minimizes a distance from a given specification.

In our work we remove these limitations by means of our new k-bisimulation. First of all, our k-bisimulation has a global view of the two processes, being able to hide moves in every point of the two labelled transition systems representing the two processes, still preserving weak equivalence. Secondly, we are able to find the minimum k such that two processes are k-bisimilar. A similar approach can be found in [22,23]. The authors propose a theoretical study of co-inductive distances and they use quantitative versions of the bisimulation game.

We instead move from the theoretical study to the practical application, proposing several heuristics to effectively compute the *k*-bisimulation. Moreover, we focus only on the weak bisimulation reaching good results. We plan to apply *k*-bisimulation in other fields, as for example secure information flow in concurrent systems [10] or for both incremental design and system evolution scenarios [26].

References

1. Van der Aalst, W., Weijters, T., Maruster, L.: Workflow mining: discovering process models from event logs. IEEE Trans. Knowl. Data Eng. **16**(9), 1128–1142 (2004)
2. Alkhammash, E., Fathabadi, A.S., Butler, M.J., Cîrstea, C.: Building traceable Event-B models from requirements. ECEASST **66**, 1–16 (2013)
3. Bolognesi, T., Brinksma, E.: Introduction to the ISO specification language LOTOS. Comput. Netw. ISDN Syst. **14**(1), 25–59 (1987)
4. Bruns, G.: A case study in safety-critical design. In: von Bochmann, G., Probst, D.K. (eds.) CAV 1992. LNCS, vol. 663, pp. 220–233. Springer, Heidelberg (1993)
5. Černý, P., Henzinger, T.A., Radhakrishna, A.: Simulation distances. In: Gastin, P., Laroussinie, F. (eds.) CONCUR 2010. LNCS, vol. 6269, pp. 253–268. Springer, Heidelberg (2010)
6. Chen, X., Deng, Y.: Game characterizations of process equivalences. In: Ramalingam, G. (ed.) APLAS 2008. LNCS, vol. 5356, pp. 107–121. Springer, Heidelberg (2008)
7. Cleaveland, R., Sims, S.: The NCSU concurrency workbench. In: Alur, R., Henzinger, T.A. (eds.) CAV 1996. LNCS, vol. 1102. Springer, Heidelberg (1996)
8. Conchon, S., Krstic, S.: Strategies for combining decision procedures. Theor. Comput. Sci. **354**(2), 187–210 (2006)
9. Cuomo, A., Santone, A., Villano, U.: CD-Form: a clone detector based on formal methods. Sci. Comput. Program. **95**, 390–405 (2014)
10. De Francesco, N., Santone, A., Tesei, L.: Abstract interpretation and model checking for checking secure information flow in concurrent systems. Fundamenta Informaticae **54**(2), 195–211 (2003)
11. De Ruvo, G., Santone, A.: Equivalence-based selection of best-fit models to support wiki design. In: Reddy, S. (ed.) WETICE 2015, pp. 204–209. IEEE Press, New York (2015)
12. Delsarte, P., Levenshtein, V.I.: Association schemes and coding theory. IEEE Trans. Inf. Theor. **44**(6), 2477–2504 (1998)
13. Garavel, H., Lang, F., Mateescu, R., Serwe, W.: CADP 2011: a toolbox for the construction and analysis of distributed processes. STTT **15**(2), 89–107 (2013)
14. van Glabbeek, R.J.: The linear time - branching time spectrum. In: Baeten, J.C.M., Klop, J.W. (eds.) CONCUR '90 Theories of Concurrency: Unification and Extension. LNCS, vol. 458, pp. 278–297. Springer, Heidelberg (1990)
15. Hamming, R.W.: Error detecting and error correcting codes. Bell Syst. Tech. J. **29**(2), 147–160 (1950)
16. Hoare, C.: Communicating sequential processes. Commun. ACM **21**(8), 666–677 (1978)
17. Jacquart, P.: Nouvelles recherches sur la distribution florale. Bull. Soc. Vand. Sci. Nat. **44**, 223–270 (1908)

18. Mazzocca, N., Santone, A., Vaglini, G., Vittorini, V.: Efficient model checking of properties of a distributed application: a multimedia case study. Softw. Test. Verif. Reliab. **12**(1), 3–21 (2002)
19. Milner, R.: Communication and Concurrency. Prentice Hall, London (1989). Prentice Hall International Series in Computer Science
20. Nguyen, H.N., Poizat, P., Zaïdi, F.: A symbolic framework for the conformance checking of value-passing choreographies. In: Liu, C., Ludwig, H., Toumani, F., Yu, Q. (eds.) Service Oriented Computing. LNCS, vol. 7636, pp. 525–532. Springer, Heidelberg (2012)
21. Palahan, S., Babic, D., Chaudhuri, S., Kifer, D.: Extraction of statistically significant malware behaviors. In: Paynre Jr., C.N. (ed.) ACSAC 2013, pp. 69–78. ACM, New York (2013)
22. Romero Hernández, D., de Frutos Escrig, D.: Defining distances for all process semantics. In: Giese, H., Rosu, G. (eds.) FORTE 2012 and FMOODS 2012. LNCS, vol. 7273, pp. 169–185. Springer, Heidelberg (2012)
23. Romero-Hernández, D., de Frutos Escrig, D.: Coinductive definition of distances between processes: beyond bisimulation distances. In: Ábrahám, E., Palamidessi, C. (eds.) FORTE 2014. LNCS, vol. 8461, pp. 249–265. Springer, Heidelberg (2014)
24. Roy, C., Cordy, J., Koschke, R.: Comparison and evaluation of code clone detection techniques and tools: a qualitative approach. Sci. Comput. Program. **74**(7), 470–495 (2009)
25. Santone, A., Vaglini, G.: Abstract reduction in directed model checking CCS processes. Acta Informatica **49**(5), 313–341 (2012)
26. Santone, A., Vaglini, G., Villani, M.L.: Incremental construction of systems: an efficient characterization of the lacking sub-system. Sci. Comput. Program. **78**(9), 1346–1367 (2013)
27. Ullah, A., Lai, R.: A systematic review of business and information technology alignment. ACM Trans. Manage. Inf. Syst. **4**(1), 1–30 (2013)
28. Zeng, Z., Tung, A.K.H., Wang, J., Feng, J., Zhou, L.: Comparing stars: on approximating graph edit distance. PVLDB **2**(1), 25–36 (2009)

Time Complexity of Concurrent Programs
– A Technique Based on Behavioural Types –

Elena Giachino[1], Einar Broch Johnsen[2], Cosimo Laneve[1], and Ka I. Pun[2(✉)]

[1] Department of Computer Science and Engineering, University of Bologna – INRIA
FOCUS, Bologna, Italy
[2] Department of Informatics, University of Oslo, Oslo, Norway
violet@ifi.uio.no

Abstract. We study the problem of automatically computing the time
complexity of concurrent object-oriented programs. To determine this
complexity we use intermediate abstract descriptions that record relevant information for the time analysis (cost of statements, creations of
objects, and concurrent operations), called *behavioural types*. Then, we
define a translation function that takes behavioural types and makes
the parallelism explicit into so-called *cost equations*, which are fed to an
automatic off-the-shelf solver for obtaining the time complexity.

1 Introduction

Computing the cost of a sequential algorithm has always been a primary question
for every programmer, who learns the basic techniques in the first years of their
computer science or engineering curriculum. This cost is defined in terms of the
input values to the algorithm and over-approximates the number of the executed
instructions. In turn, given an appropriate abstraction of the CPU speed of a
runtime system, one can obtain the expected computation time of the algorithm.

The computational cost of algorithms is particularly relevant in mainstream
architectures, such as the cloud. In that context, a service is a concurrent program that must comply with a so-called *service-level agreement* (SLA) regulat-
ing the cost in time and assigning penalties for its infringement [3]. The service
provider needs to make sure that the service is able to meet the SLA, for example
in terms of the end-user response time, by deciding on a resource management
policy and determining the appropriate number of virtual machine instances (or
containers) and their parameter settings (e.g., their CPU speeds). To help service
providers make correct decisions about the resource management before actually deploying the service, we need static analysis methods for resource-aware
services [6]. In previous work by the authors, cloud deployments expressed in
the formal modeling language ABS [8] have used a combination of cost analysis
and simulations to analyse resource management [1], and a Hoare-style proof
system to reason about end-user deadlines has been developed for sequential

Supported by the EU projects FP7-610582 ENVISAGE: Engineering Virtualized Services (http://www.envisage-project.eu).

© Springer International Publishing Switzerland 2016
C. Braga and P.C. Ölveczky (Eds.): FACS 2015, LNCS 9539, pp. 199–216, 2016.
DOI: 10.1007/978-3-319-28934-2_11

executions [7]. In contrast, we are here interested in statically estimating the computation time of concurrent services deployed on the cloud with a given dynamic resource management policy.

Technically, this paper proposes a behavioural type system expressing the resource costs associated with computations and study how these types can be used to soundly calculate the time complexity of parallel programs deployed on the cloud. To succinctly formulate this problem, our work is developed for tml, a small formally defined concurrent object-oriented language which uses asynchronous communications to trigger parallel activities. The language defines virtual machine instances in terms of dynamically created concurrent object groups with bounds on the number of cycles they can perform per time interval. As we are interested in the concurrent aspects of these computations, we abstract from sequential analysis in terms of a statement $job(e)$, which defines the number of processing cycles required by the instruction – this is similar to the sleep(n) operation in Java.

The analysis of behavioural types is defined by translating them in a code that is adequate for an off-the-shelf solver – the CoFloCo solver [4]. As a consequence, we are able to determine the computational cost of algorithms in a parametric way with respect to their inputs.

Paper overview. The language is defined in Sect. 2 and we discuss restrictions that ease the development of our technique in Sect. 3. Section 4 presents the behavioural type system and Sect. 5 explains the analysis of computation time based on these behavioural types. In Sect. 6 we outline our correctness proof of the type system with respect to the cost equations. In Sect. 7 we discuss the relevant related work and in Sect. 8 we deliver concluding remarks.

2   The Language tml

The syntax and the semantics of tml are defined in the following two subsections; the third subsection discusses a few examples.

Syntax. A tml program is a sequence of method definitions $T\ m(\overline{T\ x})\{\overline{F\ y}\ ;\ s\}$, ranged over by M, plus a main body $\{\overline{F\ z}\ ;\ s'\}$ with k. In tml we distinguish between *simple types* T which are either integers Int or classes Class (there is just one class in tml), and *types* F, which also include *future types* Fut<T>. These future types let asynchronous method invocations be typed (see below). The notation $\overline{T\ x}$ denotes any finite sequence of *variable declarations* $T\ x$. The elements of the sequence are separated by commas. When we write $\overline{T\ x}\ ;$ we mean a sequence $T_1\ x_1\ ;\ \cdots\ ;\ T_n\ x_n\ ;$ when the sequence is not empty; we mean the possibly empty sequence otherwise.

The syntax of statements s, expressions with side-effects z and expressions e of tml is defined by the following grammar:

$$s ::= x = z \ \mid\ \text{if } e \ \{s\} \text{ else } \{s\} \ \mid\ job(e) \ \mid\ \text{return } e \ \mid\ s\ ;\ s$$
$$z ::= e \ \mid\ e!m(\overline{e}) \ \mid\ e.m(\overline{x}) \ \mid\ e.\text{get} \ \mid\ \text{new Class with } e \ \mid\ \text{new local Class}$$
$$e ::= \text{this} \ \mid\ se \ \mid\ nse$$

A statement s may be either one of the standard operations of an imperative language or the job statement $\mathtt{job}(e)$ that delays the continuation by e cycles of the machine executing it.

An expression z may change the state of the system. In particular, it may be an *asynchronous* method invocation of the form $e\,!\mathtt{m}(\overline{e})$, which does not suspend the caller's execution. When the value computed by the invocation is needed, the caller performs a *non-blocking* $\mathtt{get}$ operation: if the value needed by a process is not available, then an awaiting process is scheduled and executed, i.e., *await-get*. Expressions z also include standard synchronous invocations $e.\mathtt{m}(\overline{e})$ and $\mathtt{new\ local\ Class}$, which creates a new object. The intended meaning is to create the object in the same machine – called *cog* or *concurrent object group* – of the caller, thus sharing the processor of the caller: operations in the same virtual machine interleave their evaluation (even if in the following operational semantics the parallelism is not explicit). Alternatively, one can create an object on a different cog with $\mathtt{new\ Class\ with}\ e$ thus letting methods execute in parallel. In this case, e represents the capacity of the new cog, that is, the number of cycles the cog can perform per time interval. We assume the presence of a special identifier $\mathtt{this.capacity}$ that returns the capacity of the corresponding cog.

A *pure* expression e can be the reserved identifier $\mathtt{this}$ or an integer expression. Since the analysis in Sect. 5 cannot deal with generic integer expressions, we parse expressions in a careful way. In particular we split them into *size expressions* se, which are expressions in Presburger arithmetics (this is a decidable fragment of Peano arithmetics that only contains addition), and *non-size expressions* nse, which are the other type of expressions. The syntax of size and non-size expressions is the following:

$$
\begin{aligned}
nse ::=\ & k\ \mid\ x\ \mid\ nse \le nse\ \mid\ nse\ \textbf{and}\ nse\ \mid\ nse\ \textbf{or}\ nse \\
& \mid\ nse + nse\ \mid\ nse - nse\ \mid\ nse \times nse\ \mid\ nse/nse \\
se ::=\ & ve\ \mid\ ve \le ve\ \mid\ se\ \textbf{and}\ se\ \mid\ se\ \textbf{or}\ se \\
ve ::=\ & k\ \mid\ x\ \mid\ ve + ve\ \mid\ k \times ve \\
k ::=\ & rational\ constants
\end{aligned}
$$

In the paper, we assume that sequences of declarations $\overline{T\ x}$ and method declarations $\overline{M}$ do not contain duplicate names. We also assume that $\mathtt{return}$ statements have no continuation.

Semantics. The semantics of $\mathtt{tml}$ is defined by a transition system whose states are *configurations* cn that are defined by the following syntax.

$$
\begin{aligned}
cn ::=\ & \varepsilon\ \mid\ fut(f, val)\ \mid\ ob(o, c, p, q)\ \mid\ invoc(o, f, \mathtt{m}, \overline{v}) & act ::=\ & o\ \mid\ \varepsilon \\
& \mid\ cog(c, act, k)\ \mid\ cn\ cn & val ::=\ & v\ \mid\ \bot \\
p ::=\ & \{\,l\ \mid\ s\,\}\ \mid\ \mathtt{idle} & l ::=\ & [\cdots, x \mapsto v, \cdots] \\
q ::=\ & \varnothing\ \mid\ \{\,l\ \mid\ s\,\}\ \mid\ q\ q & v ::=\ & o\ \mid\ f\ \mid\ k
\end{aligned}
$$

A *configuration* cn is a set of concurrent object groups (cogs), objects, invocation messages and futures, and the empty configuration is written as ε. The associative and commutative union operator on configurations is denoted by whitespace. A *cog* is given as a term $cog(c, act, k)$ where c and k are respectively the identifier and the capacity of the cog, and act specifies the currently active

$$\frac{\text{(COND-TRUE)}}{\text{true} = [\![e]\!]_l}{ob(o,c,\{\,l\mid \textbf{if } e \;\{\,s_1\,\}\textbf{ else }\{\,s_2\,\}\;;\;s\,\},q)} \to ob(o,c,\{\,l\mid s_1\;;\;s\,\},q)$$

$$\frac{\text{(COND-FALSE)}}{\text{false} = [\![e]\!]_l}{ob(o,c,\{\,l\mid \textbf{if } e \;\{\,s_1\,\}\textbf{ else }\{\,s_2\,\}\;;\;s\,\},q)} \to ob(o,c,\{\,l\mid s_2\;;\;s\,\},q)$$

$$\frac{\text{(NEW)}}{c' = \text{fresh}()\quad o' = \text{fresh}()\quad k = [\![e]\!]_l}{ob(o,c,\{\,l\mid x = \textbf{new Class with } e\;;\;s\,\},q)} \to ob(o,c,\{\,l\mid x = o'\;;\;s\,\},q)\; ob(o',c',\text{idle},\varnothing)\; cog(c',o',k)$$

$$\frac{\text{(NEW-LOCAL)}}{o' = \text{fresh}()}{ob(o,c,\{\,l\mid x = \textbf{new local Class }\;;\;s\,\},q)} \to ob(o,c,\{\,l\mid x = o'\;;\;s\,\},q)\; ob(o',c,\text{idle},\varnothing)$$

$$\frac{\text{(GET-TRUE)}}{f = [\![e]\!]_l\quad v \neq \bot}{ob(o,c,\{\,l\mid x = e.\textbf{get}\;;\;s\,\},q)\; fut(f,v)} \to ob(o,c,\{\,l\mid x = v\;;\;s\,\},q)\; fut(f,v)$$

$$\frac{\text{(GET-FALSE)}}{f = [\![e]\!]_l}{ob(o,c,\{\,l\mid x = e.\textbf{get}\;;\;s\,\},q)\; fut(f,\bot)} \to ob(o,c,\text{idle},q \cup \{\,l\mid x = e.\textbf{get}\;;\;s\,\})\; fut(f,\bot)$$

$$\frac{\text{(SELF-SYNC-CALL)}}{\begin{array}{c}o = [\![e]\!]_l\quad \overline{v} = [\![\overline{e}]\!]_l\quad f' = l(\text{destiny})\\ f = \text{fresh}()\quad \{\,l'\mid s'\,\} = \text{bind}(o,f,\textbf{m},\overline{v})\end{array}}{ob(o,c,\{\,l\mid x = e.\textbf{m}(\overline{e})\;;\;s\,\},q)}\\ \to ob(o,c,\{\,l'\mid s'\;;\;\textbf{cont}(f')\,\},q \cup \{\,l\mid x = f.\textbf{get}\;;\;s\,\})\; fut(f,\bot)$$

$$\frac{\text{(SELF-SYNC-RETURN-SCHED)}}{f = l'(\text{destiny})}{ob(o,c,\{\,l\mid \textbf{cont}(f)\,\},q \cup \{\,l'\mid s\,\})} \to ob(o,c,\{\,l'\mid s\,\},q)$$

$$\frac{\text{(COG-SYNC-CALL)}}{\begin{array}{c}o' = [\![e]\!]_l\quad \overline{v} = [\![\overline{e}]\!]_l\quad f' = l(\text{destiny})\\ f = \text{fresh}()\quad \{\,l'\mid s'\,\} = \text{bind}(o',f,\textbf{m},\overline{v})\\ ob(o,c,\{\,l\mid x = e.\textbf{m}(\overline{e})\;;\;s\,\},q)\\ ob(o',c,\text{idle},q')\; cog(c,o,k)\end{array}}\\ \begin{array}{c}\to ob(o,c,\text{idle},q \cup \{\,l\mid x = f.\textbf{get}\;;\;s\,\})\; fut(f,\bot)\\ ob(o',c,\{\,l'\mid s'\;;\;\textbf{cont}(f')\,\},q')\; cog(c,o',k)\end{array}$$

$$\frac{\text{(COG-SYNC-RETURN-SCHED)}}{\begin{array}{c}f = l'(\text{destiny})\\ ob(o,c,\{\,l\mid \textbf{cont}(f)\,\},q)\; cog(c,o,k)\\ ob(o',c,\text{idle},q' \cup \{\,l'\mid s'\,\})\end{array}}\\ \begin{array}{c}\to ob(o,c,\text{idle},q)\; cog(c,o',k)\\ ob(o',c,\{\,l'\mid s'\,\},q')\end{array}$$

$$\frac{\text{(ASYNC-CALL)}}{o' = [\![e]\!]_l\quad \overline{v} = [\![\overline{e}]\!]_l\quad f = \text{fresh}()}{ob(o,c,\{\,l\mid x = e!\textbf{m}(\overline{e})\;;\;s\,\},q)}\\ \to ob(o,c,\{\,l\mid x = f\;;\;s\,\},q)\; invoc(o',f,\textbf{m},\overline{v})\; fut(f,\bot)$$

$$\frac{\text{(BIND-MTD)}}{\{\,l\mid s\,\} = \text{bind}(o,f,\textbf{m},\overline{v})}{ob(o,c,p,q)\; invoc(o,f,\textbf{m},\overline{v})} \to ob(o,c,p,q \cup \{\,l\mid s\,\})$$

$$\frac{\text{(CONTEXT)}}{cn \to cn'}{cn\; cn'' \to cn'\; cn''}$$

$$\frac{\text{(RELEASE-COG)}}{ob(o,c,\text{idle},q)\; cog(c,o,k)} \to ob(o,c,\text{idle},q)\; cog(c,\varepsilon,k)$$

$$\frac{\text{(ACTIVATE)}}{ob(o,c,\text{idle},q \cup \{\,l\mid s\,\})\; cog(c,\varepsilon,k)} \to ob(o,c,\{\,l\mid s\,\},q)\; cog(c,o,k)$$

$$\frac{\text{(RETURN)}}{v = [\![e]\!]_l\quad f = l(\text{destiny})}{ob(o,c,\{\,l\mid \textbf{return } e\,\},q)\; fut(f,\bot)} \to ob(o,c,\text{idle},q)\; fut(f,v)$$

$$\frac{\text{(JOB-0)}}{[\![e]\!]_l = 0}{ob(o,c,\{\,l\mid \textbf{job}(e)\;;\;s\,\},q)} \to ob(o,c,\{\,l\mid s\,\},q)$$

$$\frac{\text{(ASSIGN-LOCAL)}}{x \in \text{dom}(l)\quad v = [\![e]\!]_l}{ob(o,c,\{\,l\mid x = e\;;\;s\,\},q)} \to ob(o,c,\{\,l\,[x \mapsto v]\mid s\,\},q)$$

Fig. 1. The transition relation of $\texttt{tml}$ – part 1.

object in the cog. An object is written as $ob(o,c,p,q)$, where o is the identifier of the object, c the identifier of the cog the object belongs to, p an *active process*, and q a pool of *suspended processes*. A *process* is written as $\{\,l\mid s\,\}$, where l denotes local variable bindings and s a list of statements. An *invocation message* is a term $invoc(o,f,\textbf{m},\overline{v})$ consisting of the callee o, the future f to which the result of the call is returned, the method name m, and the set of actual parameter values for the call. A *future* $fut(f, val)$ contains an identifier f and a reply value val, where $\bot$ indicates the reply value of the future has not been received.

The following auxiliary function is used in the semantic rules for invocations. Let $T'\; \textbf{m}(\overline{T}\; x)\{\,\overline{F}\; x';\;s\,\}$ be a method declaration. Then

$$\text{bind}(o,f,\textbf{m},\overline{v}) = \{\,[\text{destiny} \mapsto f,\overline{x} \mapsto \overline{v},\overline{x'} \mapsto \bot]\mid s\{^o/\textbf{this}\}\,\}$$

$$\frac{\text{(COND-TRUE)}}{\text{true} = [\![e]\!]_l}{ob(o,c,\{l \mid \text{if } e \{s_1\} \text{ else } \{s_2\} ; s\},q)}$$
$$\rightarrow ob(o,c,\{l \mid s_1 ; s\},q)$$

$$\frac{\text{(COND-FALSE)}}{\text{false} = [\![e]\!]_l}{ob(o,c,\{l \mid \text{if } e \{s_1\} \text{ else } \{s_2\} ; s\},q)}$$
$$\rightarrow ob(o,c,\{l \mid s_2 ; s\},q)$$

$$\frac{\text{(NEW)}}{c' = \text{fresh}() \quad o' = \text{fresh}() \quad k = [\![e]\!]_l}{ob(o,c,\{l \mid x = \text{new Class with } e ; s\},q)}$$
$$\rightarrow ob(o,c,\{l \mid x = o' ; s\},q)$$
$$ob(o',c',\text{idle},\varnothing) \quad cog(c',o',k)$$

$$\frac{\text{(NEW-LOCAL)}}{o' = \text{fresh}()}{ob(o,c,\{l \mid x = \text{new local Class} ; s\},q)}$$
$$\rightarrow ob(o,c,\{l \mid x = o' ; s\},q)$$
$$ob(o',c,\text{idle},\varnothing)$$

$$\frac{\text{(GET-TRUE)}}{f = [\![e]\!]_l \quad v \neq \bot}{ob(o,c,\{l \mid x = e.\text{get} ; s\},q) \quad fut(f,v)}$$
$$\rightarrow ob(o,c,\{l \mid x = v ; s\},q) \quad fut(f,v)$$

$$\frac{\text{(GET-FALSE)}}{f = [\![e]\!]_l}{ob(o,c,\{l \mid x = e.\text{get} ; s\},q) \quad fut(f,\bot)}$$
$$\rightarrow ob(o,c,\text{idle},q \cup \{l \mid x = e.\text{get} ; s\}) \quad fut(f,\bot)$$

$$\frac{\text{(SELF-SYNC-CALL)}}{o = [\![e]\!]_l \quad \overline{v} = [\![\overline{e}]\!]_l \quad f' = l(\text{destiny})}{f = \text{fresh}() \quad \{l' \mid s'\} = \text{bind}(o,f,\text{m},\overline{v})}{ob(o,c,\{l \mid x = e.\text{m}(\overline{e}) ; s\},q)}$$
$$\rightarrow ob(o,c,\{l' \mid s' ; \text{cont}(f')\},q \cup \{l \mid x = f.\text{get} ; s\})$$
$$fut(f,\bot)$$

$$\frac{\text{(SELF-SYNC-RETURN-SCHED)}}{f = l'(\text{destiny})}{ob(o,c,\{l \mid \text{cont}(f)\},q \cup \{l' \mid s\})}$$
$$\rightarrow ob(o,c,\{l' \mid s\},q)$$

$$\frac{\text{(COG-SYNC-CALL)}}{o' = [\![e]\!]_l \quad \overline{v} = [\![\overline{e}]\!]_l \quad f' = l(\text{destiny})}{f = \text{fresh}() \quad \{l' \mid s'\} = \text{bind}(o',f,\text{m},\overline{v})}{ob(o,c,\{l \mid x = e.\text{m}(\overline{e}) ; s\},q)}{ob(o',c,\text{idle},q') \quad cog(c,o,k)}$$
$$\rightarrow ob(o,c,\text{idle},q \cup \{l \mid x = f.\text{get} ; s\}) \quad fut(f,\bot)$$
$$ob(o',c,\{l' \mid s' ; \text{cont}(f')\},q') \quad cog(c,o',k)$$

$$\frac{\text{(COG-SYNC-RETURN-SCHED)}}{f = l'(\text{destiny})}{ob(o,c,\{l \mid \text{cont}(f)\},q) \quad cog(c,o,k)}{ob(o',c,\text{idle},q' \cup \{l' \mid s'\})}$$
$$\rightarrow ob(o,c,\text{idle},q) \quad cog(c,o',k)$$
$$ob(o',c,\{l' \mid s'\},q')$$

$$\frac{\text{(ASYNC-CALL)}}{o' = [\![e]\!]_l \quad \overline{v} = [\![\overline{e}]\!]_l \quad f = \text{fresh}()}{ob(o,c,\{l \mid x = e!\text{m}(\overline{e}) ; s\},q)}$$
$$\rightarrow ob(o,c,\{l \mid x = f ; s\},q) \quad invoc(o',f,\text{m},\overline{v}) \quad fut(f,\bot)$$

$$\frac{\text{(BIND-MTD)}}{\{l \mid s\} = \text{bind}(o,f,\text{m},\overline{v})}{ob(o,c,p,q) \quad invoc(o,f,\text{m},\overline{v})}$$
$$\rightarrow ob(o,c,p,q \cup \{l \mid s\})$$

$$\frac{\text{(CONTEXT)}}{cn \rightarrow cn'}{cn\, cn'' \rightarrow cn'\, cn''}$$

$$\frac{\text{(RELEASE-COG)}}{ob(o,c,\text{idle},q) \quad cog(c,o,k)}{\rightarrow ob(o,c,\text{idle},q) \quad cog(c,\varepsilon,k)}$$

$$\frac{\text{(ACTIVATE)}}{ob(o,c,\text{idle},q \cup \{l \mid s\}) \quad cog(c,\varepsilon,k)}{\rightarrow ob(o,c,\{l \mid s\},q) \quad cog(c,o,k)}$$

$$\frac{\text{(RETURN)}}{v = [\![e]\!]_l \quad f = l(\text{destiny})}{ob(o,c,\{l \mid \text{return } e\},q) \quad fut(f,\bot)}$$
$$\rightarrow ob(o,c,\text{idle},q) \quad fut(f,v)$$

$$\frac{\text{(JOB-0)}}{[\![e]\!]_l = 0}{ob(o,c,\{l \mid \text{job}(e) ; s\},q)}$$
$$\rightarrow ob(o,c,\{l \mid s\},q)$$

$$\frac{\text{(ASSIGN-LOCAL)}}{x \in \text{dom}(l) \quad v = [\![e]\!]_l}{ob(o,c,\{l \mid x = e ; s\},q)}$$
$$\rightarrow ob(o,c,\{l [x \mapsto v] \mid s\},q)$$

Fig. 1. The transition relation of $\texttt{tml}$ – part 1.

object in the cog. An object is written as $ob(o,c,p,q)$, where o is the identifier of the object, c the identifier of the cog the object belongs to, p an *active process*, and q a pool of *suspended processes*. A *process* is written as $\{l \mid s\}$, where l denotes local variable bindings and s a list of statements. An *invocation message* is a term $invoc(o,f,\text{m},\overline{v})$ consisting of the callee o, the future f to which the result of the call is returned, the method name m, and the set of actual parameter values for the call. A *future* $fut(f,val)$ contains an identifier f and a reply value val, where $\bot$ indicates the reply value of the future has not been received.

The following auxiliary function is used in the semantic rules for invocations. Let $T' \, \text{m}(\overline{T \, x})\{ \overline{F \, x'}; s \}$ be a method declaration. Then

$$\text{bind}(o,f,\text{m},\overline{v}) = \{ [\text{destiny} \mapsto f, \overline{x} \mapsto \overline{v}, \overline{x'} \mapsto \bot] \mid s\{^o/\texttt{this}\} \}$$

A statement s may be either one of the standard operations of an imperative language or the job statement $job(e)$ that delays the continuation by e cycles of the machine executing it.

An expression z may change the state of the system. In particular, it may be an *asynchronous* method invocation of the form $e\,!\,m(\overline{e})$, which does not suspend the caller's execution. When the value computed by the invocation is needed, the caller performs a *non-blocking* `get` operation: if the value needed by a process is not available, then an awaiting process is scheduled and executed, i.e., *await-get*. Expressions z also include standard synchronous invocations $e.m(\overline{e})$ and **new local** Class, which creates a new object. The intended meaning is to create the object in the same machine – called *cog* or *concurrent object group* – of the caller, thus sharing the processor of the caller: operations in the same virtual machine interleave their evaluation (even if in the following operational semantics the parallelism is not explicit). Alternatively, one can create an object on a different cog with **new** Class **with** e thus letting methods execute in parallel. In this case, e represents the capacity of the new cog, that is, the number of cycles the cog can perform per time interval. We assume the presence of a special identifier **this.capacity** that returns the capacity of the corresponding cog.

A *pure* expression e can be the reserved identifier **this** or an integer expression. Since the analysis in Sect. 5 cannot deal with generic integer expressions, we parse expressions in a careful way. In particular we split them into *size expressions se*, which are expressions in Presburger arithmetics (this is a decidable fragment of Peano arithmetics that only contains addition), and *non-size expressions nse*, which are the other type of expressions. The syntax of size and non-size expressions is the following:

$$
\begin{aligned}
nse ::=\ & k \ \mid\ x \ \mid\ nse \le nse \ \mid\ nse \ \textbf{and}\ nse \ \mid\ nse \ \textbf{or}\ nse \\
\mid\ & nse + nse \ \mid\ nse - nse \ \mid\ nse \times nse \ \mid\ nse/nse \\
se ::=\ & ve \ \mid\ ve \le ve \ \mid\ se \ \textbf{and}\ se \ \mid\ se \ \textbf{or}\ se \\
ve ::=\ & k \ \mid\ x \ \mid\ ve + ve \ \mid\ k \times ve \\
k ::=\ & rational\ constants
\end{aligned}
$$

In the paper, we assume that sequences of declarations $\overline{T}\,\overline{x}$ and method declarations $\overline{M}$ do not contain duplicate names. We also assume that **return** statements have no continuation.

Semantics. The semantics of tml is defined by a transition system whose states are *configurations cn* that are defined by the following syntax.

$$
\begin{aligned}
cn ::=\ & \varepsilon \ \mid\ fut(f, val) \ \mid\ ob(o, c, p, q) \ \mid\ invoc(o, f, \mathbf{m}, \overline{v}) & act ::=\ & o \ \mid\ \varepsilon \\
\mid\ & cog(c, act, k) \ \mid\ cn\ cn & val ::=\ & v \ \mid\ \bot \\
p ::=\ & \{\,l \mid s\,\} \ \mid\ \texttt{idle} & l ::=\ & [\cdots, x \mapsto v, \cdots] \\
q ::=\ & \varnothing \ \mid\ \{\,l \mid s\,\} \ \mid\ q\ q & v ::=\ & o \ \mid\ f \ \mid\ k
\end{aligned}
$$

A *configuration cn* is a set of concurrent object groups (cogs), objects, invocation messages and futures, and the empty configuration is written as ε. The associative and commutative union operator on configurations is denoted by whitespace. A *cog* is given as a term $cog(c, act, k)$ where c and k are respectively the identifier and the capacity of the cog, and act specifies the currently active

Notice that t-stable (and, consequently, strongly t-stable) configurations cannot progress anymore because every object is stuck either on a job or on unresolved get statements. The update of cn with respect to a time value t, noted $\Phi(cn, t)$ is defined in Fig. 2. Given these two notions, rule TICK defines the time progress.

The initial configuration of a program with main method $\{\,\overline{F\ x}; s\,\}$ with k is

$$ob(start, start, \{\,[destiny \mapsto f_{start}, \overline{x} \mapsto \bot]\,|\,s\,\}, \varnothing)$$
$$cog(start, start, k)$$

where start and $start$ are special cog and object names, respectively, and f_{start} is a fresh future name. As usual, $\rightarrow^*$ is the reflexive and transitive closure of $\rightarrow$.

Examples. To begin with, we discuss the Fibonacci method. It is well known that the computational cost of its sequential recursive implementation is exponential. However, this is not the case for the parallel implementation. Consider

```
Int fib(Int n) {
        if (n<=1) { return 1; }
        else {  Fut<Int> f; Class z; Int m1; Int m2;
            job(1);
            z = new Class with this.capacity ;
            f = this!fib(n-1); g = z!fib(n-2);
            m1 = f.get; m2 = g.get;
            return  m1 + m2; } }
```

Here, the recursive invocation `fib(n-1)` is performed on the `this` object while the invocation `fib(n-2)` is performed on a new cog with the same capacity (i.e., the object referenced by z is created in a new cog set up with `this.capacity`), which means that it can be performed in parallel with the former one. It turns out that the cost of the following invocation is n.

```
Class z; Int m; Int x; x = 1;
z = new Class with x;
m = z.fib(n);
```

Observe that, by changing the line x = 1; into x = 2; we obtain a cost of n/2.

Our semantics does not exclude paradoxical behaviours of programs that perform infinite actions without consuming time (preventing rule TICK to apply), such as this one

```
Int foo() { Int m; m = this.foo(); return m; }
```

This kind of behaviours are well-known in the literature, (*cf.* Zeno behaviours) and they may be easily excluded from our analysis by constraining recursive invocations to be prefixed by a `job(e)`-statement, with a positive e. It is worth to observe that this condition is not sufficient to eliminate paradoxical behaviours. For instance the method below does not terminate and, when invoked with `this.fake(2)`, where `this` is in a cog of capacity 2, has cost 1.

```
Int fake(Int n) {
        Int m; Class x;
        x = new Class with 2*n; job(1); m = x.fake(2*n); return m; }
```

$$\text{(Tick)} \quad \frac{strongstable_t(cn)}{cn \rightarrow \Phi(cn, t)}$$

where

$$
\Phi(cn, t) =
\begin{cases}
ob(o, c, \{l' \mid \texttt{job}(k') \; ; \; s\}, q) \; \Phi(cn', t) & \text{if } cn = ob(o, c, \{l \mid \texttt{job}(e) \; ; \; s\}, q) \; cn' \\
& \text{and } cog(c, o, k) \in cn' \\
& \text{and } k' = [\![e]\!]_l - k * t \\[2ex]
ob(o, c, \texttt{idle}, q) \; \Phi(cn', t) & \text{if } cn = ob(o, c, \texttt{idle}, q) \; cn' \\[2ex]
cn & \text{otherwise.}
\end{cases}
$$

Fig. 2. The transition relation of `tml` – part 2: the strongly stable case

The *transition rules* of `tml` are given in Figs. 1 and 2. We discuss the most relevant ones: object creation, method invocation, and the `job`(e) operator. The creation of objects is handled by rules NEW and NEW-LOCAL: the former creates a new object inside a new cog with a given capacity e, the latter creates an object in the local cog. Method invocations can be either synchronous or asynchronous. Rules SELF-SYNC-CALL and COG-SYNC-CALL specify synchronous invocations on objects belonging to the same cog of the caller. Asynchronous invocations can be performed on every object.

In our model, the unique operation that consumes time is `job`(e). We notice that the reduction rules of Fig. 1 are not defined for the `job`(e) statement, except the trivial case when the value of e is 0. This means that time does not advance while non-job statements are evaluated. When the configuration cn reaches a *stable* state, *i.e.*, no other transition is possible apart from those evaluating the `job`(e) statements, then the time is advanced by the minimum value that is necessary to let at least *one* process start. In order to formalize this semantics, we define the notion of stability and the *update operation* of a configuration cn (with respect to a time value t). Let $[\![e]\!]_l$ return the value of e when variables are bound to values stored in l.

Definition 1. *Let $t > 0$. A configuration cn is t-stable, written $stable_t(cn)$, if any object in cn is in one of the following forms:*

1. *$ob(o, c, \{l \mid \texttt{job}(e); s\}, q)$ with $cog(c, o, k) \in cn$ and $[\![e]\!]_l/k \geq t$,*
2. *$ob(o, c, \texttt{idle}, q)$ and*
   - *i. either $q = \varnothing$,*
   - *ii. or, for every $p \in q$, $p = \{l \mid x = e.\texttt{get}; s\}$ with $[\![e]\!]_l = f$ and $fut(f, \perp)$,*
   - *iii. or, $cog(c, o', k) \in cn$ where $o \neq o'$, and o' satisfies Definition 1.1.*

A configuration cn is strongly t-stable, written $strongstable_t(cn)$, if it is t-stable and there is an object $ob(o, c, \{l \mid \texttt{job}(e); s\}, q)$ with $cog(c, o, k) \in cn$ and $[\![e]\!]_l/k = t$.

Imagine a parallel invocation of the method `Int one() { job(1); }` on an object residing in a cog of capacity 1. At each stability point the job(1) of the latter method will compete with the job(1) of the former one, which will win every time, since having a greater (and growing) capacity it will require always less time. So at the first stability point we get job($1 - 1/2$) (for the method one), then job($1 - 1/2 - 1/4$) and so on, thus this sum will never reach 0.

In the examples above, the statement job(e) is a cost annotation that specifies how many processing cycles are needed by the subsequent statement in the code. We notice that this operation can also be used to program a timer which suspends the current execution for e units of time. For instance, let

```
Int wait(Int n) { job(n); return 0; }
```

Then, invoking `wait` on an object with capacity 1

```
Class timer; Fut<Class> f; Class x;
timer = new Class with 1;
f = timer!wait(5); x = f.get;
```

one gets the suspension of the current thread for 5 units of time.

3   Issues in Computing the Cost of `tml` Programs

The computation time analysis of `tml` programs is demanding. To highlight the difficulties, we discuss a number of methods.

```
Int wrapper(Class x) {
     Fut<Int> f; Int z;
     job(1) ; f = x!server(); z = f.get;
     return z; }
```

Method `wrapper` performs an invocation on its argument x. In order to determine the cost of `wrapper`, we notice that, if x is in the same cog of the carrier, then its cost is (assume that the capacity of the carrier is 1): $1 + cost(\text{server})$ because the two invocations are sequentialized. However, if the cogs of x and of the carrier are different, then we are not able to compute the cost because we have no clue about the state of the cog of x.

Next consider the following definition of `wrapper`

```
Int wrapper_with_log(Class x) {
     Fut<Int> f; Fut<Int> g; Int z;
     job(1) ; f = x!server(); g = x!print_log(); z = f.get;
     return z; }
```

In this case the wrapper also asks the server to print its log and this invocation is not synchronized. We notice that the cost of `wrapper_with_log` is not anymore $1 + cost(\text{server})$ (assuming that x is in the same cog of the carrier) because `print_log` might be executed *before* `server`. Therefore the cost of `wrapper_with_log` is $1 + cost(\text{server}) + cost(\text{print\_log})$.

Finally, consider the following wrapper that also logs the information received from the server on a new cog without synchronising with it:

```
Int wrapper_with_external_log(Class x) {
    Fut<Int> f; Fut<Int> g; Int z; Class y;
    job(1) ; f = x!server(); g = x!print_log(); z = f.get;
    y = new Class with 1;
    f = y!external_log(z);
    return z; }
```

What is the cost of **wrapper_with_external_log**? Well, the answer here is debatable: one might discard the cost of **y!external_log(z)** because it is useless for the value returned by **wrapper_with_external_log**, or one might count it because one wants to count every computation that has been triggered by a method in its cost. In this paper we adhere to the second alternative; however, we think that a better solution should be to return different cost for a method: a *strict cost*, which spots the cost that is necessary for computing the returned value, and an *overall cost*, which is the one computed in this paper.

Anyway, by the foregoing discussion, as an initial step towards the time analysis of **tml** programs, we simplify our analysis by imposing the following constraint:

– *it is possible to invoke methods on objects either in the same cog of the caller or on newly created cogs.*

The above constraint means that, if the callee of an invocation is one of the arguments of a method then it must be in the same cog of the caller. It also means that, if an invocation is performed on a returned object then this object must be in the same cog of the carrier. We will enforce these constraints in the typing system of the following section – see rule T-INVOKE.

4   A Behavioural Type System for tml

In order to analyse the computation time of **tml** programs we use abstract descriptions, called *behavioural types*, which are intermediate codes highlighting the features of **tml** programs that are relevant for the analysis in Sect. 5. These abstract descriptions support compositional reasoning and are associated to programs by means of a type system. The syntax of behavioural types is defined as follows:

$$
\begin{array}{llll}
t ::= & - \mid se \mid c[se] & & \text{basic value} \\
x ::= & f \mid t & & \text{extended value} \\
a ::= & e \mid \nu c[se] \mid m(\overline{t}) \to t \mid \nu f \colon m(\overline{t}) \to t \mid f^{\checkmark} & & \text{atom} \\
b ::= & a \triangleright \Gamma \mid a \,\fatsemi\, b \mid (se)\{b\} \mid b + b & & \text{behavioural type}
\end{array}
$$

where $c, c', \cdots$ range over cog names and $f, f', \cdots$ range over future names. Basic values t are either generic (non-size) expressions $-$ or size expressions se or the type $c[se]$ of an object of cog c with capacity se. The extended values add future names to basic values.

Atoms a define creation of cogs ($\nu c[se]$), synchronous and asynchronous method invocations ($m(\overline{t}) \to t$ and $\nu f \colon m(\overline{t}) \to t$, respectively), and synchronizations on asynchronous invocations ($f^{\checkmark}$). We observe that cog creations always carry a capacity, which has to be a size expression because our analysis in the next section cannot deal with generic expressions. Behavioural types $\mathbb{b}$ are sequences of atoms $\mathbb{a} \, \mathring{,} \, \mathbb{b}'$ or conditionals, typically $(se)\{\mathbb{b}\} + (\neg se)\{\mathbb{b}'\}$ or $\mathbb{b} + \mathbb{b}'$, according to whether the boolean guard is a size expression that depends on the arguments of a method or not. In order to type sequential composition in a precise way (see rule T-SEQ), the leaves of behavioural types are labelled with *environments*, ranged over by $\Gamma, \Gamma', \cdots$. Environments are maps from method names $\mathbb{m}$ to terms $(\overline{\mathbb{t}}) \to \mathbb{t}$, from variables to extended values $\mathbb{x}$, and from future names to values that are either $\mathbb{t}$ or $\mathbb{t}^\checkmark$.

The abstract behaviour of methods is defined by *method behavioural types* of the form: $\mathbb{m}(\mathbb{t}_t, \overline{\mathbb{t}})\{\mathbb{b}\} : \mathbb{t}_r$, where $\mathbb{t}_t$ is the type value of the receiver of the method, $\overline{\mathbb{t}}$ are the type value of the arguments, $\mathbb{b}$ is the abstract behaviour of the body, and $\mathbb{t}_r$ is the type value of the returned object. The subterm $\mathbb{t}_t, \overline{\mathbb{t}}$ of the method contract is called *header*; $\mathbb{t}_r$ is called *returned type value*. We assume that names in the header occur linearly. Names in the header *bind* the names in $\mathbb{b}$ and in $\mathbb{t}_r$. The header and the returned type value, written $(\mathbb{t}_t, \overline{\mathbb{t}}) \to \mathbb{t}_r$, are called *behavioural type signature*. Names occurring in $\mathbb{b}$ or $\mathbb{t}_r$ may be *not bound* by header. These *free names* correspond to new cog creations and will be replaced by fresh cog names during the analysis. We use $\mathbb{C}$ to range over method behavioural types.

The type system uses judgments of the following form:

- $\Gamma \vdash e : \mathbb{x}$ for pure expressions e, $\Gamma \vdash f : \mathbb{t}$ or $\Gamma \vdash f : \mathbb{t}^\checkmark$ for future names f, and $\Gamma \vdash \mathbb{m}(\overline{\mathbb{t}}) : \mathbb{t}$ for methods.
- $\Gamma \vdash z : \mathbb{x}, \; [\mathbb{a} \triangleright \Gamma']$ for expressions with side effects z, where $\mathbb{x}$ is the value, $\mathbb{a} \triangleright \Gamma'$ is the corresponding behavioural type, where Γ' is the environment Γ *with possible updates* of variables and future names.
- $\Gamma \vdash s : \mathbb{b}$, in this case the updated environments Γ' are inside the behavioural type, in correspondence of every branch of its.

Since Γ is a function, we use the standard predicates $x \in \mathrm{dom}(\Gamma)$ or $x \notin \mathrm{dom}(\Gamma)$. Moreover, we define

$$\Gamma[x \mapsto \mathbb{x}](y) \stackrel{def}{=} \begin{cases} \mathbb{x} & \text{if } y = x \\ \Gamma(y) & \text{otherwise} \end{cases}$$

The *multi-hole contexts* $\mathcal{C}[\,]$ are defined by the following syntax:

$$\mathcal{C}[\,] ::= \quad [\,] \quad | \quad \mathbb{a} \, \mathring{,} \, \mathcal{C}[\,] \quad | \quad \mathcal{C}[\,] + \mathcal{C}[\,] \quad | \quad (se)\{\mathcal{C}[\,]\}$$

and, whenever $\mathbb{b} = \mathcal{C}[\mathbb{a}_1 \triangleright \Gamma_1] \cdots [\mathbb{a}_n \triangleright \Gamma_n]$, then $\mathbb{b}[x \mapsto \mathbb{x}]$ is defined as $\mathcal{C}[\mathbb{a}_1 \triangleright \Gamma_1[x \mapsto \mathbb{x}]] \cdots [\mathbb{a}_n \triangleright \Gamma_n[x \mapsto \mathbb{x}]]$.

The typing rules for expressions are defined in Fig. 3. These rules are not standard because (size) expressions containing method's arguments are typed with the expressions themselves. This is crucial to the cost analysis in Sect. 5. In particular, *cog creation* is typed by rule T-NEW, with value $c[se]$, where c is the fresh name associated with the new cog and se is the value associated with the declared capacity. The behavioural type for the cog creation is $\nu c[se] \triangleright \Gamma[c \mapsto se]$, where the newly created cog is added to Γ. In this way, it is possible to verify whether the receiver of a method invocation is within a locally created cog or not by testing whether the receiver belongs to $\mathrm{dom}(\Gamma)$ or not,

$$
\begin{array}{ll}
\text{(T-Var)} & \text{(T-Method)} \\
\dfrac{x \in \mathrm{dom}(\Gamma)}{\Gamma \vdash x : \Gamma(x)} \quad \text{(T-Se)} \quad \text{(T-Nse)} & \dfrac{\Gamma(\mathtt{m}) = (\overline{\mathtt{t}}) \to \mathtt{t}' \quad fv(\mathtt{t}') \setminus fv(\overline{\mathtt{t}}) \neq \varnothing \;\; \text{implies} \;\; \sigma(\mathtt{t}') \text{ fresh}}{\Gamma \vdash \mathtt{m}(\sigma(\overline{\mathtt{t}})) : \sigma(\mathtt{t}')}
\end{array}
$$

$$
\Gamma \vdash se : se \qquad \Gamma \vdash nse : -
$$

$$
\begin{array}{ll}
\text{(T-New)} & \text{(T-New-Local)} \\
\dfrac{\Gamma \vdash e : se \quad c \text{ fresh}}{\Gamma \vdash \textbf{new Class with } e : c[se],\; \big[\nu c[se] \rhd \Gamma[c \mapsto se]\big]} & \dfrac{\Gamma \vdash \textbf{this} : c[se]}{\Gamma \vdash \textbf{new local Class} : c[se],\; \big[0 \rhd \Gamma\big]}
\end{array}
$$

$$
\begin{array}{ll}
\text{(T-Invoke-Sync)} & \text{(T-Invoke)} \\
\dfrac{\Gamma \vdash e : c[se] \quad \Gamma(\textbf{this}) = c[se]}{} & \dfrac{\Gamma \vdash e : c[se] \quad (c \in \mathrm{dom}(\Gamma) \;\; \text{or} \;\; \Gamma(\textbf{this}) = c[se])}{} \\
\dfrac{\Gamma \vdash \overline{e} : \overline{\mathtt{t}} \quad \Gamma \vdash \mathtt{m}(c[se], \overline{\mathtt{t}}) : \mathtt{t}'}{\Gamma \vdash e.\mathtt{m}(\overline{e}) : \mathtt{t}',\; \big[\mathtt{m}(c[se], \overline{\mathtt{t}}) \to \mathtt{t}' \rhd \Gamma\big]} & \dfrac{\Gamma \vdash \overline{e} : \overline{\mathtt{t}} \quad \Gamma \vdash \mathtt{m}(c[se], \overline{\mathtt{t}}) : \mathtt{t}' \quad f \text{ fresh}}{\Gamma \vdash e!\mathtt{m}(\overline{e}) : f,\; \big[\nu f \colon \mathtt{m}(c[se], \overline{\mathtt{t}}) \to \mathtt{t}' \rhd \Gamma[f \mapsto \mathtt{t}']\big]}
\end{array}
$$

$$
\begin{array}{ll}
\text{(T-Get)} & \text{(T-Get-Top)} \\
\dfrac{\Gamma \vdash e : f \quad \Gamma(f) = \mathtt{t}}{\Gamma \vdash e.\textbf{get} : \mathtt{t},\; \big[f^{\checkmark} \rhd \Gamma[f \mapsto \mathtt{t}^{\checkmark}]\big]} & \dfrac{\Gamma \vdash e : f \quad \Gamma(f) = \mathtt{t}^{\checkmark}}{\Gamma \vdash e.\textbf{get} : \mathtt{t},\; \big[0 \rhd \Gamma\big]}
\end{array}
$$

Fig. 3. Typing rules for expressions

respectively (*cf.* rule T-Invoke). *Object creation* (*cf.* rule T-New-Local) is typed as the cog creation, with the exception that the cog name and the capacity value are taken from the local cog and the behavioural type is empty. Rule T-Invoke types *method invocations* $e!\mathtt{m}(\overline{e})$ by using a fresh future name f that is associated to the method name, the cog name of the callee and the arguments. In the updated environment, f is associated with the returned value. Next we discuss the constraints in the premise of the rule. As we discussed in Sect. 2, asynchronous invocations are allowed on callees located in the current cog, $\Gamma(\textbf{this}) = c[se]$, or on a newly created object which resides in a fresh cog, $c \in \mathrm{dom}(\Gamma)$. Rule T-Get defines the *synchronization* with a method invocation that corresponds to a future f. The expression is typed with the value $\mathtt{t}$ of f in the environment and behavioural type $f^{\checkmark}$. Γ is then updated for recording that the synchronization has been already performed, thus any subsequent synchronization on the same value would not imply any waiting time (see that in rule T-Get-Top the behavioural type is 0). The *synchronous method invocation* in rule T-Invoke-Sync is directly typed with the return value $\mathtt{t}'$ of the method and with the corresponding behavioural type. The rule enforces that the cog of the callee coincides with the local one.

The typing rules for statements are presented in Fig. 4. The behavioural type in rule T-Job expresses the time consumption for an object with capacity se' to perform se processing cycles: this time is given by se/se', which we observe is in general a rational number. We will return to this point in Sect. 5.

The typing rules for method and class declarations are shown in Fig. 5.

(T-Assign)
$$\frac{\Gamma \vdash rhs : \mathbb{x}, \ [\mathbb{a} \triangleright \Gamma']}{\Gamma \vdash x = rhs : \mathbb{a} \triangleright \Gamma'[x \mapsto \mathbb{x}]}$$

(T-Job)
$$\frac{\Gamma \vdash e : se \quad \Gamma \vdash \mathtt{this} : c[se']}{\Gamma \vdash \mathtt{job}(e) : se/se' \triangleright \Gamma}$$

(T-Return)
$$\frac{\Gamma \vdash e : \mathbb{t} \quad \Gamma \vdash \mathtt{destiny} : \mathbb{t}}{\Gamma \vdash \mathtt{return} \ e : 0 \triangleright \Gamma}$$

(T-Seq)
$$\frac{\Gamma \vdash s : \mathcal{C}[\mathbb{a}_1 \triangleright \Gamma_1] \cdots [\mathbb{a}_n \triangleright \Gamma_n] \quad \Gamma_i \vdash s' : \mathbb{b}'_i}{\Gamma \vdash s \ ; \ s' : \mathcal{C}[\mathbb{a}_1 \ \mathring{,} \ \mathbb{b}'_1] \cdots [\mathbb{a}_n \ \mathring{,} \ \mathbb{b}'_n]}$$

(T-If-Nse)
$$\frac{\Gamma \vdash e : - \quad \Gamma \vdash s : \mathbb{b} \quad \Gamma \vdash s' : \mathbb{b}'}{\Gamma \vdash \mathtt{if} \ e \ \{s\} \ \mathtt{else} \ \{s'\} : \mathbb{b} + \mathbb{b}'}$$

(T-If-Se)
$$\frac{\Gamma \vdash e : se \quad \Gamma \vdash s : \mathbb{b} \quad \Gamma \vdash s' : \mathbb{b}'}{\Gamma \vdash \mathtt{if} \ e \ \{s\} \ \mathtt{else} \ \{s'\} : (se)\{\mathbb{b}\} + (\neg se)\{\mathbb{b}'\}}$$

Fig. 4. Typing rules for statements

(T-Method)
$$\frac{\Gamma(\mathtt{m}) = (\mathbb{t}_t, \overline{\mathbb{t}}) \rightarrow \mathbb{t}_r \quad \Gamma[\mathtt{this} \mapsto \mathbb{t}_t][\mathtt{destiny} \mapsto \mathbb{t}_r][\overline{x} \mapsto \overline{\mathbb{t}}] \vdash s : \mathcal{C}[\mathbb{a}_1 \triangleright \Gamma_1] \cdots [\mathbb{a}_n \triangleright \Gamma_n]}{\Gamma \vdash T \ \mathtt{m} \ (\overline{T \ x}) \ \{s\} : \mathtt{m}(\mathbb{t}_t, \overline{\mathbb{t}})\{\mathcal{C}[\mathbb{a}_1 \triangleright \varnothing] \cdots [\mathbb{a}_n \triangleright \varnothing]\} : \mathbb{t}_r}$$

(T-Class)
$$\frac{\Gamma \vdash \overline{M} : \overline{\mathbb{C}} \quad \Gamma[\mathtt{this} \mapsto start[k]][\overline{x} \mapsto \overline{\mathbb{t}}] \vdash s : \mathcal{C}[\mathbb{a}_1 \triangleright \Gamma_1] \cdots [\mathbb{a}_n \triangleright \Gamma_n]}{\Gamma \vdash \overline{M} \ \{\overline{T \ x} \ ; \ s\} \ \mathtt{with} \ k \ : \overline{\mathbb{C}}, \mathcal{C}[\mathbb{a}_1 \triangleright \varnothing] \cdots [\mathbb{a}_n \triangleright \varnothing]}$$

Fig. 5. Typing rules for declarations

Examples. The behavioural type of the `fib` method discussed in Sect. 2 is

```
fib(c[x],n) {
    (n ≤ 1){ 0 ▷ ∅ }
  + (n ≥ 2){
    1/x ⨾ d[x] ⨾ νf: fib(c[x],n-1)→ − ⨾ νg: fib(d[x],n-2)→ − ⨾
    f✓⨾ g✓⨾0 ▷ ∅ } } : −
```

5   The Time Analysis

The behavioural types returned by the system defined in Sect. 4 are used to compute upper bounds of time complexity of a `tml` program. This computation is performed by an off-the-shelf solver – the `CoFloCo` solver [4] – and, in this section, we discuss the translation of a behavioural type program into a set of *cost equations* that are fed to the solver. These cost equations are terms

$$m(\overline{x}) = exp \quad [se]$$

where m is a (cost) function symbol, *exp* is an expression that may contain (cost) function symbol applications (we do not define the syntax of *exp*, which may be derived by the following equations; the reader may refer to [4]), and se is a size expression whose variables are contained in $\bar{x}$. Basically, our translation maps method types into cost equations, where (i) method invocations are translated into function applications, and (ii) cost expressions se occurring in the types are left unmodified. The difficulties of the translation is that the cost equations must account for the parallelism of processes in different cogs and for sequentiality of processes in the same cog. For example, in the following code:

```
x = new Class with c; y = new Class with d;
f = x!m(); g = y!n(); u = g.get; u = f.get;
```

the invocations of m and n will run in parallel, therefore their cost will be $\max(t, t')$, where t is the time of executing m on x and t' is the time executing n on y. On the contrary, in the code

```
x = new local Class; y = new local Class;
f = x!m(); g = y!n(); u = g.get; u = f.get;
```

the two invocations are queued for being executed on the same cog. Therefore the time needed for executing them will be $t + t'$, where t is time needed for executing m on x, and t' is the time needed for executing n on y. To abstract away the execution order of the invocations, the execution time of *all unsynchronized* methods from the same cog are taken into account when one of these methods is synchronized with a `get`-statement. To avoid calculating the execution time of the rest of the unsynchronized methods in the same cog more than necessary, their estimated cost are ignored when they are later synchronized.

In this example, when the method invocation y!n() is synchronized with g.get, the estimated time taken is $t + t'$, which is the sum of the execution time of the two unsynchronized invocations, including the time taken for executing m on x because both x and y are residing in the same cog. Later when synchronizing the method invocation x!m(), the cost is considered to be *zero* because this invocation has been taken into account earlier.

The Translate Function. The translation of behavioural types into cost equations is carried out by the function **translate**, defined below. This function parses atoms, behavioural types or declarations of methods and classes. We will use the following auxiliary function that removes cog names from (tuples of) t terms:

$$\lfloor \_ \rfloor = \_ \qquad \lfloor e \rfloor = e \qquad \lfloor c[e] \rfloor = e \qquad \lfloor t_1, \ldots, t_n \rfloor = \lfloor t_1 \rfloor, \ldots, \lfloor t_n \rfloor$$

We will also use *translation environments*, ranged over by $\Psi, \Psi', \cdots$, which map future names to pairs $(e, \mathsf{m}(\bar{t}))$ that records the (over-approximation of the) time when the method has been invoked and the invocation.

In the case of atoms, **translate** takes four inputs: a *translation environment* Ψ, the cog name of the carrier, an over-approximated cost e of an execution branch, and the atom a. In this case, **translate** returns an updated translation environment and the cost. It is defined as follows.

$\texttt{translate}(\Psi, c, e, \texttt{a}) =$

$$\begin{cases}
(\Psi, e + e') & \text{when } \texttt{a} = e' \\[4pt]
(\Psi, e) & \text{when } \texttt{a} = \nu c[e'] \\[4pt]
(\Psi, e + \texttt{m}(\lfloor \overline{t} \rfloor)) & \text{when } \texttt{a} = \texttt{m}(\overline{t}) \to t' \\[4pt]
(\Psi[f \mapsto (e, \texttt{m}(\overline{t}))], e) & \text{when } \texttt{a} = (\nu f\colon \texttt{m}(\overline{t}) \to t') \\[4pt]
(\Psi \setminus F, e + e_1))) & \text{when } \texttt{a} = f^{\checkmark} \quad \text{and} \quad \Psi(f) = (e_f, \texttt{m}_f(c[e'], \overline{t_f})) \\
& \text{let } F = \{\, g \mid \Psi(g) = (e_g, \texttt{m}_g(c[e'], \overline{t_g})) \,\} \text{ then} \\
& \text{and } e_1 = \sum \{\, \texttt{m}_g(\lfloor \overline{t_g'} \rfloor) \mid (e_g, \texttt{m}_g(\overline{t_g'})) \in \Psi(F) \,\} \\[4pt]
(\Psi \setminus F, max(e, e_1 + e_2)) & \text{when } \texttt{a} = f^{\checkmark} \text{ and } \Psi(f) = (e_f, \texttt{m}_f(c'[e'], \overline{t_f})) \text{ and } c \neq c' \\
& \text{let } F = \{\, g \mid \Psi(g) = (e_g, \texttt{m}_g(c'[e'], \overline{t_g})) \,\} \text{ then} \\
& e_1 = \sum \{\, \texttt{m}_g(\lfloor \overline{t_g'} \rfloor) \mid (e_g, \texttt{m}_g(\overline{t_g'})) \in \Psi(F) \,\} \\
& \text{and } e_2 = max\{\, e_g \mid (e_g, \texttt{m}_g(\overline{t_g'})) \in \Psi(F) \,\} \\[4pt]
(\Psi, e) & \text{when } \texttt{a} = f^{\checkmark} \text{ and } f \notin dom(\Psi)
\end{cases}$$

The interesting case of $\texttt{translate}$ is when the atom is $f^{\checkmark}$. There are three cases:

1. The synchronization is with a method whose callee is an object of the same cog. In this case its cost must be *added*. However, it is not possible to know when the method will be actually scheduled. Therefore, we sum the costs of all the methods running on the same cog (worst case) – the set F in the formula – and we remove them from the translation environment.
2. The synchronization is with a method whose callee is an object on a different cog c'. In this case we use the cost that we stored in $\Psi(f)$. Let $\Psi(f) = (e_f, \texttt{m}_f(c'[e'], \overline{t_f}))$, then e_f represents the time of the invocation. The cost of the invocation is therefore $e_f + \texttt{m}_f(e', \lfloor \overline{t_f} \rfloor)$. Since the invocation is *in parallel* with the thread of the cog c, the overall cost is $max(e, e_f + \texttt{m}_f(e', \lfloor \overline{t_f} \rfloor))$. As in case 5, we consider the worst scheduler choice on c'. Instead of taking $e_f + \texttt{m}_f(e', \lfloor \overline{t_f} \rfloor)$, we compute the cost of all the methods running on c' – the set F in the formula – and we remove them from the translation environment.
3. The future does not belong to Ψ. That is the cost of the invocation which has been already computed. In this case, the value e does not change.

In the case of behavioural types, $\texttt{translate}$ takes as input a translation environment, the cog name of the carrier, an over-approximated cost of the current execution branch $(e_1)e_2$, where e_1 indicates the conditions corresponding to the branch, and the behavioural type a.

$\texttt{translate}(\Psi, c, (e_1)e_2, \texttt{b}) =$

$$\begin{cases}
\{\, (\Psi', (e_1)e_2') \,\} & \text{when } \texttt{b} = \texttt{a} \triangleright \Gamma \quad \text{and} \quad \texttt{translate}(\Psi, c, e_2, \texttt{a}) = (\Psi', e_2') \\[4pt]
C & \text{when } \texttt{b} = \texttt{a} \mathbin{;} \texttt{b}' \quad \text{and} \quad \texttt{translate}(\Psi, c, e_2, \texttt{a}) = (\Psi', e_2') \\
& \text{and } \texttt{translate}(\Psi', c, (e_1)e_2', \texttt{b}') = C \\[4pt]
C \cup C' & \text{when } \texttt{b} = \texttt{b}_1 + \texttt{b}_2 \quad \text{and} \quad \texttt{translate}(\Psi, c, (e_1)e_2, \texttt{b}_1) = C \\
& \text{and} \quad \texttt{translate}(\Psi, c, (e_1)e_2, \texttt{b}_2) = C' \\[4pt]
C & \text{when } \texttt{b} = (e)\{\, \texttt{b}' \,\} \quad \text{and} \quad \texttt{translate}(\Psi, c, (e_1 \wedge e)e_2, \texttt{b}') = C
\end{cases}$$

The translation of the behavioural types of a method is given below. Let $dom(\Psi) = \{\, f_1, \cdots, f_n \,\}$. Then we define $\Psi^{\checkmark} \stackrel{def}{=} f_1^{\checkmark} \mathbin{;} \cdots \mathbin{;} f_n^{\checkmark}$.

$$\texttt{translate}(\texttt{m}(c[e],\overline{t})\{\,\texttt{b}\,\}:\texttt{t}) \;=\; \left[\begin{array}{ll} \texttt{m}(e,\overline{e}) = e_1' + e_1'' & [e_1] \\ \quad\vdots & \\ \texttt{m}(e,\overline{e}) = e_n' + e_n'' & [e_n] \end{array}\right.$$

where $\texttt{translate}(\varnothing, c, 0, \texttt{b}) = \{\, \Psi_i, (e_i)e_i' \mid 1 \leq i \leq n \,\}$, and $\overline{e} = \lfloor \overline{t} \rfloor$, and $e_i'' = \texttt{translate}(\Psi_i, c, 0, \Psi_i^{\checkmark} \triangleright \varnothing)$. In addition, $[e_i]$ are the conditions for branching the possible execution paths of method $\texttt{m}(e, \overline{e})$, and $e_i' + e_i''$ is the over-approximation of the cost for each path. In particular, e_i' corresponds to the cost of the synchronized operations in each path (e.g., jobs and gets), while e_i'' corresponds to the cost of the asynchronous method invocations triggered by the method, but not synchronized within the method body.

Examples. We show the translation of the behavioural type of fibonacci presented in Sect. 4. Let $\texttt{b} = (se)\{0 \triangleright \varnothing\} + (\neg se)\{\texttt{b}'\}$, where $se = (n \leq 1)$ and $\texttt{b}' = 1/e \,\mathbf{;}\, \nu f \colon \texttt{fib}(c[e], n-1) \to -\,\mathbf{;}\, \nu g \colon \texttt{fib}(c'[e], n-2) \to -\,\mathbf{;}\, f^{\checkmark}\,\mathbf{;}\, g^{\checkmark}\,\mathbf{;}\, 0 \triangleright \varnothing\}$. Let also $\Psi = \Psi_1 \cup \Psi_2$, where $\Psi_1 = [f \mapsto (1/e, \texttt{fib}(e, n-1))]$ and $\Psi_2 = [g \mapsto (1/e, \texttt{fib}(e, n-2))]$.

The following equations summarize the translation of the behavioural type of the fibonacci method.

$\texttt{translate}(\varnothing, c, 0, \texttt{b})$
$\quad = \texttt{translate}(\varnothing, c, 0, (se)\,\{0 \triangleright \varnothing\}) \;\cup\; \texttt{translate}(\varnothing, c, 0, (\neg se)\,\{\texttt{b}'\})$
$\quad = \texttt{translate}(\varnothing, c, (se)0, \{0 \triangleright \varnothing\}) \;\cup\; \texttt{translate}(\varnothing, c, (\neg se)0, \{1/e \,\mathbf{;}\, \dots\})$
$\quad = \{\,(se)0\} \;\cup\; \texttt{translate}(\varnothing, c, (\neg se)(1/e), \{\nu f \colon \texttt{fib}(c[e], n-1) \to -\,\mathbf{;}\, \dots\})$
$\quad = \{\,(se)0\} \;\cup\; \texttt{translate}(\Psi_1, c, (\neg se)(1/e), \{\nu g \colon \texttt{fib}(c'[e], n-2) \to -\,\mathbf{;}\, \dots\})$
$\quad = \{\,(se)0\} \;\cup\; \texttt{translate}(\Psi, c, (\neg se)(1/e), \{f^{\checkmark}\,\mathbf{;}\, g^{\checkmark}\,\mathbf{;}\, \dots\})$
$\quad = \{\,(se)0\} \;\cup\; \texttt{translate}(\Psi_2, c, (\neg se)(1/e + \texttt{fib}(e, n-1)), \{g^{\checkmark}\,\mathbf{;}\, \dots\})$
$\quad = \{\,(se)0\} \;\cup\; \texttt{translate}(\varnothing, c, (\neg se)(1/e + \max(\texttt{fib}(e, n-1), \texttt{fib}(e, n-2))), \{0 \triangleright \varnothing\})$
$\quad = \{\,(se)0\} \;\cup\; \{\,(\neg se)(1/e + \max(\texttt{fib}(e, n-1), \texttt{fib}(e, n-2)))\,\}$

$\texttt{translate}(\varnothing, c, 0, 0) \;=\; (\varnothing, 0)$
$\texttt{translate}(\varnothing, c, 0, 1/e) \;=\; (\varnothing, 1/e)$
$\texttt{translate}(\varnothing, c, 1/e, \nu f \colon \texttt{fib}(c[e], n-1) \to -) \;=\; (\Psi_1, 1/e)$
$\texttt{translate}(\Psi_1, c, 1/e, \nu g \colon \texttt{fib}(c'[e], n-2) \to -) \;=\; (\Psi, 1/e)$
$\texttt{translate}(\Psi, c, 1/e, f^{\checkmark}) \;=\; (\Psi_2, 1/e + \texttt{fib}(e, n-1))$
$\texttt{translate}(\Psi_2, c, 1/e + \texttt{fib}(e, n-1), g^{\checkmark}) \;=\; (\varnothing, 1/e + \max(\texttt{fib}(e, n-1), \texttt{fib}(e, n-2)))$

$$\texttt{translate}(\texttt{fib}\ (c[e], n)\{\,\texttt{b}\,\} : -) \;=\; \begin{cases} \texttt{fib}(e, n) = 0 & [n \leq 1] \\ \texttt{fib}(e, n) = 1/e + \max(\texttt{fib}(e, n-1), \texttt{fib}(e, n-2)) & [n \geq 2] \end{cases}$$

Remark 1. Rational numbers are produced by the rule T-JOB of our type system. In particular behavioural types may manifest terms se/se' where se gives the processing cycles defined by the job operation and se' specifies the number of processing cycles per unit of time the corresponding cog is able to handle. Unfortunately, our backend solver – CoFloCo – cannot handle rationals se/se'

where se' is a variable. This is the case, for instance, of our fibonacci example, where the cost of each iteration is $1/x$, where x is a parameter. In order to analyse this example, we need to determine *a priori* the capacity to be a constant – say 2 –, obtaining the following input for the solver:

```
eq(f(E,N),0,[],[-N>=1,2*E=1]).
eq(f(E,N),nat(E),[f(E,N-1)],[N>=2,2*E=1]).
eq(f(E,N),nat(E),[f(E,N-2)],[N>=2,2*E=1]).
```

Then the solver gives nat(N-1)*(1/2) as the upper bound. It is worth to notice that fixing the fibonacci method is easy because the capacity does not change during the evaluation of the method. This is not always the case, as in the following alternative definition of fibonacci:

```
Int fib_alt(Int n) {
    if (n<=1) { return 1; }
    else { Fut<Int> f; Class z; Int m1; Int m2;
        job(1);
        z = new Class with (this.capacity*2) ;
        f = this!fib_alt(n-1); g = z!fib_alt(n-2);
        m1 = f.get; m2 = g.get;
        return m1+m2; } }
```

In this case, the recursive invocation z!fib_alt(n-2) is performed on a cog with twice the capacity of the current one and CoFloCo is not able to handle it. It is worth to observe that this is a problem of the solver, which is otherwise very powerful for most of the examples. Our behavioural types carry enough information for dealing with more complex examples, so we will consider alternative solvers or combination of them for dealing with examples like fib_alt.

6 Properties

In order to prove the correctness of our system, we need to show that (i) the behavioural type system is correct, and (ii) the computation time returned by the solver is an upper bound of the actual cost of the computation.

The correctness of the type system in Sect. 4 is demonstrated by means of a subject reduction theorem expressing that if a runtime configuration cn is well typed and $cn \rightarrow cn'$ then cn' is well-typed as well, and the computation time of cn is larger or equal to that of cn'. In order to formalize this theorem we extend the typing to configurations and we also use extended behavioural types $\Bbbk$ with the following syntax

$$\Bbbk ::= \quad \mathtt{b} \quad | \quad [\mathtt{b}]_f^c \quad | \quad \Bbbk \parallel \Bbbk \qquad \text{runtime behavioural type}$$

The type $[\mathtt{b}]_f^c$ expresses the behaviour of an asynchronous method bound to the future f and running in the cog c; the type $\Bbbk \parallel \Bbbk'$ expresses the parallel execution of methods in $\Bbbk$ and in $\Bbbk'$.

We then define a relation $\unrhd_t$ between runtime behavioural types that relates types. The definition is algebraic, and $\Bbbk \unrhd_t \Bbbk'$ is intended to mean that the computational time of $\Bbbk$ is at least that of $\Bbbk' + t$ (or conversely the computational time of $\Bbbk'$ is at most that of $\Bbbk - t$). This is actually the purpose of our theorems.

Theorem 1 (Subject Reduction). *Let cn be a configuration of a* tml *program and let* $\Bbbk$ *be its behavioural type. If cn is not strongly t-stable and cn* $\rightarrow$ *cn' then there exists* $\Bbbk'$ *typing cn' such that* $\Bbbk \unrhd_0 \Bbbk'$. *If cn is strongly t-stable and cn* $\rightarrow$ *cn' then there exists* $\Bbbk'$ *typing cn' such that* $\Bbbk \unrhd_t \Bbbk'$.

The proof of is a standard case analysis on the last reduction rule applied. The second part of the proof requires an extension of the translate function to run-time behavioural types. We therefore define a cost of the equations $\mathcal{E}_{\Bbbk}$ returned by translate($\Bbbk$) – noted $\mathsf{cost}(\mathcal{E}_{\Bbbk})$ – by unfolding the equational definitions.

Theorem 2 (Correctness). *If* $\Bbbk \unrhd_t \Bbbk'$, *then* $\mathsf{cost}(\mathcal{E}_{\Bbbk}) \geq \mathsf{cost}(\mathcal{E}_{\Bbbk'}) + t$.

As a byproduct of Theorems 1 and 2, we obtain the correctness of our technique, modulo the correctness of the solver.

7   Related Work

In contrast to the static time analysis for sequential executions proposed in [7], the paper proposes an approach to analyse time complexity for concurrent programs. Instead of using a Hoare-style proof system to reason about end-user deadlines, we estimate the execution time of a concurrent program by deriving the time-consuming behaviour with a type-and-effect system.

Static time analysis approaches for concurrent programs can be divided into two main categories: those based on type-and-effect systems and those based on abstract interpretation – see references in [9]. Type-and-effect systems (i) collect constraints on type and resource variables and (ii) solve these constraints. The difference with respect to our approach is that we do not perform the analysis during the type inference. We use the type system for deriving behavioural types of methods and, in a second phase, we use them to run a (non compositional) analysis that returns cost upper bounds. This dichotomy allows us to be more precise, avoiding unification of variables that are performed during the type derivation. In addition, we notice that the techniques in the literature are devised for programs where parallel modules of sequential code are running. The concurrency is not part of the language, but used for parallelising the execution.

Abstract interpretation techniques have been proposed addressing domains carrying quantitative information, such as resource consumption. One of the main advantages of abstract interpretation is the fact that many practically useful optimization techniques have been developed for it. Consequently, several well-developed automatic solvers for cost analysis already exist. These techniques either use finite domains or use expedients (widening or narrowing functions) to guarantee the termination of the fix-point generation. For this reason, solvers often return inaccurate answers when fed with systems that are finite but not statically bounded. For instance, an abstract interpretation technique that is very close to our contribution is [2]. The analysis of this paper targets a language with the same concurrency model as ours, and the backend solver for our analysis, CoFloCo, is a slightly modified version of the solver used by [2]. However the two techniques differ profoundly in the resulting cost equations and in the way they are produced. Our technique computes the cost by means of a type system, therefore every method has an associated type, which is parametric with respect to the arguments. Then these types are translated into a bunch of cost equations that may be *composed* with those of other methods. So our approach supports a technique similar to *separate compilation*, and is able to deal with systems that create statically an unbounded but finite number of nodes. On the contrary, the technique in [2] is not compositional because it takes the whole program and computes the parts that may run in parallel. Then the cost equations are generated accordingly. This has the advantage that their technique does not have any restriction on invocations on arguments of methods that are (currently) present in our one.

We finally observe that our behavioural types may play a relevant role in a cloud computing setting because they may be considered as abstract descriptions of a method suited for SLA compliance.

8   Conclusions

This article presents a technique for computing the time of concurrent object-oriented programs by using behavioural types. The programming language we have studied features an explicit cost annotation operation that define the number of machine cycles required before executing the continuation. The actual computation activities of the program are abstracted by job-statements, which are the unique operations that consume time. The computational cost is then measured by introducing the notion of (strong) *t-stability* (*cf.* Definition 1), which represents the ticking of time and expresses that up to t time steps no control activities are possible. A Subject Reduction theorem (Theorem 1), then, relates this stability property to the derived types by stating that the consumption of t time steps by job statements is properly reflected in the type system. Finally, Theorem 2 states that the solution of the cost equations obtained by translation of the types provides an upper bound of the execution times provided by the type system and thus, by Theorem 1, of the actual computational cost.

Our behavioural types are translated into so-called cost equations that are fed to a solver that is already available in the literature – the CoFloCo solver [4]. As discussed in Remark 1, CoFloCo cannot handle rational numbers with variables at the denominator. In our system, this happens very often. In fact, the number pc of processing cycles needed for the computation of a job(pc) is divided by the speed s of the machine running it. This gives the cost in terms of time of the job(pc) statement. When the capacity is not a constant, but depends on the value of some parameter and changes over time, then we get the untreatable rational expression. It is worth to observe that this is a problem of the solver (otherwise very powerful for most of the examples), while our behavioural types carry enough information for computing the cost also in these cases. We plan to consider alternative solvers or a combination of them for dealing with complex examples.

Our current technique does not address the full language. In particular we are still not able to compute costs of methods that contain invocations to arguments which do not live in the same machine (which is formalized by the notion of cog in our language). In fact, in this case it is not possible to estimate the cost without any indication of the state of the remote machine. A possible solution to this issue is to deliver costs of methods that are parametric with respect to the state of remote machines passed as argument. We will investigate this solution in future work.

In this paper, the cost of a method also includes the cost of the asynchronous invocations in its body that have not been synchronized. A more refined analysis, combined with the resource analysis of [5], might consider the cost of each machine, instead of the overall cost. That is, one should count the cost of a method *per* machine rather than in a cumulative way. While these values are identical when the invocations are always synchronized, this is not the case for unsynchronized invocation and a disaggregated analysis might return better estimations of virtual machine usage.

References

1. Albert, E., de Boer, F.S., Hähnle, R., Johnsen, E.B., Schlatte, R., Tarifa, S.L.T., Wong, P.Y.H.: Formal modeling of resource management for cloud architectures : an industrial case study using Real-Time ABS. J. Serv.-Oriented Comput. Appl. 8(4), 323–339 (2014)
2. Albert, E., Correas, J., Johnsen, E.B., Román-Díez, G.: Parallel cost analysis of distributed systems. In: Blazy, S., Jensen, T. (eds.) SAS 2015. LNCS, vol. 9291, pp. 275–292. Springer, Heidelberg (2015)
3. Buyya, R., Yeo, C.S., Venugopal, S., Broberg, J., Brandic, I.: Cloud computing and emerging IT platforms: vision, hype, and reality for delivering computing as the 5th utility. Future Gener. Comp. Syst. 25(6), 599–616 (2009)
4. Flores-Montoya, A., Hähnle, R.: Resource analysis of complex programs with cost equations. In: Garrigue, J. (ed.) APLAS 2014. LNCS, vol. 8858, pp. 275–295. Springer, Heidelberg (2014)
5. Garcia, A., Laneve, C., Lienhardt, M.: Static analysis of cloud elasticity. In: Proceedings of PPDP vol. 2015 (2015)
6. Hähnle, R., Johnsen, E.B.: Resource-aware applications for the cloud. IEEE Comput. 48(6), 72–75 (2015)
7. Johnsen, E.B., Pun, K.I., Steffen, M., Tarifa, S.L.T., Yu, I.C.: Meeting deadlines, elastically. In: From Action Systems to Distributed Systems: The Refinement Approach. CRC Press (to Appear, 2015)
8. Johnsen, E.B., Schlatte, R., Tarifa, S.L.T.: Integrating deployment architectures, resource consumption in timed object-oriented models. J. Logical Algebraic Meth. Program. 84(1), 67–91 (2015)
9. Trinder, P.W., Cole, M.I., Hammond, K., Loidl, H., Michaelson, G.: Resource analyses for parallel and distributed coordination. Concurrency Comput.: Pract. Experience 25(3), 309–348 (2013)

Composing Constraint Automata, State-by-State

Sung-Shik T.Q. Jongmans[1,2,3]($\boxtimes$), Tobias Kappé[4], and Farhad Arbab[3,4]

[1] School of Computer Science, Open University of the Netherlands,
Heerlen, The Netherlands
ssj@ou.nl
[2] Institute for Computing and Information Sciences,
Radboud University Nijmegen, Nijmegen, The Netherlands
[3] Centrum Wiskunde and Informatica, Amsterdam, The Netherlands
[4] Leiden Institute of Advanced Computer Science,
Leiden University, Leiden, The Netherlands

Abstract. The grand composition of n automata may have a number of states/transitions exponential in n. When it does, it seems not unreasonable for the computation of that grand composition to require exponentially many resources (time, space, or both). Conversely, if the grand composition of n automata has a number of states/transitions only linear in n, we may reasonably expect the computation of that grand composition to also require only linearly many resources.

Recently and problematically, we saw cases of linearly-sized grand compositions whose computation required exponentially many resources. We encountered these cases in the context of Reo (a graphical language for coordinating components in component-based software), constraint automata (a general formalism for modeling systems' behavior), and our compiler for Reo based on constraint automata. Combined with earlier research on constraint automata verification, these ingredients facilitate a correctness-by-construction approach to component-based software engineering—one of the hallmarks in Sifakis' "rigorous system design". To achieve that ambitious goal, however, we need to solve the previously stated problem. In this paper we present such a solution.

1 Introduction

Context. Over the past decades, coordination languages emerged for modeling and implementing interaction protocols among components in component-based software. This class of languages includes *Reo* [1,2]. Reo facilitates compositional construction of *connectors*: software entites that embody concurrency protocols for coordinating the synchronization and communication among components. Metaphorically, connectors constitute the "glue" that holds components together in component-based software and mediates their communication. Figure 1 already shows a number of example connectors in their usual graphical syntax. Briefly, a connector consists of a number of *channels* (edges), through which data can flow, and a number of *nodes* (vertices), on which channel ends coincide. The graphical appearance of a channel indicates its *type*; channels of

© Springer International Publishing Switzerland 2016
C. Braga and P.C. Ölveczky (Eds.): FACS 2015, LNCS 9539, pp. 217–236, 2016.
DOI: 10.1007/978-3-319-28934-2_12

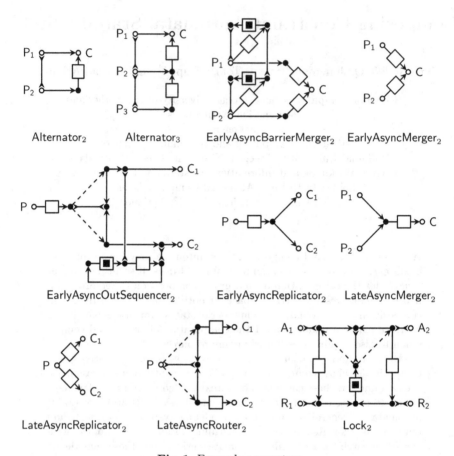

Fig. 1. Example connectors

different types have different data-flow behavior. Figure 1, for instance, includes standard synchronous channels (normal edges) and asynchronous channels with a 1-capacity buffer (rectangle-decorated edges), among others.

Reo has several formal semantics [9], with different purposes. The existence of such formal semantics forms a crucial precondition for Reo-based *rigorous system design* [16]: a design approach proposed by Sifakis centered around the principles of component-based software engineering, separation of concerns, and correctness-by-construction. In this paper, we focus on one particularly important formal semantics of Reo: *constraint automata* (CA) [5]. Constraint automata specify *when* during execution of a connector *which* data flow *where* (i.e., through which channel ends). We can compute the global CA for a connector from the local CAs for that connector's nodes and channels. As such, CAs constitute a *compositional* formal semantics of Reo. Both verification and compilation tools for Reo leverage this compositionality (e.g., [3,4,10,11,13]); the combination of such tools facilitates a correctness-by-construction approach to component-based software-engineering—one of the hallmarks in Sifakis' rigorous system design.

Problem. Reo's CA-based verification and compilation tools regularly need to compute the grand composition of the local CAs for a connector's *constituents* (i.e., its nodes/channels), to obtain its global CA for subsequent correctness analyses or code generation. The grand composition of n constraint automata, however, may yield a compound CA of a size *exponential* in n. The representation of such exponentially-sized compound CAs may require an exponential amount of space; computation of such CAs may require an exponential amount of time.

Recently, we reported on a number of experiments with our CA-based Reo-to-Java compiler [11]. In these experiments, we indeed observed exponential resource consumption for computing exponentially-sized grand compositions. Curiously, however, we also observed exponential resource consumption for computing *linearly*-sized grand compositions. Whereas exponential resource consumption seems undesirable but understandable for exponentially-sized grand compositions, it seems unacceptable and unintelligible for linearly-sized ones. Before we can achieve the ambitious goal of Reo-based rigorous system design, we must better understand this problem and find a solution.

Contribution. Based on earlier preliminary observations [11], we present a careful analysis of the previously stated problem. Essentially, as we shortly explain in more detail, our existing approach for computing grand compositions sometimes involves the computation of exponentially many "intermediately-reachable-but-finally-unreachable" states in "intermediate compounds", which become unreachable only in the "final compound". Subsequently, we present a solution for this problem in terms of a new approach for computing grand compositions; we prove the corresponding algorithm's correctness using Hoare logic. Finally, we present our implementation of this new approach and evaluate its performance.

In Sect. 2, we discuss preliminaries on Reo and CAs. In Sect. 3, we analyze the previously stated problem. In Sect. 4, we present our solution. In Sect. 5, we evaluate an implementation. Section 7 concludes this paper. An associated technical report contains all formal definitions and in-depth proofs [12].

2 Preliminaries

2.1 Reo

Reo is a graphical language for compositional construction of interaction protocols, manifested as connectors [1,2]. Connectors consist of channels and nodes, organized in a graph-like structure. Every channel consists of two ends and a constraint that relates the timing and the contents of the data-flows at those ends. Channel ends have one of two types: *source ends* accept data into their channels (i.e., a source end of a channel connects to that channel's data source/producer), while *sink ends* dispense data out of their channels (i.e., a sink end of a channel connects to that channel's data sink/consumer). Reo makes no other assumptions about channels and allows, for instance, channels with two source ends. Table 1 shows four common channels. Users of Reo may freely extend this set of common channels by defining their own channels with custom semantics.

Table 1. Graphical syntax and informal semantics of common channels

Syntax	Semantics
$e_1 \longrightarrow e_2$	Synchronously takes a datum d from its source end e_1 and writes d to its sink end e_2.
$e_1 \longrightarrow\!\!\!<\ e_2$	Synchronously takes data from both its source ends and loses them.
$e_1 \dashrightarrow e_2$	Synchronously takes a datum d from its source end e_1 and nondeterministically either writes d to its sink end e_2 or loses d.
$e_1 \ \square_x\ e_2$	Asynchronously [takes a datum d from its source end e_1 and stores d in a buffer x], then [writes d to its sink end e_2 and clears x].

Every node has at least one coincident channel end. A node with no coincident sink channel end is called a *source node*. A node with no coincident source channel end is called a *sink node*. A node with both source and sink coincident channel ends is called a *mixed node*. The set of all source nodes and sink nodes of a connector are collectively referred to as its *boundary nodes*. In Fig. 1, we distinguish connectors' white boundary nodes from their shaded mixed nodes.

Every sink channel end coincident on a node serves as a data source for that node. Analogously, every source channel end coincident on a node serves as a data sink for that node. A source node of a connector connects to an output port of a component, which will act as its data source. Similarly, a sink node of a connector connects to an input port of a component, which will act as its data sink. Source nodes permit **put** operations (for components to send data), while sink nodes permit **get** operations (for components to receive data); a connector uses its mixed nodes only for internally routing data.

Contrasting channels, all nodes have the same, fixed data-flow behavior: repeatedly, a node nondeterministically selects an available datum out of one of its data sources and replicates this datum into each of its data sinks. A node's nondeterministic selection and its subsequent replication constitute one atomic execution step; nodes cannot store, generate, or lose data. For a connector to make a global execution step—usually instigated by pending I/O-operations—its channels and its nodes must reach consensus about their combined behavior, to guarantee mutual consistency of their local execution steps (e.g., a node should not replicate a data item into a channel with an already full buffer). Subsequently, connector-wide data-flow emerges. A description of the behavior of the connectors in Fig. 1 appears elsewhere [11].

2.2 Constraint Automata

Although originally developed as a formal semantics of Reo [5], CAs constitute a general operational formalism for modeling the behavior of concurrent systems: every CA models a component, which has a number of *ports* through which it interacts with its environment. Often, we annotate ports with a direction of data-flow (i.e., a component can use a port either for producing data or for consuming data but not for both); in this paper, because these directions do not matter to our current problem, we omit them. To formalize Reo's semantics in terms of CA-based components, we view a channel as a component with two ports (one for each of its two ends), while we view a node with n coincident sink ends and m coincident source ends as a component with $n + m$ ports. Then, we can compositionally compute the CA for a connector by computing the grand composition of the CAs for its constituents. But first, we formally define CAs.

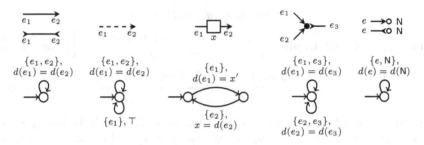

Fig. 2. Constraint automata for the channels in Table 1 (first three from the left), for a mixed node with two incoming and one outgoing channel (fourth from the left), and for two boundary nodes, each with either one incoming or one outgoing channel (fifth from the left). The latter CA is defined not only over the names of its coincident channel ends but also over its own name. (Components use node names—not channel end names—to perform I/O-operations on.)

Structurally, every CA consists of finite sets of states and transitions, which model a component's internal configurations and atomic execution steps. Every transition has a label that consists of two elements: (i) a set, typically denoted by P, containing the names of the ports that have synchronous data-flow in that transition, called a *synchronization constraint*, and (ii) a logical formula, typically denoted by ϕ, that specifies which particular data may flow through which of the ports in P, called a *data constraint*. For instance, the atomic data constraint $d(p_1) = d(p_2)$ means that the same datum flows through ports p_1 and p_2; the atomic data constraint $\top$ means that it does not matter which particular data flow where. Let $\mathbb{D}C$ denote a universal set of data constraints. More precisely, $\mathbb{D}C$ serves as the carrier set in some Boolean algebra $(\mathbb{D}C, \wedge, \vee, \neg, \bot, \top)$, including atoms of the form $d(p_1) = d(p_2)$. The details of data constraints do not matter in this paper, and therefore, we skip them. Let $\mathbb{S}T$ denote the universal set of states, let $\mathbb{P}\text{ORT}$ denote the universal set of ports, and let $\mathsf{Dc}(P)$ denote the set of data constraints in which only ports from P occur.

Definition 1. *A constraint automaton is a tuple* $(Q, P^{\text{all}}, \longrightarrow, Q_0)$*, where* $Q \subseteq \mathbb{S}\text{T}$ *is the state space,* $P^{\text{all}} \subseteq \mathbb{P}\text{ORT}$ *is the set of known ports,* $\longrightarrow \subseteq Q \times 2^{P^{\text{all}}} \times \mathsf{Dc}(P^{\text{all}}) \times Q$ *is the transition relation, and* $Q_0 \subseteq Q$ *are the initial states.* AUT *is the universal set of constraint automata, ranged over by* α*.*

Figure 2 shows example CAs. Let $\mathsf{St}(\alpha)$, $\mathsf{Port}(\alpha)$, $\mathsf{Tr}(\alpha)$, and $\mathsf{Init}(\alpha)$ denote α's state space, its set of ports, its transition relation, and its initial states.

Our behavioral equivalence in this paper is based on *bisimulation*. We define this equivalence in two steps. First, we define *simulation*.

Definition 2. $\preceq \subseteq \text{AUT} \times \text{AUT} \times 2^{\mathbb{S}\text{T} \times \mathbb{S}\text{T}}$ *is the relation defined as follows:*

$$\frac{\left[\left[\begin{bmatrix} (q_1, P, \phi, q_1') \in \mathsf{Tr}(\alpha_1) \\ \text{and } (q_1, q_2) \in R \end{bmatrix} \text{ implies } \begin{bmatrix} (q_2, P, \phi, q_2') \in \mathsf{Tr}(\alpha_2) \\ \text{and } (q_1', q_2') \in R \end{bmatrix} \text{ for some } q_2' \right] \right] \text{ for all } q_1, q_1', q_2, P, \phi}{\text{and } \left[\left[q_1 \in \mathsf{Init}(\alpha_1) \text{ implies } \begin{bmatrix} [q_2 \in \mathsf{Init}(\alpha_2) \text{ and } (q_1, q_2) \in R] \\ \text{for some } q_2 \end{bmatrix} \right] \text{ for all } q_1 \right] \\ \text{and } \mathsf{Port}(\alpha_1) = \mathsf{Port}(\alpha_2) \text{ and } R \subseteq \mathsf{St}(\alpha_1) \times \mathsf{St}(\alpha_2)}{\alpha_1 \preceq_R \alpha_2}$$

In words, α_2 simulates α_1 under *simulation relation* R—in which case $\alpha_1 \preceq_R \alpha_2$ holds true—whenever we can relate the states of α_1 and α_2 such that: (i) α_2 can mimic every transition that α_1 can make in related states, and (ii) α_2 can already perform such mimicry in any of α_1's initial states. If we care only about the existence of a simulation relation between (the states of) α_1 and α_2 but not about its exact content, we often simply write $\alpha_1 \preceq \alpha_2$. Formally, we "overload" relation symbol $\preceq$ as follows.

Definition 3. $\preceq \subseteq \text{AUT} \times \text{AUT}$ *is the relation defined as follows:*

$$\frac{\alpha_1 \preceq_R \alpha_2 \text{ for some } R}{\alpha_1 \preceq \alpha_2}$$

The definition of bisimulation now straightforwardly follows.

Definition 4. $\simeq \subseteq \text{AUT} \times \text{AUT} \times 2^{\mathbb{S}\text{T} \times \mathbb{S}\text{T}}$ *is the relation defined as follows:*

$$\frac{\alpha_1 \preceq_R \alpha_2 \text{ and } \alpha_2 \preceq_{R^{-1}} \alpha_1}{\alpha_1 \simeq_R \alpha_2}$$

We favor this automata-centric definition of bisimilarity over its definition as the maximal bisimulation on states, because automata are our primary objects of interest instead of their states. As with simulation, if we care only about the existence of a *bisimulation relation* between (the states of) α_1 and α_2 but not about its exact content, we often simply write $\alpha_1 \simeq \alpha_2$ and overload $\simeq$ accordingly.

Definition 5. $\simeq\, \subseteq \text{AUT} \times \text{AUT}$ *is the relation defined as follows:*

$$\frac{\alpha_1 \simeq_R \alpha_2 \text{ for some } R}{\alpha_1 \simeq \alpha_2}$$

Note that, as usual with (bi)simulations, $\alpha_1 \simeq \alpha_2$ implies $\big[\alpha_1 \preceq \alpha_2 \text{ and } \alpha_2 \preceq \alpha_1\big]$, but $\big[\alpha_1 \preceq \alpha_2 \text{ and } \alpha_2 \preceq \alpha_1\big]$ does *not* imply $\alpha_1 \simeq \alpha_2$.

To model component composition in terms of CAs, we define the following (synchronous) composition operation.

Definition 6. $\cdot \otimes \cdot : \text{AUT} \times \text{AUT} \to \text{AUT}$ *is the function defined as follows:*

$$\alpha_1 \otimes \alpha_2 = \left(\begin{array}{c} \text{St}(\alpha_1) \times \text{St}(\alpha_2), \text{Port}(\alpha_1) \cup \text{Port}(\alpha_2), \\[2mm] \left\{ \left(\begin{array}{c} (q_1, q_2), \\ P_1 \cup P_2, \\ \phi_1 \wedge \phi_2, \\ (q_1', q_2') \end{array} \right) \left| \begin{array}{c} \text{Port}(\alpha_1) \cap P_2 = \text{Port}(\alpha_2) \cap P_1 \\ \text{and } (q_1, P_1, \phi_1, q_1') \in \text{Tr}(\alpha_1) \\ \text{and } (q_2, P_2, \phi_2, q_2') \in \text{Tr}(\alpha_2) \end{array} \right. \right\}, \\[4mm] \text{Init}(\alpha_1) \times \text{Init}(\alpha_2) \end{array} \right)$$

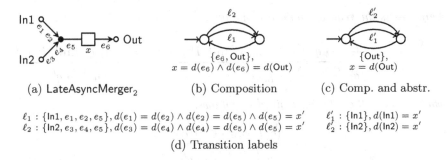

(a) LateAsyncMerger$_2$ (b) Composition   (c) Comp. and abstr.

$\ell_1 : \{\text{In1}, e_1, e_2, e_5\}, d(e_1) = d(e_2) \wedge d(e_2) = d(e_5) \wedge d(e_5) = x'$ $\ell_1' : \{\text{In1}\}, d(\text{In1}) = x'$
$\ell_2 : \{\text{In2}, e_3, e_4, e_5\}, d(e_3) = d(e_4) \wedge d(e_4) = d(e_5) \wedge d(e_5) = x'$ $\ell_2' : \{\text{In2}\}, d(\text{In2}) = x'$

(d) Transition labels

Fig. 3. Composition and abstraction of LateAsyncMerger$_2$ in Fig. 1

Essentially, the previous definition of $\otimes$ formalizes the idea that two components can fire a transition together only if they agree on the involvement of their shared ports. Our composition differs slightly from its original definition [5], where Baier et al. encode the possibility for one CA to *idle*, while the other CA makes a transition, explicitly in the definition of composition. Here, we prefer the equivalent alternative of encoding the idling of components explicitly in their CAs—instead of in the definition of composition—through self-loop transitions labeled with $\emptyset, \top$. This has the advantage of a simpler definition of composition, without losing expressiveness. We stipulate that every example CA that we show has implicit self-loops for idling in each of their states. (In principle, our theory for CAs does not require self-loops; for modeling Reo, however, CAs require self-loops.) Fig. 3 shows an example of composition. We adopt left-associative notation for $\otimes$ and omit brackets whenever possible (e.g., we write $\alpha_1 \otimes \alpha_2 \otimes \alpha_3$ for $(\alpha_1 \otimes \alpha_2) \otimes \alpha_3$). Similarly, we adopt left-associative notation for pairs of states (e.g., we write (q_1, q_2, q_3) for $((q_1, q_2), q_3)$). Behaviorally, bracketing is insignificant, because $\otimes$ is associative/commutative modulo bisimulation. However, as we reason also structurally about CAs in this paper, bracketing matters.

To compute the formal semantics of a connector, we compute the grand composition of the CAs for its constituents using $\otimes$, in an iterative manner: for an expression $\alpha_1 \otimes \cdots \otimes \alpha_n$, we first compute $\alpha := \alpha_1 \otimes \alpha_2$, then $\alpha := \alpha \otimes \alpha_3$, then $\alpha := \alpha \otimes \alpha_4$, and so on. We call every $\alpha \otimes \alpha_{i<n}$ in this computation an *intermediate compound*; we call $\alpha \otimes \alpha_n$ the *final compound*.

Beside multiplication, Baier et al. defined another operation on constraint automata: *abstraction* [5]. Abstraction removes ports from the observables of a CA, possibly *internalizing* transitions (i.e., making those transitions unobservable from the environment). In practice, abstraction can significantly reduce the size of a CA, both in terms of states and transitions. Although not the main topic of this paper, due to its practical relevance, we use abstraction in Sect. 5. Its formal definition appears below for completeness.

Definition 7. $\cdot \ominus \cdot : \text{AUT} \times \text{PORT} \to \text{AUT}$ *is the function defined as follows:*

$$\alpha \ominus p = (\text{St}(\alpha), \text{Port}(\alpha) \setminus \{p\}, \longrightarrow, \text{Init}(\alpha))$$

where $\longrightarrow$ *is the relation defined as follows:*

$$\frac{q_1 \xrightarrow{\emptyset, \phi_1}_\emptyset \cdots \xrightarrow{\emptyset, \phi_{n-1}}_\emptyset q_n \xrightarrow{P, \phi_n}_\emptyset q_{n+1} \text{ and } P \neq \emptyset}{q_1 \xrightarrow{P, \phi_1 \wedge \cdots \wedge \phi_n} q_{n+1}} \qquad \frac{q \xrightarrow{P, \phi}_\emptyset q' \text{ and } P \neq \emptyset}{q \xrightarrow{P, \phi} q'}$$

where $\longrightarrow_\emptyset$ *is the relation defined as follows:*

$$\frac{(q, P, \phi, q') \in \text{Tr}(\alpha)}{q \xrightarrow{P \setminus \{p\}, \exists p.\phi}_\emptyset q'}$$

3 Problem

In ongoing work, we are developing a CA-based Reo-to-Java compiler; in recent work, to study the effectiveness of one of our optimization techniques, we compared the performance of the code generated by our compiler with and without applying that technique [11]. Our comparison featured a number of k-parametric *families* of connectors, where k controls the size of a coordinating connector through its number of coordinated components. Figure 1 shows the $k = 2$ members of the families with which we experimented. One can extend these $k = 2$ members to their $k > 2$ versions in a similar way as how we extended Fig. 1a to b. We selected these families because each of them exhibits different behavior in terms of synchrony, exclusion, nondeterminism, direction, sequentiality, and parallelism, thereby aiming for a balanced comparison.

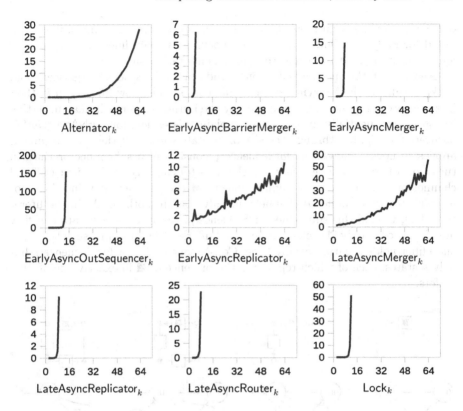

Fig. 4. Computation times (y-axis) for nine k-parametric families, for $2 \leq k \leq 64$ (x-axis). Time is measured in seconds, except for EarlyAsyncReplicator$_k$ and LateAsyncMerger$_k$, where time is measured in milliseconds.

Although we focused our attention primarily on the performance of the generated code, we also made some observations about the performance of our compiler itself. Without applying the optimization technique under investigation, our compiler uses the previously explained *iterative approach* to compute the grand composition of the CAs for a connector's constituents. Figure 4 shows the computation times measured for the k-parametric families under study, for $2 \leq k \leq 64$, averaged over sixteen runs.[1] For six families, the compiler exhausted its available resources (five minutes of time or 2 GB of heap space) long before reaching $k = 64$. The cause: "rapid"—at least exponential—growth in k. For four of these families, we have a good explanation for this phenomenon: the grand compositions computed for EarlyAsyncMerger$_k$, EarlyAsyncBarrierMerger$_k$, LateAsyncReplicator$_k$, and LateAsyncRouter$_k$ grow exponentially in k, such that the amount of resources required to compute those grand compositions logically also grows at least exponentially in k. For the other two families, in contrast,

---

[1] We recollected the data shown in Fig. 4 specifically for this paper, but we made our initial observations based on our previous data [11].

our measurements seem more difficult to explain: the grand compositions computed for EarlyAsyncOutSequencer$_k$ and Lock$_k$ grow only linearly in k, making an exponential growth in resource requirements rather surprising.

Analysis of the intermediate compounds of EarlyAsyncOutSequencer$_k$ and Lock$_k$ taught us the following: even if final compounds grow linearly in k, their intermediate compounds, as computed by the iterative approach, may nevertheless grow exponentially in k. We can explain this easiest for EarlyAsyncOutSequencer$_k$ (cf. Fig. 1e), through the size of its state space, but the same argument applies to Lock$_k$. EarlyAsyncOutSequencer$_k$ consists of a subconnector that, in turn, consists of a cycle of k buffered channels (of capacity 1). The first buffered channel initially contains a dummy datum ■ (i.e., its actual value does not matter); the other buffered channels initially contain nothing. As in the literature [1,2], we call this subconnector Sequencer$_k$. Because no new data can flow into Sequencer$_k$, only ■ cycles through the buffers—ad infinitum—such that only one buffer holds a datum at any time. Consequently, the CA for Sequencer$_k$ has only k states, each of which represents the presence of ■ in exactly one of its k buffers.

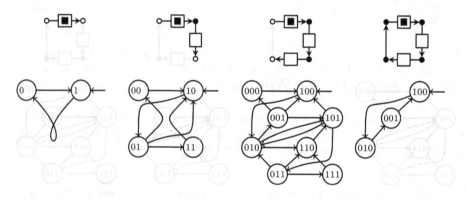

Fig. 5. Grand composition of the CAs for a cycle of three buffered channels (of capacity 1), closed by a synchronous channel. State labels xyz indicate the emptiness/fullness of buffers, where x refers to the first buffer, y to the second buffer, and z to the third buffer; we omitted transition labels to avoid clutter.

However, if we compute the grand composition of the local CAs for Sequencer$_k$'s constituents using the iterative approach, we "close the cycle" only with the very last application of ⊗: until then, this soon-to-become-cycle still appears an open-ended chain of buffered channels. Because new data can freely flow into such an open-ended chain, this chain can have a datum in any buffer at any time. Consequently, the CA for the largest chain has 2^k states. Only when we compose this penultimate compound with the last local CA, the state space collapses into k states, as we "find out" that the open-ended chain actually forms a cycle with exactly one datum. Because Sequencer$_k$ constitutes EarlyAsyncOutSequencer$_k$, also EarlyAsyncOutSequencer$_k$ suffers from this problem.

Figure 5 shows our previous analysis in pictures. Most interestingly, the intermediate compounds in Fig. 5 (i.e., the first three automata from the left) contain progressively more states with the following peculiar property: they are reachable from an initial state in those intermediate compounds, called *intermediate-reachability*, but neither those states themselves nor any compound state that they constitute, are reachable in the final compound, called *final-unreachability*. Thus, by using the iterative approach for computing a grand composition, we may spend exponentially many resources on generating a state space that we nearly completely discard in the end. This seems the heart of our problem.

4 Solution

The main idea to solve our problem is to compute grand compositions *state-by-state*, instead of iteratively. In this new approach, we start computing a grand composition from its straightforwardly computable set of initial states. Subsequently, we *expand* each of those states by computing their outgoing compound transitions. These compound transitions enter new compound states, which we subsequently recursively expand. As such, we compute only the reachable states of the final compound, avoiding the unnecessary computation of intermediately-reachable-but-finally-unreachable states. Easy to explain, the main challenge we faced consisted of finding an elegant formalization of this state-by-state approach—including an algorithm—amenable to formal reasoning and proofs. Such proofs are crucially important in the correctness-by-construction principle advocated in rigorous system design for component-based software engineering.

4.1   State-Based Decomposition/Recomposition

We start by formalizing the state-based *decomposition* of a CA into its per-state "subautomata" and the *recomposition* of that CA from those decompositions. Let σ denote the *selection function* (cf. relational algebra) that consumes as input a transition relation $\longrightarrow$ and a state q and produces as output the subrelation of $\longrightarrow$ consisting of precisely the transitions in $\longrightarrow$ that exit q.

Definition 8. $\sigma : 2^{\mathbb{ST} \times 2^{\mathbb{PORT}} \times \mathbb{DC} \times \mathbb{ST}} \times \mathbb{ST} \to 2^{\mathbb{ST} \times 2^{\mathbb{PORT}} \times \mathbb{DC} \times \mathbb{ST}}$ *is the function defined as follows:*

$$\sigma_q(\longrightarrow) = \{(q, \hat{P}, \hat{\phi}, \hat{q}') \mid q \xrightarrow{\hat{P}, \hat{\phi}} \hat{q}'\}$$

Next, let $\cdot\langle\cdot\rangle$ denote the *(state-based) decomposition function* that consumes as input an automaton α and a state q and produces as ouput a CA consisting of exactly the same set of states, set of ports, and set of initial states, and with a transition relation consisting of precisely the transitions in α that exit q.

Definition 9. $\cdot\langle\cdot\rangle : \mathrm{AUT} \times \mathbb{ST} \to \mathrm{AUT}$ *is the function defined as follows:*

$$\alpha\langle q\rangle = (\mathsf{St}(\alpha), \mathsf{Port}(\alpha), \sigma_q(\mathsf{Tr}(\alpha)), \mathsf{Init}(\alpha))$$

We call q the *significant state* in $\alpha\langle q\rangle$. The following lemma states that decomposition distributes over composition: instead of first computing the grand composition of n local CAs and then decomposing the resulting global CA with respect to a global state, we can equally first decompose every local CA with respect to its local state and then compute the grand composition of the resulting per-state decompositions. A detailed proof appears in the technical report [12].

Lemma 1. $(\alpha_1 \otimes \cdots \otimes \alpha_n)\langle(q_1,\ldots,q_n)\rangle = \alpha_1\langle q_1\rangle \otimes \cdots \otimes \alpha_n\langle q_n\rangle$

The previous definitions (and lemma) cover the essentials of state-based decomposition; in the rest of this subsection, we discuss recomposition. Let $\bigsqcup$ denote a *recomposition function* that consumes as input a set of CAs and produces as output a CA by taking the grand union of the sets of states, sets of ports, sets of transitions, and sets of initial states.

Definition 10. $\bigsqcup \cdot : 2^{\text{AUT}} \to \text{AUT}$ *is the function defined as follows:*

$$\bigsqcup A = \left(\bigcup\{\mathsf{St}(\alpha) \mid \alpha \in A\}, \bigcup\{\mathsf{Port}(\alpha) \mid \alpha \in A\}, \bigcup\{\mathsf{Tr}(\alpha) \mid \alpha \in A\}, \bigcup\{\mathsf{Init}(\alpha) \mid \alpha \in A\}\right)$$

The following lemma states that a CA equals the recomposition of its state-based decompositions. A detailed proof appears in the technical report [12].

Lemma 2. $\alpha = \bigsqcup\{\alpha\langle q\rangle \mid q \in \mathsf{St}(\alpha)\}$

The following theorem states the correctness of the state-by-state approach for grand compositions, as outlined in the beginning of this section. *Roughly*, it states that the grand composition of n local CAs equals the recomposition of that grand composition's state-based decompositions. More precisely, however, it states that this grand composition equals the recomposition of *the composition of state-based decompositions of the local CAs*. This is a subtle but important point: it means that to compute the grand composition of n local CAs, we only need to compute compositions of state-based decompositions of those local CAs. We further clarify this point in the next subsection.

Theorem 1

$$\alpha_1 \otimes \cdots \otimes \alpha_n = \bigsqcup\{\alpha_1\langle q_1\rangle \otimes \cdots \otimes \alpha_n\langle q_n\rangle \mid (q_1,\ldots,q_n) \in \mathsf{St}(\alpha_1) \times \cdots \times \mathsf{St}(\alpha_n)\}$$

Proof (Sketch). By applying Lemma 2, Definition 6 of $\otimes$, and Lemma 1. A detailed proof appears in the technical report [12]. □

4.2   Algorithm

Having formalized de/recomposition, we can now formulate an algorithm for computing the reachable fragment of grand compositions. First, we formalize reachability. We call a state q reachable iff q is an initial state or a finite sequence of k transitions exists that form a path from some initial state to q. Let Reach denote the *reachability function* that consumes as input a CA and produces as output its reachable states.

Definition 11. Reach : $\text{AUT} \to 2^{\text{ST}}$ *is the function defined as follows:*

$$\text{Reach}(\alpha) = \text{Init}(\alpha) \cup \left\{ q_k \left| \begin{array}{l} (q_1, P_1, \phi_1, q_2), \ldots, (q_{k-1}, P_{k-1}, \phi_{k-1}, q_k) \in \text{Tr}(\alpha) \\ \text{and } q_1 \in \text{Init}(\alpha) \end{array} \right. \right\}$$

Next, let $\lfloor \cdot \rfloor$ denote the *floor function*, which takes as input a CA and produces as output an equivalent—proven below—CA for its reachable states (i.e., the floor function "rounds" a CA "down" to its reachable fragment).

Definition 12. $\lfloor \cdot \rfloor : \text{AUT} \to \text{AUT}$ *is the function defined as follows:*

$$\lfloor \alpha \rfloor = \bigsqcup \{ \alpha \langle q \rangle \mid q \in \text{Reach}(\alpha) \}$$

The following lemmas state that a CA simulates its floored version and vice versa. Detailed proofs appear in the technical report [12].

Lemma 3. $\alpha \preceq_{\{(q,q)\mid q \in \text{Reach}(\alpha)\}} \lfloor \alpha \rfloor$

Lemma 4. $\lfloor \alpha \rfloor \preceq_{\{(q,q)\mid q \in \text{Reach}(\alpha)\}^{-1}} \alpha$

From these two lemmas, we can immediately conclude the following theorem, which states that a CA and its floored version are bisimulation equivalent.

Theorem 2. $\alpha \simeq_{\{(q,q)\mid q \in \text{Reach}(\alpha)\}} \lfloor \alpha \rfloor$

Proof (Sketch). By applying Lemmas 3 and 4 and Definition 4 of $\simeq$. A detailed proof appears in the technical report [12]. □

$\{\textbf{true}\}$
$A := \emptyset$
$A' := \{ \alpha_1 \langle q_1 \rangle \otimes \cdots \otimes \alpha_n \langle q_n \rangle \mid (q_1, \ldots, q_n) \in \text{Init}(\alpha_1) \times \cdots \times \text{Init}(\alpha_n) \}$
$\textbf{while } \alpha \in A' \setminus A \textbf{ for some } \alpha \textbf{ do}$
    $A := A \cup \{\alpha\}$
    $A' := A' \cup \{ \alpha_1 \langle q_1' \rangle \otimes \cdots \otimes \alpha_n \langle q_n' \rangle \mid (q, P, \phi, (q_1', \ldots, q_n')) \in \text{Tr}(\alpha) \}$
$\textbf{end while}$
$\{ \bigsqcup A = \lfloor \alpha_1 \otimes \cdots \otimes \alpha_n \rfloor \}$

Fig. 6. Algorithm for computing the grand composition of n autamata using the state-by-state approach

Figure 6 shows an algorithm for computing the grand composition of n local CAs using the state-by-state approach, including a precondition and a postcondition, formulated in terms of de/recomposition and reachability. This algorithm works as described in the beginning of this section. A denotes the subset of so-far computed state-based decompositions whose significant state the algorithm already has expanded (i.e., the algorithm has processed all CAs in A). A', in contrast, denotes the full set of so-far computed state-based decompositions (i.e., A' contains A such that $A'\backslash A$ contains the CAs that the algorithm still needs to process). After the algorithm terminates, A contains a number of state-based decompositions. The postcondition subsequently asserts that the recomposition of the CAs in A equals the reachable fragment of the grand composition.

$\{\textbf{true}\}$
$\{\textsf{invar}$
$\quad [A' := \{\alpha_1\langle q_1\rangle \otimes \cdots \otimes \alpha_n\langle q_n\rangle \mid (q_1,\ldots,q_n) \in \mathsf{Init}(\alpha_1) \times \cdots \times \mathsf{Init}(\alpha_n)\}]$
$\quad [A := \emptyset] \hfill \}$
$A := \emptyset$
$A' := \{\alpha_1\langle q_1\rangle \otimes \cdots \otimes \alpha_n\langle q_n\rangle \mid (q_1,\ldots,q_n) \in \mathsf{Init}(\alpha_1) \times \cdots \times \mathsf{Init}(\alpha_n)\}$
$\{\textsf{invar}\}$
$\textbf{while } \alpha \in A' \backslash A \textbf{ for some } \alpha \textbf{ do}$
$\quad \{\alpha \in A' \backslash A \textbf{ and } \textsf{invar} \textbf{ and } |\mathsf{St}(\alpha_1 \otimes \cdots \otimes \alpha_n)| - |A| = z\}$
$\quad \{\,[\textsf{invar} \textbf{ and } 0 \le |\mathsf{St}(\alpha_1 \otimes \cdots \otimes \alpha_n)| - |A| < z]$
$\quad\quad [A' := A' \cup \{\alpha_1\langle q_1'\rangle \otimes \cdots \otimes \alpha_n\langle q_n'\rangle \mid (q, P, \phi, (q_1',\ldots,q_n')) \in \mathsf{Tr}(\alpha)\}]$
$\quad\quad [A := A \cup \{\alpha\}] \hfill \}$
$\quad A := A \cup \{\alpha\}$
$\quad A' := A' \cup \{\alpha_1\langle q_1'\rangle \otimes \cdots \otimes \alpha_n\langle q_n'\rangle \mid (q, P, \phi, (q_1',\ldots,q_n')) \in \mathsf{Tr}(\alpha)\}$
$\quad \{\textsf{invar} \textbf{ and } 0 \le |\mathsf{St}(\alpha_1 \otimes \cdots \otimes \alpha_n)| - |A| < z\}$
$\textbf{end while}$
$\{\textsf{invar} \textbf{ and } [\alpha \notin A' \backslash A \textbf{ for all } \alpha]\}$
$\{\bigsqcup A = \lfloor \alpha_1 \otimes \cdots \otimes \alpha_n \rfloor\}$

Fig. 7. Algorithm for computing the grand composition of n autamata using the state-by-state approach, annotated with assertions for total correctness

Figure 7 shows the algorithm in Fig. 6 annotated with assertions for total correctness; Fig. 8 shows the loop invariant. This invariant consists of four conjuncts. The first conjunct states that $A \cup A'$ contains the initial states in the grand composition. The second conjunct states that the A and A' contain only state-based decompositions of the grand composition. The third conjunct states that every CA in $A \cup A'$ is a state-based decomposition of the grand composition, with respect to some reachable state in that grand composition. The fourth conjunct states that if a CA in A has a transition entering a (global) state q', $A \cup A'$ contains a decomposition of the grand composition with respect to q'. As soon as the loop terminates, the invariant and the negated loop condition imply that every CA in A has a reachable significant state ("soundness"; consequence of the third conjunct) and that, in fact, A contains a CA for every reachable state ("completeness"; consequence of the fourth conjunct).

Theorem 3. *The algorithm in Fig. 6 is correct.*

invar: $\{(\alpha_1 \otimes \cdots \otimes \alpha_n)\langle q \rangle \mid q \in \mathsf{Init}(\alpha_1 \otimes \cdots \otimes \alpha_n)\} \subseteq A \cup (A' \setminus A)$
   and $A, A' \subseteq \{(\alpha_1 \otimes \cdots \otimes \alpha_n)\langle q \rangle \mid q \in \mathsf{St}(\alpha_1 \otimes \cdots \otimes \alpha_n)\}$

and $\left[\begin{array}{c} \alpha \in A \cup (A' \setminus A) \textbf{ implies} \\ \left[\left[\begin{array}{l} \alpha = (\alpha_1 \otimes \cdots \otimes \alpha_n)\langle q \rangle \\ \textbf{and } q \in \mathsf{Reach}(\alpha_1 \otimes \cdots \otimes \alpha_n) \end{array} \right] \textbf{ for some } q \right] \end{array} \right] \textbf{ for all } \alpha]$

and $\left[\begin{array}{c} \left[\alpha \in A \textbf{ and } (q, P, \phi, q') \in \mathsf{Tr}(\alpha) \right] \textbf{ implies} \\ \left[\left[\begin{array}{l} \alpha' = (\alpha_1 \otimes \cdots \otimes \alpha_n)\langle q' \rangle \\ \textbf{and } \alpha' \in A \cup (A' \setminus A) \end{array} \right] \textbf{ for some } \alpha' \right] \end{array} \right] \textbf{ for all } \alpha, q, q', P, \phi]$

Fig. 8. Addendum to Fig. 7

Proof (Sketch). By the assertions in Fig. 7 and the axioms of Hoare logic. A detailed proof appears in the technical report [12].

Note that the invariant refers only to decompositions of the global CA with respect to a global state (e.g., $(\alpha_1 \otimes \cdots \otimes \alpha_n)\langle q \rangle$ for a global state q), whereas the algorithm refers only to decompositions of local CAs with respect to local states (e.g., $\alpha_1\langle q_1 \rangle \otimes \cdots \otimes \alpha_n\langle q_n \rangle$ for local states $q_1, \ldots, q_n$). Recognizing this difference is important, because it highlights the main advantage of the state-by-state approach: by using only decompositions of local CAs, the algorithm never needs to compute any intermediate compounds, so avoiding a potential source of exponential resource requirements.

5 Implementation, Evaluation, and Discussion

We implemented the state-by-state approach for computing grand compositions as an extension to our CA-based Reo-to-Java compiler. This compiler is implemented in Java and extends the ECT, a collection of plugins for Eclipse that serve as an IDE for Reo (see http://reo.project.cwi.nl).

To evaluate the performance of the state-by-state approach in practice, we experimented with the same k-parameteric families of connectors as those in Fig. 4. Because not only composition but also abstraction play an important role in practice (as mentioned at the end of Sect. 2), we consider three composition–abstraction approaches:

- *Alternating iterative approach.* Variant of the iterative approach where we abstract away all *internal ports* for mixed nodes (which do not contribute to the observable behavior of a connector) in intermediate compounds directly after their computation; this approach alternates between composition and abstraction. It has the advantage that intermediate compounds remain small (i.e., abstraction of internal ports eliminates internal transitions and collapses states together), thereby reducing overall resource consumption (i.e., generally, composing smaller CAs requires fewer resources than composing larger CAs).

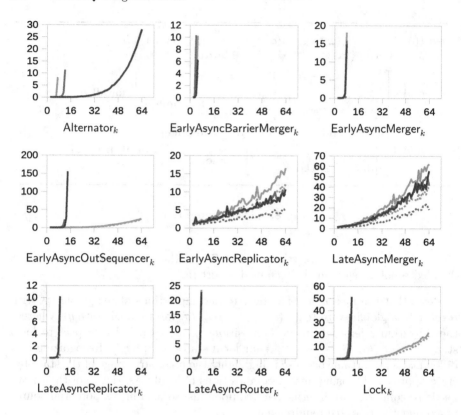

Fig. 9. Computation times (y-axis) for nine k-parametric families, for $2 \leq k \leq 64$ (x-axis), by applying the alternating iterative approach (blue lines), the phased iterative approach before abstraction (dotted-red lines) and after (solid-red lines), and the phased state-by-state approach before abstraction (dotted-yellow lines) and after (solid-yellow lines). Time is measured in seconds, except for EarlyAsyncReplicator$_k$ and LateAsyncMerger$_k$, where time is measured in milliseconds. Page-size versions of these plots appear in the technical report [12] (Color figure online).

- *Phased iterative approach.* Variant of the iterative approach where we abstract away all internal ports only in the final compound and not in intermediate compounds.
- *Phased state-by-state approach.* Variant of the state-by-state approach where we abstract away all internal ports only after the composition phase.

Figure 9 shows the computation times that we measured for the various approaches, connectors, and values of $2 \leq k \leq 64$. We set a timeout of five minutes and bounded the size of the heap at 2 GB.

The four families whose grand compositions grow exponentially in k (i.e., EarlyAsyncBarrierMerger$_k$, EarlyAsyncMerger$_k$, LateAsyncReplicator$_k$, and LateAsyncRouter$_k$) logically provoke exponential growth in resource requirements not only in the iterative approaches (as already observed in Sect. 3) but also in the phased state-by-state approach. Still, the phased state-by-state approach, performs worse than the alternating iterative approach (at least for EarlyAsyncBarrierMerger$_k$ and EarlyAsyncMerger$_k$).

For EarlyAsyncOutSequencer$_k$ and Lock$_k$, the phased state-by-state approach has substantially better performance: whereas both the alternating and the phased iterative approaches fail for $k > 14$ (because these approaches require too much resources to successfully complete their computation), the phased state-by-state approach succeeds for all values of k under study. (These two families formed the main motivation for doing the work reported on in this paper.)

For EarlyAsyncReplicator$_k$ and LateAsyncMerger$_k$, the phased state-by-state approach seems roughly twice as slow as the iterative approaches. A mundane reason may be that we have not optimized our implementation of the state-by-state approach as aggressively as the iterative approach (which has been under development for several years). Another reason may be that the state-by-state approach is not as cache/memory-friendly as the iterative approach (i.e., locality issues), because the state-by-state approach continuously accesses all local CAs. Moreover—and more seriously—Alternator$_k$ forms a problematic case for the phased state-by-state approach. Indeed, the alternating iterative approach performs much better, exactly because it abstracts away internal ports as early as possible. Interestingly, early abstraction does not have such a significant effect for all families of connectors under study. This has to do with the particular structure of Alternator$_k$, explained in detail elsewhere and considered beyond the scope of this paper [10]. Here, the important point is that, although the phased state-by-state approach dramatically improves performance in some cases, it is not a silver bullet. One piece of future work, therefore, concerns the development of heuristics about which composition approach we should apply when. Another piece of future work concerns the investigation of a variant of the state-by-state approach with early abstraction similar to the alternating incremental approach. The main challenge with this is that to perform abstraction, we require certain information that, in the state-by-state approach, seems to become available only once we have completed computing the grand composition. Therefore, we need to develop clever techniques to obtain this kind of information earlier on.

6   Related Work

The main inspiration for our solution in this paper came from Proença's distributed Reo engine [15]. On input of a connector, this engine starts an actor for each of that connector's constituents. Each of these actors has some kind of local automaton (not quite a CA but the differences and details do not matter here) for its corresponding node/channel. Together, the actors run a distributed consensus algorithm to synchronize their behavior, by composing their local behaviors into one consistent global behavior. As part of this consensus algorithm, actors exchange data structures with information about their current state and that state's outgoing transitions (called *frontiers* by Proença). By doing so, the actors effectively compute the composition of their automata at run-time, and only for their reachable states. Our state-by-state approach for computing grand compositions effectively does a similar computation at compile-time.

Some literature exists on algorithms for computing the composition of CAs. For instance, Ghassemi et al. documented that the order in which a tool composes the CAs in a grand composition matters [7]: although any order yields the same final compound (because composition exhibits associativity and commutativity), different orders may yield diffent intermediate compounds. Some orders may give rise to relatively large intermediate compounds, with high resource requirements as a result, while other orders may keep intermediate compounds small. Choosing the right order, therefore, matters significantly in practice. In the same paper, Ghassemi et al. also briefly mention the idea of computing the composition of *two* CAs in a state-by-state approach, but they do not generalize this to arbitrary grand compositions as we do in this paper. Pourvatan and Rouhy also worked on an algorithm for efficiently computing the composition of two CAs [14]. Their approach consists of a special algebraic representation of CAs, including a reformulation of the composition operation for this representation. Pourvatan and Rouhy claim that their approach computes composition twice as fast as the approach by Ghassemi et al., but evidence remains limited.

State expansion based on reachability also surfaces in what Hopcroft et al. call "lazy evaluation" of subsets in the powerset construction for determinizing a nondeterministic finite automaton in classical automata theory [8]. The fact that we need to compose CAs during the expansion of global states—and explicitly do not want to compute the grand composition beforehand—makes our situation more complex, though. Lemma 1 plays a key role in this respect.

Our work is related also to on-the-fly model checking, proposed by Gerth et al. [6], where the state space under verification is generated as needed during the actual decision procedure instead of in its entirety, beforehand. If a counterexample is found already early during state space generation/exploration, then, no effort gets wasted on precomputing the entire state space. A key difference is our use of Hoare logic to prove our technique's correctness, which to our knowledge has not been done in the context of on-the-fly model checking.

7   Conclusion

Our performance evaluation shows that our new approach for computing grand compositions substantially improves the problematic cases of the existing approach. However, in other cases, our existing approach outperformed our new approach. In future work, we want to investigate heuristics for deciding which of these two approaches we should use when.

Constraint automata comprise a general operational formalism for modeling the behavior of concurrent systems, where every CA models a component. To analyze systems modeled as CAs, efficiently computing the grand composition of those CAs is very important. This makes our work a relevant advancement to the theory and practice of component-based software engineering. In this paper, we focused on the "coordination subsystems"—connectors—among the components.

When expressed in Reo, we can compositionally compute connector behavior in terms of CAs. This enables both verification (e.g., model checking [3,4,13]) and compilation (i.e., code generation [10,11]), whose combination subsequently facilitates a correctness-by-construction approach to component-based software engineering—one of the hallmarks in Sifakis' rigorous system design [16].

We can use our new approach for computing grand compositions also beyond Reo, whenever not only the coordinating connectors' semantics exist as CAs but also the semantics of their coordinated components. For instance, the combination of CAs and Reo has been used to model and verify a simple railway network [3], a biomedical sensor network [4], and an industrial communication platform [13]. To model check temporal logic properties of the composition of the components and connectors of such systems (e.g., the composition never deadlocks), we need to compute the grand composition of the CAs for all components and connectors. Here too, our new approach for computing grand compositions constitutes a valuable alternative to the existing approach. In fact, the abstract approach of computing compound global behavior out of primitive local behavior under a "reachability-based" strategy, to avoid excessive intermediate resource consumption, does not depend on CAs and can be applied also to other models.

References

1. Arbab, F.: Reo: a channel-based coordination model for component composition. MSCS **14**(3), 329–366 (2004)
2. Arbab, F.: Puff, the magic protocol. In: Agha, G., Danvy, O., Meseguer, J. (eds.) Formal Modeling: Actors, Open Systems, Biological Systems. LNCS, vol. 7000, pp. 169–206. Springer, Heidelberg (2011)
3. Baier, C., Blechmann, T., Klein, J., Klüppelholz, S.: A uniform framework for modeling and verifying components and connectors. In: Field, J., Vasconcelos, V.T. (eds.) COORDINATION 2009. LNCS, vol. 5521, pp. 247–267. Springer, Heidelberg (2009)
4. Baier, C., Blechmann, T., Klein, J., Klüppelholz, S., Leister, W.: Design and verification of systems with exogenous coordination using Vereofy. In: Margaria, T., Steffen, B. (eds.) ISoLA 2010, Part II. LNCS, vol. 6416, pp. 97–111. Springer, Heidelberg (2010)
5. Baier, C., Sirjani, M., Arbab, F., Rutten, J.: Modeling component connectors in Reo by constraint automata. SCP **61**(2), 75–113 (2006)
6. Gerth, R., Peled, D., Vardi, M., Wolper, P.: Simple on-the-fly automatic verification of linear temporal logic. In: PSTV 1995, pp. 3–18 (1995)
7. Ghassemi, F., Tasharofi, S., Sirjani, M.: Automated mapping of Reo circuits to constraint automata. In: FSEN 2005, ENTCS, vol. 159, pp. 99–115 (2006)
8. Hopcroft, J., Motwani, R., Ullman, J.: Introduction to Automata Theory, Languages, and Computation (2001)
9. Jongmans, S.S., Arbab, F.: Overview of thirty semantic formalisms for Reo. Sci. Ann. Comput. Sci. **22**(1), 201–251 (2012)
10. Jongmans, S.S., Arbab, F.: Toward sequentializing overparallelized protocol code. In: ICE 2014, EPTCS, vol. 166, pp. 38–44 (2014)

11. Jongmans, S.S., Arbab, F.: Can high throughput atone for high latency in compiler-generated protocol code? In: Dastani, M., Sirjani, M. (eds.) FSEN 2015. LNCS, vol. 9392, pp. 238–258. Springer, Heidelberg (2015)
12. Jongmans, S.S., Kappé, T., Arbab, F.: Composing constraint automata, state-by-state (Technical report). Technical report FM-1506, CWI (2015)
13. Klein, J., Klüppelholz, S., Stam, A., Baier, C.: Hierarchical modeling and formal verification. An industrial case study using Reo and Vereofy. In: Salaün, G., Schätz, B. (eds.) FMICS 2011. LNCS, vol. 6959, pp. 228–243. Springer, Heidelberg (2011)
14. Pourvatan, B., Rouhy, N.: An alternative algorithm for constraint automata product. In: Arbab, F., Sirjani, M. (eds.) FSEN 2007. LNCS, vol. 4767, pp. 412–422. Springer, Heidelberg (2007)
15. Proença, J.: Synchronous coordination of distributed components. Ph.D. thesis, Leiden University (2011)
16. Sifakis, J.: Rigorous system design. In: PODC 2014, p. 292 (2014)

Floating Time Transition System: More Efficient Analysis of Timed Actors

Ehsan Khamespanah[1,2]($^{\boxtimes}$), Marjan Sirjani[2], Mahesh Viswanathan[3], and Ramtin Khosravi[1]

[1] School of Electrical and Computer Engineering, University of Tehran, Tehran, Iran
e.khamespanah@ut.ac.ir
[2] School of Computer Science, Reykjavik University, Reykjavik, Iceland
[3] Department of Computer Science, University of Illinois at Urbana-Champaign, Champaign, USA

Abstract. The actor model is a concurrent object-based computational model in which event-driven and asynchronously communicating actors are units of concurrency. Actors are widely used in modeling real-time and distributed systems. Floating-Time Transition System (FTTS) is proposed as an alternative semantics for timed actors, and schedulability and deadlock-freedom analysis techniques have been developed for it. The absence of shared variables and blocking send or receive, and the presence of single-threaded actors along with non-preemptive execution of each message server, ensure that the execution of message servers do not interfere with each other. The Floating-Time Transition System semantics exploits this by executing message servers in isolation, and by relaxing the synchronization of progress of time among actors, and thereby has fewer states in the transition system. Considering an actor-based language, we prove a weak bisimulation relation between FTTS and Timed Transition System, which is generally the standard semantic framework for discrete-time systems. Thus, the FTTS semantics preserves event-based branching-time properties. Our experimental results show a significant reduction in the state space for most of the examples we have studied.

Keywords: Actor model · Timed Rebeca · Verification · State space reduction · Floating Time Transition System · Timed Transition System

1 Introduction

The semantics of real-time systems is often defined assuming an ambient global time that proceeds uniformly for all participants in a distributed system. Even when individual local clocks are assumed to have skews, these skews are modelled relative to this ambient global time. For systems where the time domain is taken to be discrete (i.e., the set of natural numbers), this results in the semantics being described using a *Timed Transition System (TTS)*. In a timed transition system,

© Springer International Publishing Switzerland 2016
C. Braga and P.C. Ölveczky (Eds.): FACS 2015, LNCS 9539, pp. 237–255, 2016.
DOI: 10.1007/978-3-319-28934-2_13

transitions are partitioned into two classes: instantaneous transitions (in which time does not progress), and time ticks when the global clock is incremented. These time ticks happen when all participants "agree" for time elapse. Such TTS-based semantics is standard and has been defined for a variety of formalisms [8,12,16]. Note that, using TTS is not limited to discrete-time systems. It also has been used to give semantics for timed languages and formalisms that assume continuous or dense time domains.

The timed transition system semantics, unfortunately, suffers from the usual state space explosion problem (in addition to being infinite in many cases). The transition system contains arbitrary interleavings of independent actions of the various components of a distributed system, resulting in a large state space. In the presence of a global clock and timing information this may become even more acute.

A very different semantics, called Floating Time Transition System (FTTS), was proposed in [15] for a timed actor-based language called Timed Rebeca [22]. Timed Rebeca has been used in a number of applications. Examples of such case studies include analysis of routing algorithms and scheduling policies in NoC (Network on Chip) designs [24,25]; schedulability analysis of distributed real-time sensor network applications [19], more specifically a real-time continuous sensing application for structural health monitoring in [17]; evaluation of different dispatching policies in clouds with priorities and deadlines in Mapreduce clusters, based on the work in [10].

Floating Time Transition Systems (FTTS) define a semantics where actors in a distributed system proceed at their own rates with local clocks widely apart, instead of moving in a lock step fashion with the global time as in TTS. Recall that in the Actor model [3] of computation, actors encapsulate the concept of concurrent behavior. Each actor provides services that can be requested by other actors by sending messages to the provider. Messages are put in the message buffer of the receiver; the receiver takes the message and executes the requested service, possibly sending messages to some other actors. In FTTS semantics, each transition is the complete execution of a message server of an actor (which contains both timed and untimed statements), without any interleaving with the steps of other actors. Since actors execute a message to completion in this semantics, actors may have different local times in states of FTTS, as their local times are increased by timed statements of message servers. Relaxing the synchronization of progress of time among actors in FTTS can significantly reduce the size of the state space as it avoids many of the interleavings present in the TTS semantics.

The main contribution of this paper is the establishment of the bisimularity of the TTS and FTTS semantics for Timed Rebeca. Moreover, since the starting time of the execution of actions is also preserved, we can prove the preservation of any timed property of actions that is bisimulation invariant. Examples of such properties include μ-calculus with weak modalities. Such a logic preservation result is stronger than previous results about this and other reduction techniques, which only establish the preservation of "reachability"-type properties. In [15], we showed that FTTS preserves assertion-based properties like schedulability and deadlock avoidance. Similarly, many other works on reduction techniques for asynchronous systems papers like [7,11,18] consider assertion-based properties.

For timed systems, the norm is to show that there is a timed weak bisimulation relation between two timed transition systems to prove that they preserve the same set of timed branching-time properties (e.g. TCTL). Proving the existence of such a relation is impossible when one of the transition systems does not have progress-of-time transitions which is the case of relation between TTS and FTTS. In this paper, we proved that the actions and the execution time of the actions are preserved in FTTS using an innovative approach for defining relation between the states of a TTS and its corresponding FTTS.

Our bisimulation proof relies on observing that the FTTS semantics exploits key features of the actor model of computation. In such a model there is no shared memory, and sends and receives are non-blocking. Moreover, actors are single-threaded, with message servers being executed non-preemptively. This means that message servers can be executed in an isolated fashion, as is carried out in FTTS, without compromising the semantics of the model. Since our correctness proof of FTTS relies only on certain features of the actor model (rather than something specific to timed Rebeca), it suggests that FTTSs can be used in the analysis of other actor models and languages, and more generally, in other asynchronous event-based models.

We present experimental results that demonstrate the savings obtained from using FTTS. We have developed a toolset for generating the state space of a given Timed Rebeca model based on both the TTS and FTTS semantics that is accessible through the Rebeca homepage [1]. We show that using the FTTS semantics results in a smaller state space, fewer transitions, and less model checking time when compared with the TTS semantics (Sect. 4). In some case studies, using FTTS results in a state space which is 10 times smaller than its observational equivalent state space in TTS semantics.

2 Background

2.1 Timed Rebeca

Timed Rebeca is an extension of Rebeca [26] with time-related features for modeling and verification of time-critical systems. We describe Timed Rebeca language constructs using a simple ticket service example (see Fig. 1).

Each Timed Rebeca model consists of a number of *reactive classes*, each describing the type of a certain number of *actors* (called *rebecs* in Timed Rebeca). In this example (Fig. 1), we have three reactive classes TicketService, Agent, and Customer. Each reactive class declares a set of *state variables* which define the local state of the rebecs of that class (like issueDelay of TicketService which defines the time needed to issue a ticket). Following the actor model, the communication in the model takes place by rebecs sending asynchronous messages to each other. Each rebec has a set of *known rebecs* to which it can send messages. For example, a rebec of type TicketService knows a rebec

```
 1 reactiveclass TicketService {        24   }
 2   knownrebecs {Agent a;}             25   msgsrv ticketIssued(int id) {
 3   statevars {                        26     c.ticketIssued(id);
 4     int issueDelay, nextId;          27   }
 5   }                                  28 }
 6   msgsrv initial(int myDelay) {      29 reactiveclass Customer {
 7     issueDelay = myDelay;            30   knownrebecs {Agent a;}
 8     nextId = 0;                      31   msgsrv initial() {
 9   }                                  32     self.try();
10   msgsrv requestTicket() {           33   }
11     delay(issueDelay);               34   msgsrv try() {
12     a.ticketIssued(nextId);          35     a.requestTicket();
13     nextId = nextId + 1;             36   }
14   }                                  37   msgsrv ticketIssued(int id) {
15 }                                    38     self.try() after(30);
16 reactiveclass Agent {                39   }
17   knownrebecs {                      40 }
18     TicketService ts;                41
19     Customer c;                      42 main {
20   }                                  43   Agent a(ts, c):();
21   msgsrv requestTicket() {           44   TicketService ts(a):(3);
22     ts.requestTicket()               45   Customer c(a):();
23         deadline(5);                 46 }
```

Fig. 1. The Timed Rebeca model of ticket service system.

of type Agent (line 2), to which it can send messages (line 12). Reactive classes declare the messages to which they can respond. The way a rebec responds to a message is specified in a *message server*. A rebec can change its state variables through assignment statements (line 13), make decisions through conditional statements (not appearing in our example), and communicate with other rebecs by sending messages (line 12). Iterative behavior is modeled by rebecs sending messages to themselves (line 38). Since the communication is asynchronous, each rebec has a *message bag* from which it takes the next incoming message. A rebec takes the first message from its bag, executes the corresponding message server atomically, and then takes the next message (or waits for the next message to arrive) and so on.

Timed Rebeca allows nondeterministic assignment to model nondeterministic behavior of message servers. In this paper we consider the fragment of language *without* such nondeterministic assignment. Thus, message servers in this paper specify deterministic behavior. Note, however, that even the Timed Rebeca language considered in this paper exhibits nondeterminism that results from the interleaving of the executions of different rebecs due to concurrency; more details follow in the section defining the semantics.

Finally, the main block is used to instantiate the rebecs in the system. In our example (lines 43–45), three rebecs are created receiving their known rebecs and the arguments to their inital message servers upon instantiation.

In a Timed Rebeca model, although there is a notion of global time, each rebec has its own local clock. The local clocks can be considered as synchronized distributed clocks. Though methods (message servers) are executed atomically, passing of time while executing a method can still be modeled. In addition, instead of a queue for messages, there is a bag of messages for each rebec, ordering its messages based on their arrival time.

Timed Rebeca adds three primitives to Rebeca to address timing issues: *delay*, *deadline* and *after*. A *delay* statement models the passing of time for a rebec during execution of a message server (line 11). Note that all other statements are assumed to execute instantaneously. The keywords *after* and *deadline* can be used in conjunction with a method call. The term `after` n indicates that it takes n units of time (based on the local time of the sender) for the message to be delivered to its receiver. For example, the periodic task of requesting a new ticket is modeled in line 38 by the customer sending a `try` message to itself and letting the receiver (itself) take it from its bag only after 30 units of time. The term `deadline` n shows that if the message is not taken in n units of time, it will be purged from the receiver's bag automatically. For example, line 23 indicates that a `requestTicket` message to the ticket service must be started to execute before five units from sending the message. Note that, the deadline is counted from the time of the sending of the message.

2.2 Semantics of Timed Rebeca

Prior to the detailed definition of semantics of Timed Rebeca, we formalize the definition of a rebec and a model in Timed Rebeca. A rebec r_i with the unique identifier i is defined as the tuple $(\mathcal{V}_i, \mathcal{M}_i, \mathcal{K}_i)$ where $\mathcal{V}_i$ is the set of its state variables, $\mathcal{M}_i$ is the set of its message servers, and $\mathcal{K}_i$ is the set of its known rebecs. The set of all the values of the state variables of r_i is denoted by $Vals_i$. For a Timed Rebeca model $\mathcal{M}$, there is a universal set $\mathcal{I}$ which contains identifiers of all the rebecs of $\mathcal{M}$.

A (timed) message is defined as $tmsg = ((sid, rid, mid), ar, dl)$, where rebec r_{sid} sends the message $m_{mid} \in \mathcal{M}_{rid}$ to rebec r_{rid}. This message is delivered to the rebec r_{rid} at $ar \in \mathbb{N}_0$ as its arrival time and the message should be served before $dl \in \mathbb{N}_0$ as its deadline. For the sake of simplicity, we assume parametrized messages as different messages (i.e. the value of parameters are in the name of the message) without loss of generality. Each rebec r_i has a message bag $\mathcal{B}_i$ which can be defined as a multiset of timed messages. $\mathcal{B}_i$ stores the timed messages which are sent to r_i. The set of possible states of $\mathcal{B}_i$ is denoted by $Bags_i$.

In the following sections, two different semantics for Timed Rebeca models are defined, called *timed transition system* and *floating time transition system*. FTTS is defined in [15] as the natural semantics of Timed Rebeca but the relation between TTS and FTTS for Timed Rebeca has not been investigated before. Timed transition system is generally the standard semantic framework for timed systems, and we define the formal semantics of Timed Rebeca in TTS in Sect. 2.3. Floating time transition system exploits key features of actor models to generate smaller transition systems compared to TTS. The absence of shared variables, and blocking send or receive, and the presence of single threaded actors along with non-preemptive execution of each message server, ensures that the execution of a message server does not interfere with the execution of another message server of a different rebec. The floating time transition system semantics exploits this by executing message servers in isolation, and thereby having fewer states in the transition system.

2.3   Semantics of Timed Rebeca in Timed Transition System

Timed Transition System of the Timed Rebeca model $\mathcal{M}$ is a tuple of $TTS = (S, s_0, Act, \rightarrow)$ where S is the set of states, s_0 is the initial state, Act is the set of actions, and $\rightarrow$ is the transition relation.

States. A state $s \in S$ consists of the local states of the rebecs, together with the current time of the state. The local state of rebec r_i in state s is defined as the tuple $(V_{s,i}, B_{s,i}, pc_{s,i}, res_{s,i})$, where

- $V_{s,i} \in Vals_i$ is the values of the state variables of r_i
- $B_{s,i} \in Bags_i$ is the message bag of r_i
- $pc_{s,i} \in \{null\} \cup (\mathcal{M}_i \times \mathbb{N})$ is the program counter, tracking the execution of the current message server ($null$ if r_i is idle in s)
- $res_{s,i} \in \mathbb{N}_0$ is the resuming time, if r_i is executing a delay in s

So, state $s \in S$ can be defined as $\left(\prod_{i \in \mathcal{I}} (V_{s,i}, B_{s,i}, pc_{s,i}, res_{s,i}), now_s \right)$ where $now_s \in \mathbb{N}$ is the current time of s.

Initial State. s_0 is the initial state of the Timed Rebeca model $\mathcal{M}$ where the state variables of the rebecs are set to their initial values , the initial message is put in the bag of all rebecs having such a message server (their arrival times are set to zero), the program counters of all rebecs are set to $null$, and the resuming time of all rebecs and the time of the state are set to zero.

Actions. There are three possible types of actions: taking a message $tmsg$, executing a statement by an actor (which we consider as an internal transition τ), and progress of $n \in \mathbb{N}$ units of time. Hence, the set of actions is $Act = \bigcup_{i \in \mathcal{I}} ((\mathcal{I} \times i \times \mathcal{M}_i) \times \mathbb{N} \times \mathbb{N}) \cup \{\tau\} \cup \mathbb{N}$.

Transition Relations. Before defining the transition relation, we introduce the notation $E_{s,i}$ which denotes the set of *enabled messages* of rebec r_i in state s which contains the messages whose arrival time is less than or equal to now_s. The transition relation $\rightarrow \subset S \times Act \times S$ is defined such that $(s, act, t) \in \rightarrow$ if and only if one of the following conditions holds.

1. **(Taking a Message for Execution).** In state s, there exists r_i such that $pc_{s,i} = null$ and there exists $tmsg \in E_{s,i}$. Here, we have a transition of the form $s \xrightarrow{tmsg} t$. This transition results in extracting $tmsg$ from the message bag of r_i, setting $pc_{t,i}$ to the first statement of the message server corresponding to $tmsg$, and setting $res_{t,i}$ to now_t (which is the same as now_s). Note that $V_{t,i}$ remains the same as $V_{s,i}$. These transitions are called *taking-event transitions* and r_i is called *enabled rebec*.

2. **(Internal Action).** In state s, there exist r_i such that $pc_{s,i} \neq null$ and $res_{s,i} = now_s$ (the value of $res_{s,i}$ does not change during the execution of a message, except for running a delay statement). The statement of message server of r_i specified by $pc_{s,i}$ is executed and one of the following cases occurs based on the type of the statement. Here, we have a transition of the form $s \xrightarrow{\tau} t$.

   (a) Non-delay statement: the execution of such a statement may change the value of a state variable of rebec r_i or send a message to another rebec. Here, $pc_{t,i}$ is set to the next statement (or $null$ if there is no more statements). In this case $now(t)$ and $now(s)$ are the same.

   (b) Delay statement with parameter $d \in \mathbb{N}$: the execution of a delay statement sets $res_{t,i}$ to $now_s + d$. All other elements of the state remain unchanged. Particularly, $pc_{t,i} = pc_{s,i}$ because the execution of delay statement is not yet complete. The value of the program counter will be set to the next statement after completing the execution of delay (as will be shown in the third case).

   These transitions are called *internal transitions*.

3. **(Progress of Time).** If in state s none of the conditions in cases 1 and 2 hold, meaning that $\nexists r_i \cdot ((pc_{s,i} = null \wedge E_{s,i} \neq \emptyset) \vee (pc_{s,i} \neq null \wedge res_{s,i} = now_s))$, the only possible transition is progress of time. In this case, now_t is set to $now_s + d$ where $d \in \mathbb{N}$ is the minimum value which makes one of the aforementioned conditions become true. The transition is of the form $s \xrightarrow{d} t$. For any rebec r_i, if $pc_{s,i} \neq null$ and $res_{s,i} = now_t$ (the current value of $pc_{s,i}$ points to a delay statement), $pc_{t,i}$ is set to the next statement (or to $null$ if there are no more statements). These transitions are called *time transitions*. Note that when such a transition exists, there is no other outgoing transition from s.

Later, for each state of a TTS we need to find messages which are sent by a given rebec. Therefore, we define the following function which returns a bag of messages which are sent by a rebec.

Definition 1 (Sent Messages in TTS). *For a given state $s \in S$ and rebec r_i, function $sent(s, r_i)$ returns bag of messages which are sent by r_i in state s. In other words, $tmsg \in sent(s, r_i)$ if and only if for message $tmsg = ((sid, rid, mid), ar, dl)$ there is $\exists r_j \cdot tmsg \in B_{s,j} \wedge sid = r_i$.* □

2.4 Semantics of Timed Rebeca in Floating Timed Transition System

The notion of floating time transition system (FTTS) as a semantics for Timed Rebeca has been introduced in [15]. States in floating time transition system contain the local times of each rebec, in addition to values of their state variables and the bag of their received messages. However, the local times of rebecs in a state can be different, and there is no unique value for time in each state. Such a semantics is reasonable when one is only interested in the order of visible events. FTTS may not be appropriate for analyses that require reasoning about all synchronized global states of a Timed Rebeca model. The key features of Rebeca actors that make FTTS a reasonable semantics are having no shared variables, no blocking send or receive, single-threaded actors, and atomic (non-preemptive) execution of each message server which give us an isolated message server execution. This means that the execution of a message server of a rebec will not interfere with execution of a message server of another rebec. Therefore, we can execute all the statements of a given message server (even delay statements) during a single transition. This makes the transition system significantly smaller, because there will be only one kind of action, which is taking a message and executing the corresponding message server entirely.

The operational semantics of a Timed Rebeca model $\mathcal{M}$ is defined as a floating time transition system $FTTS = (S', s'_0, Act', \hookrightarrow)$ and is as described below. In this paper, we use the primed version for letters and notations related to FTTS except for transitions which are shown by $\hookrightarrow$ (for TTS we use the unprimed letters).

States. Similar to TTS, a state $s \in S'$ consists of the local states of the rebecs. However, the current time is kept separately for each rebec, denoted by $now_{s',i}$. We will see shortly, the message servers are executed entirely in one transition; therefore, there is no need to keep track of the program counter and the resuming time. So, the state $s' \in S'$ is defined as $s' = \prod_{i \in \mathcal{I}} (V_{s',i}, B_{s',i}, now_{s',i})$.

Initial State. s'_0 is the initial state of the Timed Rebeca model $\mathcal{M}$ where the state variables of the rebecs are set to their initial values (according to their types), the `initial` message is put in the bag of rebecs (their arrival times are set to zero), and the current times of all the rebecs are set to zero.

Actions. As mentioned before, there is only one kind of action, which is taking a message and executing the corresponding message server entirely. Therefore, $Act' = \bigcup_{i \in \mathcal{I}} ((\mathcal{I} \times \{i\} \times \mathcal{M}_i) \times \mathbb{N} \times \mathbb{N})$ is defined as the set of all the possible timed messages.

Transition Relations. We first define the notion of *release time* of a message. A rebec r_i in a state $s' \in S'$ has a number of timed messages in its bag. The release time of $tmsg = ((sid, rid, mid), ar, dl) \in B_{s',i}$ is defined as $rt_{tmsg} = \max(now_{s',i}, ar)$ (Note that $ar < now_{s',i}$ means that $tmsg$ has arrived at some time when r_i has been busy executing another message server. Hence, $tmsg$ is ready to be processed at $now_{s',i}$). Consequently, the set of enabled messages of rebec r_i in state s' is $E_{s',i} = \{tmsg \in B_{s',i} | \forall tmsg' \in B_{s',i} \cdot rt_{tmsg} \leq rt_{tmsg'}\}$ which are the messages with the smallest release time. For a set of enabled messages $E_{s',i}$, enabling time $ET_{s',i}$ is the release time of the members of $E_{s',i}$.

Now we define the transition relation $\hookrightarrow \subset S' \times Act' \times S'$ such that for every pair of states $s', t' \in S'$, we have $(s', tmsg, t') \in \hookrightarrow$ for every $tmsg \in E_{s',i} \wedge (\forall j \in \mathcal{I} \cdot ET_{s',i} \leq ET_{s',j})$. All the transitions of FTTS are called taking-event transitions and as a result of a taking-event transition labeled with $tmsg$, $tmsg$ is extracted from the bag of r_i, the local time of r_i is set to $ET_{s',i}$, and all the statements in the message server corresponding to $tmsg$ are executed sequentially. Here, r_i is called *enabled rebec*. The effect of executing non-delay statements is changing the state variables of r_i and sending some messages to s_i or other rebecs. The effect of executing a delay statement with parameter $d \in \mathbb{N}$ is increasing the local time of r_i by d units of time.

We define bag of sent messages in FTTS the same as what we defined in TTS.

Definition 2 (Sent Messages in FTTS). *For a given state $s' \in S'$ and rebec r_i, function $sent(s', r_i)$ returns bag of messages which are sent by r_i in state s'. In the other words, $tmsg \in sent(s', r_i)$ if and only if for message $tmsg = ((sid, rid, mid), ar, dl)$ there is $\exists \, r_j \cdot tmsg \in B_{s',j} \wedge sid = r_i$.*   □

There is no explicit reset operator for the time in Timed Rebeca, so, progress of time results in an infinite number of states in the transition systems of both FTTS and TTS. However, Timed Rebeca models are models of reactive systems which generally show periodic or recurrent behaviors. Hence, if we ignore the absolute time of the states, usually finite number of untimed traces are generated for Timed Rebeca models. Based on this fact, in [15] we presented a new notion for equivalence relation between two states to make the transition systems finite, called *shift equivalence relation*. In shift equivalence relation two states are equivalent if and only if they are the same except for the value of parts which are related to the time (value of *now*, arrival times of messages, and deadlines of messages) and shifting the value of parts which are related to the time in one state makes it the same as the other one. This way, instead of preserving absolute value of time, only the relative difference of timing parts of states are preserved. As discussed in [15], shift equivalence relation makes transition systems of the majority of Timed Rebeca models finite.

3 An Action-Based Weak Bisimulation Between TTS and FTTS

As described in Sect. 2.4, in FTTS representation of a Timed Rebeca model, all the statements of a message server are executed at once during a single transition. In contrast, the TTS semantics executes one statement at a time, and interleaves the execution of different message servers. We demonstrate despite these differences, these semantics are equivalent in some sense. To this end, we define an action-based weak bisimulation (observational equivalence) relation between $TTS = (S, s_0, Act, \rightarrow)$ and $FTTS = (S', s'_0, Act', \hookrightarrow)$ for a given Timed Rebeca model $\mathcal{M}$. Note that in the following text we denote the states of FTTS as the primed version of the states in TTS.

This definition is valid for Zeno-free Timed Rebeca models. As the model of time in Timed Rebeca is discrete, the execution of infinite number of message servers in zero time is the only scenario resulting Zeno behavior. So, the Zeno behavior happens if and only if there is a cycle of message servers invocations among different actors without progress of time, can be detected by performing a depth-first-search (DFS) in both TTS and FTTS [14].

Prior to the formal definition of the relation between the states of FTTS and TTS the following definitions and proposition are required to make the relation easy to understand.

We begin by defining the observable and τ actions in both transitions systems. All actions in FTTS are observable. In the TTS, only *taking-event transitions* are observable. Therefore, *time transitions* and *internal transitions* in TTS are assumed to be τ transitions. In other words, only taking-event actions are observable in TTS and FTTS. This definition conforms the definition of *events* and *observer primitives* in the actor model which is introduced by Agha et al. in [2] as a reference actor framework. Next, we define the notion of a *completing trace* for a rebec r_i in TTS state s as an execution which results in completing the execution of the message server of r_i that has already commenced in state s. Note that during a completing trace for r_i the other rebecs, may complete their servers (or not), and may start the execution of new message servers. We begin by first defining an execution.

Definition 3 (Execution Trace). *Execution trace from state s in TTS is a sequence of transitions from state s to one of its reachable states u, shown by $s \xrightarrow{act_1} s_1 \xrightarrow{act_2} \cdots \xrightarrow{act_n} u$.* □

Definition 4 (Completing Trace for a Rebec). *A given execution trace from state s to state u in TTS is a completing trace for rebec r_i if and only if r_i does not execute any taking-event transition from s to u, $pc_{u,i} = null$, and there is no other state in the trace where the program counter of r_i is null. Here, we also define $CT_{s,i}$ as one of the completing traces from s for rebec r_i (no matter which one in the case there are more than one completing traces from s for rebec r_i). In case of $pc_{s,i} = null$, there is $CT_{s,i} = \epsilon$ as no more action is needed for completing the execution of a message server of r_i in s.* □

Note that, as there is no preemption in the message server execution and there is no infinite message server body in Timed Rebeca, there is a completing trace for all the rebecs from all the states.

We define three functions on the completing traces. The first one returns the value of the state variables of the specific rebec at the last state of the trace (the rebec that the completing trace is defined for). The second one returns the time of the last state of the trace. The third one returns the bag of messages that are sent by the specific rebec during this trace.

Definition 5 (Three Functions on Completing Traces). *The values of state variables of r_i in the target state of trace $CT_{s,i}$ is return by function $state_i(CT_{s,i})$. Function $now_i(CT_{s,i})$ returns the time of the target state of trace $CT_{s,i}$. Function $sent_i(CT_{s,i})$ returns a bag of messages where $tmsg = ((sid, rid, mid), ar, dl) \in sent_i(CT_{s,i})$ if and only if $tmsg$ is sent during the execution of completing trace $CT_{s,i}$ and $sid = r_i$.* □

Based on the isolated execution of rebecs (no shared variables and no preemption of a message server) we can easily conclude that in case of more than one completing trace for a rebec, any of the completing traces ends in the same values for state variables, the same state time, and the same bag of sent messages.

Proposition 1 (Completing Traces End in the Same Final Condition).
Assume that there are two different completing traces $CT_{s,i}^1$ and $CT_{s,i}^2$ from a given state $s \in S$ and rebec r_i. We have $sent_i(CT_{s,i}^1) = sent_i(CT_{s,i}^2)$, $now_i(CT_{s,i}^1) = now_i(CT_{s,i}^2)$, and $state_i(CT_{s,i}^1) = state_i(CT_{s,i}^2)$. This proposition is valid when there is no nondeterminism in the body of message servers. At the beginning of this section we made clear that in this work we address Timed Rebeca models which do not have nondeterministic assignments.

Proof. As mentioned in the semantics of Timed Rebeca, execution of a message server is not interfered with the execution of other rebecs because in Timed Rebeca there is no shared variable or any kind of preemption of execution of a message server while its executing. In addition, we assumed that there is no non-deterministic expression in messages servers of rebecs. Therefore, in all the completing traces from state s, execution of τ transitions which are related to r_i ends in the same values for state variables and bag of sent messages. On the other hand, as *delay* statements which are related to the execution of r_i are the same in two different competing traces, the time at the target states of $CT_{s,i}^1$ and $CT_{s,i}^2$ are the same.   □

Next, we define a projection function for states of TTS and FTTS. Projection functions extract values of state variables and the collection of messages which are sent by one rebec from a given TTS or FTTS state. Using these projection functions, we get uniform views from states of TTS and FTTS which are necessary for the definition of the action-based weak bisimulation relation. To this aim, as the execution of a message in TTS is completed in several steps, the projection function in TTS is defined based on completing traces to be able to have access to the valuation of state variables and bags of sent messages after completing the execution of currently executing messages.

Definition 6 (Projection Function in TTS). *For a given TTS state $s \in S$ and rebec r_i, projection function $Proj(s, i)$ returns a collection of $state_i(CT_{s,i})$, $now_i(CT_{s,i})$, and $sent(s, i) \cup sent_i(CT_{s,i})$. Here, $CT_{s,i}$ is one of completing traces of rebec r_i in state s.*   □

Definition 7 (Projection Function in FTTS). *For a given FTTS state $s' \in S'$ and rebec r_i, projection function $Proj(s', i)$ returns a collection of the values of state variables of r_i in s', $now(s', i)$, and $sent(s', i)$.*   □

Using the above definitions, we define the action-based weak bisimulation relation among states of TTS and FTTS. Two states in TTS and FTTS are in the relation if and only if the projection of states to each rebec is the same. This way, we will prove that two states have the same future behavior in Theorem 1. Figure 2 shows how states in TTS are mapped to their corresponding states in FTTS. As the observational behavior of s_1 and s_1' are the same (only the

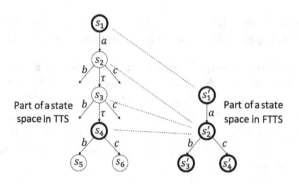

Fig. 2. How states in TTS are mapped to states of FTTS with the same future behaviors.

observable action a is enabled), s_1 is mapped to s'_1 and as the observational behavior of s_2, s_3, and s_4 are the same as the observational behavior of s'_2 (the observable actions b and c are enabled), they are mapped to s'_2.

Definition 8 (Relation among States of TTS and FTTS). *Two states $s \in S$ and $s' \in S'$ are in relation $\mathcal{R} \subseteq S \times S'$ if and only if $Proj(s, i) = Proj(s', i)$ holds for every rebec r_i.*   □

Directly from the definition of relation $\mathcal{R}$ it is concluded that the bag of enabled taking-event messages in s and s' are the same.

Proposition 2 (Relation $\mathcal{R}$ Preserves Enabled Messages). *Two states $s \in S$ and $s' \in S'$ which are in relation $\mathcal{R}$ and $E_{s,i} \neq \emptyset$, have the same bag of enabled messages and the enabled messages have the same enabling time.*

Proof. Assume that for given states $s \in S$ and $s' \in S'$ there is $s \, \mathcal{R} \, s'$. Then, $\forall \, i \in \mathcal{I} \cdot Proj(s, i) = Proj(s', i)$ which results in $\forall \, i \in \mathcal{I} \cdot sent(s, i) \cup sent_i(CT_{s,i}) = sent(s', i)$. As a result, there is $\bigcup_{i \in \mathcal{I}} (sent(s, i) \cup sent_i(CT_{s,i})) = \bigcup_{i \in \mathcal{I}} (sent(s', i))$ which implies that $\bigcup_{i \in \mathcal{I}} (B_{s,i}) \cup \bigcup_{i \in \mathcal{I}} sent_i(CT_{s,i}) = \bigcup_{i \in \mathcal{I}} (B_{s',i})$. As the messages in $\bigcup_{i \in \mathcal{I}} sent_i(CT_{s,i})$ will be send in the future, none of the enabled messages in s are in $\bigcup_{i \in \mathcal{I}} sent_i(CT_{s,i})$. Therefore, enabled messages in $\bigcup_{i \in \mathcal{I}} (B_{s',i})$ are in $\bigcup_{i \in \mathcal{I}} (B_{s,i})$. On the other hand, based on the definition of enabled messages in TTS, enabled rebecs are not busy with the execution of messages in s. So, their completing trace are empty trace. Assume that r_i is one of the enabled rebecs of s. Having $CT_{s,i} = \emptyset$ results in $now_i(CT_{s,i}) = now(s)$. Therefore, as $Proj(s, i) = Proj(s', i)$ there is $now(s', i) = now_i(CT_{s,i}) = now(s)$. So, for enabled rebecs in s, their local times in s' is the same as the time of state s.

Finally, as in s and s' there are the same messages in the bag of enabled rebecs and their times are the same, based on the definition of enabled rebecs in Sect. 2.2, s and s' have the same bag of enabled rebecs. This property holds for both conditions one and two.   □

Having the same enabled messages (messages with the same signature and the same execution time) in two given states $s \in S$ and $s' \in S'$ where $s \mathcal{R} s'$, we are able to prove that s and s' have the same future behavior. To this aim, we have to prove that $\mathcal{R}$ is an action-based weak bisimulation relation.

Definition 9 (Action-Based Weak Bisimulation Relation). *A relation $\mathcal{P}$ over two transition systems $TS_1 = (S_1, s_{1_0}, Act_1, \rightarrow_1)$ and τ-free transition system $TS_2 = (S_2, s_{2_0}, Act_2, \rightarrow_2)$, is an action-based weak bisimulation relation if the following conditions hold for states of TS_1 and TS_2.*

1. *$\forall s_1, t_1 \in S_1$ and $s_2 \in S_2$ where $s_1 \mathcal{P} s_2$, in case of $s_1 \xrightarrow{\alpha}_1 t_1$ where $\alpha \in Act_1$ then $\exists\, t_2 \in S_2$ such that $s_2 \xrightarrow{\alpha}_2 t_2$ and $t_1 \mathcal{P} t_2$ and in case of $s_1 \xrightarrow{\tau}_1 t_1$ there is $t_1 \mathcal{P} s_2$.*
2. *$\forall s_2, t_2 \in S_2$ and $s_1 \in S_1$ where $s_1 \mathcal{P} s_2$, for a message $\alpha \in Act_2$ such that $s_2 \xrightarrow{\alpha}_2 t_2$ then $\exists\, s', s'', \ldots, s^{(k)}, t_1 \in S_1$ (for $k \geq 0$) such that $s_1 \xrightarrow{\tau}_1 s' \xrightarrow{\tau}_1 s'' \xrightarrow{\tau}_1 \cdots \xrightarrow{\alpha}_1 t_1$ and $t_1 \mathcal{P} t_2$.* □

Theorem 1. *The relation $\mathcal{R}$ is an action-based weak bisimulation relation between states of TTS and FTTS.*

Proof. It is presented in Appendix A.

We discussed in Sect. 2.4 that in actor systems we are interested in relation among actions of systems and the time where they are triggered (messages are taken from bags). So, we have to find the most expressive action-based logic which is preserved in action-based weak bisimulation relation. As mentioned in [27], weak bisimulation relation preserves properties in form of modal μ-calculus with weak modalities. Weak-bisimulation relation does not preserve complete modal μ-calculus. Weak modal μ-calculus has the same syntax as modal μ-calculus, where we assume that the diamond ($\langle a \rangle \varphi$) and box ($[a]\varphi$) modalities are restricted to observable transitions, i.e., action a must be a taking-event transition. The semantics of this logic is identical to that of μ-calculus, except for the semantics of the diamond and box operators — a state s satisfies $\langle a \rangle \varphi$ if there is an execution starting from state s to t, such that a is the only visible action, and t satisfies (inductively) φ. The semantics of box is defined dually.

Corollary 1. *Transition systems of Timed Rebeca models in TTS and FTTS are equivalent with respect to all formulas that can be expressed in modal μ-calculus with weak modalities where the actions are taking messages from bags.* □

4   Experimental Results

We developed a toolset for the model checking of Timed Rebeca models based on the semantics of both FTTS and TTS, as a part of the Afra project[1]. The current version of the model checking toolset supports schedulability and deadlock-freedom analysis and assertion based verification of Timed Rebeca models. The

---

[1] The latest version of the toolset (version 2.5.0) is accessible from http://www.rebeca-lang.org/wiki/pmwiki.php/Tools/RMC

Timed Rebeca code of the case studies and the model checking toolset are accessible from Rebeca homepage [1]. We provide four case studies of different sizes to illustrate the reduction in state space size, number of transitions, and time consumption of model checking using FTTS in comparison with TTS. The host computer of model checking toolset was a desktop computer with 1 CPU (2 cores) and 6GB of RAM storage, running Microsoft Windows 7 as the operating system. The selected case studies are the models of a *Wireless Sensor and Actuator Networks (WSAN)*, the simplified version of *Scheduler of Hadoop*, a *Ticket Service* system, and simplified version of *802.11 Wireless Protocol*.

The details of the *Ticket Service* case study is explained in Sect. 2.1. Catching the deadline of issuing the ticket is the main property of this model. We created different sizes of ticket service model by varying the number of customers, which results in four to ten rebecs in the model. In the case of the simplified version of *802.11 Wireless Protocol*, we modeled three wireless nodes which are communicating via a medium. The medium sets random back-off time when more than one node starts to send data, to resolve data collision in the medium. Deadlock avoidance is the main property of this model. In the third case study, a WSAN is modeled as a collection of actors for sensing, radio communication, data processing, and actuation. Schedulability of the model is verified as the main property of this model. Finally, we modeled a simplified version of the behavior of MapReduce of Hadoop system, called YARN. We modeled one client which submits jobs to YARN resource manager. The resource manager distributes the submitted job among application masters and application masters split the job into some tasks and distribute tasks among some nodes. This model has 32 rebecs and is model checked to meet deadline of jobs.

Using FTTS results in significant reduction in the size of the state space for the majority of timed actor models. As shown in Table 1, in *Yarn* model we have about 90 % of reduction. The reason is many delay statements in the message servers of *Yarn* model which results in splitting the execution of message servers in TTS. Interleaving of the execution of these parts results in larger state spaces in TTS. The same argument is valid to support results of *Ticket Service* and *WSAN*. In the case of *WSAN*, in each row, the size (the numbers which are separated by comma) is a combination of the sampling rate, the number of nodes, the packet size, and the sensor task delay of the model, respectively. As the complexity of these examples are less than *Yarn* model, the reduction is about 50 %. There are some exceptional models in which the state space size and the number of transitions in TTS and FTTS are close to each other. The model of *802.11 prot.* is one of them. As there is no delay statement in the body of the message servers of *802.11 prot.*, the execution of the message servers is without progress of time. Therefore, atomic execution of message servers in FTTS and the rather fine-grain execution of message servers in TTS results in state spaces with comparable sizes. The effectiveness of FTTS is reduced in this kind of models. Table 1 also shows that using FTTS reduces the model checking time consumption (even in case of *802.11 prot.*). It is because of the simplicity of the generated state space in FTTS, using atomic execution of message servers.

Table 1. Number of states and transitions, time consumption, and reduction ratio in model checking based on floating time transition system and timed transition system.

Problem	Size	Using FTTS			Using TTS			Reduction	
		states	trans	time	states	trans	time	states	trans
Yarn	-	1.30K	5.71K	< 1 sec	11.03K	61.08K	6 secs	88 %	91 %
IWSAN	**33,6,4,2**	977	1.5K	< 1 sec	1.92K	2.52K	< 1 sec	49 %	41 %
	25,5,4,10	1.85K	2.54K	< 1 sec	3.72K	4.55K	< 1 sec	50 %	44 %
	30,6,4,2	4.75K	5.78K	< 1 sec	9.35K	10.46K	2 secs	50 %	45 %
	25,6,4,2	17.02K	20K	5 secs	34.5K	37.85K	24 secs	51 %	47 %
	20,6,4,2	28.19K	32.19K	16 secs	57.62K	62.21K	64 secs	51 %	48 %
Ticket Service	1	5	6	< 1 sec	8	9	< 1 sec	38 %	33 %
	2	51	77	< 1 sec	77	107	< 1 sec	34 %	28 %
	3	252	418	< 1 sec	360	550	< 1 sec	30 %	24 %
	4	1.29K	2.21K	< 1 sec	1.82K	2.89K	< 1 sec	30 %	24 %
	5	7.53K	12.8K	< 1 sec	10.7K	16.9K	< 1 sec	30 %	24 %
	6	51.6K	84.7K	2 secs	73.5K	114K	2 secs	30 %	26 %
	7	408K	650K	18 secs	582K	884K	24 secs	30 %	26 %
802.11 Prot.	2	1.12K	2.09K	2 secs	1.92K	2.62K	2 secs	10 %	4 %
	3	59K	196K	122 secs	61K	198K	153 secs	3 %	1 %

5   Related Work

Here, we give an overview of the approaches which are used for dealing with time in some widely used real-time system modeling and verification languages.

Real-Time Maude. Real-Time Maude [20,21] is a high level declarative programming language supporting specification of real-time and hybrid systems in timed rewriting logic. Real-Time Maude supports both discrete and continuous time models. A set of tools are developed for time-bounded analysis of real-time Maude. *Timed rewrite* and *Timed search* build traces of the model from its initial state and checks whether a specific state is reachable or not. *Timed model checking* verifies models against time-bounded TLTL formulas. Recently, Real-Time Maude is equipped with a model checker for TCTL properties [16]. In [23] we used these facilities for the model checking of Timed Rebeca models against TCTL formulas. Comparing to FTTS, the mentioned tools are working on lock step fashion which results in generating timed transition systems of the Timed Rebeca models. To the best of our knowledge, no reduction technique is implemented for real-time Maude models to relax lock step fashion. In addition, timed transition systems of real-time Maude models are generated to the defined time-bound. In contrary, using shift equivalence relation in FTTS, there is no need to define time-bound to achieve finite transition system.

Timed Automata. Timed automata [4] model the behavior of timed systems using a set of automata that is equipped with the set of clock variables. Although clocks are the system variables, their values can only be checked or set to zero.

The values of all clocks are increased in the same rate or can be reset to zero while moving from one state to other states. Constraints over clocks can be added as enabling conditions on both states and transitions. Timed automata support parallel composition as a convenient approach for modeling complex systems. As described in [6], parallel composition of timed automata is based on the hand-shaking actions. Timed automata support both continuous and discrete timed models [9,13]. UPPAAL [8] generates region transition system of timed automata (symbolic representation of timed transition system of the timed automata) and apply verification techniques on it. Modeling of real-time distributed systems with asynchronous message passing between components using synchronous communication of automata increases the number of states dramatically (because of many synchronizations among automta for model asynchronous behavior, as shown in [15] in detail). In contrast, using FTTS requires fewer synchronizations, because messages are executed atomically.

Erlang. Erlang is a dynamically-typed general-purpose programming language which was developed in 1986 [5]. The concurrency model of Erlang is based on the actor model. Fredlund et al. in [12] proposed a timed extension of McErlang as a model checker of timed Erlang programs. In comparison with FTTS, McErlang provides fine-grain model checker for Erlang systems which results in generating timed transition system; however, states in FTTS are coarse-grain and more abstract than that of McErlang. Experimental results in [15] show very well the efficiency of FTTS in comparison with the results of the approach of McErlang.

Partial Order Reduction. The reduction from TTS to FTTS has aspects that are similar to partial order reduction (POR). In fact the relationship between POR and FTTS is subtle. FTTS is unaware of any independence relation, persistence/ample sets for timed actor systems that will result in POR techniques producing FTTS as the reduced transition system. Moreover, not only is the formal relationship between FTTS and POR nontrivial, POR techniques for timed systems were empirically compared against the FTTS semantics and found that the FTTS results in smaller transition systems in [15].

6   Conclusion

In this paper we proved that there is a weak bisimulation relation between timed transitions system (TTS) – as a standard semantics of discrete time systems – and floating time transitions system (FTTS) – as a natural semantics for time actor systems. FTTS was previously introduced in [15] along with an algorithm for schedulability and deadlock freedom analysis. Proving the weak bisimilarity of TTS and FTTS, enables one to use FTTS for verification of branching-time properties in addition to previously proposed analyses. Experimental evidence supports our theoretical observation that FTTS of Timed Rebeca models are smaller than TTS in general. In case of models with many concurrently executing actors, FTTS is up to 90 % smaller than TTS. Therefore, we can efficiently model check more complicated models. In addition, our technique and the proofs are based on the actor model of computation where the interaction is solely based on asynchronous message passing between the components. So, they are generalized enough to be applied to computation models which have message-driven communication and autonomous objects as units of concurrency such as agent-based systems.

Acknowledgements. This work has been partially supported by the project "Timed Asynchronous Reactive Objects in Distributed Systems: TARO" (nr. 110020021) of the Icelandic Research Fund.

A   Proof of Theorem 1

To prove that the first condition of action-based weak bismulation holds for $\mathcal{R}$, based on the type of $tmsg$ the following two cases are possible.

- $s \xrightarrow{tmsg} t$: Based on the definition of relation $\mathcal{R}$, in this case projection function for all the rebecs in s and t return the same value except for the sender and receiver of $tmsg$. For the sender rebec (assume that it is r_i) the difference is in the bag of sent messages, results in $sent_{t,i} = sent_{s,i} - tmsg$. On the other hand, projection function in s' and t' have the same value for all the rebecs except the sender and receiver of $tmsg$. For the sender rebec (assume that it is r_i) the difference is in the bag of sent messages, results in $sent_{t',i} = sent_{s',i} - tmsg$.

  For the receiver rebec (assume that it is r_j), there is a completing trace $CT_{t,j}$ such that $Proj(t, j)$ returns valuation of state variables of r_j from the target state of $CT_{t,j}$ and messages which are sent by r_j in t in union with messages which are sent during $CT_{t,j}$. In FTTS state t', projection function returns valuation of state variables and the sent messages of r_j after the execution of all the statements of $tmsg$ (i.e. doing transition $tmsg$ in FTTS) which is the same as what projection function returns in t. Therefore, there is $t \mathcal{R} t'$ as the results of projection function in t and t' are the same for all the rebecs.
- $s \xrightarrow{\tau} t$: As transition from s to t is not observable, we have to show that there is relation $\mathcal{R}$ between t and s'. This way, doing a τ transition from s results in stuttering in s' as one of the properties of action-based weak bismulation relations.

  Assume that τ transition belongs to rebec r_i. Doing τ transition by r_i makes projection function return the same result in s and t for all the rebecs except r_i. It is because of the fact that only r_i has progress which may result in changing the valuation of its state variables or sending a message to other rebec. For r_i in state s one of the completing traces is a trace which contains τ transition from s to t as its first transition. Therefore, completing traces of r_i which are started from s and t are ended in the same target state, results in $Proj(s, i) = Proj(t, i)$. Therefore, result of projection function for all the rebecs in TTS and FTTS are the same and t is in relation $\mathcal{R}$ with s'.

To prove the second condition, as all the transitions in FTTS are taking-event transitions, $tmsg$ must be taking-event transition. On the other hand, transition $tmsg$ is enabled in s as we discussed in Proposition 2. Now we can prove that

t and t' are in relation $\mathcal{R}$ with the argument the same as what we did in case $s \overset{tmsg}{\rightarrow} t$ of condition one.

Finally, we have to show that the initial states of the transitions systems are in relation $\mathcal{R}$. As the program counter of all of the rebecs in s_0 is set to null, the completing traces started from s_0 are ϵ. So, for any given rebec r_i, $state_i(CT_{s,i}) = state(s, i) = state(s', i)$, $sent(CT_{s,i}) = \emptyset \rightarrow sent(s_0, i) = sent(s'_0, i)$, and $now(CT_{s,i}) = now(s) = now(s', i) = 0$, results in $s_0 \mathcal{R} s'_0$. $\square$

References

1. Rebeca Home Page. http://www.rebeca-lang.org
2. Agha, G., Mason, I.A., Smith, S.F., Talcott, C.L.: A foundation for actor computation. J. Funct. Program. **7**(1), 1–72 (1997)
3. Agha, G.A.: ACTORS - A Model of Concurrent Computation in Distributed Systems. MIT Press series in artificial intelligence. MIT Press, Cambridge (1990)
4. Alur, R., Dill, D.L.: A theory of timed automata. Theor. Comput. Sci. **126**(2), 183–235 (1994)
5. Armstrong, J.: A history of Erlang. In: Ryder, B.G., Hailpern, B. (eds.) HOPL, pp. 1–26. ACM (2007)
6. Baier, C., Katoen, J.P.: Principles of Model Checking. MIT Press, Cambridge (2008)
7. Bultan, T., Ouederni, M., Basu, S.: Synchronizability for verification of asynchronously communicating systems. In: Kuncak, V., Rybalchenko, A. (eds.) VMCAI 2012. LNCS, vol. 7148, pp. 56–71. Springer, Heidelberg (2012)
8. Bengtsson, J., Larsen, K.G., Larsson, F., Pettersson, P., Yi, W.: UPPAAL - a tool suite for automatic verification of real-time systems. In: Alur, R., Henzinger, T.A., Sontag, E.D. (eds.) Hybrid Systems. LNCS, vol. 1066, pp. 232–243. Springer, Heidelberg (1995)
9. Bozga, M., Maler, O., Tripakis, S.: Efficient verification of timed automata using dense and discrete time semantics. In: Pierre, L., Kropf, T. (eds.) CHARME 1999. LNCS, vol. 1703, pp. 125–141. Springer, Heidelberg (1999)
10. Cho, B., Rahman, M., Chajed, T., Gupta, I., Abad, C., Roberts, N., Lin, P.: Natjam: design and evaluation of eviction policies for supporting priorities and deadlines in mapreduce clusters. In: Lohman, G.M. (ed.) SoCC, p. 6. ACM (2013)
11. Desai, A., Garg, P., Madhusudan, P.: Natural proofs for asynchronous programs using almost-synchronous reductions. In: Black, A.P., Millstein, T.D. (eds.) Proceedings of the 2014 ACM International Conference on Object Oriented Programming Systems Languages & Applications, OOPSLA 2014, part of SPLASH 2014, 20–24 October 2014, Portland, OR, USA, pp. 709–725. ACM (2014)
12. Fredlund, L.Å., Earle, C.B.: Verification of timed Erlang programs using McErlang. In: Giese, H., Rosu, G. (eds.) FORTE 2012 and FMOODS 2012. LNCS, vol. 7273, pp. 251–267. Springer, Heidelberg (2012)
13. Ibarra, O.H., Su, J.: Generalizing the discrete timed automaton. In: Yu, S., Păun, A. (eds.) CIAA 2000. LNCS, vol. 2088, p. 157. Springer, Heidelberg (2001)
14. Khamespanah, E., Khosravi, R., Sirjani, M.: Efficient TCTL model checking algorithm for timed actors. In: Boix, E.G., Haller, P., Ricci, A., Varela, C. (eds.) Proceedings of the 4th International Workshop on Programming based on Actors Agents & Decentralized Control, AGERE! 2014, 20 October 2014, Portland, OR, USA, pp. 55–66. ACM (2014)

15. Khamespanah, E., Sirjani, M., Sabahi-Kaviani, Z., Khosravi, R., Izadi, M.: Timed Rebeca schedulability and deadlock freedom analysis using bounded floating time transition system. Sci. Comput. Program. **98**, 184–204 (2015)
16. Lepri, D., Ábrahám, E., Ölveczky, P.C.: Timed CTL model checking in real-time Maude. In: Durán, F. (ed.) WRLA 2012. LNCS, vol. 7571, pp. 182–200. Springer, Heidelberg (2012)
17. Linderman, L.E., Mechitov, K., Spencer, B.F.: TinyOS-based real-time wireless data acquisition framework for structural health monitoring and control. Struct. Control Health Monit. **20**(6), 1007–1020 (2013)
18. Manohar, R., Martin, A.J.: Slack elasticity in concurrent computing. In: Jeuring, J. (ed.) MPC 1998. LNCS, vol. 1422, p. 272. Springer, Heidelberg (1998)
19. Mechitov, K.A., Khamespanah, E., Sirjani, M., Agha, G.: A Model Checking Approach for Schedulability Analysis of Distributed Real-Time Sensor Network Applications (2015). Submitted for Publication
20. Ölveczky, P.C., Meseguer, J.: Specification and analysis of real-time systems using real-time Maude. In: Wermelinger, M., Margaria-Steffen, T. (eds.) FASE 2004. LNCS, vol. 2984, pp. 354–358. Springer, Heidelberg (2004)
21. Ölveczky, P.C., Meseguer, J.: Real-time Maude 2.1. Electr. Notes Theor. Comput. Sci. **117**, 285–314 (2005)
22. Reynisson, A.H., Sirjani, M., Aceto, L., Cimini, M., Jafari, A., Ingólfsdóttir, A., Sigurdarson, S.H.: Modelling and simulation of asynchronous real-time systems using timed Rebeca. Sci. Comput. Program. **89**, 41–68 (2014)
23. Khamespanah, E., Ölveczky, P.C., Sirjani, M., Khosravi, R., Sabahi-Kaviani, Z.: Formal semantics and analysis of timed Rebeca in real-time Maude. In: Artho, C., Ölveczky, P.C. (eds.) FTSCS 2013. CCIS, vol. 419, pp. 178–194. Springer, Heidelberg (2014)
24. Sharifi, Z., Mohammadi, S., Sirjani, M.: Comparison of NoC routing algorithms using formal methods. In: PDPTA (2013)
25. Sharifi, Z., Mosaffa, M., Mohammadi, S., Sirjani, M.: Functional and performance analysis of network-on-chips using actor-based modeling and formal verification. ECEASST **66** (2013)
26. Sirjani, M., Movaghar, A., Shali, A., de Boer, F.S.: Modeling and verification of reactive systems using Rebeca. Fundam. Inform. **63**(4), 385–410 (2004)
27. Sprenger, C.: A verified model checker for the modal μ-Calculus in Coq. In: Steffen, B. (ed.) TACAS 1998. LNCS, vol. 1384, p. 167. Springer, Heidelberg (1998)

Configuration Logics: Modelling Architecture Styles

Anastasia Mavridou, Eduard Baranov, Simon Bliudze$^{(\boxtimes)}$, and Joseph Sifakis

École Polytechnique Fédérale de Lausanne,
Station 14, 1015 Lausanne, Switzerland
{anastasia.mavridou,eduard.baranov,simon.bliudze,
joseph.sifakis}@epfl.ch

Abstract. We study a framework for the specification of architecture styles as families of architectures involving a common set of types of components and coordination mechanisms. The framework combines two logics: (1) interaction logics for the specification of architectures as generic coordination schemes involving a configuration of interactions between typed components; (2) configuration logics for the specification of architecture styles as sets of interaction configurations. The presented results build on previous work on architecture modelling in BIP. We show how propositional interaction logic can be extended into a corresponding configuration logic by adding new operators on sets of interaction configurations. We provide a complete axiomatisation of the propositional configuration logic, as well as a decision procedure for checking that an architecture satisfies given logical specifications. To allow genericity of specifications, we study first-order and second-order extensions of the propositional logic. We provide examples illustrating the application of the results to the characterization of architecture styles. Finally, we provide an experimental evaluation using the Maude rewriting system to implement the decision procedure for the propositional logic.

1 Introduction

Architectures are common means for organizing coordination between components in order to build complex systems and to make them manageable. They depict generic coordination principles between components and embody design rules that can be understood by all. Architectures allow thinking on a higher plane and avoiding low-level mistakes. They are a means for ensuring global coordination properties between components and thus, achieving correctness by construction [1]. Using architectures largely accounts for our ability to master complexity and develop systems cost-effectively. System developers extensively use reference architectures ensuring both functional and non-functional properties, e.g. fault-tolerant, time-triggered, adaptive, security architectures.

Informally architectures are characterized by the structure of the interactions between a set of typed components. The structure is usually specified as a relation, e.g. connectors between component ports.

© Springer International Publishing Switzerland 2016
C. Braga and P.C. Ölveczky (Eds.): FACS 2015, LNCS 9539, pp. 256–274, 2016.
DOI: 10.1007/978-3-319-28934-2_14

Architecture styles characterize not a single architecture but a family of architectures sharing common characteristics such as the type of the involved components and the topology induced by their coordination structure. Simple examples of architecture styles are Pipeline, Ring, Master/Slave, Pipe and Filter. For instance, Master/Slave architectures integrate two types of components, masters and slaves, such that each slave can interact only with one master. Figure 1 depicts four Master/Slave architectures involving master components M_1, M_2 and slave components S_1, S_2. Their communication ports are respectively m_1, m_2 and s_1, s_2. The architectures correspond to interaction configurations: $\{\{s_1, m_1\}, \{s_2, m_2\}\}$, $\{\{s_1, m_1\}, \{s_2, m_1\}\}$, $\{\{s_1, m_2\}, \{s_2, m_1\}\}$ and $\{\{s_1, m_2\}, \{s_2, m_2\}\}$. The set $\{s_i, m_j\}$ denotes an interaction between ports s_i and m_j. A configuration is a non-empty set of interactions. The Master/Slave architecture style characterizes all the Master/Slave architectures for arbitrary numbers of masters and slaves.

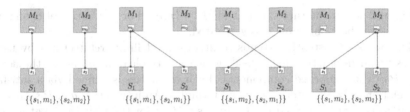

Fig. 1. Master/Slave architectures

The paper studies the relation between architectures and architecture styles. This relation is similar to the relation between programs and their specifications. As program specifications can be expressed by using logics, e.g. temporal logics, architecture styles can be specified by configuration logics characterizing classes of architectures.

We propose a propositional configuration logic whose formulas represent, for a given set of components, the allowed configuration sets. Then, we introduce first-order and second-order logics as extensions of the propositional logic. These allow genericity of description as they are defined for types of components.

The meaning of a configuration logic formula is a set of configurations, each representing a particular architecture. Defining configuration logics requires considering three hierarchically structured semantic domains:

The lattice of interactions. An interaction a is a non-empty subset of P, the set of ports of the integrated components. Its execution implies the atomic synchronization of all component actions (at most one action per component) associated with the ports of a.

The lattice of configurations. Configurations are non-empty sets of interactions characterizing architectures.

The lattice of configuration sets. Sets of configurations are properties described by the configuration logic.

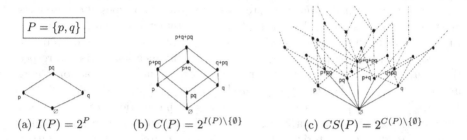

(a) $I(P) = 2^P$ (b) $C(P) = 2^{I(P)\setminus\{\emptyset\}}$ (c) $CS(P) = 2^{C(P)\setminus\{\emptyset\}}$

Fig. 2. Lattices of interactions (a), configurations (b) and configuration sets (c).

Figure 2 shows the three lattices for $P = \{p, q\}$. For the lattice of configuration sets, we show only how it is generated.

This work consistently extends results on modelling architectures by using propositional interaction logic [2–4], which are Boolean algebras on the set of ports P of the composed components. Their semantics is defined via a satisfaction relation between interactions and formulas. An interaction $a \subseteq P$ satisfies a formula ϕ (we write $a \models_i \phi$) if ϕ evaluates to *true* for the valuation that assigns *true* to the ports belonging to a and *false* otherwise. It is characterized exactly by the formula $\bigwedge_{p \in a} p \wedge \bigwedge_{p \notin a} \overline{p}$.

Configuration logic is a powerset extension of the interaction logic. Its formulas are generated from the formulas of the propositional interaction logic by using the operators union, intersection and complementation as well as a *coalescing operator* $+$. To avoid ambiguity, we refer to the formulas of the configuration logic that syntactically are also formulas of the interaction logics as *interaction formulas*. The semantics of the configuration logic is defined via a satisfaction relation $\models$ between configurations $\gamma = \{a_1, ..., a_n\}$ and formulas. An interaction formula f represents any configuration consisting of interactions satisfying it; that is $\gamma \models f$ if, for all $a \in \gamma$, $a \models_i f$. For set-theoretic operators we take the standard meaning. The meaning of formulas of the form $f_1 + f_2$ is all configurations γ that can be decomposed into γ_1 and γ_2 ($\gamma = \gamma_1 \cup \gamma_2$) satisfying respectively f_1 and f_2. The formula $f_1 + f_2$ represents configurations obtained as the union of configurations of f_1 with configurations of f_2.

Despite its apparent complexity, configuration logic is easy to use because of its stratified construction. From interaction logic it inherits the Boolean connectives of conjunction ($\wedge$), disjunction ($\vee$) and negation ($^-$). It also uses the set-theoretic operations of union ($\sqcup$), complementation ($\neg$) and coalescing ($+$). It can be shown that intersection coincides with conjunction.

Formulas of the form $f + true$, denoted $\sim f$, present a particular interest for writing specifications. Their characteristic configuration set is the largest set containing configurations satisfying f.

We provide a full axiomatisation of the propositional configuration logic and a normal form similar to the disjunctive normal form in Boolean algebras. The existence of such normal form implies the decidability of formula equality and of satisfaction of a formula by an architecture model.

To allow genericity of specifications, we study first-order and second-order extensions of the propositional logic. First-order logic formulas involve quantification over component variables. Second-order logic formulas involve additionally quantification over sets of components. Second-order logic is needed to express interesting topological properties, e.g. the existence of interaction cycles.

A complete presentation, with proofs and additional examples, of the results in this paper can be found in the technical report [22].

The paper is structured as follows. Section 2 recalls some basic facts about the interaction logic. Section 3 presents the propositional configuration logic, its properties and the definition of a normal form. Section 4 proposes a methodology for the specification of architecture styles. Section 5 presents first-order and second-order extensions of the logic and illustrates their use by several architecture style examples. Section 6 presents the results of an implementation of the decision procedure in the Maude rewriting system. Section 7 discusses related work. Section 8 concludes the paper.

2   Propositional Interaction Logic

The propositional interaction logic (PIL), studied in [2,3], is a Boolean logic used to characterize the interactions between components on a global set of ports P. In this section, we present only the results needed to introduce the propositional configuration logic (Sect. 3). Below, we assume that the set P is given.

Definition 1. *An* interaction *is a set of ports $a \subseteq P$ such that $a \neq \emptyset$.*

Syntax. The propositional interaction logic is defined by the grammar:

$$\phi ::= true \mid p \mid \overline{\phi} \mid \phi \vee \phi, \qquad \text{with any } p \in P.$$

Conjunction is defined as usual: $\phi_1 \wedge \phi_2 \overset{def}{=} \overline{(\overline{\phi_1} \vee \overline{\phi_2})}$. To simplify the notation, we omit it in monomials, e.g. writing pqr instead of $p \wedge q \wedge r$.

Semantics. The meaning of a PIL formula ϕ is defined by the following satisfaction relation. Let $a \subseteq P$ be a non-empty interaction. We define: $a \models_i \phi$ iff ϕ evaluates to *true* for the valuation $p = true$, for all $p \in a$, and $p = false$, for all $p \notin a$. Thus, the semantic domain of PIL is the lattice of configurations $C(P) = 2^{I(P)\backslash\{\emptyset\}}$, where $I(P) = 2^P$ (Fig. 2).

The operators meet the usual Boolean axioms and the additional axiom $\bigvee_{p \in P} p = true$ meaning that interactions are non-empty sets of ports.

An interaction a can be associated to a characteristic monomial $m_a = \bigwedge_{p \in a} p \wedge \bigwedge_{p \notin a} \overline{p}$ such that $a' \models_i m_a$ iff $a' = a$.

Example 1. Consider a system consisting of three components: a sender with port p and two receivers with ports q and r respectively. We can express the following interaction patterns:

- *Strong synchronization* between the components is specified by a single interaction involving all components, represented by the single monomial pqr.
- *Broadcast* defines weak synchronization among the sender and any number of the receivers: $\{\{p\}, \{p,q\}, \{p,r\}, \{p,q,r\}\}$, represented by the formula p, which can be expanded to $p\bar{q}\bar{r} \vee pq\bar{r} \vee p\bar{q}r \vee pqr$.

3 Propositional Configuration Logic

3.1 Syntax and Semantics

Syntax. The propositional configuration logic (PCL) is a powerset extension of PIL defined by the following grammar:

$$f ::= true \mid \phi \mid \neg f \mid f + f \mid f \sqcup f,$$

where ϕ is a PIL formula; $\neg$, $+$ and $\sqcup$ are respectively the *complementation*, *coalescing* and *union* operators.

We define the usual notation for intersection and implication: $f_1 \sqcap f_2 \overset{def}{=} \neg(\neg f_1 \sqcup \neg f_2)$ and $f_1 \Rightarrow f_2 \overset{def}{=} \neg f_1 \sqcup f_2$.

The language of PCL formulas is generated from PIL formulas by using union, coalescing and complementation operators. The binding strength of the operators is as follows (in decreasing order): PIL negation, complementation, PIL conjunction, PIL disjunction, coalescing, union. Henceforth, to avoid confusion, we refer as *interaction formulas* to the subset of PCL formulas that syntactically are also PIL formulas. Furthermore, we will use Latin letters f, g, h for general PCL formulas and Greek letters ϕ, ψ, ξ for interaction formulas. Interaction formulas inherit all axioms of PIL.

Semantics. Let P be a set of ports. The semantic domain of PCL is the lattice of configuration sets $CS(P) = 2^{C(P)\setminus\{\emptyset\}}$ (Fig. 2(c)). The meaning of a PCL formula f is defined by the following satisfaction relation. Let $\gamma \in C(P)$ be a non-empty configuration. We define:

$$\gamma \models true, \qquad \text{always,}$$

$\gamma \models \phi,$ if $\forall a \in \gamma, a \models_i \phi$, where ϕ is an interaction formula and $\models_i$ is the satisfaction relation of PIL,

$\gamma \models f_1 + f_2,$ if there exist $\gamma_1, \gamma_2 \in C(P) \setminus \{\emptyset\}$, such that $\gamma = \gamma_1 \cup \gamma_2$, $\gamma_1 \models f_1$ and $\gamma_2 \models f_2$,

$\gamma \models f_1 \sqcup f_2,$ if $\gamma \models f_1$ or $\gamma \models f_2$,

$\gamma \models \neg f,$ if $\gamma \not\models f$ (i.e. $\gamma \models f$ does not hold).

In particular, the meaning of an interaction formula ϕ in PCL is the set $2^{I_a} \setminus \{\emptyset\}$, with $I_a = \{a \in I(P) \mid a \models_i \phi\}$, of all configurations involving any number of interactions satisfying ϕ in PIL.

We say that two formulas are equivalent $f_1 \equiv f_2$ iff, for all $\gamma \in C(P)$ such that $\gamma \neq \emptyset$, $\gamma \models f_1 \Leftrightarrow \gamma \models f_2$.

Proposition 1. *Equivalence $\equiv$ is a congruence w.r.t. all PCL operators.*

Example 2. The Master/Slave architecture style for two masters M_1, M_2 and two slaves S_1, S_2 with ports m_1, m_2, s_1 and s_2 respectively characterizes the four configurations of Fig. 1 as the union:

$$\bigsqcup_{i,j \in \{1,2\}} (\phi_{1,i} + \phi_{2,j}),$$

where, for $i \neq i'$ and $j \neq j'$, the monomial $\phi_{i,j} = s_i \, m_j \, \overline{s_{i'}} \, \overline{m_{j'}}$ defines a binary interaction between ports s_i and m_j.

3.2   Conservative Extension of PIL Operators

Notice that from the PCL semantics of interaction formulas, it follows immediately that PCL is a conservative extension of PIL. Below we extend the PIL conjunction and disjunction operators to PCL.

PCL intersection is a conservative extension of PIL conjunction.

Proposition 2. $\phi_1 \wedge \phi_2 \equiv \phi_1 \sqcap \phi_2$, *for any interaction formulas* ϕ_1, ϕ_2.

Thus, conjunction and intersection coincide on interaction formulas. In the rest of the paper, we use the same symbol $\wedge$ to denote both operators.

Disjunction can be conservatively extended to PCL with the following semantics: for any PCL formulas f_1 and f_2,

$$\gamma \models f_1 \vee f_2, \qquad\qquad \text{if} \gamma \models f_1 \sqcup f_2 \sqcup f_1 + f_2. \qquad (1)$$

Proposition 3. *For any interaction formulas* ϕ_1 *and* ϕ_2 *and any* $\gamma \in C(P)$ *such that* $\gamma \neq \emptyset$, *we have* $\gamma \models \phi_1 \vee \phi_2$ *iff* $\forall a \in \gamma, a \models_i \phi_1 \vee \phi_2$.

3.3   Properties of PCL Operators

Union, complementation and conjunction have the standard set-theoretic meaning and consequently, they satisfy the usual axioms of propositional logic.

Coalescing $+$ combines configurations, as opposed to union $\sqcup$, which combines configuration sets. Coalescing has the following properties:

Proposition 4. $+$ *is associative, commutative and has an absorbing element* $false \stackrel{def}{=} \neg true$.

Proposition 5. *For any formulas* f, f_1, f_2 *and any interaction formula* ϕ, *we have the following distributivity results:*

1. $f \vee (f_1 \sqcup f_2) \equiv (f \vee f_1) \sqcup (f \vee f_2)$,
2. $f + (f_1 \vee f_2) \equiv (f + f_1) \vee (f + f_2)$,
3. $f + (f_1 \sqcup f_2) \equiv f + f_1 \sqcup f + f_2$,
4. $\phi \wedge (f_1 + f_2) \equiv (\phi \wedge f_1) + (\phi \wedge f_2)$.

Associativity of coalescing and union, together with the distributivity of coalescing over union, immediately imply the following generalisation of the extended semantics of disjunction (1).

Corollary 1. *For any set of formulas* $\{f_i\}_{i \in I}$, *we have*

$$\bigvee_{i \in I} f_i \equiv \bigsqcup_{\emptyset \neq J \subseteq I} \sum_{j \in J} f_j \,,$$

where $\sum_{j \in J} f_j$ *denotes the coalescing of formulas* f_j, *for all* $j \in J$.

Example 3. A configuration γ satisfying the formula $f = f_1 \vee f_2 \vee f_3$ can be partitioned into $\gamma = \gamma_1 \cup \gamma_2 \cup \gamma_3$, such that $\gamma_i \models f_i$. By the semantics of disjunction, some γ_i can be empty. On the contrary, the semantics of coalescing requires all elements of such partition to be non-empty. Hence, in order to rewrite f without the disjunction operator, we take the union of all possible coalescings of f_1, f_2 and f_3. Thus, we have $f \equiv f_1 \sqcup f_2 \sqcup f_3 \sqcup (f_1+f_2) \sqcup (f_1+f_3) \sqcup (f_2+f_3) \sqcup (f_1+f_2+f_3)$.

Notice that in general coalescing does not distribute over conjunction.

Example 4. Let $P = \{p, q\}$ and consider $f = p \sqcup q$, $f_1 = p$ and $f_2 = q$. Configuration $\{\{p\}, \{q\}\}$ satisfies $(f + f_1) \wedge (f + f_2)$, but not $f + (f_1 \wedge f_2)$.

Coalescing with *true* presents a particular interest for writing specifications, since they allow adding any set of interactions to the configurations satisfying f. Notice that *true* is not a neutral element of coalescing: only the implication $f \Rightarrow f + true$ holds in general.

Definition 2. *For any formula* f, *the* closure operator $\sim$ *is defined by putting* $\sim f \stackrel{def}{=} f + true$. *We give* $\sim$ *the same binding power as* $\neg$.

Example 5. For $P = \{p, q, r\}$ the formula f characterizing all the configurations such that p must interact with both q and r, is $f = \sim(pq + qr) = pq + pr + true$. Notice that the only constraint imposed by the formula f is that configurations that satisfy it must contain an interaction pqr or both interactions pq and qr. Configurations satisfying f can contain any additional interactions.

Proposition 6. *For any formula* f, *we have* $\sim\sim f \equiv \sim f$.

The closure operator can be interpreted as a modal operator with existential quantification. The formula $\sim f$ characterizes configurations γ, such that there *exists* a sub-configuration of γ satisfying f. Thus, $\sim f$ means "possible f". Dually $\neg \sim \neg f$ means "always f" in the following sense: if a configuration γ satisfies $\neg \sim \neg f$, *all* sub-configurations of γ satisfy f. Below, we show that, for an interaction formula ϕ, holds the equivalence $\sim\neg\phi \equiv \neg\phi$, which implies $\neg\sim\neg\phi \equiv \neg\neg\phi \equiv \phi$. However, this is not true in general. Consider $f = m_a + m_b$, where m_a and m_b are characteristic monomials of interactions a and b respectively. The only configuration satisfying f is $\gamma = \{a, b\}$. In particular, none of the sub-configurations $\{a\}, \{b\} \subset \gamma$ satisfies f. Thus, $\neg\sim\neg(m_a + m_b) \equiv false$.

Proposition 7. *For any f_1 and f_2, we have*

1. $\sim(f_1 \sqcup f_2) \equiv \sim f_1 \sqcup \sim f_2 \equiv \sim(f_1 \vee f_2)$,
2. $\sim(f_1 + f_2) \equiv \sim f_1 + \sim f_2 \equiv \sim f_1 \wedge \sim f_2$.

The following proposition allows us to address the relation between complementation and negation.

Proposition 8. *For any interaction formula ϕ, we have*

$$\phi \sqcup \overline{\phi} \sqcup (\overline{\phi} + \phi) \equiv true.$$

Notice that the three terms on the left are mutually disjoint and therefore, for any interaction formula ϕ, we have

$$\neg\phi \equiv \overline{\phi} \sqcup (\phi + \overline{\phi}) \equiv \overline{\phi} + true \equiv \sim\overline{\phi}. \tag{2}$$

This means that complementation can also be interpreted as a modality. Proposition 8 shows that the complementation of an interaction formula ϕ represents all configurations that contain $\overline{\phi}$. Equivalences $\neg\overline{\phi} \equiv \sim\phi$, $\neg\sim\phi \equiv \overline{\phi}$, $\neg\sim\overline{\phi} \equiv \phi$ and $\sim\neg\phi \equiv \neg\phi$, for interaction formulas ϕ, are direct corollaries of Propositions 6 and 8. Proposition 9 generalises (2) to coalescings of interaction formulas.

Proposition 9. *For any set of interaction formulas Φ, we have*

$$\neg\left(\sum_{\phi\in\Phi}\phi\right) \equiv \bigsqcup_{\phi\in\Phi}\overline{\phi} \sqcup \sim\left(\bigwedge_{\phi\in\Phi}\overline{\phi}\right).$$

Example 6. Consider a formula $f = \neg(pq + pr)$ and a configuration $\gamma \models f$. The PCL semantics requires that γ cannot be split into two non-empty parts $\gamma_1 \models pq$ and $\gamma_2 \models pr$. This can happen in two cases: (1) there exists $a \in \gamma$ such that a does not satisfy neither pq nor pr; (2) one of the monomials is not satisfied by any interaction in γ. The former case can be expressed as $\sim(\overline{pq}\ \overline{pr})$ and the latter as $\overline{pq} \sqcup \overline{pr}$. The union of these formulas gives the equivalence $\neg(pq + pr) \equiv \overline{pq} \sqcup \overline{pr} \sqcup \sim(\overline{pq}\ \overline{pr})$.

Proposition 9 allows the elimination of complementation. It is also possible to eliminate conjunction of coalescings by using the following distributivity results to push it down within the formula.

Proposition 10. *For two sets of interaction formulas Φ and Ψ, we have*

$$\sum_{\phi\in\Phi}\phi \wedge \sum_{\psi\in\Psi}\psi \equiv \sum_{\xi\in\Phi\cup\Psi}\left(\xi \wedge \bigvee_{(\phi,\psi)\in\Phi\times\Psi}(\phi\wedge\psi)\right).$$

Example 7. Consider a formula $f = (\phi_1 + \phi_2) \wedge (\phi_3 + \phi_4)$, where ϕ_1, ϕ_2, ϕ_3 and ϕ_4 are interaction formulas, and a configuration $\gamma \models f$. The semantics requires that there exists two partitions of γ: $\gamma = \gamma_1 \cup \gamma_2$ and $\gamma = \gamma_3 \cup \gamma_4$, such that $\gamma_i \models \phi_i$ for $i \in [1, 4]$. Considering an intersection $\gamma_{i,j} = \gamma_i \cap \gamma_j$ we have $\gamma_{i,j} \models \phi_i \wedge \phi_j$. Thus, $\gamma = \bigcup \gamma_{i,j}$ satisfies $\phi_1\phi_3 \vee \phi_1\phi_4 \vee \phi_2\phi_3 \vee \phi_2\phi_4$ even if some $\gamma_{i,j}$ are empty. However, disjunction allows configurations such that no interaction satisfy one of the disjunction terms and consequently some ϕ_i. A coalescing of ϕ_i allows only configurations such that each ϕ_i is satisfied by at least one interaction. Thus, the conjunction of these formulas gives the equivalent representation:

$$
\begin{aligned}
f &\equiv (\phi_1\phi_3 \vee \phi_1\phi_4 \vee \phi_2\phi_3 \vee \phi_2\phi_4) \wedge (\phi_1 + \phi_2 + \phi_3 + \phi_4) \\
&\equiv \phi_1 \wedge (\phi_1\phi_3 \vee \phi_1\phi_4 \vee \phi_2\phi_3 \vee \phi_2\phi_4) \; + \; \phi_2 \wedge (\phi_1\phi_3 \vee \phi_1\phi_4 \vee \phi_2\phi_3 \vee \phi_2\phi_4) \\
&+ \phi_3 \wedge (\phi_1\phi_3 \vee \phi_1\phi_4 \vee \phi_2\phi_3 \vee \phi_2\phi_4) \; + \; \phi_4 \wedge (\phi_1\phi_3 \vee \phi_1\phi_4 \vee \phi_2\phi_3 \vee \phi_2\phi_4) .
\end{aligned}
$$

The PCL lattice is illustrated in Fig. 3. The circle nodes represent interaction formulas, whereas the red dot nodes represent all other formulas. Notice that the PCL lattice has two sub-lattices generated by monomials:

– through disjunction and negation (isomorphic to the PIL lattice);
– through union and complementation (disjunction is not expressible).

Notice that coalescing cannot be expressed in any of these two sub-lattices. Although some formulas involving the closure operator can be expressed in the second sub-lattice, e.g. $\sim\overline{\phi} \equiv \neg\phi$, in general this is not the case, e.g. the formulas $\sim(\overline{\phi} \wedge \overline{\psi})$ and $\sim\phi \sqcup \sim\psi$ are not part of either sub-lattice. However, the closure operator is expressible by taking as generators the interaction formulas:

Proposition 11. *The lattice generated by interaction formulas through union and complementation is closed under the closure operator $\sim$.*

3.4   Deciding Equivalence and Satisfaction

In this subsection, we present an axiomatisation of the PCL equivalence $\equiv$, which is sound and complete with respect to the definition in Sect. 3.1. This axiomatisation allows us to define a normal form for PCL formulas, similar to the disjunctive normal form in Boolean algebras. The existence of such a normal form immediately implies the decidability of (1) the equivalence of two PCL formulas and (2) the satisfaction of a formula by a configuration.

Axioms. PCL operators satisfy the following axioms (for any formulas f, f_1 and f_2 and any sets of interaction formulas Φ and Ψ):

1. The PIL axioms for interaction formulas.
2. The usual axioms of propositional logic for $\sqcup$, $\wedge$, $\neg$.
3. $+$ is associative, commutative and has an absorbing element *false*.
4. $f + (f_1 \sqcup f_2) \equiv f + f_1 \sqcup f + f_2$.

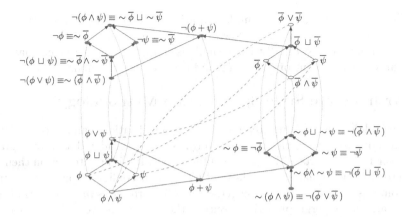

Fig. 3. PCL lattice (the blue arrows represent implications; red dashed and green solid lines represent, respectively, PIL negation and complementation). (Color figure online)

5. $\displaystyle\sum_{\phi\in\Phi}\phi\wedge\sum_{\psi\in\Psi}\psi\equiv\sum_{\xi\in\Phi\cup\Psi}\Big(\xi\wedge\bigvee_{(\phi,\psi)\in\Phi\times\Psi}(\phi\wedge\psi)\Big).$

6. $\displaystyle\neg\Big(\sum_{\phi\in\Phi}\phi\Big)\equiv\bigsqcup_{\phi\in\Phi}\overline{\phi}\sqcup\sim\Big(\bigwedge_{\phi\in\Phi}\overline{\phi}\Big).$

Theorem 1. *The above set of axioms is sound and complete for the equivalence $\equiv$ in PCL.*

Applying the axioms above, one can remove or push PCL operators down in the expression tree of the formula. For instance, Ax. 5 allows one to push the conjunction down, Ax. 6 removes the complementation.[1]

Definition 3. *A PCL formula is in* normal form *iff it has the form* $\bigsqcup_{i\in I}\sum_{j\in J_i}\bigvee_{k\in K_{i,j}}m_{i,j,k}$, *where all $m_{i,j,k}$ are monomials.*

Theorem 2. *Any PCL formula has an equivalent normal form formula.*

Example 8. The following example illustrates the normalization process:

$$
\begin{aligned}
(pq\sqcup r)\wedge(pr+\neg q) &\equiv (pq\sqcup r)\wedge(pr+\overline{q}+true) && //\text{ Ax. 6}\\
&\equiv (pq\wedge(pr+\overline{q}+true))\sqcup(r\wedge(pr+\overline{q}+true)) && //\text{ Ax. 2}\\
&\equiv ((pq\wedge pr)+(pq\wedge\overline{q})+(pq\wedge true)) && //\text{ Ax. 5}\\
&\quad\ \sqcup((r\wedge pr)+(r\wedge\overline{q})+(r\wedge true))\\
&\equiv (pqr+false+pq)\sqcup(pr+r\overline{q}+r) && //\text{ Ax. 1}\\
&\equiv pr+r\overline{q}+r. && //\text{ Ax. 2, 3}
\end{aligned}
$$

---

[1] Full details of the normal form derivation can be found in the technical report [22].

The first step removes the complementation. Then the application of distributivity rules pushes conjunction down in the expression tree of the formula, to the level of monomials. Finally, the formula is simplified, by observing that *false* is the absorbing element of coalescing and the identity of union.

4 Architecture Style Specification Methodology

The methodology for writing architecture style specifications can be conceptually simplified due to the fact that an architecture can be considered as a hypergraph whose vertices are ports and edges are interactions. If a is an interaction then, its characteristic monomial m_a specifies in PCL a single configuration (hypergraph) that contains only the interaction (edge) a. The formula $\sim m_a$ specifies all the configurations (hypergraphs) that contain the interaction (edge) a. It can be considered as a predicate on ports expressing their connectivity.

A key idea in writing architecture style specifications is that these can be expressed as logical relations between connectivity formulas of the form $\sim \phi$ where ϕ is an interaction formula. This allows simplification through separation of concerns: first configurations are specified as the conjunction of formulas on Boolean variables representing connectivity formulas; then, after simplification, the connectivity formulas are replaced. This may require another round of simplifications based on specific properties of PCL. This idea is illustrated in Example 9.

Example 9. Consider a system with three ports p, q, r and the following connectivity constraint: *If any port is connected to the two others, the latter have to be connected between themselves.* In order to specify this constraint in PCL, we first define three predicates $X = \sim (pq)$, $Y = \sim (qr)$ and $Z = \sim (pr)$. The constraint we wish to impose is then specified by the conjunction of the three implications: $(X \wedge Y \Rightarrow Z) \wedge (Y \wedge Z \Rightarrow X) \wedge (Z \wedge X \Rightarrow Y) \equiv \neg Z \wedge \neg Y \sqcup \neg Y \wedge \neg X \sqcup \neg X \wedge \neg Z \sqcup X \wedge Y \wedge Z$. Substituting $\sim (pq)$, $\sim (qr)$, $\sim (pr)$ for X, Y, Z, respectively, we obtain:

$$(\overline{p} \vee \overline{r}) \wedge (\overline{q} \vee \overline{r}) \sqcup (\overline{q} \vee \overline{r}) \wedge (\overline{p} \vee \overline{q}) \sqcup (\overline{p} \vee \overline{q}) \wedge (\overline{p} \vee \overline{r})$$
$$\sqcup \sim (pq) \wedge \sim (qr) \wedge \sim (pr)$$
$$\equiv \neg(\overline{r} \vee \overline{p}\,\overline{q}) \wedge \neg(\overline{q} \vee \overline{p}\,\overline{r}) \wedge \neg(\overline{p} \vee \overline{q}\,\overline{r}) \Rightarrow \sim (pq) \wedge \sim (qr) \wedge \sim (pr)$$
$$\equiv \sim (pr \vee qr) \wedge \sim (qr \vee pq) \wedge \sim (pq \vee pr) \Rightarrow \sim (pq) \wedge \sim (qr) \wedge \sim (pr)$$
$$\equiv \sim (pr) \wedge \sim (qr) \sqcup \sim (qr) \wedge \sim (pq) \sqcup \sim (pq) \wedge \sim (pr)$$
$$\Rightarrow \sim (pq) \wedge \sim (qr) \wedge \sim (pr)$$
$$\equiv \sim (pr + qr) \sqcup \sim (pq + qr) \sqcup \sim (pq + pr) \Rightarrow \sim (pq + qr + pr).$$

5 First and Second Order Extensions of PCL

PCL is defined for a given set of ports and a given set of components. In order to specify architecture styles, we need quantification over component variables. We make the following assumptions:

- A finite set of component types $T = \{T_1, \ldots, T_n\}$ is given. Instances of a component type have the same interface and behaviour. We write $c : T$ to denote a component c of type T.
- The interface of each component type has a distinct set of ports. We write $c.p$ to denote the port p of component c and $c.P$ to denote the set of ports of component c.

5.1   First-Order Configuration Logic

Syntax. The language of the formulas of the first-order configuration logic extends the language of PCL by allowing set-theoretic predicates on component variables, universal quantification and a specific coalescing quantifier $\Sigma c{:}T$. Let ϕ denote any interaction formula:

$$F ::= true \mid \phi \mid \forall c{:}T\big(\Phi(c)\big).F \mid \Sigma c{:}T\big(\Phi(c)\big).F \mid F \sqcup F \mid \neg F \mid F + F ,$$

where $\Phi(c)$ is some set-theoretic predicate on c (omitted when $\Phi = true$).

Semantics. The semantics is defined for closed formulas, where, for each variable in the formula, there is a quantifier over this variable in a higher nesting level. We assume that the finite set of component types $T = \{T_1, \ldots, T_n\}$ is given. Models are pairs $\langle B, \gamma \rangle$, where B is a set of component instances of types from T and γ is a configuration on the set of ports P of these components. For quantifier-free formulas, the semantics is the same as for PCL formulas. For formulas with quantifiers, the satisfaction relation is defined as follows:

$$\langle B, \gamma \rangle \models \forall c{:}T\big(\Phi(c)\big).F , \qquad \text{iff } \gamma \models \bigwedge_{c':T \in B \wedge \Phi(c')} F[c'/c],$$

$$\langle B, \gamma \rangle \models \Sigma c{:}T\big(\Phi(c)\big).F , \qquad \text{iff } \gamma \models \sum_{c':T \in B \wedge \Phi(c')} F[c'/c],$$

where $c' : T$ ranges over all component instances of type $T \in T$ satisfying Φ and $F[c'/c]$ is obtained by replacing all occurrences of c in F by c'.

For a more concise representation of formulas, we introduce the notation $\sharp(c_1.p_1, \ldots, c_n.p_n)$, which expresses an exact interaction, i.e. all ports in the arguments and only they participate in the interaction:

$$\sharp(c_1.p_1, \ldots, c_n.p_n) \stackrel{def}{=} \bigwedge_{i=1}^{n} c_i.p_i \wedge \bigwedge_{i=1}^{n} \bigwedge_{p \in c_i.P \setminus \{p_i\}} \overline{c_i.p}$$

$$\wedge \bigwedge_{T \in T} \bigwedge_{c:T \notin \{c_1, \ldots, c_n\}} \bigwedge_{p \in c.P} \overline{c.p} . \tag{3}$$

Example 10. The Star architecture style is defined for a set of components of the same type. One central component s is connected to every other component through a binary interaction, and there are no other interactions. It can be specified as follows:

$$\exists s\!:\!T.\ \forall c\!:\!T(c \neq s).\ \big(\sim(c.p\ s.p)\ \wedge\ \forall c'\!:\!T(c' \notin \{c,s\}).\,(\overline{c'.p\ c.p})\big)$$
$$\wedge \big(\forall c\!:\!T.\ \neg \sim\!\sharp(c.p)\big).\quad (4)$$

The three conjuncts of this formula express respectively the properties: (1) any component is connected to the center; (2) components other than the center are not connected; and (3) unary interactions are forbidden.

Notice that the semantics of the first part of the specification, $\forall c : T(c \neq s).\ \sim (c.p\ s.p)$, is a conjunction of closure formulas. In this conjunction, the closure operator also allows interactions in addition to the ones explicitly defined. Therefore, to correctly specify this style, we need to forbid all other interactions with the second and third conjuncts of the specification. A simpler alternative specification uses the Σ quantifier:

$$\exists s\!:\!T.\ \Sigma c\!:\!T(c \neq s).\ \sharp(c.p,\ s.p).\quad (5)$$

The $\sharp$ notation requires interactions to be binary and the Σ quantifier allows configurations that contain only interactions satisfying $\sharp(c.p,\ s.p)$, for some c. Thus, contrary to (4), we do not need to explicitly forbid unary interactions and connections between non-center components.

Example 11. The Pipes and Filters architecture style [13] involves two types of components, P and F, each having two ports *in* and *out*. Each input (resp. output) of a filter is connected to an output (resp. input) of a single pipe. The output of any pipe can be connected to at most one filter. This style can be specified as follows:

$$\forall f\!:\!F.\ \exists p\!:\!P.\ \sim(f.in\ p.out) \wedge \forall p'\!:\!P(p \neq p').\,(\overline{f.in\ p'.out})\quad (6)$$

$$\wedge\, \forall f\!:\!F.\ \exists p\!:\!P.\ \sim(f.out\ p.in) \wedge \forall p'\!:\!P(p \neq p').\,(\overline{f.out\ p'.in})\quad (7)$$

$$\wedge\, \forall p\!:\!P.\ \exists f\!:\!F.\ \forall f'\!:\!F(f \neq f').\,(\overline{p.out\ f'.in})\quad (8)$$

$$\wedge\, \forall p\!:\!P.\ \big(\overline{p.in\ p.out} \wedge \forall p'\!:\!P(p \neq p').\,(\overline{p.in\ p'.in} \wedge \overline{p.in\ p'.out})\big)\quad (9)$$

$$\wedge\, \forall f\!:\!F.\ \big(\overline{f.in\ f.out} \wedge \forall f'\!:\!F(f \neq f').\,(\overline{f.in\ f'.in} \wedge \overline{f.in\ f'.out})\big).\quad (10)$$

The first conjunct (6) requires that the input of each filter be connected to the output of a single pipe. The second conjunct (7) requires that the output of each filter be connected to the input of a single pipe. The third conjunct (8) requires that the output of a pipe be connected to at most one filter. The fourth and fifth conjuncts (9), (10) require that pipes only be connected to filters and vice-versa.

5.2   Second-Order Configuration Logic

Properties stating that two components are connected through a chain of interactions, are essential for architecture style specification. For instance, the property that all components form a single ring and not several disjoint ones can be reformulated as such a property. In [18], it is shown that transitive closure, necessary to specify such reachability properties, cannot be expressed in the first-order logic. This motivates the introduction of the second-order configuration logic with quantification over sets of components.

This logic further extends PCL with variables ranging over component sets. We write $C:T$ to denote a component set C of type T. Additionally, we denote C_T the set of all the components of type T. Finally, we assume the existence of the universal component type U, such that any component or component set is of this type. Thus, C_U represents all the components of a model.

Syntax. The syntax of the second-order configuration logic is defined by the following grammar (ϕ is an interaction formula):

$$S ::= true \mid \phi \mid \forall c{:}T\big(\Phi(c)\big).S \mid \Sigma c{:}T\big(\Phi(c)\big).S \mid S \sqcup S \mid \neg S \mid S + S$$
$$\mid \forall C : T\big(\Psi(C)\big).S \mid \Sigma C : T\big(\Psi(C)\big).S\,,$$

where $\Phi(c)$, $\Psi(C)$ are some set-theoretic predicates (omitted when *true*).

Semantics. Models are pairs $\langle B, \gamma \rangle$, where B is a set of component instances of types from T and γ is a configuration on the set of ports P of these components. The meaning of quantifier-free formulas or formulas with quantification only over component variables is as for first-order logic. We define the meaning of quantifiers over component set variables:

$$\langle B, \gamma \rangle \models \forall C{:}T\big(\Psi(C)\big).S\,, \qquad \text{iff}\, \gamma \models \bigwedge_{C'{:}T\subseteq B \wedge \Psi(C')} S[C'/C],$$

$$\langle B, \gamma \rangle \models \Sigma C{:}T\big(\Psi(C)\big).S\,, \qquad \text{iff}\, \gamma \models \sum_{C'{:}T\subseteq B \wedge \Psi(C')} S[C'/C],$$

where $C'{:}T$ ranges over all sets of components of type T that satisfy Ψ.

Example 12. The Repository architecture style [7] consists of a repository component r with a port p and a set of data-accessor components of type A with ports q. We provide below a list of increasingly strong properties that may be used to characterize this style:

1. The basic property *"there exists a single repository and all interactions involve it"* is specified as follows:

$$SingleRepo \overset{def}{=} \exists r{:}R.\ (r.p) \wedge \forall r{:}R.\ \forall r'{:}R(r' \neq r).\ false.$$

2. The additional property *"there are some data-accessors and any data-accessor must be connected to the repository"* is enforced as follows:

$$DataAccessor \overset{def}{=} SingleRepo \wedge \exists a{:}A.\ true \wedge \forall a{:}A.\ \exists r{:}R.\ {\sim}(r.p\ a.q).$$

3. Finally, the additional property *"there are no components of other types than Repository and Data-accessor"* is enforced by the formula:

$$DataAccessor \; \wedge \; \forall c{:}U(c \notin C_R \wedge c \notin C_A). \; false.$$

Example 13. In the Ring architecture style (with only one component type T), all components form a single ring by connecting their *in* and *out* ports. This style can be specified as follows:

$$\Sigma c{:}T. \; \exists c'{:}T(c \neq c'). \; \sharp(c.in, \; c'.out) \wedge \Sigma c{:}T. \; \exists c'{:}T(c \neq c'). \; \sharp(c.out, \; c'.in)$$
$$\wedge \forall C{:}T(C \neq U). \; (\exists c{:}T(c \in C). \; \exists c'{:}T(c' \notin C). \; \sim(c.in \; c'.out)) \, .$$

The last conjunct requires that there be a single ring and not several disjoint ones.

6   Implementation of the Decision Procedure

The PCL decision procedure is based on the computation of the normal form followed by a decision whether a model satisfies at least one union term of the normal form or not. For the first- and second-order extensions, satisfaction of a formula by a model can be decided by reduction to the decision procedure of PCL. Indeed, given a model, all quantifiers can be effectively eliminated, transforming a formula into a PCL one. More details can be found in [22].

We implemented the decision procedure for PCL using Maude 2.0. Maude is a language and an efficient rewriting system supporting both equational and rewriting logic specification and programming for a wide range of applications. In the experimental evaluation we used a set of architecture styles including Star, Ring, Request-Response [9], Pipes-Filters, Repository and Blackboard [8]. We used configuration logic formulas (all formulas can be found in [22]) and models of different sizes, including both correct and incorrect models. Quantifiers were eliminated externally and the decision procedure was applied to quantifier-free formulas. All experiments were performed on a 64-bit Linux machine with a 2.8 Ghz Intel i7-2640M CPU with 1 Gb memory limit and 600 sec time limit.

Figure 4 shows the average duration of the decision procedure for the six examples, as a function of the total number of ports involved in the formula. Simple architecture styles like Star are decidable within seconds even for 50 ports. For architecture styles requiring more complex specifications, the number of ports that can be managed in 600 sec is smaller. For the Ring architecture the memory limit is attained for the model with 24 ports.

7   Related Work

A plethora of approaches exist for characterizing architecture styles. Patterns [9,16] are commonly used for this purpose in practical applications. They incorporate explicit constructs for architecture modelling but, lacking formal semantics, are not amenable to formal analysis. Among the formal approaches for representing and analysing architecture styles, we distinguish two main categories:

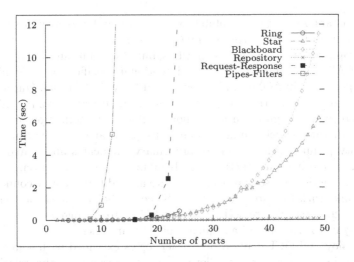

Fig. 4. Decision procedure for architecture styles

- *Extensional approaches*, where one explicitly specifies all interactions among the components (cf. the specification (5) of the Star pattern). All connections, other than the ones specified, are excluded.
- *Intentional approaches*, where one does not explicitly specify all connections among the components, but these are derived from a set of logical constraints, formulating the intentions of the designer (cf. the specification (4) of the Star pattern). In this case specifications are conjunctions of logical formulas.

The proposed framework encompasses both approaches. It allows explicit specification of individual interactions, e.g. with interaction formulas, as well as explicit specification of configuration sets, e.g. with formulas of the form $\sim f$.

A large body of literature, originating in [15,21], studies the use of graph grammars and transformations [24] to define software architectures. Although this work focuses mainly on dynamic reconfiguration of architectures, e.g. [6,19,20], graph grammars can be used to extensionally define architecture styles: a style admits all the configurations that can be derived by its defining grammar. The main limitations, outlined already in [21], are the following: (1) the difficulty of understanding the architecture style defined by a grammar; (2) the fact that the restriction to context-free grammars precludes the specification of certain styles (e.g. trees with unbounded number of components or interactions, square grids); (3) the impossibility of combining several styles in a homogeneous manner. To some extent, the latter two are addressed, respectively, by considering synchronised hyperedge replacement [11], context-sensitive grammars [10,27] and architecture views [23]. Our approach avoids these problems. Combining the extensional and intentional approaches allows intuitive specification of architecture styles. The higher-order extensions of PCL allow imposing global constraints necessary to specify styles that are not expressible by context-free graph grammars. Finally, the combination of several architecture styles is defined by the conjunction of the corresponding PCL formulas.

The proposed framework has similarities, but also significant differences, with the use of Alloy [17] and OCL [26] for intentional specification of architecture styles, respectively, in ACME and Darwin [12,14] and in UML [5]. Our approach achieves a strong semantic integration between architectures and architecture styles. Moreover, configuration logic allows a fine characterization of the coordination structure by using n-ary connectivity predicates. On the contrary, the connectivity primitives in [12,14,26] are binary predicates and cannot tightly characterize coordination structures involving multiparty interaction. To specify an n-ary interaction, these approaches require an additional entity connected by n binary links with the interacting ports. Since the behaviour of such entities is not part of the architecture style, it is impossible to distinguish, e.g., between an n-ary synchronisation and a sequence of n binary ones.

Both Alloy and OCL rely on first-order logics extended with some form of the Kleene closure operator that allows to iterate over a transitive relationship. In particular, this operator allows defining reachability among components. It is known that the addition of the Kleene closure increases the expressive power w.r.t. a first-order logic [18]. To the best of our knowledge, the expressiveness relation between a first-order logic extended with Kleene closure and a corresponding second-order logic remains to be established.

8   Conclusion

The presented work is a contribution to a long-term research program that we have been pursuing for more than 15 years. The program aims at developing the BIP component framework for rigorous systems design [25]. BIP is a language and a set of supporting tools including code generators, verification and simulation tools. So far the theoretical work has focused on the study of expressive composition frameworks and their algebraic and logical formalization. This led in particular, to the formalization of architectures as generic coordination schemes applied to sets of components in order to enforce a given global property [1].

The presented work nicely complements the existing component framework with logics for the specification of architecture styles. Configuration logic formulas characterize interaction configurations between instances of typed components. Quantification over components and sets of components allows the genericity needed for architecture styles. We have shown through examples that configuration logic allows full expressiveness combined with ease of use. It is integrated in a unified semantic framework which is equipped with a decision procedure for checking that a given architecture model meets given style requirements.

As part of the future work, we will extend our results in several directions. From the specification perspective, we are planning to incorporate hierarchically structured interactions and data transfer among the participating ports. From the analysis perspective, we will study techniques for deciding satisfiability of higher-order extensions of PCL. Finally, from the practical perspective, we also plan to extend to the higher-order logics the Maude implementation of the decision procedures. We will also study sublogics that are practically relevant and for which more efficient decision procedures can be applied.

In parallel, we are currently using configuration logic to formally specify reference architectures for avionics systems, in a project with ESA.

References

1. Attie, P., Baranov, E., Bliudze, S., Jaber, M., Sifakis, J.: A general framework for architecture composability. In: Giannakopoulou, D., Salaün, G. (eds.) SEFM 2014. LNCS, vol. 8702, pp. 128–143. Springer, Heidelberg (2014)
2. Bliudze, S., Sifakis, J.: The algebra of connectors–structuring interaction in BIP. IEEE Trans. Comput. **57**(10), 1315–1330 (2008)
3. Bliudze, S., Sifakis, J.: Causal semantics for the algebra of connectors. FMSD **36**(2), 167–194 (2010)
4. Bliudze, S., Sifakis, J.: Synthesizing glue operators from glue constraints for the construction of component-based systems. In: Apel, S., Jackson, E. (eds.) SC 2011. LNCS, vol. 6708, pp. 51–67. Springer, Heidelberg (2011)
5. Booch, G., Rumbaugh, J., Jacobson, I.: The Unified Modeling Language User Guide. Addison-Welsley Longman Inc, Boston (1999)
6. Bruni, R., Lluch-Lafuente, A., Montanari, U., Tuosto, E.: Style-based architectural reconfigurations. Bull. EATCS **94**, 161–180 (2008)
7. Clements, P., Garlan, D., Bass, L., Stafford, J., Nord, R., Ivers, J., Little, R.: Documenting Software Architectures: Views and Beyond. Pearson Education, New York (2002)
8. Corkill, D.D.: Blackboard systems. AI Expert **6**(9), 40–47 (1991)
9. Daigneau, R.: Service Design Patterns: Fundamental Design Solutions for SOAP/WSDL and Restful Web Services. Addison-Wesley, Boston (2011)
10. Ehrig, H., König, B.: Deriving bisimulation congruences in the DPO approach to graph rewriting. In: Walukiewicz, I. (ed.) FOSSACS 2004. LNCS, vol. 2987, pp. 151–166. Springer, Heidelberg (2004)
11. Ferrari, G.-L., Tuosto, E., Hirsch, D., Lanese, I., Montanari, U.: Synchronised hyperedge replacement as a model for service oriented computing. In: de Boer, F.S., Bonsangue, M.M., Graf, S., de Roever, W.-P. (eds.) FMCO 2005. LNCS, vol. 4111, pp. 22–43. Springer, Heidelberg (2006)
12. Garlan, D., Monroe, R., Wile, D.: Acme: An architecture description interchange language.In: Proceedings CASCON 1997, pp. 159–173. IBM Press (1997)
13. Garlan, D., Shaw, M.: An introduction to software architecture. In: Advances in Software Engineering and Knowledge Engineering, pp. 1–39. World Scientific Publishing Company (1993)
14. Georgiadis, I., Magee, J., Kramer, J.: Self-organising software architectures for distributed systems. In: Proceedings of the First Workshop on Self-Healing Systems, pp. 33–38. ACM (2002)
15. Hirsch, D., Inverardi, P., Montanari, U.: Modeling software architectures and styles with graph grammars and constraint solving. In: Donohoe, P. (ed.) Software Architecture. IFIP—The International Federation for Information Processing, vol. 12, pp. 127–143. Springer, US (1999)
16. Hohpe, G., Woolf, B.: Enterprise Integration Patterns: Designing, Building, and Deploying Messaging Solutions. Addison-Wesley Longman Publishing Co., Inc., Boston (2003)

17. Jackson, D.: Alloy: a lightweight object modelling notation. ACM Trans. Softw. Eng. Methodol. **11**(2), 256–290 (2002)
18. Keller, U.: Some remarks on the definability of transitive closure in first-order logic and Datalog. Internal report, Digital Enterprise Research Institute (DERI), University of Innsbruck (2004)
19. Koehler, C., Lazovik, A., Arbab, F.: Connector rewriting with high-level replacement systems. Electron. Notes Theor. Comput. Sci. **194**(4), 77–92 (2008)
20. Krause, C., Maraikar, Z., Lazovik, A., Arbab, F.: Modeling dynamic reconfigurations in Reo using high-level replacement systems. Sci. Comp. Prog. **76**(1), 23–36 (2011)
21. Le Métayer, D.: Describing software architecture styles using graph grammars. IEEE Trans. Softw. Eng. **24**(7), 521–533 (1998)
22. Mavridou, A., Baranov, E., Bliudze, S., Sifakis, J.: Configuration logics - modelling architecture styles. Technical report EPFL-REPORT-206825, EPFL IC IIF RiSD, March 2015. http://infoscience.epfl.ch/record/206825
23. Perry, D.E., Wolf, A.L.: Foundations for the study of software architecture. ACM SIGSOFT Softw. Eng. Notes **17**(4), 40–52 (1992)
24. Rozenberg, G. (ed.): Handbook of Graph Grammars and Computing by Graph Transformation. World Scientific, Singapore (1997)
25. Sifakis, J.: Rigorous system design. Found. Trends Electron. Des. Autom. **6**, 293–362 (2012)
26. Warmer, J.B., Kleppe, A.G.: The Object Constraint Language: Precise Modeling With UML. Addison-Wesley, Boston (1998)
27. Zhang, D.-Q., Zhang, K., Cao, J.: A context-sensitive graph grammar formalism for the specification of visual languages. Comput. J. **44**(3), 186–200 (2001)

Learning-Based Compositional Model Checking of Behavioral UML Systems

Yael Meller[1]([⊠]), Orna Grumberg[1], and Karen Yorav[2]

[1] CS Department, Technion, Haifa, Israel
{ymeller,orna}@cs.technion.ac.il
[2] IBM Research, Haifa, Israel
yorav@il.ibm.com

Abstract. This work presents a novel approach for applying compositional model checking of behavioral UML models, based on learning. The *Unified Modeling Language* (UML) is a widely accepted modeling language for embedded and safety critical systems. As such the correct behavior of systems represented as UML models is crucial. *Model checking* is a successful automated verification technique for checking whether a system satisfies a desired property. However, its applicability is often impeded by its high time and memory requirements. A successful approach to tackle this limitation is *compositional model checking*. Recently, great advancements have been made in this direction via automatic learning-based Assume-Guarantee reasoning.

In this work we propose a framework for automatic Assume-Guarantee reasoning for behavioral UML systems. We apply an off-the-shelf learning algorithm for incrementally generating environment assumptions that guarantee satisfaction of the property. A unique feature of our approach is that the generated assumptions are UML state machines. Moreover, our Teacher works at the UML level: all queries from the learning algorithm are answered by generating and verifying behavioral UML systems.

1 Introduction

This work presents a novel approach for learning-based compositional model checking of behavioral UML systems. Our work focuses on systems that rely on *UML state machines*, a standard graphical language for modeling the behavior of event-driven software components. The *Unified Modeling Language* (UML) [3] is becoming the dominant modeling language for specifying and constructing embedded and safety critical systems. As such, the correct behavior of systems represented as UML models is crucial and model checking techniques applicable to such models are required.

Model checking [7] is a successful automated verification technique for checking whether a given system satisfies a desired property. The system is usually described as a finite state model such as a state transition graph, where nodes represent the current state of the system and edges represent transitions of the

---

An extended version including full proofs is published as a technical report in [22].

© Springer International Publishing Switzerland 2016
C. Braga and P.C. Ölveczky (Eds.): FACS 2015, LNCS 9539, pp. 275–293, 2016.
DOI: 10.1007/978-3-319-28934-2_15

system from one state to another. The specification is usually given as a temporal logic formula. The model checking algorithm traverses *all* of the system behaviors (i.e., paths in the state transition graph), and either concludes that all system behaviors are correct w.r.t. to the checked property, or provides a *counterexample* that demonstrates an erroneous behavior.

Model checking is widely recognized as an important approach to increase the reliability of hardware and software systems and is vastly used in industry. Unfortunately, its applicability is often impeded by its high time and memory requirements. One of the most appealing approaches to fighting these problems is *compositional model checking*, where parts of the system are verified separately. The construction of the entire system is avoided and consequently the model checking cost is reduced. Due to dependencies among components' behaviors, it is usually impossible to verify one component in complete isolation from the rest of the system. To take such dependencies into account the Assume-Guarantee (**AG**) paradigm [14,17,27] suggests how to verify a component based on an *assumption* on the behavior of its environment, which consists of the other system components. The environment is then verified in order to guarantee that the assumption is actually correct.

Learning [2] has become a major technique to construct assumptions for the **AG** paradigm automatically. An automated *learning-based **AG** framework* was first introduced in [9]. It uses iterative **AG** reasoning, where in each iteration an assumption is constructed and checked for suitability, based on learning and on model checking. Many works suggest optimizations of the basic framework and apply it in the context of different **AG** rules (e.g. [4,6,11,16,24,25]).

In this paper we propose a framework for automated learning-based **AG** reasoning *for UML state machines*. Our framework is similar to the one presented in [9], with the main difference being that our framework remains at the state machine level. That is, the system's components are state machines, and the learned assumptions are *state machines* as well. This is in contrast to [9], where the system's components and the learned assumptions are all presented as Labeled Transition Systems (LTSs), which are a form of low-level state transition graphs. To the best of our knowledge, this is the first work that applies learning-based assume guarantee reasoning in the context of behavioral UML systems.

A naive implementation of our framework might translate a given behavioral UML system into LTSs and apply the algorithm from [9] on the result. However, due to the hierarchical and orthogonal structure of state machines such translation would result in LTSs that are exponentially larger than the original UML system. Moreover, state machines communicate via event queues. Such translation must also include the event queues, which would also increase the size of the LTSs by an order of magnitude. We therefore choose to define a framework for automated learning-based **AG** reasoning *directly on the state machine level*. Another important advantage of working with state machines is that it enables us to exploit high level information to make the learning much more efficient. It also enables us to apply model checkers designed for *behavioral UML systems* (e.g. [1, 5, 8, 10, 15, 19, 20, 23, 29]). Such model checkers take into account the specific structure and semantics of UML, and are therefore more efficient than model checkers designed for low-level representations (such as state transition graphs).

We use the standard **AG** rule below, where M_1 and M_2 are UML state machines. We replace $\langle A \rangle$ with $[A]$, to emphasize that A is a state machine playing the role of an *assumption* on the environment of M_1. The first premise (*Step* 1) holds iff $A \| M_1$ satisfies φ, and the second one (*Step* 2) holds iff every execution of M_2 in any environment has a representative in A. Together they guarantee that $M_1 \| M_2$ satisfies φ in any environment.

$$
\textbf{Rule AG-UML} \qquad
\begin{array}{l}
(Step\ 1)\ \ [A]\ M_1\ \langle\varphi\rangle \\
(Step\ 2)\ \ \langle true\rangle\ M_2\ [A] \\
\hline
\qquad \langle true\rangle\ M_1 \| M_2\ \langle\varphi\rangle
\end{array}
$$

We assume φ is a safety property, and use the learning algorithm L^* [2, 28] to iteratively construct assumptions A_i until both premises of the rule hold for A_i, implying $M_1 \| M_2 \models \varphi$, or until a real counterexample is found, demonstrating that $M_1 \| M_2 \not\models \varphi$.

UML state machines communicate via *asynchronous events* using thread-local event queues. When a state machine receives an event, it makes a *run-to-completion (RTC)* step, in which it processes the event and continues execution until it cannot continue anymore. During its execution, the state machine may send events to other state machines. We exploit the notion of RTC steps for defining the alphabet Σ of the learned assumptions. We define an alphabet over *sequences of events*, where a letter (i.e., a sequence of events) represents a single RTC step of the assumption. A word w over these letters corresponds to an execution of the assumption. It also represents the equivalence class of all executions of the checked system, which are interleaved with w. Our alphabet is defined based on statically analyzing the behavior of M_2.

Learning words over sequences of events makes L^* highly efficient, as it avoids learning sequences that can never occur in M_2 and therefore should not be considered in an assumption. Moreover, our learning is executed w.r.t. *equivalence classes of executions*. Even though our learning process is over equivalence classes, we show that our framework is sound and complete. That is, we do not lose information from grouping executions according to their representative word.

The remainder of the paper is organized as follows. Some background on UML and **AG** reasoning is given in Sect. 2. UML computations, executions, words and their relations are defined in Sect. 3. In Sect. 4 we present our framework, implementing **Rule AG-UML** for UML systems. We conclude in Sect. 5.

2 Preliminaries

2.1 UML Behavioral Systems

We present here a brief overview of behavioral UML systems, and in particular, UML state machines. We refer the interested reader to the UML specification [13].

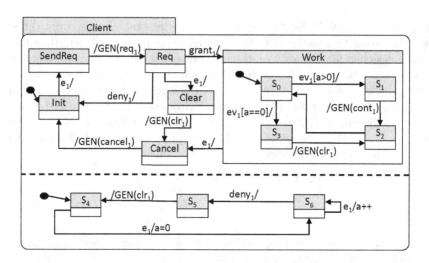

Fig. 1. Example State Machine of Class *client*

Behavioral UML systems include objects (instances of classes) that process events. Event processing is performed by state machines, which include complex features such as hierarchy, concurrency and communication. UML objects communicate by sending each other events (asynchronous messages) that are kept in *event queues* (EQs). Every object is associated with a single EQ, and several objects can be associated with the same EQ. In a multi-threaded system there are several EQs, one for each thread. Each thread executes a loop, taking an event from its EQ, and dispatching it to the target object, which then makes an RTC step. Only when the target object finishes its RTC step, the thread dispatches the next event available in its EQ. RTC steps of different threads are interleaved.

Figure 1 describes the state machine of class *client*. UML state machines include hierarchical states (states $Work$ and $Client$ in Fig. 1), a single initial state in each hierarchical state (e.g., state s_0 in $Work$), and transitions between states. Each transition is labeled with $t[g]/a$, where t, g and a are *trigger, guard,* and *action,* respectively. Each of them is independently optional. A trigger is an event name, a guard is a Boolean expression over local and global variables, and an action is a piece of code in the underlying language used by the model. Actions can include statements generating event e and sending it to the relevant EQ. We represent such statements as "GEN(e)". An event e includes the name of the event and the state machine to which the event is sent. The set of events of a system includes events sent by a state machine in the system, and events sent by the "environment" of the system (to be formally defined later).

A transition from state s is *enabled* if s is part of the current (possibly hierarchical) active state, the trigger (if there is one) matches the current event dispatched, and the guard holds (an empty guard is equivalent to *true*). Further, all transitions contained in s are disabled. For example, in Fig. 1, the transition from $Work$ to $Cancel$ is enabled only if $Work$ is active, the event dispatched is e_1, and the transitions from s_0, s_1, s_2 and s_3 are disabled. When a transition is taken, the action labeling it is executed, and the state machine moves to the target state. An object executes an RTC step by traversing on enabled transitions, until it cannot continue anymore.

A state can include multiple orthogonal regions, separated by a dashed line, which corresponds to the parallel execution of the state machines contained in them (e.g., state $Client$ has two orthogonal regions). When an event is dispatched to a state machine, and it has no enabled transitions, then the event is *discarded* and the RTC step terminates immediately. Otherwise, if there exists an enabled transition, we say that the event is *consumed*. In each RTC step only the first transition may consume an event. An exception is the case of orthogonal regions that share the same trigger. These transitions are executed simultaneously. Since the semantics of simultaneous execution is unclear, we assume that the actions of transitions in orthogonal regions labeled with the same trigger do not affect other transitions. That is, firing them in any order yields the same effect on the system.

A *computation* of a system is defined as a sequence of system configurations. A *system configuration* includes information about the current state of each state machine in the system, the contents of all the EQs, and the value of all variables in the system. The initial configuration in a computation matches the initial state of the system, and the system moves from configuration c to configuration c' by executing an enabled transition or by receiving an event from the environment. A formal definition of computations can be found in [21].

2.2   Assume Guarantee Reasoning and Compositional Verification

[9] presents a framework for automatically constructing assumption A in an iterative fashion for applying the standard **AG** rule, where M_1 and M_2 are $LTSs$ and φ is a safety property. At each iteration i, an assumption A_i is constructed. Afterwards, *Step 1* ($\langle A_i \rangle M_1 \langle \varphi \rangle$) is applied in order to check whether M_1 guarantees φ in an environment that satisfies A_i. A *false* result means that this assumption is too *weak*, i.e., A_i does not restrict the environment enough for φ to be satisfied. Thus, the assumption needs to be *strengthened* (which corresponds to removing behaviors from it) with the help of the counterexample produced by *Step 1*. If *Step 1* returns *true* then A_i is strong enough for the property to be satisfied. To complete the proof, *Step 2* ($\langle true \rangle M_2 \langle A_i \rangle$) must be applied to discharge A_i on M_2. If *Step 2* returns *true*, then the compositional rule guarantees $\langle true \rangle M_1 || M_2 \langle \varphi \rangle$. That is, φ holds in $M_1 || M_2$. If it returns *false*, further analysis is required to identify whether $M_1 || M_2$ violates φ or whether A_i is stronger than necessary. Such analysis is based on the counterexample returned by *Step 2*. If A_i is too strong it must be *weakened* (i.e., behaviors must be added) in iteration $i+1$. The new assumption may be too weak, and thus the entire process must be repeated. The framework in [9] uses a learning algorithm for generating assumptions A_i and a model checker for verifying the two steps in the rule.

2.3   The L^* Algorithm

The learning algorithm used in [9] was developed by [2], and later improved by [28]. The algorithm, named L^*, learns an unknown regular language and produces a minimal deterministic finite automaton (DFA) that accepts it. Let U be an unknown regular language over some alphabet Σ. In order to learn U, L^* needs to interact with a *Minimally Adequate Teacher*, called Teacher. A Teacher must be able to correctly answer two types of questions from L^*. A *membership query*, consists of a string $w \in \Sigma^*$. The answer is *true* if $w \in U$, and *false* otherwise. A *conjecture* offers a candidate DFA C and the Teacher responds with *true* if $L(C) = U$ (where $L(C)$ denotes the language of C) or returns a counterexample, which is a string w s.t. $w \in L(C) \setminus U$ or $w \in U \setminus L(C)$.

3   Representing Executions as Words

A behavioral UML system with n state machines is denoted by $Sys = M_1||...||M_n$. We assume state machines communicate only through events (all variables are local), and assume also that every RTC step is finite. These assumptions enable us to define sequences of events representing a single RTC step, which will be the letters of our alphabet (formally defined later). For simplicity of presentation, we assume the following restrictions: (a) Transitions with triggers do not generate events, and each transition may generate at most one event, (b) A state machine does not generate events to itself, (c) An event e cannot be generated by more than one state machine, and (d) Each state machine runs in a separate thread[1].

Given a state machine M, $Con(M)$ and $Gen(M)$ denote the events that M can consume and generate, respectively. An over-approximation of these sets can be found by static analysis. The events of a system include events sent by a state machine in the system denoted $ESys$, and events sent by the "environment" of the system denoted $EEnv$. For a system Sys, $ESys(Sys) = Gen(M_1) \cup ... \cup Gen(M_n)$, and $EEnv(Sys) = \{Con(M_1) \cup ... \cup Con(M_n)\} \setminus \{Gen(M_1) \cup ... \cup Gen(M_n)\}$. We denote $EV(Sys) = ESys(Sys) \cup EEnv(Sys)$. We assume the most general environment, that can send any environment event at any time. Note that the environment of a system might send events that will always be discarded by the target state machine. Since we are handling safety properties, such behaviors do not affect the satisfaction of the property, and we can therefore ignore them.

Recall that a computation of Sys is a series of configurations. Based on the above assumptions on Sys, each move from configuration c to configuration c' in a computation is labeled by at most one of $tr(e)$ and $gen(e)$, where $tr(e)$ denotes that when moving from c to c' event e was dispatched to the target state machine, and $gen(e)$ denotes that event e was either generated by a state machine in Sys (if $e \in ESys(Sys)$) or sent by the environment of Sys (if $e \in EEnv(Sys)$). Note that it is possible that a move is denoted with neither (labeled with ϵ).

---

[1] The case where several state machines run on the same thread is simpler, however presentation of both is cumbersome. We present only the more complex case.

Note that events are always generated before they are dispatched. UML2 places no restrictions on the implementation of the EQs, and neither do we. However, a specific implementation implies restrictions on the possible order of events. For example, if the EQs are FIFOs, then if e was generated before e' and the target of both events is M, then e will be dispatched before e'. Given a set of events EV, a sequence of labels over $\{tr(e), gen(e) | e \in EV\}$ is an *execution* over EV if it adheres to the above ordering requirements. A computation matches an execution ex if ex is the sequence of non-ϵ labels of the computation. We denote the set of executions of Sys by $L_{ex}(Sys)$. Note that every computation matches a single execution. However, different computations may match the same execution.

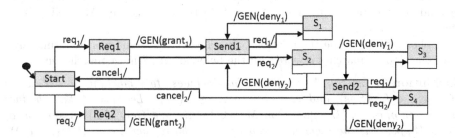

Fig. 2. Example State Machine for Class *server*

Example. *Consider the system $Sys = server\|client$ where client and server are presented in Figs. 1 and 2, respectively. Then $gen(e_1), tr(e_1), gen(req_1), tr(req_1), gen(grant_1) \in L_{ex}(Sys)^2$. However, $gen(e_1), tr(e_1), gen(cancel_1) \notin L_{ex}(Sys)$, since client, when in initial state, cannot generate $cancel_1$ after consuming e_1.*

From here on we do not address computations of a system, and consider only executions. We say that "execution ex satisfies a property φ" iff *all computations* that match ex satisfy φ. Let $EV' \subseteq EV$ be a set of events, and ex be an execution over EV. The *projection of ex w.r.t. EV'*, denoted $ex \downarrow_{EV'}$, is the projection of ex on $\{tr(e), gen(e) | e \in EV'\}$. The following theorem is a result of the fact that state machines communicate only through events.

Theorem 1. *Let $Sys = M_1\|...\|M_n$, and let ex be an execution over $EV(Sys)$. Then, $ex \in L_{ex}(Sys)$ iff for every $i \in \{1, ..., n\}$, $ex \downarrow_{EV(M_i)} \in L_{ex}(M_i)$.*

In order to later apply the L^* algorithm for learning assumptions on state machines, we first need to define an alphabet.

Definition 2. *Let M be a state machine. $\sigma = (t, (e_1, .., e_n))$ is in the alphabet of M, $\Sigma(M)$, if $t \in Con(M)$ and there exists an RTC step of M that starts by consuming or discarding t, and continues by generating a sequence of events $e_1, ..., e_n$.*

---

[2] In the examples throughout the paper we assume EQs are implemented as FIFOs.

Letters in $\Sigma(M)$ where n is 0 are denoted (t, ϵ). The idea behind our definition is that since the state machines in our systems communicate only through events, the alphabet maintains only the event information of the state machines. Since every RTC is finite, then an over-approximation of $\Sigma(M)$ can be found by static analysis (by traversing the graph of M), and the over-approximation is finite.

Example. *Let* $M = client$ *(Fig. 1). Then* $\Sigma(M) = \{(e_1, (req_1)), (deny_1, \epsilon),$ $(e_1, (clr_1, cancel_1)), (e_1, \epsilon), (deny_1, (clr_1)), (grant_1, \epsilon), (ev_1, (clr_1)), (ev_1, (cont_1)),$ (ev_1, ϵ). *For example,* $(e_1, (clr_1, cancel_1)) \in \Sigma(M)$ *(resulting from a possible RTC step that starts when* M *is in state* Req). *Also* $(ev_1, \epsilon) \in \Sigma(M)$, *since client can discard* ev_1 *(e.g., when in initial state).*

For a letter $\sigma = (t, (e_1, ..., e_n))$, $trig(\sigma) = t$ and $evnts(\sigma) = \{e_1, .., e_n\}$. We extend these notations to the alphabet Σ in the obvious way. Also, $EV(\Sigma) = trig(\Sigma) \cup evnts(\Sigma)$.

Following, we define the relation between executions and words. Intuitively, an execution ex matches a word w if the behavior of M in ex matches w.

Definition 3. *Let* Sys *be a system that includes state machine* M, *let* $ex = f_1, f_2, ... \in L_{ex}(Sys)$, *and let* $w = \sigma_1, \sigma_2, ... \in \Sigma(M)^*$. *Let* $\xi_1 = f'_1, f'_2, ...$ *be the projection of* ex *on* $\{tr(e) | e \in Con(M)\} \cup \{gen(e) | e \in Gen(M)\}$. *Assume also* $\xi_2 = f''_1, f''_2, ...$ *is the sequence created from* w *by replacing* $\sigma = (t, (e_1, ..., e_n))$ *with* $tr(t), gen(e_1), ..., gen(e_n)$. *Then* ex *matches* w, *denoted* $ex \triangleright w$, *iff* $\xi_1 = \xi_2$.

Note that an immediate result of the above definition is that if $ex \triangleright w$ where $w \in \Sigma^*$, then adding or removing from ex occurrences of events not in $EV(\Sigma)$ results in a sequence ex' s.t. $ex' \triangleright w$ still holds. Another important thing to note is that different executions can match the same word w. Thus w represents all the different executions under which the behavior of M matches w.

Example. *Consider execution* $ex = gen(e_1), tr(e_1), \mathbf{gen(req_1)}\ tr(req_1),$ $gen(grant_1), gen(ev_1), \mathbf{tr(ev_1)} \in L_{ex}(server \| client)$. *We denote with* **bold** *the parts of the execution that represent behavior of client. For the word* $w = (e_1, req_1), (ev_1, \epsilon) \in \Sigma(client)^*$, $ex \triangleright w$. *It also holds that for the execution* $ex' = gen(e_1), gen(ev_1), \mathbf{tr(e_1)}, \mathbf{gen(req_1)}, tr(req_1), \mathbf{tr(ev_1)}, gen(grant_1), ex' \triangleright w$.

We consider safety properties over events, based on predicates such as $InQ(e)$, denoting that e is in the EQ, $BeforeQ(e, e')$ indicating that e is before e' in the EQ, and $gen(e)$ (or $tr(e)$), indicating that e is generated (or dispatched). We handle safety properties over LTL_x, which is the Linear-time Temporal Logic (LTL) [26] without the next-time operator. Model checking safety properties can be reduced to handling properties of the form $\forall Gp$ for a state formula p[3] [18], which means that along every execution path, p globally holds (every execution path satisfies Gp). That is, every reachable configuration satisfies p. We therefore assume $\varphi = \forall Gp$. The following theorem states that if an execution ex satisfies Gp, then adding or removing occurrences that do not influence p, results in an execution that satisfies Gp.

---

[3] In LTL, the syntax of this property is AGp. We choose to denote it by $\forall Gp$ in order to differentiate the property from **AG** (which stands for Assume-Guarantee).

Theorem 4. *Let ex be an execution over EV and let p be a property over events* $EV' \subseteq EV$. *Then* $ex \models Gp$ *iff* $ex \downharpoonright_{EV'} \models Gp$.

4   AG for State Machines

Our goal is to efficiently adapt the **AG** framework for UML state machines. Following, we first show that **Rule AG-UML** (presented in Sect. 1) holds for UML state machines, and present a framework for applying **Rule AG-UML** for UML state machines (Sect. 4.1). We give a detailed description of the framework in Sects. 4.2 and 4.3, discuss its correctness in Sect. 4.4, and present a performance analysis in Section 4.5.

4.1   A Framework for Employing Rule AG-UML and Its Correctness

First, we formally define the meaning of the two premises in **Rule AG-UML**: $[A]M\langle \forall Gp \rangle$ holds iff for every $ex \in L_{ex}(A||M)$, $ex \models Gp$. $\langle true \rangle M[A]$ holds iff $EV(A) \subseteq EV(M)$ and for every $ex \in L_{ex}(M)$, $ex \downharpoonright_{EV(A)} \in L_{ex}(A)$.

Theorem 5. *Let* M_1, M_2 *and* A *be state machines s.t.* $EV(A) \subseteq EV(M_2)$, *let* p *be a property over events* $EV' \subseteq (EV(A) \cup EV(M_1))$, *and let* $\varphi = \forall Gp$. *Then* **Rule AG-UML** *is sound.*

We use L^* to iteratively construct assumptions A, until either both premises of **Rule AG-UML** hold, or until a real counterexample is found. L^* learns a language over *words*, where each word represents an equivalence class of executions.

In order to apply the L^* algorithm we define Σ, the alphabet of the language learned by L^*. Intuitively, Σ includes details of M_2 that are relevant for proving φ with M_1. The alphabet $\Sigma(M_2)$ (Definition 2) may include events of M_2 which are irrelevant. We therefore restrict $\Sigma(M_2)$ to Σ by keeping only elements of $EV(M_2)$ that are relevant for the interaction with M_1 and for φ.

Definition 6. *Let* $M_1||M_2$ *be a system and* φ *be a safety property.* Σ, *the assumption alphabet of* M_2 *w.r.t.* M_1 *and* φ, *is the maximal set, s.t. for every* $\sigma = (t, (e_{i_1}, ..., e_{i_n})) \in \Sigma$ *there exists* $\sigma' = (t, (e_1, ..., e_m)) \in \Sigma(M_2)$ *s.t. both requirements hold:*

1. $(e_{i_1}, ..., e_{i_n})$ *is the maximal sub-vector of* $(e_1, ..., e_m)$ *(i.e.,* $1 \leq i_1 < i_2 < ... < i_n \leq m$) *where each* e_{i_j} *is consumed by* M_1 *or part of the property* φ.
2. *If* $t \in EEnv(M_1||M_2)$ *and* $n = 0$: *add* (t, ϵ) *to* Σ *only if either* t *is part of* φ *or there exists* $\sigma_1 = (t, (e'_1, ..., e'_k)) \in \Sigma$ *s.t.* $k > 0$.

Example. Let $Sys = server||client$ *where* $server$ *is* M_1 *and* $client$ *is* M_2, *and let* $\varphi = \forall G(\neg(InQ(grant_1) \land InQ(deny_1))$. *The events of* φ *are* $grant_1$ *and* $deny_1$. Σ, *the assumption alphabet of* M_2 *w.r.t.* M_1 *and* φ, *is* $\{(e_1, (req_1)), (e_1, \epsilon), (grant_1, \epsilon), (deny_1, \epsilon), (e_1, (cancel_1))\}$. *Note that although* $(deny_1, (clr_1)) \in \Sigma(client)$, *since* clr_1 *is not consumed by the server and is not* part of φ, then it is not included in Σ. Similarly, $(e_1, (clr_1, cancel_1)) \in \Sigma(client)$, but only $(e_1, (cancel_1)) \in \Sigma$. Note also that Σ includes all the interface information between client and server. Thus, $(e_1, (req_1)) \in \Sigma$, although neither e_1 nor req_1 are part of φ.

We define the notion of *weakest assumption* in the context of state machines.

Definition 7. *A language $A_w \subseteq \Sigma^*$ is the* weakest assumption *w.r.t. M_1 and φ if the following holds: $w \in A_w$ iff for every execution ex over $EV(\Sigma) \cup EV(M_1)$, if $ex \triangleright w$ and $ex \lfloor_{EV(M_1)} \in L_{ex}(M_1)$, then $ex \models Gp$.*

Assume we could construct a state machine M_{A_w} that *represents* A_w. That is, for every execution ex over $EV(\Sigma)$, $ex \in L_{ex}(M_{A_w})$ iff there exists $w \in A_w$ s.t. $ex \triangleright w$. Then, M_{A_w} describes exactly those executions over Σ that when executed with M_1 do not violate Gp. The following theorem states that $\langle true \rangle M_1 || M_2 \langle \varphi \rangle$ holds iff every execution of M_2 matches a word in A_w.

Theorem 8. *$\langle true \rangle M_1 || M_2 \langle \varphi \rangle$ holds iff for every execution $ex \in L_{ex}(M_2)$, there exists $w \in A_w$ s.t. $ex \triangleright w$, where A_w is the weakest assumption w.r.t. M_1 and φ.*

Proof Sketch. *The proof of direction $\Leftarrow$ is based on the definitions of executions (full proof available in [22]). For the proof of direction $\Rightarrow$, assume there exists an execution $ex_1 \in L_{ex}(M_2)$ and no word $w \in A_w$ s.t. $ex_1 \triangleright w$. Thus, there exists a word $w \in \Sigma^* \setminus A_w$ s.t. $ex_1 \triangleright w$. We show that $\langle true \rangle M_1 || M_2 \langle \varphi \rangle$ does not hold. If $w \notin A_w$, then there exists an execution ex_2 over $EV(\Sigma) \cup EV(M_1)$ s.t. $ex_2 \lfloor_{EV(M_1)} \in L_{ex}(M_1)$, $ex_2 \triangleright w$, and $ex_2 \not\models Gp$. We then construct an execution ex by combining ex_1 and ex_2. Our construction ensures that $ex \lfloor_{EV(M_i)} \in L_{ex}(M_i)$ for $i \in \{1,2\}$. We conclude that $ex \in L_{ex}(M_1 || M_2)$, and show that $ex \not\models Gp$ as well. Note that the construction of ex is not straightforward; ex_1 and ex_2 both match w, however the other parts of the executions might not match, i.e., the interleaving of M_2 and the environment in ex_2 may be different from the interleaving of M_1 and Σ in ex_1. Our construction of ex actually shows that there exists an interleaving that is possible by both M_1 and M_2, and that still violates Gp.*   □

From the definition of A_w and from the above theorem we conclude the following corollary, which states that **Rule AG-UML** holds if we replace A with M_{A_w}.

Corollary 9. *Let A_w be the weakest assumption w.r.t. M_1 and φ. Assume there exists a state machine M_{A_w} that represents A_w. Then **Rule AG-UML** holds when replacing A with M_{A_w}.*

The goal of L^* is therefore to learn A_w. To automate L^* in our setting we now show how to construct a Teacher that answers membership and conjecture queries. The Teacher answers queries by "translating" the queries into state machines, and verifying properties on state machines via a model checker for behavioral UML systems. The model checker must be able to always return a definite answer (*true* or *false*) for properties of type $\forall Gp$. Also, when answering *false* it should give a counterexample. Model checkers for behavioral UML systems verify the behavior w.r.t. system configurations. Thus, a counterexample is a computation of the system. It is straightforward to translate the counterexample into a counterexample execution or word. Although our goal is to learn A_w, our automatic framework may stop with a definite *true* or *false* answer before A_w is constructed.

For a membership query on w, the Teacher constructs a state machine for w, and checks if, when executed with M_1, φ is violated. For conjecture queries, the Teacher constructs a state machine $A(C)$ from conjecture C, and verifies *Step 1* and *Step 2* of **Rule AG-UML** w.r.t. $A(C)$.

From now on, in our following constructions, we sometimes include an *err* state in state machines. For simplicity of presentation, for a given system Sys where some of its state machines include *err* state, $L_{ex}(Sys)$ represents only the executions that do not reach *err* state on any of its state machines.

4.2   Membership Queries

To answer a membership query for $w \in \Sigma^*$, the Teacher must return *true* iff $w \in A_w$. The Teacher creates a state machine $M(w)$ s.t. $\Sigma(M(w)) \subseteq \Sigma$. $M(w)$ is constructed s.t. for every ex over $EV(\Sigma) \cup EV(M_1)$: $ex \in L_{ex}(M(w)\|M_1)$ iff $ex \downharpoonright_{EV(M_1)} \in L_{ex}(M_1)$ and $ex \triangleright w$. If this holds, then (by the definition of A_w in Definition 7) $w \in A_w$ iff for every execution $ex \in L_{ex}(M(w)\|M_1)$, $ex \models Gp$.

Let $w = \sigma_1, \sigma_2, ..., \sigma_m$ and let $\sigma_i = (t_i, (e^i_1, e^i_2, ..., e^i_{k_i}))$, for $i \in \{1, ..., m\}$. The state machine $M(w)$ is presented in Fig. 3. A transition labeled with a set of triggers T (e.g., the transition from s_1 to err) is a shorthand for a set of transitions, each labeled with a single trigger $t \in T$. For $\sigma = (t, (e^1, ..., e^k))$, a compound transition, denoted as a double arrow $\Rightarrow$, labeled with $trig[grd]/GEN(\sigma)$ is a shorthand for a sequence of states and transitions, where the first transition is labeled with $trig[grd]$, the second is labeled with action $GEN(e^1)$, the third with action $GEN(e^2)$, etc. The idea behind splitting the compound transition into intermediate states is to enable all possible interleaving between $M(w)$ and M_1, thus ensuring that every execution over $EV(\Sigma) \cup EV(M_1)$ that represents an execution of M_1 and matches w is indeed a possible execution of $M(w)\|M_1$.

We explicitly define at each state s_i the behavior of $M(w)$ in response to any possible event $t \in trig(\Sigma)$. Not specifying such a behavior implies that if t is dispatched to $M(w)$ then $M(w)$ discards t and remains in the same state.

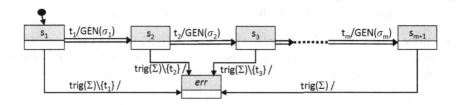

Fig. 3. $M(w)$ constructed for w

This is an undesired behavior of $M(w)$, which is supposed to execute w with *no additional intermediate letters*. Thus, transitions that do not match w are sent to state *err*. The following theorem describes the executions of $M(w)$.

Theorem 10. *Let $M(w)$ be the state machine constructed for word $w \in \Sigma^*$. For every execution ex over $EV(\Sigma)$: $ex \in L_{ex}(M(w))$ iff there exists a prefix w' of w s.t. $ex \triangleright w'$.*

Once $M(w)$ is constructed, the Teacher model checks $M(w) \| M_1 \models \forall G(p \vee IsIn(err))$, where $IsIn(s)$ denotes that s is part of the current state of the system. The model checker returns *true* iff for every execution one of the following holds: (1) the execution does not reach state *err*, i.e. the execution matches a prefix of w, and p is satisfied along the entire execution, or (2) the execution reaches state *err*, meaning that the execution does not match w and therefore we do not need to require p[4]. The Teacher returns *true*, indicating $w \in A_w$ iff the model checker returns *true*. The following theorem defines the correctness of the Teacher.

Theorem 11. $M(w) \| M_1 \models \forall G(p \vee IsIn(err))$ *iff $w \in A_w$.*

4.3   Conjecture Queries

A conjecture of the L^* algorithm is a DFA over Σ. Our framework first transforms this DFA, C, into a state machine $A(C)$. Then, *Step 1* and *Step 2* are applied in order to verify the correctness of $A(C)$.

Constructing a State Machine from a DFA: A DFA is a five tuple $C = (Q, \alpha, \delta, q_0, F)$, where Q is a finite non-empty set of states, α is the alphabet, $\delta \subseteq Q \times \alpha \times Q$ is a deterministic transition relation, $q_0 \in Q$ is the initial state, and $F \subseteq Q$ is a set of accepting states. For a string w, $\delta(q, w)$ denotes the state that C arrives at after reading w, starting from state q. A string w is *accepted* by C iff $\delta(q_0, w) \in F$. The language of C, denoted $L(C)$, is the set $\{w | \delta(q_0, w) \in F\}$. The DFAs returned by the L^* algorithm are complete, minimal, and prefix-closed. Thus they contain a single non-accepting state, q_{err}, and for every $\sigma \in \alpha$ and $q \in Q$, $\delta(q, \sigma)$ is defined.

The alphabet α of the DFA in our framework is exactly Σ. Given a DFA $C = (Q, \Sigma, \delta, q_0, Q \setminus \{q_{err}\})$, we construct a state machine $A(C)$ where $EV(A(C)) = EV(\Sigma)$. We then show that $A(C)$ *represents* $L(C)$, i.e., for every execution ex over $EV(\Sigma)$, $ex \in L_{ex}(A(C))$ iff there exists $w \in L(C)$ s.t. $ex \triangleright w$.

Definition 12 ($A(C)$ Construction). *Let $C = (Q, \Sigma, \delta, q_0, Q \setminus \{q_{err}\})$. $A(C)$ includes 3 states: init, end and err, where init is the initial state. $A(C)$ includes a single variable qs whose domain is Q, initialized to q_0. $A(C)$ has the following transitions:*

---

[4] It is ok to require p on a prefix leading to state *err*, since A_w is prefix closed for safety properties.

(1) For every $q \in Q$ and $\sigma = (t, (e_1, .., e_n)) \in \Sigma$ where $\delta(q, \sigma) = q'$ add a compound transition labeled with $t[qs = q]/qs := q'; GEN(\sigma)$ from init to end (if $q' \neq q_{err}$) or to err (if $q' = q_{err}$).

(2) Add a transition with no trigger, guard or action from end to init.

Example. For $Sys = server \| client$ and $\varphi = \forall G(\neg(InQ(grant_1) \wedge InQ(deny_1))$, the conjecture DFA C returned from the L^* algorithm, and state machine $A(C)$ representing $L(C)$, are presented in Fig. 4.

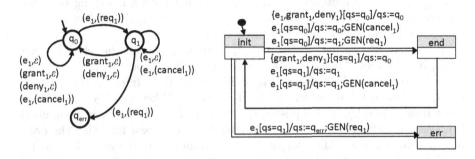

Fig. 4. The conjecture DFA C (left) and the state machine $A(C)$ (right)

The construction ensures that for every $t \in trig(\Sigma)$ and for every $q \in Q$ there exists a transition with trigger t and guard $qs = q$. That is, as long as $A(C)$ is at state *init* in the beginning of an RTC step, it does not discard events. Also, according to the semantics of state machines, every RTC step that starts at state *init*, either moves to state *err*, which is a sink state, or moves to state *end* and returns to state *init*. The following theorem states that $A(C)$ is indeed a state machine representing $L(C)$.

Theorem 13. Let $A(C)$ be the state machine constructed for DFA C. For every execution ex over $EV(\Sigma)$: $ex \in L_{ex}(A(C))$ iff there exists $w \in L(C)$ s.t. $ex \triangleright w$.

After creating $A(C)$, the Teacher uses two oracles and a counterexample analysis to answer conjecture queries.

Check $[A(C)]M_1\langle\varphi\rangle$: Oracle 1 performs *Step* 1 in the compositional rule by model checking $A(C)\|M_1 \models \forall G(p \vee IsIn(err))$. If the model checker returns *false* with a counterexample execution *cex*, the Teacher informs L^* that the conjecture is incorrect, and gives it the word $w \in \Sigma^*$ s.t. $cex \triangleright w$ to witness this fact ($w \in L(C)$ and $w \notin A_w$). If the model checker returns *true*, indicating that $[A(C)]M_1\langle\varphi\rangle$ holds, then the Teacher forwards $A(C)$ to Oracle 2.

Check $\langle true \rangle M_2[A(C)]$: Oracle 2 preforms *Step* 2 in the compositional rule. That is, check that for every execution $ex \in L_{ex}(M_2)$, $ex \downarrow_{EV(A(C))} \in L_{ex}(A(C))$. Note that this is a language containment check. In state machines there is no known algorithm for checking language containment. We present here a method for this check in the special case where the abstract state machine is the state machine $A(C)$ previously defined. *Step* 2 is done by constructing a single state machine, and applying model checking on the resulting state machine.

Given the state machines M_2 and $A(C)$, Oracle 2 constructs a new state machine, $\mathcal{M}$, that is composed from modifications of M_2 and $A(C)$ as two orthogonal regions. $\mathcal{M}$ is constructed so that the behavior of M_2 is *monitored* by $A(C)$ after every RTC step. $\mathcal{M}$ includes a synchronization mechanism, so that when an event is dispatched, first the region that includes M_2 executes the RTC step. When it finishes, the region that includes $A(C)$ executes its step *only if* $A(C)$ *has a behavior that matches* M_2. If $A(C)$ does not have a matching behavior, then $\mathcal{M}$ moves to an error state, indicating that $\langle true \rangle M_2[A(C)]$ does not hold. The general structure of $\mathcal{M}$ is presented in Fig. 5.

From here on, we denote M_2 and $A(C)$ that are regions in $\mathcal{M}$ as $\hat{M}_2$ and $\hat{A}(C)$, respectively. We add a local queue, IQ, and two local variables, rtc and tr, to $\mathcal{M}$. tr "records" the event e dispatched to $\mathcal{M}$, if $e \in trig(\Sigma)$. IQ "records" events generated by $\hat{M}_2$ which are from $evnts(\Sigma)$. Whenever $\hat{M}_2$ generates an event from $evnts(\Sigma)$, it also pushes the event to IQ. $\hat{A}(C)$ will, in turn, check if it has a matching behavior by observing IQ. rtc is used for fixing the order of execution along an RTC step of $\mathcal{M}$. It is initialized to 0, and as long as the monitoring is successful, the value of rtc at the end of the RTC step of $\mathcal{M}$ is 0. $rtc = 3$ indicates that $\hat{M}_2$ is executing an RTC step that should be monitored. $rtc = 2$ indicates that $\hat{M}_2$ finished its execution, and $\hat{A}(C)$ can monitor the behavior. $rtc = 1$ indicates that the monitoring step of $\hat{A}(C)$ was successful, i.e., $\hat{A}(C)$ has a behavior that matches $\hat{M}_2$. If the monitoring of $\hat{A}(C)$ failed, then rtc at the end of the RTC step is 2, indicating an error.

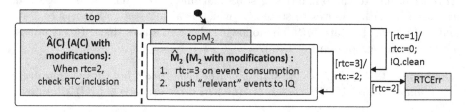

Fig. 5. General scheme for $\mathcal{M}$ created from $A(C)$ and M_2

The following modifications are applied to M_2 for constructing $\hat{M}_2$: Set rtc to 3 on transitions that consume event $e \in trig(\Sigma)$, and add $IQ.push(e')$ on transitions that generate event $e' \in gen(\Sigma)$.

The following modifications are applied to $A(C)$ (Definition 12) for constructing $\hat{A}(C)$:

1. Add a new state called *step* to $A(C)$, and for every $t \in trig(\Sigma)$, add a transition from *init* to *step* labeled $t/tr := t$.
2. Every compound transition from *init* to *end* labeled with:
   $t[qs = q]/qs := q'; GEN(e_1); ...; GEN(e_n)$ s.t. $n > 0$
   is replaced with a transition from *step* to *end* labeled with:
   $[tr = t \wedge qs = q \wedge rtc = 2 \wedge IQ = (e_1, ..., e_n)]/qs := q'; rtc := 1$

3. Every compound transition from *init* to *end* labeled with: $t[qs = q]/qs := q'$
   (no event generation), is replaced with a transition from *step* to *end* labeled
   with: $[tr = t \wedge qs = q \wedge ((rtc = 2 \wedge IQ = ()) \vee rtc = 0)]/ qs := q'; rtc := 1$
4. Every compound transition from *init* to *err* labeled with:
   $t[qs = q]/qs := q'; GEN(e_1); ...; GEN(e_n)$ s.t. $n > 0$
   is replaced with a transition from *step* to *err* labeled with:
   $[tr = t \wedge qs = q \wedge rtc = 2 \wedge IQ = (e_1, ..., e_n)]/qs := q'; rtc := 2$
5. Every compound transition from *init* to *err* labeled with: $t[qs = q]/qs := q'$
   (no event generation), is replaced with a transition from *step* to *err* labeled
   with: $[tr = t \wedge qs = q \wedge ((rtc = 2 \wedge IQ = ()) \vee rtc = 0)]/ qs := q'; rtc := 2$

If $\hat{A}(C)$ is at state *step* and $rtc = 0$ holds, then $\hat{M}_2$ discarded the event in
the current RTC step. $\hat{A}(C)$ has a matching behavior if it has a behavior that
consumes an event and does not generate events. The transitions described in
(3) and (5) monitor RTC steps of $\hat{M}_2$ that consume event t and do not generate
any events, and also RTC steps that discard t. Note that items (2) and (4)
(respectively, (3) and (5)) are distinct in the target state (*end* or *err*) and in
the assignment to rtc on the action. The transitions in (2) and (3) monitor RTC
steps that are legal in $\hat{A}(C)$, and transitions in (4) and (5) monitor RTC steps
that are not legal in $\hat{A}(C)$.

The correctness of our construction is captured in the following theorem.

Theorem 14. *For every* $ex \in L_{ex}(\mathcal{M})$: *ex reaches state RTCErr iff*
$ex \downharpoonleft_{EV(M_2)} \in L_{ex}(M_2)$ *and* $ex \downharpoonleft_{EV(A(C))} \notin L_{ex}(A(C))$.

After constructing $\mathcal{M}$, Oracle 2 model checks $\mathcal{M} \models \forall G(\neg IsIn\ (RTCErr))$.
If the model checker returns *true*, then the Teacher returns *true* and our frame-
work terminates the verification, because according to **Rule AG-UML**, φ has
been proved on $M_1||M_2$. Otherwise, if the model checker returns *false* with a
counterexample execution *cex*, then *cex* is analyzed as follows.

Counterexample Analysis: Note that only $\hat{M}_2$ generates events. Thus, by
projecting the execution *cex* on $\{tr(e)|e \in trig(\Sigma)\} \cup \{gen(e)|e \in evnts(\Sigma)\}$ we
can obtain $w \in \Sigma^*$ s.t. $cex \triangleright w$. The Teacher executes a membership query on w,
for checking whether w is in A_w (as presented in Sect. 4.2). If the membership
query succeeds (i.e., $w \in A_w$), the Teacher informs L^* that the conjecture is
incorrect, and gives it w to witness this fact (since $w \in A_w$ but $w \notin L(C)$). If the
membership query fails then the Teacher concludes that $\langle true \rangle M_1||M_2 \langle \varphi \rangle$ does
not hold, since $cex \downharpoonleft_{EV(M_2)} \in L_{ex}(M_2)$, $cex \downharpoonleft_{EV(M_2)} \triangleright w$ and $w \notin A_w$ (Theorem 8).
The Teacher then returns *false*.

Example. *Consider the system* server||client *and the assumption* $A(C)$ *(Fig. 4).*
When checking $\langle true \rangle client[A(C)]$, *the model checker may return a counterexample cex, represented by the word* $w = (e_1, (req_1)), (e_1, (cancel_1)), (e_1, (req_1))$
$(cex \triangleright w)$. $cex \downharpoonleft_{EV(M_2)} \in L_{ex}(client)$, $cex \downharpoonleft_{EV(M_2)} \triangleright w$ *and* $w \notin L(C)$.

*During counterexample analysis, the Teacher performs a membership query
on* w. *This check fails, since there exists an execution of* $M(w)||server$ *that vio-
lates the property* $\forall G(\neg(InQ(grant_1) \wedge InQ(deny_1)))$. *Note that the property is*

violated even though server receives the event $cancel_1$ before it receives the second req_1. However, there exists a behavior of the environment of $M(w)\|server$ that causes violation of the property: if server receives event req_2 after $cancel_1$, then when it receives the second req_1 it will send $deny_1$. Note that since every state machine runs on a different thread, it is possible that the event $grant_1$, previously sent to client, was not yet dispatched. Thus, when $deny_1$ is added to the EQ of client, the property is violated. Since the membership query fails, we conclude that $server\|client \not\models \varphi$.

4.4   Correctness

We first argue correctness of our approach, and then the fact that it terminates.

Theorem 15. *Given state machines M_1 and M_2, and a property $\forall Gp$, our framework returns true if $M_1\|M_2 \models \forall Gp$ and false otherwise.*

Termination: Assuming the number of configurations of $M_1\|M_2$ is finite, the weakest assumption w.r.t. M_1 and φ, A_w, is a regular language. To prove this, we construct an accepting automaton for A_w similarly to the construction in [12]. Since A_w is a regular language, then by correctness of the L^* algorithm, we are guaranteed that if it keeps receiving counterexamples, it will eventually produce A_w. The Teacher will then apply *Step* 2, which will return, based on Theorem 8, either *true* or a counterexample.

4.5   Performance Analysis

Our framework for automated learning-based **AG** reasoning is applied directly at the state machine level. That is, the system's components and the learned assumptions are state machines. However, the learning is done by applying an off-the-shelf L^* algorithm, whose conjectures are DFAs and its membership queries are words. Thus we need to translate DFAs and words into state machines. On the other hand we never need to translate from state machines back to low level representation (such as LTSs or DFAs). It is important to emphasize that, as shown above, the translation from DFAs and words to UML state machines is simple and straightforward, since the state machines created do not include complex features (such as hierarchy or orthogonality). On the other hand, a translation from UML state machines to LTSs may result in an exponential blowup, since the hierarchy and orthogonal structure should be flattened. Moreover, the event queues need to be represented explicitly, causing another blowup. Note that applying such a translation to LTSs does not influence the number of the membership or conjecture queries, as the learned assumption remains the same. However, it complicates the model checking used to answer these queries, since the system is much larger.

Our framework learns assumptions over an alphabet consisting of *sequences of events* representing RTC steps of M_2. We refer to this alphabet as *RTC alphabet.* Note that it is also possible to apply the framework (with minor modifications) over an alphabet consisting of single event occurrences (called *event alphabet*) rather then over the RTC alphabet, while still keeping the learning at the UML level. However, learning over the RTC alphabet is often better, as discussed below.

The complexity of the L^* algorithm can be represented by the number of membership and conjecture queries it needs in order to learn an unknown language U. As shown in [9,28], the number of membership queries of L^* is $O(n^2 \cdot k + n \cdot log(m))$ and the number of conjecture queries is at most $n - 1$, where n represents the number of states in the learned DFA, k is the size of the alphabet, and m is the size of the longest counterexample returned by the Teacher. This results from the characteristics of L^*, which learns the minimal automaton for U, and from the fact that each conjecture is smaller than the next one.

In theory, the size of the RTC alphabet might be much larger than the size of the event alphabet. This happens when every possible sequence of events is a possible RTC step of M_2. However, in practice typical state machines exhibit only a much smaller number of different RTC steps. Moreover, the number of states in the DFA Q_{RTC} learned over the RTC alphabet may be much smaller than the number of states in the DFA Q_{evnt} over the event alphabet. This is because a single transition in Q_{RTC} might be replaced by a sequence of transitions in Q_{evnt}, one for each of the events in the RTC.

The above observations are demonstrated in the following example.

Example. *We re-visit the example presented throughout Sect. 4.* $\varphi = \forall G(\neg(InQ(grant_1) \wedge InQ(deny_1)))$, *and* $Sys = server||client$ *where server is* M_1, *client is* M_2. *The final DFA learned when using event sequences is presented in Fig. 4(a). The total number of membership queries is* $O(3^2 \cdot 5 + 3 \cdot log2)$ *and there are 2 conjecture queries.*

If we apply learning over single event occurrence, then there are $O(4^2 \cdot 5 + 4 \cdot log3)$ *membership queries and 3 conjecture queries, since the resulting DFA has 4 states and the alphabet is* $\{tr(e_1), tr(grant_1), tr(deny_1), gen(req_1), gen(cancel_1)\}$.

5   Conclusion

We presented a framework for applying learning-based compositional verification of behavioral UML systems. Note that our framework is completely automatic; we use an off-the-shelf L^* algorithm. However, our Teacher works at the UML level. In particular, the assumptions generated throughout the learning process are state machines. From the regular automaton learned by the L^* algorithm, we construct a *state machine* which is a conjecture on M_2. Also, the Teacher answers membership and conjecture queries by "translating" them to model checking queries on state machines. Our framework is presented for $Sys = M_1||M_2$ where both M_1 and M_2 are state machines. However, M_1 and M_2 can both be systems that include *several state machines*, as long as the state machines of M_2 run on a single thread. If M_2 includes multiple state machines $M_1^2||...||M_k^2$ that run on a single thread, then we can construct a single state machine $\widetilde{M}_2$ where each M_i^2 is an orthogonal region in $\widetilde{M}_2$. The executions of $\widetilde{M}_2$ are equivalent to those of M_2. We can then apply our framework on $M_1 \| \widetilde{M}_2$.

In the future we plan to investigate other assume-guarantee rules in the context of behavioral UML system. For example, we would like to define a framework for checking $[A_1]M[A_2]$. Such a framework will enable us to apply recursive invocation of the **AG** rule, where M_2 includes several state machines.

References

1. Majzik, I., Darvas, A., Beny, B.: Verification of UML statechart models of embedded systems. In: Design and Diagnostics of Electronic Circuits and Systems Workshop (DDECS 2002), pp. 70–77. IEEE (2002)
2. Angluin, D.: Learning regular sets from queries and counterexamples. Inf. Comput. **75**(2), 87–106 (1987)
3. Booch, G., Rumbaugh, J.E., Jacobson, I.: The unified modeling language user guide. J. Database Manag. **10**(4), 51–52 (1999)
4. Strichman, O., Chaki, S.: Optimized L*-based assume-guarantee reasoning. In: Grumberg, O., Huth, M. (eds.) TACAS 2007. LNCS, vol. 4424, pp. 276–291. Springer, Heidelberg (2007)
5. Chan, W., Anderson, R.J., Beame, P., Burns, S., Modugno, F., Notkin, D., Reese, J.D.: Model checking large software specifications. IEEE Trans. Softw. Eng. **24**(7), 498–520 (1998)
6. Chen, Y.-F., Tsay, Y.-K., Clarke, E.M., Farzan, A., Wang, B.-Y.: Learning minimal separating DFA's for compositional verification. In: Kowalewski, S., Philippou, A. (eds.) TACAS 2009. LNCS, vol. 5505, pp. 31–45. Springer, Heidelberg (2009)
7. Clarke, E.M., Grumberg, O., Peled, D.A.: Model Checking. MIT press, Cambridge (1999)
8. Clarke, E.M., Heinle, W.: Modular translation of statecharts to SMV. Technical report CMU-CS-00-XXX, Carnegie-Mellon University School of Computer Science (2000)
9. Cobleigh, J.M., Giannakopoulou, D., Păsăreanu, C.S.: Learning assumptions for compositional verification. In: Garavel, H., Hatcliff, J. (eds.) TACAS 2003. LNCS, vol. 2619, pp. 331–346. Springer, Heidelberg (2003)
10. Dubrovin, J., Junttila, T.A.: Symbolic model checking of hierarchical UML state machines. In: Application of Concurrency to System Design (ACSD 2008), pp. 108–117. IEEE (2008)
11. Farzan, A., Tsay, Y.-K., Chen, Y.-F., Wang, B.-Y., Clarke, E.M.: Extending automated compositional verification to the full class of omega-regular languages. In: Ramakrishnan, C.R., Rehof, J. (eds.) TACAS 2008. LNCS, vol. 4963, pp. 2–17. Springer, Heidelberg (2008)
12. Giannakopoulou, D., Păsăreanu, C.S., Barringer, H.: Component verification with automatically generated assumptions. Autom. Softw.Eng. **12**(3), 297–320 (2005)
13. Object Management Group. OMG Unified Modeling Language (UML) Superstructure, version 2.4.1. formal/2011-08-06 (2011)
14. Grumberg, O., Long, D.E.: Model checking and modular verification. ACM Trans. Program. Lang. Syst. **16**(3), 843–871 (1994)

15. Meller, Y., Yorav, K., Grumberg, O.: Applying software model checking techniques for behavioral UML models. In: Giannakopoulou, D., Méry, D. (eds.) FM 2012. LNCS, vol. 7436, pp. 277–292. Springer, Heidelberg (2012)
16. Gupta, A., McMillan, K.L., Fu, Z.: Automated assumption generation for compositional verification. Form. Methods Syst. Des. **32**(3), 285–301 (2008)
17. Jones, C.B.: Specification and design of (parallel) programs. In: IFIP Congress, pp. 321–332 (1983)
18. Kupferman, O., Vardi, M.Y.: Model checking of safety properties. Form. Methods Syst. Des. **19**(3), 291–314 (2001)
19. Latella, D., Majzik, I., Massink, M.: Automatic verification of a behavioural subset of UML statechart diagrams using the spin model-checker. Formal Asp. Comput. **11**(6), 637–664 (1999)
20. Madhukar, K., Metta, R., Singh, P., Venkatesh, R.: Reachability verification of rhapsody statecharts. In: International Conference on Software Testing, Verification and Validation Workshops (ICSTW 2013), pp. 96–101. IEEE (2013)
21. Grumberg, O., Meller, Y., Yorav, K.: Verifying behavioral UML systems via CEGAR. In: Albert, E., Sekerinski, E. (eds.) IFM 2014. LNCS, vol. 8739, pp. 139–154. Springer, Heidelberg (2014)
22. Meller, Y., Grumberg, O., Yorav, K.: Learning-based compositional model checking of behavioral UML systems. Technical report CS-2015-05, Department of Computer Science, Technion - Israel Institute of Technology (2015)
23. Mikk, E., Lakhnech, Y., Siegel, M., Holzmann, G.J.: Implementing statecharts in PROMELA/SPIN. In: Workshop on Industrial-Strength Formal Specification Techniques (WIFT 1998), pp. 90–101. IEEE (1998)
24. Nam, W., Madhusudan, P., Alur, R.: Automatic symbolic compositional verification by learning assumptions. Form. Methods Syst. Des. **32**(3), 207–234 (2008)
25. Pasareanu, C.S., Giannakopoulou, D., Bobaru, M.G., Cobleigh, J.M., Barringer, H.: Learning to divide and conquer: applying the L* algorithm to automate assume-guarantee reasoning. Form. Methods Syst. Des. **32**(3), 175–205 (2008)
26. Pnueli, A.: The temporal logic of programs. In: Proceedings of the Eighteenth Annual Symposium on Foundations of Computer Science (FOCS 1977) (1977)
27. Pnueli, A.: In transition from global to modular temporal reasoning about programs. In: Apt, K.R. (ed.) Formal Models of Concurrent Systems, pp. 123–144. Springer-Verlag, Berlin (1985)
28. Rivest, R.L., Schapire, R.E.: Inference of finite automata using homing sequences. In: Symposium on Theory of Computing (STOC 1989), pp. 411–420. ACM (1989)
29. Schinz, I., Toben, T., Mrugalla, C., Westphal, B.: The rhapsody UML verification environment. In: Software Engineering and Formal Methods (SEFM 2004), pp. 174–183. IEEE (2004)

Typed Connector Families

José Proença[1,2]($\boxtimes$) and Dave Clarke[3]

[1] HASLab – INESC TEC and Universidade Do Minho, Braga, Portugal
`jose.proenca@cs.kuleuven.be`
[2] IMinds-DistriNet, Department of Computer Science, Ku Leuven, Belgium
[3] Department of Information Technology, Uppsala University, Uppsala, Sweden
`dave.clarke@it.uu.se`

Abstract. Typed models of connector/component composition specify interfaces describing ports of components and connectors. Typing ensures that these ports are plugged together appropriately, so that data can flow out of each output port and into an input port. These interfaces typically consider the direction of data flow and the type of values flowing. Components, connectors, and systems are often parameterised in such a way that the parameters affect the interfaces. Typing such *connector families* is challenging. This paper takes a first step towards addressing this problem by presenting a calculus of connector families with integer and boolean parameters. The calculus is based on monoidal categories, with a dependent type system that describes the parameterised interfaces of these connectors. As an example, we demonstrate how to define n-ary Reo connectors in the calculus. The paper focusses on the structure of connectors—*well-connectedness*—and less on their behaviour, making it easily applicable to a wide range of coordination and component-based models. A type-checking algorithm based on constraints is used to analyse connector families, supported by a proof-of-concept implementation.

1 Introduction

Software product lines provide the flexibility of concisely specifying a family of software products, by identifying common features of functionality among these products and automatising the creation of products from a selection of relevant features. Interesting challenges in this domain include how to specify families and combinations of features, how to automatise the creation process, how to identify features from a collection of products, and how to reason about (e.g., verify) whole families of products.

This paper investigates such variability in coordination languages, i.e., it studies *connector families* that exogenously describe how (families of) components are connected. The key problem is that different connectors from a single family can have different interfaces, i.e., different ways of connecting to other connectors. Hence, specifying and composing such families of connectors while guaranteeing that interfaces still match becomes non-trivial.

This research is supported by the FCT grant SFRH/BPD/91908/2012.

C. Braga and P.C. Ölveczky (Eds.): FACS 2015, LNCS 9539, pp. 294–311, 2016.
DOI: 10.1007/978-3-319-28934-2_16

Consider, for example a component c that produces 3 values, and a family of connectors ∇_n that merge n values into a single output. We say the interface of c has 3 output ports, and the interface of each ∇_n has n input ports and 1 output port. This paper provides a calculus to compose such n-ary connectors while guaranteeing that all their ports can be properly connected. For example, "$c\,; \nabla_3$" denotes the sequential composition of c and a merger with 3 inputs, connecting the output ports of the first to the input ports of the second, resulting in a well-connected connector with 0 inputs and 1 outputs.

Fig. 1. Example of the composition of connectors.

Figure 1 exemplifies more complex compositions of n-ary connectors. The left presents the composition of m parallel instances of the component c, written as c^m, with a merger with n inputs. This composition yields a new connector that, given some n and m values, produces a new connector with a single (output) port. This paper provides a type system that checks if such n and m values exist, and their relation: n must be 3 times larger than m. More formally, the connector is written as $\lambda m : \mathbb{N}, n : \mathbb{N} \cdot (c^m\,; \nabla_n)$, and the type system yields both the type $\forall m : \mathbb{N}, n : \mathbb{N} \cdot 0 \to 1$ and the constraint $n = m * 3$. This means that both the connector and the type are parameterised by two numbers m and n, the connector has type $0 \to 1$, and $n = m * 3$ must hold for the connector to be well typed. The right example of Fig. 1 shows a variation of this example, where the instances of c are composed with k instances of a binary merger ∇_2. The type of the composed connector is $\forall m : \mathbb{N}, k : \mathbb{N} \cdot 0 \to k$ constrained by $3 * m = 2 * k$, which means that $3 * m = 2 * k$ must hold for the connector to be well typed, yielding a connector with 0 inputs and k outputs. By writing this connector as $\lambda m : \mathbb{N}, k : \mathbb{N} \cdot (c^{2*m}\,; \nabla_2^k)$ the type becomes $\forall m : \mathbb{N}, k : \mathbb{N} \cdot 0 \to 3 * m$, constrained by $k = 3 * m$.

To increase compositionality, parameterised connectors can also be composed. Hence $(\lambda m : \mathbb{N} \cdot c^m)\,; (\lambda n : \mathbb{N} \cdot \nabla_n)$ has the same type as the left composition of Fig. 1. Finally, extra constraints can be added to parameterised connectors. For example, $\lambda m : \mathbb{N} \cdot (c^m \,|_{m \leq 10})$ represents a parameterised connector that can have at most 10 instances of the connector c. We call *connector families* such connectors that can be parameterised, constrained, and composed.

Summarising, the main contributions of this paper are:

- a calculus for families of connectors with constraints;
- a type system to describe well-defined compositions of such families; and
- a constraint-based type-checking algorithm for this type system.

Connectors are defined incrementally. We start by defining a basic connector calculus for composing connectors inspired by Bruni et al.'s connector algebra [3,5] (Sect. 2). This calculus is then extended with parameters and expressions, over both integers and booleans (Sect. 3), being now able to specify connectors (and interfaces) that depend on input parameters. Both the basic and the extended calculus are accompanied by a type system; the latter is an extension of the former, allowing integer and boolean parameters (and effectively becoming a dependent type system). Section 4 introduces *connector families*, by explicitly incorporating constraints over the parameters, and by lifting the composition of connectors to the composition of constrained and parameterised connectors. Section 5 describes an algorithm to type-check connector families with untyped ports, i.e., when the type flowing over each port is not relevant, and presents our prototype implementation. This paper wraps up with related work (Sect. 6), conclusions and future work (Sect. 7).

2   Basic Connector Calculus

This section describes an algebraic approach to specify connectors (or components) with a fixed interface, that is, with a fixed sequence of input and output ports that are used to send and receive data. The main goal of this algebraic approach is to describe the structure of connectors and not so much their behaviour. We illustrate the usage of this algebra by using Reo connectors [2], which have well-defined semantics, although our approach can be applied to any connector-like model that connects entities with input and output interfaces.

We start by presenting an overview of how to specify connectors using our calculus. We then describe the syntax of the basic connector calculus and a type system to verify if connectors are well-connected, followed by a brief discussion on how to describe the semantics of connectors orthogonally to this calculus.

2.1   Overview

Our *basic connector calculus* is based on monoidal categories—more specifically on traced monoidal categories [14]—where connectors are morphisms, ";" is the composition of morphisms with identity id, and "⊗" is the tensor product. The operator "⊗" composes connectors in parallel, while the operator ";" connects the ports of the given connectors. Objects of this category are *interfaces*, which correspond to ports in our connectors and include the unit of the tensor product represented by 0. The commutativity of the tensor product is captured by a family of symmetries that swap the order of ports in parallel. Loops can be represented via *traces*, which plug part of the right interface to the left interface of the same connector.

The connector in Table 1 helps understanding the intuition behind our algebra of connectors. Our algebra is inspired by the graphical notation used for monoidal categories (see, e.g., Selinger's survey [14]), and by Bruni et al.'s connector algebra [3,5]. The Reo connector on the left is composed out of smaller subconnectors, connected with each other via shared ports $(\bullet)$. The second column describes a possible representation of the same connector, writing the names of each subconnector parameterised by its ports. For example, the connector '$\rightarrowtail$' is written as $\mathsf{sdrain}(a, b)$ to mean that it has two ports named a and b. Composing connectors is achieved via the $\bowtie$ operator, which connects ports with the same names – this is the most common way to compose Reo connectors in the literature. In this paper we will use instead the algebraic representation on the right of Table 1, where port names are not necessary. The connector $\Delta \otimes \Delta$, for example, puts two duplicator channels in parallel, yielding a new connector with 2 input ports and 4 output ports. This can be composed via "$;$" with $\mathsf{id} \otimes \mathsf{sdrain} \otimes \mathsf{fifo}$ because this connector has 4 input ports: both the id and the fifo channels have one input port and the sdrain has 2 input ports.

Table 1. Specification of the alternator connector with port names and algebraically.

Graphical	With port names	Algebraic term
	$\Delta(a, a_1, a_2) \bowtie \Delta(b, b_1, b_2) \bowtie$ $\mathsf{sdrain}(a_2, b_1) \bowtie$ $\mathsf{id}(a_1, c_1) \bowtie \mathsf{fifo}(b_2, c_2) \bowtie$ $\triangledown(c_1, c_2, c)$	$\Delta \otimes \Delta;$ $\mathsf{id} \otimes \mathsf{sdrain} \otimes \mathsf{fifo};$ $\triangledown$

2.2 Syntax

The syntax of connectors and interfaces of our basic connector calculus is presented in Fig. 2. Each connector has a signature $I \to J$ consisting of an input interface I and an output interface J. For example, the identity connector id_I has the same input and output interface I, written $\mathsf{id}_I : I \to I$. Ports of an interface are identified simply with a capital letter, such as A, which capture the type of messages that can be sent via that port. In our examples we assume that A can only be the type 1, which represents any port type. This more specific model is also exploited in our algorithm for constraint solving (later in Sect. 5).

The intuition of these connectors becomes clearer with the visual representations exemplified in Fig. 3. All connectors are depicted with their input interface on the left side and the output interface on the right side. Each *identity* connector id_I has the same input and output interface I; each *symmetry* $\gamma_{I,J}$ swaps the top interface I with the bottom interface J, hence it has input interface $I \otimes J$ and output interface $J \otimes I$; and each *trace* $\mathsf{Tr}_I(c)$ creates a loop from the bottom output interface I of c with the bottom input interface I of c, hence if c has input interface $I' \otimes I$ and output interface $J' \otimes I$ then the trace has input and output interaces I' and J', respectively.

Parallelism is represented by tensor products, plugging of connectors by morphism composition, swapping order of parameters by symmetries, and loops by traces. Connectors and types obey a set of *Equations for Connectors* that allow their algebraic manipulation and capture the intuition behind the above mentioned representations. Figure 4 presents *some* of these equations, which reflect

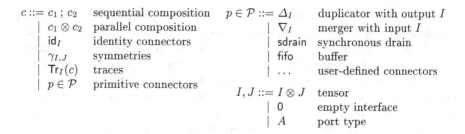

Fig. 2. Connectors (left), primitive connectors (top-right), interfaces (bottom-right).

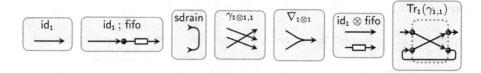

Fig. 3. Visual representation of simple connectors.

properties of traced monoidal categories. For example, the fact that two symmetries in sequence with swapped interfaces are equivalent to the identity connector, or how the trace of the symmetry $\gamma_{1,1}$ is also equivalent to the identity.

2.3   Type Rules

Every connector c has an input interface I and an output interface J, written $c : I \to J$. We call these two interfaces the *type* of the connector. Every primitive has a fixed type, for example, $\mathsf{fifo} : 1 \to 1$ and $\nabla_{1 \otimes 1} : 1 \otimes 1 \to 1$. The typing rules for connectors (Fig. 5) reflect the fact that two connectors can only be composed sequentially if the output interface of the first connector matches the input interface of the second one. A connector is well-connected if and only if it is well-typed.

For example, using these type rules it is possible to infer the type of the connector $\mathsf{Tr}_{1 \otimes 1}(\gamma_{1 \otimes 1,1} \,;\, (\mathsf{fifo} \otimes \mathsf{fifo} \otimes \mathsf{fifo}))$ to be $1 \to 1$, but no type could be inferred after removing one occurence of fifo. This connector is chaining in sequence 3 parallel fifo connectors.

$$
\begin{aligned}
\mathsf{id}_I \,;\, c &= c = c \,;\, \mathsf{id}_J \quad (\text{if } c : I \to J) & \mathsf{Tr}_I(\gamma_{I,I}) &= \mathsf{id}_I \\
\gamma_{I,J} \,;\, \gamma_{J,I} &= \mathsf{id}_{I \otimes J} & \mathsf{Tr}_0(c) &= c \\
(c_1 \otimes c_2) \otimes c_3 &= c_1 \otimes (c_2 \otimes c_3) & c_1 \,;\, \mathsf{Tr}_I(c_2) &= \mathsf{Tr}_I(c_1 \otimes \mathsf{id}_I \,;\, c_2) \\
0 \otimes I &= I = I \otimes 0 & \mathsf{Tr}_I(c_1) \,;\, c_2 &= \mathsf{Tr}_I(c_1 \,;\, c_2 \otimes \mathsf{id}_I) \\
(I_1 \otimes I_2) \otimes I_3 &= I_1 \otimes (I_2 \otimes I_3) & \mathsf{Tr}_I(\mathsf{Tr}_J(c)) &= \mathsf{Tr}_{I \otimes J}(c)
\end{aligned}
$$

Fig. 4. Equations for Connectors – based on properties of traced monoidal categories.

(sequence)
$$\frac{\vdash c_1 : I_1 \to J \quad \vdash c_2 : J \to J_2}{\vdash c_1 \,;\, c_2 : I_1 \to J_2}$$

(parallel)
$$\frac{\vdash c_1 : I_1 \to J_1 \quad \vdash c_2 : I_2 \to J_2}{\vdash c_1 \otimes c_2 : I_1 \otimes I_2 \to J_1 \otimes J_2}$$

(trace)
$$\frac{\vdash c : I_1 \otimes J \to I_2 \otimes J}{\vdash \mathsf{Tr}_J(c) : I_1 \to I_2}$$

(sym)
$$\vdash \gamma_{I,J} : I \otimes J \to J \otimes I$$

(id)
$$\vdash \mathsf{id}_I : I \to I$$

(prim)
$$\frac{p : I \to J \in \mathcal{P}}{\vdash p : I \to J}$$

Fig. 5. Type rules for basic connectors.

The type rules from Fig. 5 rely on the syntactic comparison of interfaces, e.g., rule (sequence) allows c_1 and c_2 to be composed only if the output interface J of c_1 is syntactically equivalent to the input interface of c_2. To support more complex notions of interfaces we use the constraint-based type rules from Fig. 6, which explicitly compare interfaces that must be *provably equivalent* instead of syntactically comparing them. Rules (sym), (id), and (prim) remain the same, only with the context. The typing judgments now include a context $\Gamma \mid \phi$ consisting both of a set of typed variables Γ (that will only be used in the next section) and a set of constraints ϕ that must hold for the connector to be well-typed. The context must be always well-formed, i.e., Γ cannot have repeated variables and ϕ must have at least one solution, but for simplicity we do not include these global restrictions in the type rules.

(sequence)
$$\frac{\Gamma \mid \phi \vdash c_1 : I_1 \to J_1 \quad \Gamma \mid \phi \vdash c_2 : I_2 \to J_2}{\Gamma \mid \phi, J_1 = I_2 \vdash c_1 \,;\, c_2 : I_1 \to J_2}$$

(parallel)
$$\frac{\Gamma \mid \phi \vdash c_1 : I_1 \to J_1 \quad \Gamma \mid \phi \vdash c_2 : I_2 \to J_2}{\Gamma \mid \phi \vdash c_1 \otimes c_2 : I_1 \otimes I_2 \to J_1 \otimes J_2}$$

(trace)
$$\frac{\Gamma \mid \phi \vdash c : J_1 \to J_2}{\Gamma \mid \phi, J_1 = X_I \otimes I, J_2 = X_J \otimes I \vdash \mathsf{Tr}_I(c) : X_I \to X_J}$$

Fig. 6. Constraint-based type rules.

2.4 Connector Behaviour

Semantics for the behaviour of connectors can be given in various ways. For this paper we use the Tile Model [7], as it aligns closely with the algebraic presentation of connectors. We also use the Reo coordination language—more specifically its context independent semantics [3]—as the behaviour of our primitive connectors, whose visual representation has been being used.

We use the same ideas from the Tile Model proposed for Reo [3], using a variation of the category used to describe connectors. Each connector in the Tile Model consists of a set of tiles, one for each possible behaviour, as exemplified in Fig. 7. Each of these tiles contains 4 objects of a double category (two categories with the same objects) and four morphisms between pairs of objects. Visually, a tile is depicted as a square with an object in each corner and with morphisms on the sides of this square. These morphisms go from left to right and from top to bottom: horizontal morphisms are from one category, describing the construction of a connector, and the vertical morphisms are from another category, describing the evolution in time of the connector. More specifically, horizontal morphisms are connectors as specified in Fig. 2, and objects are interfaces. Vertical morphisms are either flow, noFlow, or a tensor product of these, representing a step where data flows over the ports where the flow morphism is applied, and data does not flow over the ports where noFlow is applied.

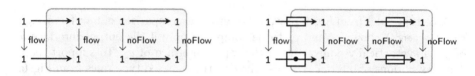

Fig. 7. Tiles for the behaviour of the id_1 (left) and the empty fifo (right) connectors.

Tiles can be composed vertically or horizontally when their adjacent morphisms match, or composed in parallel using the tensor product $\oplus$. Note that two morphisms being the same also implies that their domain and codomain must be the same (i.e., the source and destination of the arrows). The rest of this paper will focus on the horizontal composition of connectors, i.e., on the structural composition of connectors, and not on the behaviour of connectors—the vertical composition. This focus also makes the results presented here more easily applicable to any other coordination or component model where connectors or components have a set of interfaces that can be composed using our calculus.

3   Parameterised Connector Calculus

Connectors are now extended in two ways: (i) by adding integer and boolean expressions to control n-ary replication and conditional choice, and (ii) by adding free variables that can be instantiated with either natural numbers or booleans. These variables are also used in the connector types, previously written as $I \to J$, which are now given by the grammar:

$$T \quad ::= \quad I \to J \quad | \quad \forall x : P \cdot T$$

where x is a variable and $P \in \{\mathbb{N}, \mathbb{B}\}$ represents a primitive type that can be either the natural numbers ($\mathbb{N}$) or booleans ($\mathbb{B}$).

This section introduces the extended syntax and some of its properties, describes motivating examples, and extends the type rules for the connector types described above with boolean and integer parameters.

$$
\begin{array}{ll}
c ::= \ldots & \text{connectors} \\
\quad\mid c^{x \leftarrow \alpha} & n\text{-ary parallel replication} \\
\quad\mid c_1 \oplus^\phi c_2 & \text{conditional choice} \\
\quad\mid \lambda x : P \cdot c & \text{parameterised connector} \\
\quad\mid c(\phi) & \text{bool-instantiation} \\
\quad\mid c(\alpha) & \text{int-instantiation}
\end{array}
\qquad
\begin{array}{ll}
I ::= \ldots & \text{interfaces} \\
\quad\mid I^\alpha & n\text{-ary parallel replication} \\
\quad\mid I \oplus^\phi J & \text{conditional choice} \\
& \\
\alpha, \beta & \text{integer expressions} \\
\phi, \psi & \text{boolean expressions}
\end{array}
$$

Fig. 8. Extended syntax of connectors (left) and interfaces (right).

3.1 Syntax

The extended syntax of connectors and interfaces with integers and booleans is defined in Fig. 8. We write c^α instead of $c^{x \leftarrow \alpha}$ when x is not a free variable in c.

This paper does not formalise integer and boolean expressions with typed variables, since the details of these expressions are not relevant. The semantics of the n-ary parallel replication, the conditional choice, and the instantiation of parameters[1] is captured by the new Equations for Connectors in Fig. 9. These equations include a new notation—$c[v/x]$—that stands for the substitution of all variables x in c that appear freely (i.e., not bounded by a λ quantifier) by the expression v. This paper does not formalise free variables nor substitution, which follow the standard definitions.

$$
\begin{array}{rcl}
c^{x \leftarrow \alpha} &=& = c[0/x] \otimes \ldots \otimes c[\alpha-1/x] \\
c_1 \oplus^{true} c_2 &=& c_1 \\
c_1 \oplus^\phi c_2 &=& c_2 \oplus^{\neg\phi} c_1 \\
(\lambda x : P \cdot c)(v) &=& c[v/x]
\end{array}
\qquad
\begin{array}{rcl}
I^\alpha &=& I \otimes \ldots \otimes I \quad (\alpha \text{ times}) \\
I_1 \oplus^{true} I_2 &=& I_1 \\
I_1 \oplus^\phi I_2 &=& I_2 \oplus^{\neg\phi} I_1
\end{array}
$$

Fig. 9. Equations for Connector – replication, choice, and instantiation.

Although this extension allows an n-ary composition in parallel of connectors and not in sequence, n-ary sequences of connectors can also be expressed by using traces, as exemplified in the general sequence of fifo connectors on the top-left corner of Fig. 10. We write expressions such as $n-1$ instead of the interface 1^{n-1} for simplicity, when it is clear that these expressions represent interfaces. Observe that this example has been mentioned in the end of Sect. 2.3, for the specific case of 3 fifos in sequence, already defined using traces and parallel replication. The bottom example is more complex, and is based on the sequencer connector found in Reo-related literature [2]. This connector forces n (synchronous) streams of data to alternate between which one has dataflow. It uses the zip and unzip connectors to combine γ connectors (symmetries) in order to regroup sequences of pairs into a pair of sequences and vice-versa. The top-right corner instantiates the zip connector to illustrate the overal idea; the visual representation unfolds the trace, used to produce a sequence of connectors (as in *seq-fifo*).

---

[1] Known as β-reduction in lambda calculus.

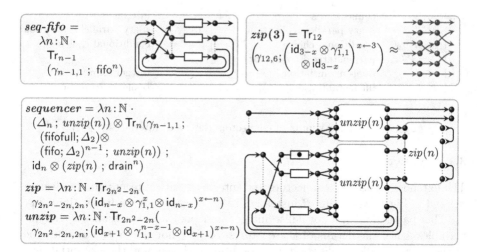

Fig. 10. A sequence of n fifo connectors (top-left), an instance of the *zip* connector (top-right), and an n-ary sequencer connector (bottom).

The details about the behaviour of the sequencer connector are out of the scope of this paper. However, observe that the visual representation is no longer precise enough, since the dotted lines only help to provide intuition but do not specify completely the connector. The parameterised calculus, on the other hand, precisely describes how to build a n-ary sequencer for any $n \geq 0$.

3.2 Parameterised Type Rules

The extended type rules are presented in Fig. 11, which now use the context Γ consisting of a set of variables and their associated primitive type ($\mathbb{B}$ or $\mathbb{N}$).

As mentioned before, the context cannot contain repeated variables, but this restriction is omitted from the type rules. The actual verification of the type of the boolean and integer variables is done during the type-checking of boolean and integer expressions, which is well known and not defined in this paper. Hence the new type rules have some gray premises, corresponding to the type rules for booleans and integer expressions. The typing judgment $\Gamma \mid \phi \vdash e : P$ for integer and boolean expressions means that $\Gamma \vdash e : P$ (i.e., the variables in the boolean or integer expression e have the type specified in Γ) in a context where ϕ is satisfiable. The notation $I[e/x]$ denotes the substitution of free occurrences of x in I by the expression e, similarly to the substitution in connectors, also not formalised here. Observe that the constraint ψ in the (choice) rule does not influence the typing of c_1 and c_2. Intuitively, if ψ and $\neg\psi$ was to be added to the context when typing c_1 and c_2, respectively, then very likely one of these branches would have *false* in the context, meaning it could not be typed.

We illustrate the usage of these type rules by building the *derivation tree* for the *seq-fifo* connector (Fig. 12), where we illustrate how to calculate the type of this connector by consecutively applying type rules. At every step of this

$$
\begin{array}{c}
\text{(parameterisation)} \\
\dfrac{\Gamma, x : P \mid \phi \vdash c : T \quad x \notin \phi}{\Gamma \mid \phi \vdash \lambda x : P \cdot c : \forall x : P \cdot T}
\end{array}
\qquad
\begin{array}{c}
\text{(instantiation)} \\
\dfrac{\Gamma \mid \phi \vdash v : P \quad \Gamma \mid \phi \vdash c : \forall x : P \cdot T}{\Gamma \mid \phi \vdash c(v) : T[v/x]}
\end{array}
$$

$$
\begin{array}{c}
\text{(replication)} \\
\Gamma \mid \phi \vdash \alpha : \mathbb{N} \qquad \Gamma, x : \mathbb{N} \mid \phi \vdash c : I \to J \\
\phi_1 = \big(X_I = I[0/x] \otimes \ldots \otimes I[\alpha - 1/x]\big) \\
\phi_2 = \big(X_J = J[0/x] \otimes \ldots \otimes J[\alpha - 1/x]\big) \\
\hline
\Gamma \mid \phi, \phi_1, \phi_2 \vdash c^{x \leftarrow \alpha} : X_I \to X_J
\end{array}
$$

$$
\begin{array}{c}
\text{(choice)} \\
\Gamma \mid \phi \vdash \psi : \mathbb{B} \\
\Gamma \mid \phi \vdash c_1 : I_1 \to J_1 \\
\Gamma \mid \phi \vdash c_2 : I_2 \to J_2 \\
\hline
\Gamma \mid \phi \vdash c_1 \oplus^\psi c_2 : I_1 \oplus^\psi I_2 \to J_1 \oplus^\psi J_2
\end{array}
$$

Fig. 11. Parameterised type rules—$x \notin \phi$ means x does not appear in ϕ. Previous type rules remain unchanged.

$$
\varnothing \mid 1 \otimes (n-1) = 1^n, (n-1) \otimes 1 = X_I \otimes (n-1), 1^n = X_J \otimes (n-1)
$$
$$
\vdash \lambda n : \mathbb{N} \cdot \mathsf{Tr}_{n-1}(\gamma_{n-1,1} \; ; \; \mathsf{fifo}^n) : \forall n : \mathbb{N} \cdot X_I \to X_J
$$

Fig. 12. Derivation tree for the *seq-fifo* connector; contexts are represented grey.

derivation tree the context is well-formed (Γ has no repeated variables and ϕ is always satisfiable). From the existence of this derivation tree one can conclude that the *seq-fifo* connector is well-typed, and by further analysing the constraints in the context it is possible to simplify the type to $\forall n : \mathbb{N} \cdot 1 \to 1$.

4 Connector Families

This section introduces *connector families*: parameterised connectors that can (i) be *restricted* by given constraints ψ, written $c \mid_\psi$, and (ii) be *composed* with each other—sequentially, in parallel, via the choice or replication operators, or within traces. These restricted and composable connector families represent families in the same sense as software families in the context of software product lines (SPL) engineering [12]. The added constraints represent the family, which in the SPL community are often derived from feature models.

4.1 Restricted Connectors and Types

Connectors can now be written as $c \mid_\psi$, meaning that the connector c is restricted by the constraint ψ. For example, the connector with at most 5 **fifo** connectors

(restriction)
$$\frac{\Gamma \mid \phi \vdash \psi \quad \Gamma \mid \phi, \psi \vdash c : T}{\Gamma \mid \phi \vdash c \mid_\psi : T \mid_\psi}$$

(parallel)
$$\frac{\Gamma \mid \phi \vdash c_1 : I_1 \to J_1 \mid_{\psi_1} \quad \Gamma \mid \phi \vdash c_2 : I_2 \to J_2 \mid_{\psi_2}}{\Gamma \mid \phi \vdash c_1 \otimes c_2 : I_1 \otimes I_2 \to J_1 \otimes J_2 \mid_{\psi_1, \psi_2}}$$

Fig. 13. Adding restrictions to types. Other rules remain almost the same, adapted in a similar way to the (parallel) rule.

in parallel can be written as $\lambda n : \mathbb{N} \cdot (\text{fifo}^n \mid_{n \leq 5})$. The type of this connector is written similarly as $\forall n : \mathbb{N} \cdot n \to n \mid_{n \leq 5}$. More formally, types now include these constraints, following the following syntax.

$$T ::= I \to J \quad | \quad \forall x : P \cdot T \quad | \quad T \mid_\psi$$

The main type rules are presented in Fig. 13. The new rule (restriction) introduces a constraint ψ from the connector to the context. All other rules are adapted in a similar way to the (parallel) rule, by simply collecting the restriction constraints in the conclusions of the rules. For readability we write 'ψ_1, ψ_2' to denote '$\psi_1 \wedge \psi_2$'. A connector c is now *well-typed* if there is a derivation tree $\emptyset \mid \phi \vdash c : T \mid_\psi$ such that $\phi \wedge \psi$ is satisfiable, i.e., ψ has at least one solution that does not contradict at least one solution of ϕ. This approach resembles Jones's qualified types [9], where types can be qualified with general predicates; in our work predicates can include only integer and boolean variables, and are not over type variables.

The example with a parameterised sequence of fifos from Fig. 12 can be adapted to restrict to sequences of at most 5 fifos, yielding the typing judgment:

$$\emptyset \mid 1 \otimes (n-1) = 1^n \;\;, \;\; (n-1) \otimes 1 = X_I \otimes (n-1) \;\;, \;\; 1^n = X_J \otimes (n-1)$$
$$\vdash \lambda n : \mathbb{N} \cdot (\text{Tr}_{n-1}(\gamma_{n-1,1} \; ; \; \text{fifo}^n) \mid_{n \leq 5}) \;\; : \;\; \forall n : \mathbb{N} \cdot X_I \to X_J \mid_{n \leq 5}$$

The conjunction of the above constraints is satisfiable: the possible solutions map X_I and X_J to 1, and map n to any value between 0 and 5. Hence the connector is well-typed.

4.2 Family Composition

Parameterised connectors (Sect. 3) allow integer and boolean expressions to influence the final connector. However, the existing type rules for composing connectors do not describe how to compose connectors with parameters. The type rules in Fig. 14 add support for composing connector families: the composition of two parameterised connectors produces a new connector parameterised by the parameters of both connectors. We write $\forall \overline{x : P}$ to represent a (possibly empty) sequence of nested pairs $\forall x : P$. Note that connectors without parameters are specific instances of connector families; indeed, the new rules (fam-*) coincide with their simpler counterparts whenever the set of parameters is empty.

For example, both connectors below have the same type: $\forall x_1 : \mathbb{N}, x_2 : \mathbb{N}, x_3 : \mathbb{N} \cdot 1^{x_1} \to 1^{x_2} \otimes 1^{x_3}$, under a context where $1^{x_1} = 1^{x_2} \otimes 1^{x_3}$. The first composes 3 connector families, while the second is a family that composes 3 connectors.

$$(\text{fam-parallel})$$
$$\frac{\Gamma \mid \phi \vdash c_1 : \forall x_1 : T_1 \cdot I_1 \to J_1 \mid_{\psi_1} \quad \Gamma \mid \phi \vdash c_2 : \forall x_2 : T_2 \cdot I_2 \to J_2 \mid_{\psi_2} \quad \overline{x_1} \cap \overline{x_2} = \varnothing}{\Gamma \mid \phi \vdash c_1 \otimes c_2 : \forall x_1 : T_1, x_2 : T_2 \cdot I_1 \otimes I_2 \to J_1 \otimes J_2 \mid_{\psi_1, \psi_2}}$$

$$(\text{fam-sequence})$$
$$\frac{\Gamma \mid \phi \vdash c_1 : \forall x_1 : T_1 \cdot I_1 \to J_1 \mid_{\psi_1} \quad \Gamma \mid \phi \vdash c_2 : \forall x_2 : T_2 \cdot I_2 \to J_2 \mid_{\psi_2} \quad \overline{x_1} \cap \overline{x_2} = \varnothing}{\Gamma \mid \phi, J_1 = I_2 \vdash c_1 \; ; \; c_2 : \forall x_1 : T_1, x_2 : T_2 \cdot I_1 \to J_2 \mid_{\psi_1, \psi_2}}$$

$$(\text{fam-replication})$$
$$\frac{\begin{array}{c} \Gamma \mid \phi \vdash \alpha : \mathbb{N} \\ \Gamma, x : \mathbb{N} \mid \phi \vdash c : \forall \overline{x'} : P \cdot I \to J \mid_\psi \\ \phi_1 = \big(X_I = I[0/x] \otimes \ldots \otimes I[\alpha - 1/x]\big) \\ \phi_2 = \big(X_J = J[0/x] \otimes \ldots \otimes J[\alpha - 1/x]\big) \end{array}}{\begin{array}{c} \Gamma \mid \phi, \phi_1, \phi_2 \\ \vdash \; c^{x \leftarrow \alpha} : \forall \overline{x'} : P \cdot X_I \to X_J \mid_\psi \end{array}}$$

$$(\text{fam-choice})$$
$$\frac{\begin{array}{c} \Gamma \mid \phi \vdash \psi : \mathbb{B} \\ \Gamma \mid \phi \vdash c_1 : \forall x_1 : T_1 \cdot I_1 \to J_1 \mid_{\psi_1} \\ \Gamma \mid \phi \vdash c_2 : \forall x_2 : T_2 \cdot I_2 \to J_2 \mid_{\psi_2} \end{array}}{\begin{array}{c} \Gamma \mid \phi \vdash c_1 \oplus^\psi c_2 : \forall x_1 : T_1, x_2 : T_2 \cdot \\ I_1 \oplus^\psi I_2 \to J_1 \oplus^\psi J_2 \mid_{\psi_1, \psi_2} \end{array}}$$

$$(\text{fam-trace})$$
$$\frac{\Gamma \mid \phi \vdash c : \forall x : P \cdot J_1 \to J_2 \mid_\psi}{\Gamma \mid \phi, I_1 = X_I \otimes I, I_2 = X_J \otimes I \vdash \mathsf{Tr}_I(c) : \forall x : P \cdot X_I \to X_J \mid_\psi}$$

Fig. 14. Type rules for the lifted composition operators of connectors.

$$(\lambda x_1 : \mathbb{N} \cdot \mathsf{id}_1^{x_1}) \; ; \; (\lambda x_2 : \mathbb{N} \cdot \mathsf{id}_1^{x_2}) \otimes (\lambda x_3 : \mathbb{N} \cdot \mathsf{id}_1^{x_3})$$
$$\lambda x_1 : \mathbb{N}, x_2 : \mathbb{N}, x_3 : \mathbb{N} \cdot (\mathsf{id}_1^{x_1} \; ; \; \mathsf{id}_1^{x_2} \otimes \mathsf{id}_1^{x_3})$$

Observe that the modularity gain with the composition of families is achieved by serialising all input arguments. As a consequence the tensor product $\otimes$ no longer obeys the property $(c_1 \otimes c_2); (c_3 \otimes c_4) = (c_1; c_3) \otimes (c_2; c_4)$ with connector families, since the serialisation of the arguments produces different orders.

5   Solving Type Constraints

This section describes an algorithm to check if the constraints produced by the type rules are satisfiable; if so, this algorithm also provides an assignment of variables to values or to other variables.

Constraint-based approaches to type-checking are well-known, for example, for the lambda calculus [11, Chap. 22], where constraints are solved using an unification algorithm. However, the unification algorithm used for the lambda calculus is not enough for our calculus, because interfaces can include complex expressions that cannot be just syntactically compared. Hence our algorithm performs algebraic rewritings, uses an unification algorithm (for the simpler cases), and invokes a constraint solver (for the more complex cases).

We focus only on untyped ports, represented by 1, which mean that any data can go through these ports. Consequently, interfaces are interpreted as integer expressions, denoting the number of ports, as we will shortly explain.

5.1   Overview

In our type-checking algorithm interfaces are interpreted as integers, by mapping constructors of interfaces to integer operations. For example, $(\![I \otimes J]\!) = (\![I]\!) + (\![J]\!)$ and $(\![I^\alpha]\!) = (\![I]\!) * \alpha$, where $(\![I]\!)$ represents the interpretation of I as an integer. Both the constraints that appear in the context and the constraints that appear in the type are combined, hence producing a type $\forall x : P \cdot I \rightarrow J \mid_\psi$, where ψ represents the conjunction of these constraints.

We exemplify our approach using the *zip* connector (Fig. 10), restricted to when n is at least 5. The type rules produce the type $\forall n : \mathbb{N} \cdot x_3 \rightarrow x_4 \mid_\psi$, where ψ is as follows (after interpreting the interfaces as integer expressions).

$$x_3 + ((2*n)*(n-1)) = ((2*n)*(n-1)) + (2*n) \ , \ \ x_4 + ((2*n)*(n-1)) = x_2 \ ,$$
$$x_1 = \sum_{0 \le x < n}(((n-x) + (2*x)) + (n-x)) \ , \ \ x_2 = \sum_{0 \le x < n}(((n-x) + (2*x)) + (n-x)) \ ,$$
$$(2*n) + ((2*n)*(n-1)) = x_1 \ \ , \ \ n < 5$$

Using algebraic laws such as distributivity, commutativity, and associativity of sums and multiplications, the constraints are simplified as follows.

$$x_3 = 2n \ , \ -2n + 2n^2 + x_4 = x_2 \ , \ x_1 = 2n^2 \ , \ x_2 = 2n^2 \ , \ 2n^2 = x_1 \ , \ n < 5$$

The unification algorithm then produces the sequence of substitutions below, leaving the $n < 5$ constraint to be handled in a later phase.

$$[2n/x_3] \ \circ \ [x_4 + 2n^2 - 2n/x_2] \ \circ \ [2n^2/x_1] \ \circ \ [2n/x_4]$$

The final step is to verify that the remaining constraint $(n < 5)$ is satisfiable using a constraint solver, allowing us to conclude that the connector is well-typed. Furthermore, applying the substitution above to the type produced by the type rules gives the most general type $\forall n : \mathbb{N} \cdot 2n \rightarrow 2n \mid_{n<5}$. The constraint solver provides a solution, say $\{n \mapsto 0\}$, which can be used to produce an instance of the general type: $0 \rightarrow 0$.

5.2   Three-Phase Solver

This section explains in more detail the three-phase algorithm used to reason about constraints, exemplified in the previous subsection. These phases are performed in sequence, and consist of the *simplification* phase, the *unification* phase, and the *constraint-solving* phase, explained below.

Simplification. This first phase prepares the constraints obtained by the type rules to be used by the unification phase. More specifically, it rewrites the constraints by applying algebraic laws of sums and multiplications, building a polinomial and manipulating the coefficients. For example, sums like $\sum_{n1 \le x < n2}(5*x)$, where $5*x$ is linear on x, are rewritten into $(5*n2 + 5*n1)*(n2 - n1)/2$; to avoid integer divisions the denominator 2 is dropped and the other coefficients are multiplied by 2. Equalities are rewritten to match, if possible, the pattern $x = \alpha$, which is exploited by the unification phase.

Note that the type rules, apart from (restriction), only produce equalities of integer expressions. Our choice of rewrites included in the prototype implementation took into account the constraints generated by the type rules using a

$$\begin{aligned}
&\mathsf{unify}(\phi) = \\
&\quad \mathsf{unify}(\phi\,;\, \mathit{true})\\[4pt]
&\mathsf{unify}(\mathit{true}, \phi\,;\, \psi) = \\
&\quad \mathsf{unify}(\phi\,;\, \psi)
\end{aligned}$$

$$\mathsf{unify}(\alpha = \alpha', \phi\,;\, \psi) = \\
\begin{cases}
\mathsf{unify}(\phi\,;\, \psi) & \text{if } \alpha \equiv \alpha' \\
\mathsf{unify}(\phi[\alpha'/x]\,;\, \psi) \circ [\alpha'/x] & \text{if } \alpha \equiv x \text{ and } x \notin \mathit{fv}(\alpha') \\
\mathsf{unify}(\phi[\alpha/x]\,;\, \psi) \circ [\alpha/x] & \text{if } \alpha' \equiv x \text{ and } x \notin \mathit{fv}(\alpha) \\
\mathsf{unify}(\phi\,;\, \psi, \alpha = \alpha') & \text{otherwise}
\end{cases}$$

Fig. 15. Unification algorithm for constraints over boolean and integer variables.

range of different connectors. These rewrites are able to simplify all the examples presented in this paper that do not use inequalities, most of which involve only linear expressions or are reduced to linear expressions, to a point where the constraint solving phase was not needed. Furthermore, other fast off-the-shelf technologies, such as computer algebra systems, could be used to quickly manipulate and simplify more complex expressions.

Unification. The second phase consists of a traditional unification algorithm [11, Chap. 22] adapted to our type system, which produces both an *unification* and a set of constraints postponed to the constraint solving phase. An unification is formally a sequence of substitutions $\sigma_1 \circ \cdots \circ \sigma_n$, and applying a unification to a connector or interface t consists of applying the substitutions in sequence $((t\,\sigma_1)\ldots)\,\sigma_n$. For example, unifying the constraints $x = 2 + y, z = 3 + x, y = w$ produces the sequence of substitutions $[2+y/x] \circ [3+2+y/z] \circ [w/y]$. Applying this unification to an interface means first substituting x by $2 + y$, followed by the substitutions of z and y. The resulting interface is guaranteed to have no occurrences of x, y, nor z, and not to have w bound by any constraint.

The unification algorithm is described by the unify function (Fig. 15) that, given a set of constraints ϕ to be solved, returns a pair with a unification and a set of postponed constraints. The core of unify is defined in the right side of Fig. 15. For every equality $\alpha = \alpha'$, it first checks if they are syntactically equivalent (using $\equiv$). It then checks if either the left or the right side is a variable that does not occur on the other side; if so, it adds the equality to the resulting unification. If none of these cases apply, it postpones the analysis of the constraint for the third phase, by using the second argument of unify as an accumulator.

Constraint Solving. The last phase consists of collecting the constraints postponed by the unification phase and use an off-the-shelf constraint solver. This will tell us if the constraints are satisfiable, producing a concrete example of a substitution that satisfies the constraints. In the example of the sequence of fifos with at most 5 fifos (Sect. 5.1), a possible solution for the constraints is $\{n \mapsto 4, x_1 \mapsto 1, x_2 \mapsto 1\}$. This substitution, when applied to the type obtained for *seq-fifo*, yields a concrete type instance *seq-fifo* : $1 \rightarrow 1$. In this example the concrete type instance matches its general type ($\forall n : \mathbb{N} \cdot 1 \rightarrow 1$), since the value of n does not influence the type of the connector.

Note that a wide variety of approaches for solving constraints exist. One can use, for example, numerical methods to find solutions, or SMT solvers over some

```
import paramConnectors.DSL._
val x ="x":I   ;   val n = "n":I   ;   val b = "b":B

//----- λx:ℕ · (fifoˣ |ₓ>₅) -----//
typeOf( lam(x, (fifo^x) | (x>5)) )
// returns ∀x:I . x -> x | x > 5
typeInstance( lam(x, (fifo^x) | (x>5)) )
// returns © 6 -> 6
typeSubstitution( lam(x, (fifo^x) | (x>5)) )
// returns © [x:I -> 6]

//----- seq-fifo -----//
typeOf(   lam(x, Tr(x-1, sym(x-1,1) & (fifo^x))) )
// returns ∀x:I . 1 -> 1   [type obtained only after
    constraint solving]
typeTree( lam(x, Tr(x-1, sym(x-1,1) & (fifo^x))) )
// returns ∀x:I . x1 -> x2 | ((x1 + (x - 1)) == ((x - 1) +
    1))
//    & ((x2 + (x - 1)) == x) & ((1 + (x - 1)) == x) & (x1 >=
    0) & (x2 >= 0)

//----- sequencer -----//
val sequencer = ....
typeOf( sequencer )
// returns ∀n:I . n -> n
```

Listing 1. Calculating the type of connectors using our tools.

specific theory. The expressive power supported by the constraint solver dictates the expressivity of the expressions α and ϕ used in the connector, which we are abstracting away in this paper. The choices made in our proof-of-concept implementation, briefly explained in the next subsection, are therefore not strict and can be rethought if necessary.

5.3 Implementation

We developed a proof-of-concept implementation in the Scala that covers all the examples described in this paper, which can be found online.[2] Listing 1 exemplifies the usage of this library—more examples can be also found online.

This implementation includes a simple domain specific language to specify connectors, making them similar to the syntax used throughout this paper. It provides three main top-level functions: typeTree, typeOf, typeInstance, and typeSubstitution. The first creates the derivation tree (if it exists); typeOf simplifies the constraints, uses the unification algorithm, invokes the constraint solver, and returns the most general type found; and typeInstance and type-Substitution perform the same steps as typeOf, but the former returns the

---

[2] https://github.com/joseproenca/parameterised-connectors.

result of the constraint solving phase (even if the type is not the most general one) and the latter returns the substitutions obtained by the unification and the constraint solver phases. Hence the result of `typeInstance` never includes constraints. The constraint solving phase uses the Choco solver[3] to search for solutions of the constraints.

Observe that the resulting type instance and substitution of the first connector start with © — this means that the resulting type is a concrete instance of a type, i.e., the constraint solving phase found more than one solution for the variables of the inferred type (after unification). However, if we would ask for a type instance of $(\lambda x : \mathbb{N} \cdot \mathsf{fifo}^x | x > 5)(7)$, for example, the result would be also its (general) type $7 \to 7$, without the ©. Typing the connector $(\lambda x : \mathbb{N} \cdot \mathsf{fifo}^x | x > 5)(2)$ gives a type error, because the constraints are not satisfied.

6 Related Work

Algebras of Connectors. The usage of symmetric monoidal categories to represent Reo connectors (and others) has been introduced by Bruni et al. [5], where they introduce an algebra of stateless connectors with an operational semantics expressed using the Tile Model [7]. The authors focus on the behavioural aspects, exploiting normalisation and axiomatisation techniques. An extension of this work dedicated to Reo connectors [3] investigates more complex semantics of Reo (with context dependent connectors) using the Tile Model. Other extensions to connector algebras exist. For example, Sobocinski [15], and more recently Bonchi et al. [4], present stateful extensions to model and reason about the behaviour of Petri Nets and of Signal Flow Graphs, respectively. The latter also describes the usage of traces (Tr) as a possible way to specify loops in their algebra. In all these approaches, interfaces (objects of the categories) can be either input or output ports, independently of being on the left or right side of the connector (morphism), focusing on the behaviour of connectors instead of how to build families of these connectors.

In our work we do not distinguish input from output ports, assuming data always flows from left to right, and use traces to support loops and achieve the same expressivity. As a result, we found the resulting connectors to be easier to read and understand. For example the connector fifo has type $\bullet\circ \to 0$ in Bruni et al.'s algebra, meaning that the left side has 2 ports: an input $\bullet$ and an output $\circ$ one. Composing two fifos in sequence uses extra connectors (called nodes) and has type $0 \to \circ\bullet$ — for a more complete explanation see [7]. Indeed, our algebra has stronger resemblances with lambda calculus (and with pointfree style in functional programming [8]), facilitating the extension to families of connectors, which is the main novelty of this work.

Analysis of Software Product Lines. In the context of software product lines Kästner et al. [10], for example, investigated how to lift a type-checking algorithm from programs to families of programs. They use featherweight Java

---

[3] http://choco-solver.org.

annotated with constraints used during product generation, and present a type-checking approach that preserves types during this product generation. Their focus is on keeping the constraints being solved as small as possible, unlike previous approaches in the generative programming community (e.g., by Thaker et al. [16]) that compile a larger global set of constraints. Many other verification approaches for software product lines have been investigated [1,6,13,17]. Post and Sinz [13] verify families of Linux device drivers using the CBMC bouned model checker, and Apel et al. [1] verify more general families of C programs using the CPAchecker symbolic checker. More recently Thüm et al. [17] presents an approach to use the KeY theorem prover to verify a feature-oriented dialect of Java with JML annotations. They encode such annotated families of Java programs into new (traditional) Java programs with new JML annotations that can be directly used by KeY to verify the family of products. Dimovski et al. [6] take a more general view and provide a calculus for modular specification of variability abstractions, and investigate tradeoffs between precision and time when analysing software product lines and abstractions of them.

Our approach targets connector and component interfaces instead of typed languages, and explicitly uses parameters that influence the connectors. Consequently, feature models can contribute not only with feature selections but also with values used to build concrete connectors. Our calculus is simpler than other more traditional programming languages since it has no statements, no notion of heap or memory, nor tables of fields or methods.

7   Conclusion and Future Work

This paper formalises a calculus for connector families, i.e., for connectors (or components) with an open number of interfaces and restricted to given constraints. A dependant type system guarantees well-connectedness of such families, i.e., that interfaces of subconnectors can be composed as long as the parameters obey the constraints in the type. These constraints are reducible to nonlinear constraints on integers when considering untyped ports (only the type 1), in which case arithmetic properties and integer constraint solvers can be used to check the constraints under which a connector family is well-connected.

In the future we will investigate connector families where the type of the data passing through the ports is also checked. Finally, we also plan to investigate how to reduce the size of the constraints being solved, by using the more dedicated contexts while building the type tree instead of collecting the constraints for a follow-up phase, similarly to the work of Kästner et al. [10].

References

1. Apel, S., Speidel, H., Wendler, P., von Rhein, A., Beyer, D.: Detection of feature interactions using feature-aware verification. In: Proceedings of the 2011 26th IEEE/ACM International Conference on Automated Software Engineering, ASE 2011, pp. 372–375. IEEE Computer Society, Washington, DC (2011)

2. Arbab, F.: Reo: a channel-based coordination model for component composition. Math. Struct. Comput. Sci. **14**(3), 329–366 (2004)

3. Arbab, F., Bruni, R., Clarke, I., Lanese, I., Montanari, U.: Tiles for Reo. In: Corradini, A., Montanari, U. (eds.) WADT 2008. LNCS, vol. 5486, pp. 37–55. Springer, Heidelberg (2009)

4. Bonchi, F., Sobocinski, P., Zanasi, F.: Full abstraction for signal flow graphs. In: Proceedings of the 42nd Annual Symposium on Principles of Programming Languages, POPL 2015, pp. 515–526. ACM, New York (2015)

5. Bruni, R., Lanese, I., Montanari, U.: A basic algebra of stateless connectors. Theor. Comput. Sci. **366**(1–2), 98–120 (2006)

6. Dimovski, A.S., Brabrand, C., Wasowski, A.: Variability abstractions: Trading precision for speed in family-based analyses (extended version) CoRR. abs/1503.04608 (2015)

7. Gadducci, F., Montanari, U.: The tile model. In: Plotkin, G.D., Stirling, C., Tofte, M. (eds.) Proof, Language, and Interaction, Essays in Honour of Robin Milner, pp. 133–166. The MIT Press (2000)

8. Gibbons, J.: A pointless derivation of radix sort. J. Funct. Program. **9**(3), 339–346 (1999)

9. Jones, M.P.: A theory of qualified types. Sci. Comput. Program. **22**(3), 231–256 (1994)

10. Kastner, C., Apel, S.: Type-checking software product lines - a formal approach. In: Proceedings of the 2008 23rd IEEE/ACM International Conference on Automated Software Engineering, ASE 2008, pp. 258–267. IEEE Computer Society, Washington, DC (2008)

11. Pierce, B.C.: Types and Programming Languages. MIT Press, Cambridge (2002)

12. Pohl, K., Böckle, G., van der Linden, F.: Software Product Line Engineering. Springer, Heidelberg (2005)

13. Post, H., Sinz, C., Configuration lifting,: Verification meets software configuration. In Proceedings of the 23rd International Conference on Automated Software Engineering, ASE '08, pp. 347–350. IEEE Computer Society, 2008. (2008)

14. Selinger, P.: A survey of graphical languages for monoidal categories. In: Coecke, B. (ed.) New Structures for Physics. Lecture Notes in Physics, vol. 813, pp. 289–355. Springer, Berlin Heidelberg (2011)

15. Selinger, P.: A survey of graphical languages for monoidal categories. In: Coecke, B. (ed.) New Structures for Physics. Lecture Notes in Physics, vol. 813, pp. 289–355. Springer, Heidelberg (2011)

16. Thaker, S., Batory, D., Kitchin, D., Cook, W.: Safe composition of product lines. In Proceedings of the 6th International Conference on Generative Programming and Component Engineering, GPCE 2007, pp. 95–104. ACM (2007)

17. Thüm, T., Schaefer, I., Apel, S., Hentschel, M.: Family-based deductive verification of software product lines. In: Proceedings of the 11th International Conference on Generative Programming and Component Engineering, GPCE 2012, pp. 11–20. ACM, New York (2012)

Formal Architecture Modeling of Sequential C-Programs

Jonas Westman$^{(\boxtimes)}$ and Mattias Nyberg

Royal Institute of Technology (KTH), Stockholm, Sweden
`jowestm@kth.se`

Abstract. To enable verification of a complex C-program, so called compositional verification can be used where the specification for the C-program is split into a set of specifications organized such that the fact that the C-program satisfies its specification can be inferred from verifying that parts of the C-program satisfy their specifications. To support the approach in practice, specifications must be organized in parallel to a formal *architecture model* capturing the C-program as a hierarchical structure of components with well-defined interfaces. Previous modeling approaches lack support for formal architecture modeling of C-programs. Therefore, a general and formal approach for architecture modeling of sequential C-programs is presented, to support compositional verification, as well as to aid design and management of such C-programs in general.

1 Introduction

Consider that, due to required effort/cost, it is infeasible to use a direct verification approach to ensure that a complex C-program satisfies its specification. A solution to such an issue is to use so called *compositional verification* [20] where the specification is decomposed into a set of specifications organized such that the fact that the C-program satisfies its specification can be inferred from verifying that parts of the C-program satisfy their specifications. In addition, compositional verification enables the verification of *open systems*, i.e. systems to which the environment is unknown [20]. Thus, as shown in scenarios in [25], compositional verification supports parallel development and outsourcing.

While providing a means to manage the development of complex C-programs, as well as systems in general, compositional verification requires the effort of iteratively decomposing specifications into lower-level specifications that can be satisfied by parts of a system. As made clear in [27], in order to support such an effort in practice, the specifications must be decomposed in parallel to an *architecture model* of a system where the model formally captures a structure of the system as a hierarchy of components with well-defined interfaces over which specifications are expressed.

Hence, in order to provide practical support for compositional verification of C-programs, an architecture model of a C-program is needed. Considering

© Springer International Publishing Switzerland 2016
C. Braga and P.C. Ölveczky (Eds.): FACS 2015, LNCS 9539, pp. 312–329, 2016.
DOI: 10.1007/978-3-319-28934-2_17

current approaches for architecture modeling, general purpose Modeling Languages (MLs) such as SysML [8] or UML [21] and Architecture Description Languages (ADLs) such as AADL [7] are often used for modeling C-programs, but since there exists no uniform mapping from a C-program to these languages, the modeling is essentially ad-hoc. Models of C-programs are used in approaches for formal verification of C-programs (see e.g. [5,10] or [9] for an overview) where a C-program is translated into a formal model that is fed into a tool for semi or fully automated analysis. However, these formal models do not capture a C-program as a hierarchical structure of components, and do not, therefore, provide support for decomposing specifications.

Thus, despite the fact that the C-language is one of the most popular programming languages [4], there exists limited support for architecture modeling of C-programs. The need for such support is crucial to manage the development of embedded SoftWare (SW) that is typically implemented as C-code. Moreover, considering automotive embedded SW, the idea of compositional verification has been adopted by the automotive functional safety standard ISO 26262 [11]. According to ISO 26262, top-level SW safety specifications must be decomposed all the way down to low-level safety specifications for SW units, such that the top-level SW safety specifications are satisfied, if the low-level safety specifications are satisfied [24,26]. In addition to providing support for compositional verification as a means to manage the complexity of C-programs, as well as to facilitate compliance with ISO 26262, architecture models can also serve as high-level descriptions of C-programs. Considering these aspects, as the main contribution, the present paper introduces a general and formal approach for architecture modeling of C-programs intended for sequential execution.

More specifically, the proposed architecture model captures built-in means of encapsulation in the C-language, i.e. C-modules and C-functions, as well as higher-level encapsulation of C-modules into packages and layers that are introduced by engineers to structure the C-program into e.g. Operating System (OS) services (e.g. scheduling) and communication services (Controller Area Network (CAN), I/O, etc.). Hence, the architecture model does not only provide a foundation for organizing specifications hierarchically as required by ISO 26262, but also allows capturing intended service dependencies [18] between layers and packages in the manner in which the specifications are organized. Each level of the program structure is modeled as a component with a well-defined interface, providing fundamental support for expressing specifications. Furthermore, explicit support is given for expressing specifications as *contracts* [3,17,22,25,26].

The architecture model is obtained by refining the well-established general compositional framework [3,22] for *Cyber-Physical Systems* [16], i.e. systems composed of heterogeneous parts, e.g. SW, HW, and physical, in a context of C-programs. The framework [3,22] relies on a general formalism where component interfaces are modeled as sets of variables and where *assertions*, i.e. sets of value sequences (runs), are used for modeling specifications and component behaviors over the interfaces. Considering the generality of the framework [3,22], the number of ways to model a C-program using the framework is practically infinite. The refinement reduces the abstract notion of interfaces to instead model constructs in the C-language, e.g. C-function prototypes, allowing a *unique* mapping from a C-program to an architecture model. Component behaviors and specifications are intentionally left expressed in the abstract form of assertions to both allow the architecture model and its specifications to be combined with models of, and specifications for, parts in other domains, as well as to support the instantiation of a more concrete formalism, e.g. a specific ML or ADL, suitable for a particular use-case. To illustrate support for the latter, it is shown how assertions can be expressed as Labeled Transition Systems (LTSs), which are used in approaches for SW verification, e.g. [5,23].

The proposed architecture model can be compared with formal models in SW compositional frameworks (see e.g. [1,15,23] or [20] for a survey). Out of these, the works [1,23] are the most similar to the present paper since the interfaces of components are clear. However, the model in [23] does not support modeling encapsulation of local C-variables and is tailored for capturing safety control flow properties, whereas the architecture model in the present paper is not limited to capturing any property in particular. In contrast to [1], the architecture model in the present paper supports modeling recursion and global variables that are written to by different parts of a C-program. Moreover, the works [1,23] do not provide specific guidance on how a C-program can be modeled whereas the present paper provides a unique mapping from a C-program to an architecture model.

The paper is organized as follows. Sections 2 and 3 present relevant concepts in the C-language and originating from the framework [3,22], respectively. Section 4 presents a refinement of [3,22] and the proposed formal approach for architectural modeling of C-programs. Section 5 presents an industrial case-study and Sect. 6 summarizes the paper and draws conclusions.

2   The C-Language

This section introduces concepts describing constructs in the C-language [14] or the manner in which C-code is organized into a program. The concepts will be frequently used in Sect. 4 that presents the proposed general approach for architecture modeling of sequential C-programs.

A *C-module* is a preprocessed .c-file, i.e. a file where all preprocessing directives, e.g. `#include`, as well as constants and macro definitions, have been replaced by a preprocessor. A *C-variable* is a variable that is declared in a C-module. A *C-function* is a block of C code consisting of: a *prototype* [14], i.e. a full declaration of the C-function including the return type, the number and order of arguments, and their types; and a *body*, i.e. a list of declarations and statements, enclosed in brackets. In the following, a prototype that is part of a C-function, but not within the body of the C-function, will be referred to as *the* prototype of the C-function.

For example, consider the .c-files mod.c and mMod.c, shown in Fig. 1. Preprocessed versions `mod` and `mMod` of mod.c and mMod.c, respectively, are C-modules. The .c-file mod.c contains a C-function `step` that increases the value

```
 1   // --------------mod.c--------------
 2   int c=0; //initialization of global counter 'c'
 3   int add(int a, int b) //C-function returning the sum a+b
 4           {int s=0; s = a+b; return s;}
 5   void step(void) //C-function that increases counter by 1
 6           {c=add(c,1);}
```

```
 7   // --------------mMod.c-------------
 8   extern int c;
 9   int main (void) //repeated step-wise counting from 0 to 10
10           {while (1){step(); if(c==10){c=0;}}}
```

Fig. 1. Code of c-files mod.c and mMod.c.

of a global C-variable c by 1 and a C-function add that returns the sum of the values of two formal parameters a and b. The C-function main calls step repeatedly, resetting c to 0 when it reaches 10. The block of code consisting of the lines 3-4 in Fig. 1 is the C-function add, contained in mod where code line 3 is the prototype of add and where code line 4 is the body of add.

A *C-program* is the resulting binary from a successful compilation of a set of C-modules. For example, a successful compilation of mod and mMod, shown in Fig. 1, is a C-program. The set of C-modules of which the C-program is a compilation of, is typically structured into packages and layers (see e.g. AUTOSAR model [2] or Open Systems Interconnection (OSI)-layer model [12]) that encapsulate certain functionalities/services as part of the SW.

For example, Fig. 2 shows a structure of a C-program executing on an Electric Control Unit (ECU) in a vehicle. The C-program consists of an application, a middleware, and a basic SW layer that are further structured into packages of C-modules (each shown as a white rectangles with a folded corner) according to e.g. vehicle features (Braking, fuel estimation, etc.), communication (Controller Area Network (CAN), I/O, etc.), or Operating System (OS) services and HW interaction (Scheduling, Analogue to Digital Conversion (ADC) etc.).

The structure of the C-program provides an overview and captures the overall dependencies of services [18] between different parts of the C-program at different levels. For example, the application layer relies on the middleware layer to provide values that correspond to CAN-signals or sensor readings and the middleware layer expects that basic SW layer delivers voltage values of the pins of the ECU. Thus, as shown in [18,26], organizing the specifications in parallel to the SW structure, provides a straightforward way of capturing the dependencies of services in the specifications.

A *structure of a C-program* will be considered to be a rooted tree where:

– the root node in the structure represents the C-program;
– each C-module that is compiled with other C-modules into the C-program, is represented by a node in the tree;

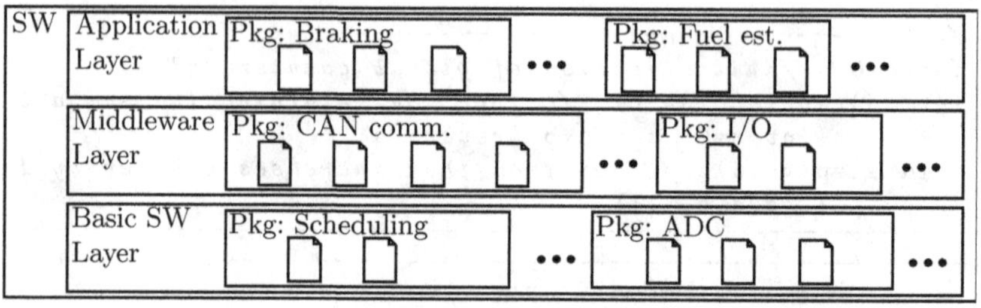

Fig. 2. A structure of a C-program executing on an ECU.

- the children of each node representing a C-module, represent the C-functions contained in the C-module and these constitute the leaf nodes in the C-program structure; and
- the children of each non-leaf node that does not represent a C-module, represent the packages/layers/C-modules that either the C-program or a package/layer, consists of.

Given a C-program structure, the term *structure entity* will be used to denote any C-function/C-module/package/layer/C-program that is represented by a node in the C-program structure. Furthermore, for convenience, the nodes in a C-program structure will be referred to as structure entities themselves, despite the fact that the nodes are only representations of structure entities. Terminology from graph theory [6] will be borrowed to describe positions of structure entities, relative to each other.

3   General Compositional Framework

This section summarizes relevant concepts originating from the compositional framework in [3,22] where specifications are expressed as *contracts* [17]. Specifically, the concepts presented in this section are based on a generalization [25,26] of [3,22]. The generalization is chosen over the original work since the concept of an architecture, which is an essential concept in the present paper, is more explicit in [25,26] than in [3,22]. In contrast to the framework in [25,26] where the number of ways to model a C-program is practically infinite, Sect. 4 will present a *unique* mapping from a C-program to an architecture model based on a refinement of [25,26].

Let Ξ denote a global set of variables in the considered context. Given a set of variables $X = \{x_1, \ldots, x_N\}$, let v_{x_i} denote a value of x_i. Consider a set $v_{X,t} = (v_{x_i})_{x_i \in X}$, called *a value set*, labeled with a time-point t in a given time-window T and ordered according to a total ordering on Ξ. A *run* for X, denoted ω_X, is an ordered set consisting of a value set $v_{X,t}$ for each $t \in T$, where ω_X is ordered such that $v_{X,t} < v_{X,t'}$, if $t < t' \in T$.

An *assertion* W *over* X is a possibly empty set of runs for X. The *projection of* W *onto a set of variables* $X' \subseteq X$, denoted $proj_{X'}(\mathsf{W})$, is the assertion obtained by removing the value of each variable $x \notin X'$ from each value set in each run in W. Given a set of variables $X'' \supseteq X$, let $\widehat{proj}_{X''}(\mathsf{W})$ denote the assertion obtained by extending each run in W with all possible runs for $X'' \setminus X$, i.e. $\widehat{proj}_{X''}(\mathsf{W}) = \{\omega_{X''} | proj_X(\{\omega_{X''}\}) \in \mathsf{W}\}$. In the following, let W^{Ξ} denote $\widehat{proj}_{\Xi}(\mathsf{W})$.

An *element* is a pair $\mathbb{E} = (X, \mathsf{B})$ consisting of: a set of variables X, called the *interface* of $\mathbb{E}$ and where each $x \in X$ is called a *port variable*; and an assertion B over X, called the *behavior* of $\mathbb{E}$. An element is an abstract concept that can be refined to model any part in general, such as a SW, hardware, or physical part, as well as logical and functional design parts, e.g. as a SysML block [8] or as a Heterogeneous Rich Component (HRC) [13].

3.1 Architecture

A set of elements can be organized into a hierarchy of elements called an *architecture* that models the structural relations between parts and where *sharing of port variables* between element interfaces models interaction points between the parts. Formally, in accordance with [25, 26], an *architecture* is a set of elements organized into a rooted tree, such that:

(a) for any non-leaf node $\mathbb{E} = (X, \mathsf{B})$, with children $\{(X_i, \mathsf{B}_i)\}_{i=1}^{N}$, it holds that $\mathsf{B} = proj_X(\bigcap_{i=1}^{N} \mathsf{B}_i^{\Xi})$ and $X \subseteq \bigcup_{i=1}^{N} X_i$; and
(b) if there is a child $\mathbb{E}' = (X', \mathsf{B}')$ and a non-descendent $\mathbb{E}'' = (X'', \mathsf{B}'')$ of $\mathbb{E} = (X, \mathsf{B})$, such that $x \in X'$ and $x \in X''$, then it holds that $x \in X$.

The *environment of an element* $\mathbb{E}$ *in an architecture*, is the set of elements $\{\mathbb{E}_j\}_{i=1}^{M}$ such that $\mathbb{E}_j$ is either a sibling or a sibling of a proper ancestor of $\mathbb{E}$.

As expressed in part (a) of the definition, the individual behaviors of the children of an element $\mathbb{E}$ is combined and abstracted by restricting their intersection to the interface of $\mathbb{E}$ using projection. Note that since the individual behaviors might be over dissimilar sets of variables, prior to using the intersection operator, the behavior of each child is transformed into an assertion over the global set of variables Ξ, using the operator $\widehat{proj}$. This is also done in general when comparing or combining assertions with set-theoretic operations and relations. Part (b) of the definition expresses that if a variable x is part of the interface of both a child of an element $\mathbb{E}$ and an element in the environment of $\mathbb{E}$, then x must also be part of the interface of $\mathbb{E}$.

To get a grasp of what an architecture is, as well as to give a preview of the architecture modeling approach that will be presented in Sect. 4, Fig. 3a shows an architecture that models a structure as shown in Fig. 3b of a C-program count10 containing the C-modules mod.c and mMod.c shown in Fig. 1. In Fig. 3a, the rectangles filled with gray and the boxes on their edges represent the elements in the architecture and their port variables, respectively, and where boxes are connected with a line or present on several edges of rectangles if they represent *a shared port variable*. The fact that a rectangle representing an element $\mathbb{E}'$ is within another rectangle representing an element $\mathbb{E}$, represents that $\mathbb{E}'$ is a proper descendant of $\mathbb{E}$.

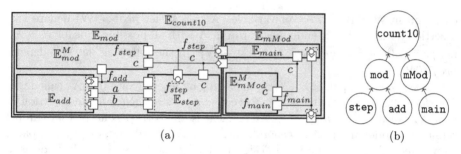

(a)   (b)

Fig. 3. In (a), an architecture is shown modeling the structure of `count10` shown in (b).

The elements $\mathbb{E}_{count10}$, $\mathbb{E}_{mod}$, $\mathbb{E}_{mMod}$, $\mathbb{E}_{step}$, $\mathbb{E}_{add}$, $\mathbb{E}_{main}$ model `count10`, `mod`, `mMod`, `step`, `add`, and `main`, respectively. The elements are actually refined types of elements called *components* that will be formally introduced in Sect. 4.1 and that have interfaces modeling constructs such as C-function prototypes and C-variables. The behaviors of $\mathbb{E}_{mod}^{M}$ and $\mathbb{E}_{mMod}^{M}$ model properties of the memory. The specifics regarding the mapping of `count10` in Fig. 3b to the architecture shown in Fig. 3a, as well as general principles of mapping a C-program structure to an architecture, will be presented in Sects. 4.2 and 4.3, respectively.

The next section will show how the framework [25,26] supports specifying and structuring contracts in parallel to an architecture to allow compositional verification. The support is given for an architecture in general, which means the same support is provided for an architecture model of a C-program where the model is obtained by following the mapping principles that will be presented in Sect. 4.

3.2   Compositional Verification

A specification for an element $\mathbb{E} = (X, \mathsf{B})$ is expressed as a *contract*, which is a pair $(\mathcal{A} = \{\mathsf{A}_1, \ldots, \mathsf{A}_N\}, \mathsf{G})$ where each A_i and G are assertions called an *assumption* and the *guarantee*, respectively. The guarantee expresses an intended property under the responsibility of the element, given *any* architecture where the environment of the element fulfills the assumptions. The element $\mathbb{E}$ *satisfies* the contract if $\mathsf{A}_1^{\Xi} \cap \ldots \cap \mathsf{A}_N^{\Xi} \cap \mathsf{B}^{\Xi} \subseteq \mathsf{G}^{\Xi}$.

Consider that a contract $(\{\mathsf{A}_1, \ldots, \mathsf{A}_N\}, \mathsf{G})$ is expressed for each element $\mathbb{E}$ in an architecture. The intent is that there are guarantees $G_{i,1}, \ldots, G_{i,N_i}$ of other contracts in the environment of $\mathbb{E}$ for each assumption A_i, as well as guarantees $G_1, \ldots, G_M$ of contracts for elements that are children of $\mathbb{E}$, such that $\mathsf{G}_{i,1}^{\Xi} \cap \ldots \cap \mathsf{G}_{i,N_i}^{\Xi} \subseteq \mathsf{A}_i^{\Xi}$ holds for each i and $\mathsf{G}_1^{\Xi} \cap \ldots \cap \mathsf{G}_M^{\Xi} \subseteq \mathsf{G}^{\Xi}$.

In accordance with [25,26], a Directed Acyclic Graph (DAG) is assumed to be created where the nodes in the graph represent the assumptions and the guarantees of the contracts and where the edges represent the intended relations. Ignoring a few technicalities that are presented in depth in [25], given that all the intended relations represented by the edges in the DAG hold, it can be shown that the root element satisfies its contract, if the leaf elements in the architecture satisfy their contracts. Thus, allowing compositional verification.

4 Architecture Modeling of Sequential C-Programs

This section presents the proposed formal approach for architectural modeling of C-programs intended for sequential execution, i.e. with a single stack. As argued in Sect. 1, such an approach is needed to support compositional verification of C-programs, as well as to support their design and management in general. The architecture model is complemented with a graphical representation for practical application.

This is done by first formally introducing a refined type of element called a *component* where a component models any type of structure entity of a C-program structure as described in Sect. 2. Similar to [23], the behavior of a component is specified given an infinite time-window where each time-point models an execution state of the C-program from the moment when a C-function in the C-program is either called or returned to, up until and including the moment when the C-function either calls another C-function or it returns. The first time-step in the time-window models an invocation of the C-function `main`, which is modeled to be invoked only one time.

In accordance with Sect. 3, it is then shown how structure entities in a C-program structure can be mapped to components in an architecture that models the structure of the C-program in a context of a HW platform consisting of a processor, memory, and a set of I/O-devices. The root element of the architecture is a component with a behavior that models the execution of the C-program on HW consisting of the processor and the memory. The interface of this component models interaction points with the I/O-devices.

4.1 Function Interfaces and Components

Prior to introducing the definition of a component, the concept of *function interfaces*, modeling C-function prototypes, is introduced. A *function interface* $\mathcal{F}$ is an ordered set of variables $(f, (x_1, \ldots, x_N))$. The variable f is a pair (f_s, f_r) of variables where f_r models the return value of the C-function. The variable f_s takes values from $\{0, 1, 2\}$ and models the execution state of the C-function that the function interface models the prototype for. The values 0, 1 and 2 model that the C-function is not on the stack, that it is on the stack and executing, and that it is on the stack but not executing, respectively.

Each variable x_i models an argument where the identifiers of $x_1, \ldots, x_N$ are mapped to the identifiers of the formal parameters of the C-function, e.g. a function interface $(f_{add}, (a, b)))$ models the prototype of the C-function `add` shown in Fig. 1. The value domain of each variable x_i corresponds to the data type of its mapped formal parameter, except that the value domain of x_i also includes a value *nil* that models that no data is currently passed to the C-function. Variables modeling arguments that are addresses or values of structs, have value domains that include variable identifiers and nested ordered sets of values, respectively. The definition of a component now follows.

A *component* is an element $\mathbb{E} = (X, \mathsf{B})$ where X is partitioned into sets $X_1^F, \ldots, X_N^F$ and X', such that:

- each set X_i^F is organized as a function interface $\mathcal{F}_i$ labeled as either *internal* or *external* of $\mathbb{E}$; and
- each port variable in X' is either labeled as *internal* or *external* of $\mathbb{E}$.

The behavior B models the properties imposed by a structure entity on non-descendent C-modules of the structure entity, as well as on HW, considering its constraints on the C-functions modeled by $\mathcal{F}_1, \ldots, \mathcal{F}_N$ and C-variables modeled by port variables in X'. Each $x \in X'$ has a value domain that corresponds to the data type of the C-variable that x models. If x models a C-variable that is not persistent in memory, then the value domain of x also includes a *nil* value, modeling the fact that the C-variable does not exist on the stack.

For example, consider the component $\mathbb{E}_{add} = (X_{add}, \mathsf{B}_{add})$ that is shown in Fig. 3a and that models add shown in Fig. 1, as well as the structure of the C-program count10 as shown in Fig. 3b in a context of a HW platform consisting solely of a processor and memory. The entire interface X_{add} is organized as a function interface $(f_{add}, (a, b))$ modeling the prototype of add. In general, if a subset of a component interface is organized as a function interface $\mathcal{F}$ modeling the prototype of a descendent of a structure entity (including itself), then $\mathcal{F}$ is labeled as internal of the component modeling the structure entity. Hence, the function interface $(f_{add}, (a, b))$ is labeled as internal of $\mathbb{E}_{add}$. In this case, since $\mathbb{E}_{add}$ models a C-function, i.e. add, it means that $(f_{add}, (a, b))$ models the prototype of add. The C-variable s is not modeled as a port variable since s is not read or written to by either step, main, or an I/O-device.

4.2   Representing and Modeling a C-Program Structure

This section introduces principles for architecture modeling of a C-program structure, as well as how it can be represented, by mapping the structure of the C-program count10 shown in Fig. 3b to the architecture shown in Fig. 3a.

Mapping C-Functions to Leaf Components. In Fig. 3a, the boxes representing the port variables that constitute the function interface $(f_{add}, (a, b))$ as previously introduced, are enclosed in brackets. The fact that $(f_{add}, (a, b))$ is labeled as internal of $\mathbb{E}_{add}$ is captured by a hollow circle and triangles attached to an edge of each of the boxes representing f_{add}, as well as a and b, respectively where the edges are within the rectangle that represents $\mathbb{E}_{add}$. The hat on the hollow circle represents that f_{add} is not of the type void.

Regarding $\mathbb{E}_{step}$, the subset X_{add} of X_{step} is organized as the function interface $(f_{add}, (a, b))$ labeled as external of $\mathbb{E}_{step}$. This models the fact that step calls add in an execution path of the C-program. Furthermore, the set $\{f_{step}\} \subset X_{step}$ is organized as a function interface $(f_{step}, ())$ modeling the prototype of step where $(f_{step}, ())$ is labeled as internal of $\mathbb{E}_{step}$. Since step is of type void, no hat is placed on the hollow circle attached to the box representing f_{step}.

The port variable c models the counter in the code shown in Fig. 1. The counter is read and written to by both step and main and is, therefore, a port variable of both $\mathbb{E}_{step}$ and $\mathbb{E}_{main}$. Since the counter is not initialized in either step or main, the port variable c is labeled as external of both $\mathbb{E}_{step}$ and $\mathbb{E}_{main}$.

The prototype of main is modeled as a function interface $(f_{main}, ())$. As previously indicated, $(f_{main}, ())$ is labeled as internal of $\mathbb{E}_{main}$ as shown in Fig. 3a since $(f_{main}, ())$ models the prototype of main and $\mathbb{E}_{main}$ models main. Considering that main calls step, $(f_{step}, ())$ is labeled as external of $\mathbb{E}_{main}$.

Specifying Behaviors and Contracts Using LTSs. As previously presented, behaviors of components are defined in the general form of assertions, which can, however, be specified using more concrete formalisms. Specifically, this section shows how behaviors, and also contracts, can be specified as LTSs. Technical details are presented in the end of this section.

In Fig. 4a, an example is shown on how the behavior of the component $\mathbb{E}_{step} = (X_{step}, \mathsf{B}_{step})$ can be specified as an LTS such that it models the static and dynamic properties imposed by step on the rest of the code of the C-program and on HW. A label on a state s is a constraint specifying a set of values of the port variables in X_{step} where all values of a port variable are in the set if it is not constrained. Each transition (s, s') corresponds to a time-step and a label on (s, s') specifies a relation on the labels of the two states where a primed x' and non-primed version x of a port variable x, refer to the new and old values of x, respectively.

The initial state s_0 models that step is not on the call stack. The transition (s_0, s_1) models an invocation of step. The transition (s_1, s_2) models a function call from step to add where the value of c and 1 are passed as arguments a and b. The transition (s_2, s_3) models a return of add to step. The transition (s_3, s_0) models a return of step where the value of c is assigned to be equal to $f_{add,r}$ modeling the return value of add.

In general, the behavior of a component modeling a C-function that is not of type void, will constrain the port variable modeling the return value of the C-function to only have a value that is not equal to nil for each time-point that models an execution state where the C-function has just returned. For example, $f_{add,r}$ is not equal to nil in state s_3, but will be constrained to be nil at state s_2 by B_{add}. However, since step is of type void, the port variable $f_{step,r}$ modeling the return value of step, is nil for each run and time-step as shown in Fig. 4a.

Furthermore, the behavior of a component modeling a C-function with formal parameters, will constrain the port variables modeling each argument to only have a value that is not equal to nil for each time-point that models an execution state where the C-function has just been called. For example, the port variables a and b have values that are not nil in the state s_2, but will be constrained to be nil at state s_3 by B_{add}.

Consider an informal requirement on step: *"the value of the counter when the C-function returns, shall be equal to a step increase of the value of the counter at the time when the C-function is called."* As can be seen in Fig. 1, for step to be able to guarantee this requirement, it requires functionality provided by the C-function add, i.e. that *"add returns the sum of its arguments to its caller".*

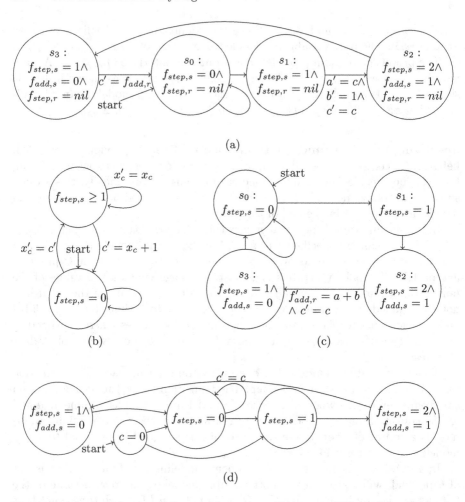

Fig. 4. In (a), the behavior of $\mathbb{E}_{step}$ is shown, specified as an LTS. In (b) and (c), the guarantee G_{step} and the intersection of the assumptions in $\mathcal{A}_{step}$ of a contract for $\mathbb{E}_{step}$ are shown, respectively. In (d), the behavior of $\mathbb{E}_{mod}^M$ is shown, specified as an LTS

Considering the interface of $\mathbb{E}_{step}$, a contract $(\mathcal{A}_{step}, \mathsf{G}_{step})$ that expresses the informal requirement and the required functionality can be formulated as shown in Fig. 4c and 4b. The guarantee G_{step} is equal to the projection of the assertion specified by the LTS in Fig. 4b onto $\{f_{step,s}, c\}$. Hence, the variable x_c is simply used as a support variable in order to specify that the value of c directly after a time-step where the value of $f_{step,s}$ switches from 1 to 0, shall be equal to a step increase of the value of c at the time-point after the latest time-step where the value of $f_{step,s}$ switched from 0 to 1.

In Fig. 4c, the intersection of the assumptions in $\mathcal{A}_{step}$ is shown where the intersection is specified as an LTS. The LTS captures the functionality that step requires from add by having the label on the transition (s_2, s_3) modeling a return of add to step, constrain the port variable $f_{add,r}$ to be equal to the sum of the old values of the port variables a and b. Additionally, the LTS in Fig. 4c specifies that the port variable c is to remain constant in states that model step being on the stack, but when step is not executing.

Consider the constraint specified in Fig. 4c to hold the counter constant if step is on the stack but not executing, as well as the fact that the counter is initialized to 0 as shown in Fig. 1. Notably, as can be seen in Fig. 4a, neither of these constraints are captured in the behavior of $\mathbb{E}_{step}$. The reason why the latter constraint is not captured is because c is initialized in mod rather than in step. The former constraint is not captured since it is a property of the memory, rather than of step. Such constraints are instead captured separately in the behaviors of the elements $\mathbb{E}_{mod}^M$ and $\mathbb{E}_{mMod}^M$ in Fig. 3.

As an example of how a behavior modeling properties of the memory can be captured, consider the element $\mathbb{E}_{mod}^M = (X_{mod}^M, \mathsf{B}_{mod}^M)$. The interface $X_{mod}^M = \{f_{add}, f_{step}, c\}$, i.e. X_{mod}^M contains the port variable f of each function interface $(f, (x_1, \ldots, x_M))$ labeled as internal of siblings of $\mathbb{E}_{step}^M$, as well as each port variable labeled as external or internal of siblings of $\mathbb{E}_{step}^M$. The behavior B_{mod}^M is shown in Fig. 4d and constrains the port variable c to be constant in states that model when step is on the stack but not executing. The behavior also models the initialization of the counter.

The elements modeling constraints on the memory are necessary in order for the behavior of the component modeling the C-program to capture *the execution of the C-program* on HW consisting of a processor and memory. Hence, if only the *structure of a C-program* is of interest, elements such as $\mathbb{E}_{mod}^M$ and $\mathbb{E}_{mMod}^M$ can be removed from a representation such as the one shown in Fig. 3.

In the examples shown in Fig. 4, the exact mapping between assertions and LTSs was not explained in detail. The details of such a mapping follow. Each assertion is specified as an LTS $(S, I \subseteq S, R, L_S, L_R)$ where each state $s \in S$ has a label $L_S(s)$ equal to a set of value sets and each transition $(s, s') \in R \subseteq S \times S$ has a label $L_R((s, s')) \subseteq L_S(s) \times L_S(s')$. For a given set of variables X and time-window $T = (t_0, t_1, t_2, \ldots)$, the assertion specified as an LTS, consists of each run $(v_{X,t_0}, v_{X,t_1}, v_{X,t_2}, \ldots,)$ where there exists a sequence $(s_0 \in I, s_1, s_2, \ldots)$ such that for each $i \geq 0$, it holds that $(s_i, s_{i+1}) \in R$ and $(v_{X,t_i}, v_{X,t_{i+1}}) \in L_R((s_i, s_{i+1}))$. Note that instead of declaring each value set in a label $L_S(s)$, the label can be specified by a constraint. Similarly, instead of declaring the set of pairs of value sets in a label $L_R((s, s'))$, the label can be specified by a constraint that restricts the set $L_S(s) \times L_S(s')$ to the set $L_R((s, s'))$.

Mapping Non-leaf Structure Entities to Components. Consider the components $\mathbb{E}_{mod} = (X_{mod}, \mathsf{B}_{mod})$ and $\mathbb{E}_{mMod} = (X_{mMod}, \mathsf{B}_{mMod})$ modeling the respective C-modules mod and mMod shown in Fig. 3. The C-function add is neither the main C-function nor an Interrupt Service Routine (ISR), nor is it called by any non-descendent C-function of mod. Therefore, the port variables f_{add}, a, and b are not part of X_{mod}. Since step is both a descendent C-function of mod and called by the non-descendent and descendent C-function main of mod and mMod, respectively, $\{f_{step}\}$ is organized as the function interface $(f_{step}, ())$ labeled as internal and external of $\mathbb{E}_{mod}$ and $\mathbb{E}_{mMod}$, respectively. Due to the fact that main is the main C-function of the C-program and a descendent of mMod, the function interface $(f_{main}, ())$ is labeled as internal of $\mathbb{E}_{mMod}$. The C-function main is not called by a descendent C-function of mod, and, hence $f_{main} \notin X_{mod}$.

Furthermore, since the counter is read and written to by both the non-descendent and descendent C-functions main and step of mod, respectively, the port variable c is part of both X_{mod} and X_{mMod}. Considering that the counter is initialized in mod, the port variable c is labeled as internal and external of $\mathbb{E}_{mod}$ and $\mathbb{E}_{mMod}$, respectively. The fact that c is labeled as internal of $\mathbb{E}_{mod}$ is represented by attaching a hollow diamond to an edge of the box representing c where the edge is within the rectangle representing $\mathbb{E}_{mod}$.

Regarding the component $\mathbb{E}_{count10} = (X_{count10}, \mathsf{B}_{count10})$ modeling the C-program count10, since step is neither the main C-function nor an ISR, f_{step} is not part of $X_{count10}$. Due to same reasons, the port variable f_{main} is, however, part of $X_{count10}$ and is organized as the function interface $(f_{main}, ())$ labeled as internal of $\mathbb{E}_{count10}$. The counter is not read or written to by an I/O-device and, hence, c is not part of $X_{count10}$.

4.3   Modeling C-Program Structures as Architectures

Consider a C-program structure in a context of a HW platform. This section generalizes principles introduced in Sect. 4.2 into the general approach of how structure entities can be mapped to components in an architecture modeling the C-program structure.

The leaf components in the architecture, model the C-functions while the root component models the C-program itself. The set $\{\mathbb{E}_i = (X_i, \mathsf{B}_i)\}_{i=1}^N$ of children of a component $\mathbb{E} = (X, \mathsf{B})$ that models a structure entity, consists of components modeling each child of the structure entity, as well as a leaf element modeling properties of the memory if there exists a port variable x of a component $\mathbb{E}_i$ where x models a C-variable and is either: not part of each interface X_i; or not part of the interface X and $\mathbb{E}$ is not the root component. Considering the architecture shown in Fig. 3, that is why the root component $\mathbb{E}_{count10}$ does not have a child that models properties of the memory.

The interface X of the component $\mathbb{E}$ is partitioned into sets $X_1^F, \ldots, X_M^F$ and X' where $X_1^F, \ldots, X_M^F$ are organized into function interfaces $\mathcal{F}_1, \ldots, \mathcal{F}_M$.

C-Variables. Port variables in X' model each C-variable that is neither a pointer nor *compound data structure*, i.e. arrays and structs, and where the C-variable is either read or written to (including initialization), in an execution path of the C-program both by a descendent C-function of the structure entity and by either a non-descendent C-function of the structure entity or an I/O-device. Note that this assumes that the C-program does not read or write to addresses that are not associated with a C-variable. A trivial extension to this case is to also model addresses as port variables.

If a port variable $x \in X'$ models a C-variable that is initialized in either a descendent C-function or a C-module of the structure entity, then x is labeled as internal of $\mathbb{E}$. Otherwise, the port variable x is labeled as external of $\mathbb{E}$. In the architecture, two different port variables do not model the same C-variable.

C-Functions, Interrupts, and Recursion. Function interfaces $\mathcal{F}_1, \ldots, \mathcal{F}_M$ model:

- the prototype of each descendent C-function of the structure entity where either $\mathbb{E}$ models the C-function, the C-function is an ISR or the C-function main of the C-program, or a non-descendent C-function of the structure entity calls the C-function in an execution path of the C-program; and
- the prototype of each non-descendent C-function of the structure entity where a descendent C-function of the structure entity calls the C-function in an execution path of the C-program.

If $\mathcal{F}_j$ models the prototype of a descendent C-function of the structure entity, then $\mathcal{F}_j$ is labeled as internal of the component. Otherwise, $\mathcal{F}_j$ is labeled as external of the component.

Interrupts that are predicted to preempt certain C-functions and where the triggered ISRs do not call other C-functions, can be modeled by a port variable $f_{ISR,s}$ modeling the execution state of an ISR, first switching from 0 to 1 and then back to 0, simultaneously as a port variable f_s modeling the execution state of the interrupted C-function, switching from 1 to 2 and then back to 1. Since the interrupt is predicted, the behavior of the component modeling the C-function can be specified such that f_s switches simultaneously as $f_{ISR,s}$ despite $f_{ISR,s}$ not necessarily being part of the interface of the component.

To capture other forms of interrupts where ISRs also calls other C-functions, each port variable $f_{ISR,s}$ modeling the execution state of an ISR can be included in the interface of each leaf component in the architecture. Hence, the behavior of each component modeling a C-function foo, can be specified such that in any time-point modeling an execution of foo, if a port variable $f_{ISR,s}$ switches from 0 to 1 in the next time-step, then the port variable $f_{foo,s}$ modeling the execution state of foo switches from 1 to 2 in the same time-step. The variable $f_{foo,s}$ can then be specified to be equal to 2 until $f_{ISR,s}$ switches back to 0.

To model a C-program where *indirect recursion* is used, i.e. when a C-function calls another C-function on the stack, two separate components need to model the same C-function. If indirect recursion is not used, only one component is needed to model a C-function. This includes *direct recursion*, i.e. when a C-function calls itself, which can be captured in the behavior of a single component.

Compound Data Structures. If a component has port variables that model each C-variable in a compound data structure, then these port variables are organized into an ordered set, which can be represented by enclosing these port variables in brackets similar to how function interfaces are represented. Hierarchies of compound data structures are organized as nested ordered sets and represented accordingly.

Pointers. As previously discussed, C-variables that are pointers, are not modeled as port variables of a component. Rather, if there exists an execution path of the C-program where the C-function either reads or writes to a C-variable indirectly through the use of a pointer, then the C-variable to which the pointer ultimately points to, is modeled as a port variable of the component. This also holds true for C-function pointers, i.e. if a C-function foo calls another C-function foo' indirectly through a function pointer, then a function interface modeling a prototype of foo', will be labeled as external of a component modeling foo.

Properties of Memory. If an element (X^M, B^M), modeling properties of the memory, has a parent that models a C-module, then X^M contains each port variable f of each function interface $(f, (x_1, \ldots, x_M))$ labeled as internal of its siblings, as well as each variable x labeled as external or internal of its siblings. The behavior B^M constrains each port variable x to be constant in states modeling the execution of descendent C-functions of the C-module where these C-functions never write or read to the C-variable modeled by x. The behavior B^M also models the initialization constraints on C-variables that are initialized in the C-module. An example of such an element was previously shown in Fig. 4d.

In the case where the parent of (X^M, B^M) is not a C-module, the interface X^M contains each port variable f of each function interface $(f, (x_1, \ldots, x_M))$ labeled as internal of its siblings, as well as each port variable x labeled as external or internal of its siblings where x is either not in the interface of the parent component of the element or not in the interface of each sibling component of the element. In case of the former, the behavior B constrains x to be constant during states where none of the descendent C-functions of the structure entity modeled by the parent component of the element, are executing. In case of the latter, the behavior B constrains x to be constant during states modeling the execution of non-descendent C-functions of structure entities modeled by each sibling component of the element where the interface of the sibling component does not contain x.

5   Industrial Case Study - Reading the Fuel Sensor

This section presents a case study where a subset of the structure of a real industrial C-program is modeled as an architecture as shown in Fig. 5 using the concepts described in Sect. 4. The modeled subset is part of a C-program executing on an ECU in a Scania truck and is the part of the C-program that manages the transformation from the digitally converted voltage value at a pin connected to a fuel sensor, to a C-variable storing an estimated fuel level value.

To save space, components and port variables will in the following be referred to as structure entities and C-variables/arguments. Elements modeling properties of the memory are omitted from the representation shown in Fig. 5.

The C-program $\mathbb{E}_{SW}$ contains an application layer $\mathbb{E}_{APPL}$, a middleware layer $\mathbb{E}_{MIDD}$, a basic SW layer $\mathbb{E}_{BIOS}$, and a C-module $\mathbb{E}_{sigDB}$ that serves as a communication interface between $\mathbb{E}_{APPL}$ and $\mathbb{E}_{MIDD}$. The main C-function

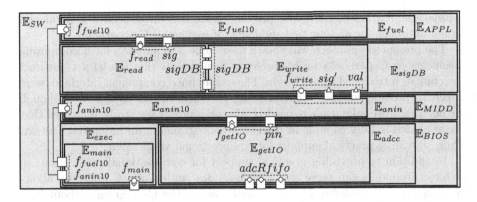

Fig. 5. An architecture modeling a subset of a structure of a C-program in an ECU.

$\mathbb{E}_{main}$ in the C-module $\mathbb{E}_{exec}$ calls the C-functions $\mathbb{E}_{anin10}$ and $\mathbb{E}_{fuel10}$ in that order. The C-function $\mathbb{E}_{anin10}$ in the C-module $\mathbb{E}_{anin}$ calls the C-function $\mathbb{E}_{getIO}$ in the C-module $\mathbb{E}_{adcc}$, passing an integer as an argument pin that maps to a specific pin on the ECU. If pin maps to the pin connected to the fuel sensor, then $\mathbb{E}_{getIO}$ will return the average of the values of the C-variables in the array $adcRfifo$. Each C-variable in the array maps to a specific part of the registry of an ADC where that part of the registry stores a sampled voltage value of the pin connected to the fuel sensor. The initialization and termination of the sampling, which is done by deactivating and activating Direct Memory Access Channels (DMACs), is not considered due to space restrictions.

After $\mathbb{E}_{getIO}$ returns, the C-function $\mathbb{E}_{anin10}$ proceeds to call the C-function $\mathbb{E}_{write}$ with the arguments sig' and val where sig' is an enum value corresponding to an ID of a general I/O and where val is the corresponding value of the I/O. If $sig' = fuelSensorLevel$, then val corresponds to an estimation of the fuel level acquired by transforming the averaged voltage value of the pin of the fuel sensor. The estimated fuel level is stored in a specific position in an array $sigDB$ where the position maps to the ID $fuelSensorLevel$. The C-function $\mathbb{E}_{fuel10}$ in the C-module $\mathbb{E}_{fuel}$ calls the C-function $\mathbb{E}_{read}$ with the argument $sig = fuelSensorLevel$. The C-function fetches the estimated fuel level from the array and returns the value to $\mathbb{E}_{fuel10}$. The C-function $fuel10$ relies on the estimated fuel level to calculate the fuel volume in the tank.

6 Conclusion

Compositional verification provides a means to manage the development of complex C-programs, but in order to support compositional verification in practice, an *architecture model* of a C-program is needed. Such support is paramount for the embedded domain, in general, and the automotive domain, in particular, since compositional verification is an essential concept in the automotive standard ISO 26262. Due to the lack of such much needed support in current approaches [1,5,7–10,21,23], the present paper has introduced a general and formal approach for architecture modeling of sequential C-programs.

The presented approach was shown to provide a foundation for decomposing specifications in parallel to a hierarchy of *components* that model a *C-program structure* as introduced by engineers. The well-defined component interfaces were shown to provide support for expressing specifications as *contracts*. Although further practical validation is needed, the presented case study indicates that the approach is fully capable of modeling C-programs in an industrial context. Thus, providing practical support for compositional verification.

In addition to providing practical support for compositional verification, an architecture model can serve as a high-level description of a C-program, allowing developers to understand, assess, and manage the C-program without having to understand the intricate complexity of the code implementation. Given a C-program, the presented approach provides a foundation for automatic generation of an architecture model from code using e.g. architecture recovery [19], ensuring a high-level description that is consistent with the code. The architecture model can then also be used to verify the consistency of manually implemented models, e.g. UML and SysML models, if they are mapped to the architecture model.

References

1. Alur, R., Grosu, R.: Modular refinement of hierarchic reactive machines. ACM Trans. Program. Lang. Syst. **26**(2), 339–369 (2004)
2. AUTOSAR: AUTomotive Open System ARchitecture. http://www.autosar.org/
3. Ferrari, A., Sofronis, C., Benveniste, A., Mangeruca, L., Passerone, Roberto, Caillaud, Benoît: Multiple viewpoint contract-based specification and design. In: de Boer, F.S., Bonsangue, M.M., Graf, S., de Roever, W.-P. (eds.) FMCO 2007. LNCS, vol. 5382, pp. 200–225. Springer, Heidelberg (2008)
4. Cass, S.: Top 10 programming languages, July 2014. http://spectrum.ieee.org/computing/software/top-10-programming-languages
5. Chaki, S., Clarke, E., Groce, A., Jha, S., Veith, H.: Modular verification of software components in C. In: Proceedings of the 25th International Conference on Software Engineering, ICSE 2003, pp. 385–395, IEEE Computer Society, Washington (2003). http://dl.acm.org/citation.cfm?id=776816.776863
6. Diestel, R.: Graph Theory. Graduate Texts in Mathematics, vol. 173. Springer, Heidelberg (2010)
7. Feiler, P.H., Gluch, D.P.: Model-Based Engineering with AADL: An Introduction to the SAE Architecture Analysis & Design Language, 1st edn. Addison-Wesley Professional, Boston (2012)
8. Friedenthal, S., Moore, A., Steiner, R.: A Practical Guide to SysML: Systems Modeling Language. Morgan Kaufmann Inc., San Francisco (2008)
9. Greenaway, D.: Automated proof-producing abstraction of C code. Ph.D. thesis, University of New South Wales (2014)
10. Henzinger, T.A., Jhala, R., Majumdar, R., Sutre, G.: Software verification with BLAST. In: Ball, T., Rajamani, S.K. (eds.) SPIN 2003. LNCS, vol. 2648, pp. 235–239. Springer, Heidelberg (2003)
11. ISO 26262: Road vehicles-Functional safety (2011)

12. ISO 7498-1: Information technology - OSI - Basic Reference Model (1994)
13. Josko, B., Ma, Q., Metzner, A.: Designing embedded systems using heterogeneous rich components. In: Proceedings of the INCOSE International Symposium (2008)
14. Kernighan, B.W.: The C Programming Language, 2nd edn. Prentice Hall Professional Technical Reference, New York (1988)
15. Laster, K., Grumberg, O.: Modular model checking of software. In: Steffen, B. (ed.) TACAS 1998. LNCS, vol. 1384, pp. 20–35. Springer, Heidelberg (1998)
16. Lee, E.: Cyber physical systems: design challenges. In: 11th IEEE International Symposium on Object Oriented Real-Time Distributed Computing (ISORC), pp. 363–369, May 2008
17. Meyer, B.: Applying "Design by Contract". Computer **25**(10), 40–51 (1992). http://dx.doi.org/10.1109/2.161279
18. Nyberg, M.: Failure propagation modeling for safety analysis using causal bayesian networks. In: 2013 Conference on Control and Fault-Tolerant Systems (SysTol), pp. 91–97, October 2013
19. Rasool, G., Asif, N.: Software architecture recovery. Int. J. Comput. Inf. Syst. Sci. Eng. **1**(3), 206 (2007)
20. de Roever, W.-P.: The need for compositional proof systems: a survey. In: Roever, W-Pl, Langmaack, H., Pnueli, A. (eds.) COMPOS 1997. LNCS, vol. 1536, p. 1. Springer, Heidelberg (1998)
21. Rumbaugh, J., Jacobson, I., Booch, G.: Unified Modeling Language Reference Manual. Pearson Higher Education, London (2004)
22. Dr, Taming, Sangiovanni-Vincentell, A.L., Damm, W., Passerone, R.: Taming Dr. Franken: contract-based design for cyber-physical systems. Eur. J. Control **18**(3), 217–238 (2012)
23. Soleimanifard, S., Gurov, D.: Algorithmic verification of procedural programs in the presence of code variability. Sci. Comput. Program (2015). http://www.sciencedirect.com/science/article/pii/S0167642315002592
24. Westman, J., Nyberg, M.: Extending contract theory with safety integrity levels. In: 2015 IEEE 16th International Symposium on HASE, pp. 85–92, January 2015
25. Westman, J., Nyberg, M.: Environment-centric contracts for design of cyber-physical systems. In: Dingel, J., Schulte, W., Ramos, I., Abrahão, S., Insfran, Emilio (eds.) MODELS 2014. LNCS, vol. 8767, pp. 218–234. Springer, Heidelberg (2014)
26. Westman, J., Nyberg, M.: Contracts for specifying and structuring requirements on cyber-physical systems. In: Rawat, D.B., Rodriques, J., Stojmenovic, I. (eds.) Cyber Physical Systems: From Theory to Practice. Taylor & Francis (2015)
27. Whalen, M.W., Gacek, A., Cofer, D., Murugesan, A., Heimdahl, M.P., Rayadurgam, S.: Your what is my how: iteration and hierarchy in system design. IEEE Softw. **30**(2), 54–60 (2013)

Author Index